Building English Skills

is an English series for grades K–12 designed to lead students toward mastery of essential writing and related language skills. This *Silver Level* text is suggested for use at grade 5.

Building English Skills is built upon several key beliefs:

1. To insure learning, each topic or skill should be developed completely in one place rather than in several places throughout the text.

2. To insure mastery, a large number and variety of exercises should be provided at key intervals.

3. To insure understanding, the reading level should be on or below the suggested grade level.

4. To insure consistency and transference of learning, English should be taught from year to year using a consistent philosophy, terminology, and approach.

How *Building English Skills* illustrates this teaching philosophy

1. *Building English Skills* develops each topic or skill completely, one step at a time, in one unit or chapter. Research by Jerome Bruner and others has shown that any topic can be taught successfully if it is presented in a meaningful, step-by-step, success-directed way—with illustrations, models, and exercises that are directly related to the students' needs and experiences.

Furthermore, students gain a sense of the relative importance of ideas and skills when they are presented together and follow logically from one concept to the next.

In contrast, most series are based on the premise that students' attention span is short and that they need to be continually jolted by a new topic every few pages in order to sustain interest. This fragmented, "scattershot" approach hides the overall structure of the subject from students and prevents them from obtaining a holistic view of a topic. Such an approach not only confuses most students and impedes the learning process but, more detrimentally, hides the relative importance of different ideas and skills.

2. *Building English Skills* includes numerous practice exercises in each text at frequent appropriate intervals. These exercises are designed to provide adequate practice to insure that the student has mastered the individual concept or skill before moving to the next topic.

3. The reading level of each *Building English Skills* text has been carefully controlled, so that reading difficulties do not interfere with the students' ability to learn essential writing and related language skills. At the lower grades, readability is on or below grade level; at the upper grades, reading level is at least one grade, and sometimes two grades, below the suggested grade level. Readability has also been enhanced by large type, clear, open format, and, perhaps most importantly, clarity of style and presentation of ideas.

4. *Building English Skills* presents a complete, consistent series for teaching basic English skills, grades K–12. The philosophy, terminology, teaching approach, and topical emphasis are consistent from grade to grade, even as the vocabulary, skills, and practice exercises grow in sophistication and difficulty.

In contrast, few other textbook series are conceived as K–12 series. They are instead more commonly conceived as separate elementary and secondary series and executed by different authors and editors. The important underlying consistencies are absent—a fact that becomes more apparent and confusing to the student as he or she moves from a grade six book in one series to a grade seven book in another.

In the *Building English Skills* book for grades K to 6, the chapters are presented in an order that provides a balanced program of language skills, and a suggested teaching sequence. In the books for grades 7 to 12, the composition chapters are presented in the first half of the book, and the grammar chapters in the second half. This organization provides the teacher with the maximum flexibility of use.

The Organization of the Text

In *Building English Skills, Silver Level*, chapters devoted to composition, grammar, and other language skills provide for steady development in the use of language. Each chapter builds on what has been presented in the preceding chapters. For example, the text opens with a chapter on individual words and vocabulary development, progresses to the study of sentences, and builds to a complete presentation of paragraphs and longer forms of writing. Chapters on research skills (using the dictionary and using the library) are presented before chapters on writing a composition requiring research.

The presentation of grammar is placed in strategic positions throughout the text. Each grammar chapter follows logically from the grammar chapter that precedes it. Each is a self-contained unit: everything about nouns is presented in one chapter, everything about pronouns in another chapter. The text defines each term when it is first used, then reviews and builds on that definition in later references. Grammar chapters need not be taught in the order in which they are presented in the book. It is better for the learner, however, that they be taught in the sequence in which they are presented.

Sentence patterns are presented systematically in this text, following certain grammar chapters. These are the pages with a green tint (pages 63, 123, 150, 151, and 234). The sentence patterns discussed are those that linguists have found to be used most frequently in speech and writing by pupils at this stage of language development. The patterns are presented in such a way that each one flows naturally from the grammar that has just been presented in the chapter. The patterns presented in *Building English Skills, Silver Level* are the N V, N V N, N LV N, and N LV Adj patterns.

The last three chapters of the *Silver Level* comprise the Handbook: Mechanics of Writing. These chapters on capitalization, punctuation, and spelling present rules and examples in an orderly, easy-to-consult form that makes the chapters not only a clear and complete instrument for direct teaching, but also a valuable reference source for students.

The Organization of Individual Chapters

Every chapter is devoted to a single topic, and all information on that topic is presented together in the chapter. Every chapter is divided into Parts. Each Part deals with a separate skill. Each Part then concludes with exercises on the skill developed. Wherever possible, there are several exercises using a variety of approaches to the same skill. All grammar, usage, and mechanics chapters are also followed by Additional Exercises, one for each Part. The quantity and variety of exercises provide the teacher with ample material for reinforcement, enrichment, and review.

The Organization of the *Building English Skills* Series

Cherry Level
Recommended for Kindergarten

Skills covered in the text include the following:

Listening Skills
  Hearing beginning sounds
  Hearing rhymes
  Listening for information
  Following directions
  Listening to stories and poems

Speaking Skills
  Speaking clearly
  Taking turns
  Telling about a thing
  Telling a story

Reading and Writing Readiness
  Using *left* and *right*
  Recognizing colors and numbers
  Recognizing shapes
  Seeing likenesses and differences
  Putting things into groups
  Putting events in order

Pink Level
Recommended for grade 1

Chapter
1. Speaking and Listening
2. Fun with the ABC's
3. All About Words
4. Sentences
5. Talking About Books
6. Naming Words
7. Doing Words
8. Writing
9. Words To Use

Plum Level
Recommended for grade 2

Chapter
1. Speaking and Listening
2. Sentences
3. Fun with Words
4. Nouns
5. Books and Stories
6. Verbs
7. Writing
8. Words That Describe
   Picture Dictionary

Brown Level
Recommended for grade 3

Chapter
1. Our Growing Language
2. Learning New Words
3. Talking with Others
4. Learning About Sentences
5. Learning About Nouns
6. Learning About Pronouns
7. Writing Paragraphs
8. Thinking Clearly
9. Improving Your Speaking and Listening Skills
10. Giving and Following Directions
11. Learning About Verbs
12. Using Verbs Correctly
13. Writing a Story
14. Making Clear Explanations
15. Learning About Adjectives
16. Telling Stories
17. Writing a Description
18. Getting Inside a Poem
19. Making Friends with Books
20. Writing a Report
21. Writing Letters
   Handbook
22. Using Capital Letters
23. Using Punctuation Marks

Aqua Level
Recommended for grade 4

Chapter
1. Learning New Words
2. Levels of Language
3. Getting Acquainted with Others
4. Learning About Sentences
5. Writing Good Sentences
6. Using Nouns
7. Using Pronouns
8. Using the Exact Word
9. Writing Paragraphs
10. Improving Your Speaking and Listening Skills
11. Talking in Groups
12. Using Verbs
13. Using Verbs Correctly
14. Telling Stories
15. Writing About Things That Happened
16. Improving Your Handwriting
17. Using Adjectives
18. Using Adverbs
19. Writing Descriptions
20. Writing Paragraphs That Explain Why
21. Writing a Story
22. Using the Dictionary
23. Using the Library
24. Enjoying Poetry
25. Writing a Report
26. Writing Friendly Letters
27. Writing Business Letters
   Handbook: The Mechanics of Writing
28. Using Capital Letters
29. Using Punctuation Marks
30. Improving Your Spelling

Silver Level
Recommended for grade 5

Chapter
1. Learning New Words
2. Learning Word Meaning from Context
3. Improving Your Reading and Study Skills
4. Learning About Sentences
5. Writing Good Sentences
6. Writing Good Paragraphs
7. Ways of Developing Paragraphs
8. Kinds of Paragraphs
9. Using Nouns
10. Using Verbs
11. Using Pronouns
12. Using Irregular Verbs Correctly
13. Improving Your Handwriting
14. Using the Library
15. Using the Dictionary
16. Using Adjectives
17. Using Adverbs
18. Making Language Lively
19. Writing a Composition
20. Writing a Story
21. Group Discussion
22. Telling Stories
23. Oral and Written Reports
24. Writing Letters
   Handbook: The Mechanics of Writing
25. Capitalization
26. Punctuation
27. Improving Your Spelling

Gold Level
Recommended for grade 6

Chapter
1. How Our Language Grows
2. Developing a Vocabulary of Specific Words
3. Learning About Sentences
4. Writing Good Paragraphs
5. Ways of Developing a Paragraph
6. Different Kinds of Paragraphs
7. Using Nouns
8. Using Verbs
9. Using Pronouns
10. Using the Dictionary
11. Using the Library
12. Writing Compositions and Reports
13. Different Kinds of Compositions
14. Using Adjectives
15. Using Adverbs
16. Using Prepositions and Conjunctions
17. Writing Letters
18. Making Subjects and Verbs Agree
19. Using Irregular Verbs
20. Improving Your Speaking Skills
21. Improving Your Listening Skills
   Handbook: The Mechanics of Writing
22. Capitalization
23. Punctuation
24. Spelling

Books recommended for levels above Grade 6:

Purple Level
Recommended for grade 12

Yellow Level
Recommended for grade 11

Blue Level
Recommended for grade 10

Orange Level
Recommended for grade 9

Green Level
Recommended for grade 8

Red Level
Recommended for grade 7

The Help Provided in This Teacher's Edition

1. The entire student text is reproduced exactly as in the student edition.

2. Teaching Suggestions for the pages of the student text are provided in the outside margins.

Chapter 16

Using Adjectives

Chapter Objectives

1. To understand the function of adjectives and to identify them in sentences
2. To identify adjectives that tell *what kind*
3. To identify adjectives that tell *how many*
4. To identify the demonstrative adjectives *this*, *that*, *these*, and *those*
5. To identify articles and to use them correctly
6. To differentiate between *them* and *those*, and to use the demonstrative adjectives with the words *kind* and *kinds* correctly
7. To form the comparative and superlative forms of adjectives, and to use them correctly

Preparing the Students

Discuss the picture on page 219. Have students tell what people and things they see in the picture. Write those nouns on the board. Then ask for words that describe those people and things, and write them in front of the nouns. Point out that those descriptive words help us understand what someone is talking about.

Additional Resources

Diagnostic Test—page 433 in this T.E. Recommended for use before teaching the chapter.
Mastery Test—pages 472 and 473 in this T.E. Recommended for use after teaching the chapter.
Additional Mastery Test—Recommended for use after any necessary reteaching. (In separate booklet, *Mastery Tests, Silver Level*, pages 35 and 36.)
Skills Practice Book—pages 82–88
Duplicating Masters—pages 82–88

Part 1 What Are Adjectives?

What picture do you see in your mind when you read this sentence?

I saw a dog.

Although the sentence expresses a complete idea, it does not make the idea clear. It needs words to describe *dog* more exactly. Here are a few ways the sentence could be improved:

I saw a huge, furry dog.
I saw a small, playful dog.
I saw a vicious, wild dog.
I saw four lovable, eager dogs.

Chapter Objectives On the first page of each chapter is a list of the skills each student is expected to master in the study of the chapter.

Preparing the Students A lesson to orient the students to the subject of the chapter is provided at the beginning of each chapter.

Additional Resources This list directs teachers to additional instructional materials provided in this Teacher's Edition, and to other supporting materials that are coordinated with the chapter.

Diagnostic Test This entry lets the teacher know that a diagnostic test is provided at the back of this book for pretesting the topics and skills of this chapter.

Mastery Test The teacher is directed to the pages at the back of this text on which are reproducible tests covering the material presented in this chapter.

Additional Mastery Test The teacher is directed to the pages in a separate booklet of tests covering the material presented in this chapter.

Skills Practice Book This entry refers the teacher to the pages of a separate workbook coordinated with this chapter.

Duplicating Masters This entry refers the teacher to the duplicating master form of the *Skills Practice Book*.

Part 8 The Subject in Imperative Sentences

An imperative sentence makes a request, or gives directions or orders. Study these examples of imperative sentences. Look for the subjects.

> Switch off the light.
> Turn left at the gas station.
> Don't wake the baby.

In each of these sentences, the subject is not expressed. The subject is understood to be *you*.

> (You) Switch off the light.
> (You) Turn left at the gas station.
> (You) Don't wake the baby.

Exercises Finding the Subject

A. Copy the following sentences. Some are imperative sentences. Draw two lines under the verb in each sentence. Draw one line under the subject of the verb. If the subject is not given in the sentence, write it in parentheses in the place where it is understood.

> Example: Wait here for me.
>
>   (You) Wait here for me.

1. Try it again. (You) try
2. Deliver the papers before school. (You) deliver
3. Karen took the message.
4. Have a second helping. (You) have
5. Stay in your seats. (You) stay
6. Who wants chocolate ice cream?
7. Look at that fancy car. (You) look
8. Add one cup of flour. (You) add

Part 8

Objective
To identify the simple subject, or subject of the verb

Presenting the Lesson
1. If necessary, review the definition of an imperative sentence. Read and discuss page 61. Ask students for further examples. Ask them how many different subjects there are for imperative sentences. Point out that knowing that *you* is the only subject makes it much easier to find.
2. You may want to do Exercise A on pages 61 and 62 with the students. Assign and discuss Exercise B on page 62.
3. Use Exercise H on page 67 for additional practice or review.

Optional Practice
Give the following directions to your students:
Imagine you are the adult leader of a scout troop (or other social organization). You are going to take your group to a play. Write six imperative sentences telling them how you want them to behave. Leave a space before each sentence. After you finish, go back and write the understood subject *you* in parentheses in that space. Be ready to read one of your sentences aloud.

Extending the Lesson
Have each student write three imperative sentences which tell another student to do something in the classroom. (Examples: Write

---

Objective The skill each student is expected to master in this Part is specified at the beginning of the Part.

Presenting the Lesson Step-by-step suggestions are provided for teaching each Part in the chapter, stressing points of emphasis and offering suggestions for use of the exercises.

Optional Practice An additional teaching resource is frequently provided for drill or review of materials.

Extending the Lesson An enrichment lesson or exercise that approaches the material in another way is frequently suggested.

Answer Key Answers to questions are overprinted on the student text.

The Help Provided in This Teacher's Edition (continued)

3. Additional teaching aids, located at the back of this book, on the pages marked with gray tabs:

Practice Pages on Irregular Verbs (Pages 405–424) Eighteen practice pages (one page on each of eighteen verbs) provide for drill and practice. McDougal, Littell & Company hereby grants you permission to reproduce these pages for your students' use. A pretest (page 405) will enable you to assess student needs.

Diagnostic Tests (Pages 428–437) These tests are provided so that you can pretest students before you teach the chapters on grammar, usage, and mechanics. The Diagnostic Tests cover essential topics and skills presented at the preceding level of *Building English Skills*. The tests will help you tailor the presentation of the chapter to the needs of the class. McDougal, Littell & Company hereby gives you permission to reproduce these pages for your students' use.

Mastery Tests (Pages 438–496) Mastery tests are provided for all chapters except those on speaking and listening. They test the specific skills presented in each chapter. You may use them at the completion of each chapter to determine student weaknesses and any needs for reteaching. Midyear and end-of-year tests are also provided. These are cumulative, testing all the skills covered in the individual mastery tests. McDougal, Littell & Company hereby gives you permission to reproduce these pages for your students' use.

A class record sheet is provided on pages 426 and 427, listing all diagnostic and mastery tests and providing space for students' scores.

Letters to Parents (Pages 497–498) Two letters to parents are provided to help you inform parents of the program and of ways they can reinforce your teaching. The letters are designed to be sent home at the beginning and at the end of the school year. McDougal, Littell & Company hereby gives you permission to reproduce these pages.

Additional Supporting Materials

Besides the exercises and drills provided in the student text and the Teacher's Edition, additional supporting materials are available. These are coordinated with the chapters in *Building English Skills, Silver Level*. The relevant pages in each of these outside sources are listed under "Additional Resources" in the teaching suggestions for each chapter:

1. Skills Practice Book This consumable workbook provides additional practice and reinforcement, keyed to the chapters in the text.

2. Mastery Tests This consumable booklet provides a new set of Mastery Tests for each chapter. The tests are similar in form to the Mastery Tests provided at the back of this Teacher's Edition, but are different in content. If, after administering the Mastery Tests provided in this Teacher's Edition, you feel it necessary to do some reteaching, you may use the additional Mastery Tests for further retesting. The additional Mastery Tests also provide a convenient basic testing program if you prefer to use tests that are already in handy consumable booklets, one booklet for each student.

3. Duplicating Masters These provide an alternate form of the pages in the *Skills Practice Book*.

Building English Skills

Purple Level

Yellow Level

Blue Level

Orange Level

Green Level

Red Level

Gold Level

SILVER LEVEL

Aqua Level

Brown Level

Plum Level

Pink Level

Cherry Level (K)

Building English Skills

Silver Level

McDougal, Littell & Company

Evanston, Illinois
Sacramento, California

Authors

Kathleen L. Bell, Arizona State University. Formerly, Chairperson, English Department, Lincoln Junior High School, Mount Prospect, Illinois

Frances Freeman Paden, Consultant in Language and Speech, Evanston, Illinois

Susan Duffy Schaffrath, Specialist in Educational Materials for the Elementary and Middle Grades, Chicago, Illinois

Consultants

Linda Coleman, Teacher, District 109, Deerfield, Illinois
Ann Curry Hemwall, Teacher, District 65, Evanston, Illinois
Roberta T. McCollister, Teacher, District 65, Evanston, Illinois
Marguerite Opaskar, Teacher, Cleveland Public Schools, Cleveland, Ohio

WARNING: No part of this book may be reproduced or transmitted in any form or by any means, electronic or mechanical, including photocopying, recording, or by any information storage and retrieval system, without permission in writing from the Publisher.

Editorial Direction: **Joy Littell**

Associate Editor: **Patricia Opaskar**

Design: **William A. Seabright**

Acknowledgments: See page 404.

ISBN: 0-88343-571-3

Copyright © 1980 by McDougal, Littell & Company
Box 1667, Evanston, Illinois 60204
All rights reserved. Printed in the United States of America

Chapters 4, 5, 9, 10, 11, 12, 13, 16, 17, 25, 26, and 27 contain, in revised form, some materials that appeared originally in *The Macmillan English Series, Grade 5,* by Thomas Clark Pollock et al., copyright © 1963 by The Macmillan Company. Used by arrangement.

Contents

Chapter 1 **Learning New Words**   1

    Part 1   Base Words   2
    Part 2   Prefixes   4
    Part 3   Suffixes   7

           Additional Exercises   11

Chapter 2 **Learning Word Meaning from Context**   13

    Part 1   A Definition in Context   14
    Part 2   A Restatement in Context   16
    Part 3   An Example in Context   18

           Additional Exercises   21

Chapter 3 **Improving Your Reading and Study Skills**   23

    Part 1   Getting Ready To Study   24
    Part 2   Improving Your Reading   27

           Additional Exercises   36

Chapter 4 Learning About Sentences — 39

- Part 1 What Is a Sentence? 40
- Part 2 Different Kinds of Sentences 44
- Part 3 Punctuating Sentences 48
- Part 4 Parts of the Sentence 50
- Part 5 The Simple Predicate, or Verb 53
- Part 6 The Simple Subject, or Subject of the Verb 56
- Part 7 The Subject in Unusual Positions 59
- Part 8 The Subject in Imperative Sentences 61

Sentence Patterns: Word Order and Meaning 63

Additional Exercises 64

Chapter 5 Writing Good Sentences — 69

- Part 1 Avoiding Run-on Sentences 69
- Part 2 Avoiding Stringy Sentences 72

Additional Exercises 74

Chapter 6 Writing Good Paragraphs — 77

- Part 1 What Is a Paragraph? 78
- Part 2 The Topic Sentence 82
- Part 3 Writing Good Topic Sentences 85

Additional Exercises 89

Chapter 7 Ways of Developing Paragraphs — 91

- Part 1 Developing a Paragraph by Using Details 92
- Part 2 Developing a Paragraph by Using an Example 95

Additional Exercises 97

Chapter 8 Kinds of Paragraphs   99

- Part 1 The Narrative Paragraph   100
- Part 2 The Descriptive Paragraph   104
- Part 3 The Explanatory Paragraph   108

   Additional Exercises   111

Chapter 9 Using Nouns   113

- Part 1 What Are Nouns?   113
- Part 2 Common Nouns and Proper Nouns   115
- Part 3 Singular and Plural Nouns   117
- Part 4 Making Nouns Show Possession   120

   Sentence Patterns: The N V Pattern   123

   Additional Exercises   124

Chapter 10 Using Verbs   127

- Part 1 What Are Verbs?   127
- Part 2 Main Verbs and Helping Verbs   131
- Part 3 Direct Objects of Verbs   136
- Part 4 Using the Right Form of *Be*   138
- Part 5 Using the Right Verb After *There, Here,* and *Where*   140
- Part 6 Some Confusing Verbs   143
- Part 7 Using Contractions   147
- Part 8 Using Negatives Correctly   148

   Sentence Patterns: The N V N Pattern   150

   Sentence Patterns: The N LV N Pattern   151

   Additional Exercises   152

Chapter 11 Using Pronouns 157

- Part 1 Substituting Pronouns for Nouns 157
- Part 2 Using Pronouns as Subjects 161
- Part 3 Using Pronouns After State-of-Being Verbs 164
- Part 4 Using Pronouns as Objects 165
- Part 5 Using *We* and *Us* 167
- Part 6 Possessive Pronouns 168

  Additional Exercises 171

Chapter 12 Using Irregular Verbs Correctly 175

- Part 1 Regular Verbs 175
- Part 2 Irregular Verbs 180

Chapter 13 Improving Your Handwriting 183

- Part 1 Studying Handwriting 183
- Part 2 Learning Different Ways of Writing 185
- Part 3 Shaping Letters Carefully 187

  Additional Exercises 189

Chapter 14 Using the Library 191

- Part 1 Two Kinds of Books 192
- Part 2 Finding a Particular Book 196
- Part 3 How To Find Information in a Book 202

Chapter 15 Using the Dictionary 205

- Part 1 Using Alphabetical Order 206
- Part 2 Finding the Word You Want 207
- Part 3 The Dictionary Entries 211

Chapter 16　Using Adjectives　219

- Part 1　What Are Adjectives?　219
- Part 2　Some Adjectives Tell *What Kind*　222
- Part 3　Some Adjectives Tell *How Many*　223
- Part 4　Some Adjectives Tell *Which Ones*　224
- Part 5　Articles　226
- Part 6　Using Adjectives Correctly　228
- Part 7　Making Comparisons with Adjectives　230

   Sentence Patterns: The N LV Adj Pattern　234

   Additional Exercises　235

Chapter 17　Using Adverbs　239

- Part 1　What Are Adverbs?　239
- Part 2　Making Comparisons with Adverbs　242
- Part 3　Adjective or Adverb?　244

   Additional Exercises　248

Chapter 18　Making Language Lively　251

- Part 1　Using Strong Verbs　252
- Part 2　Writing Similes　254
- Part 3　Writing Metaphors　257

Chapter 19　Writing a Composition　261

- Part 1　What Is a Composition?　262
- Part 2　Finding a Subject　265
- Part 3　Planning the Composition　267
- Part 4　Writing the Introductory Paragraph　270
- Part 5　Writing the Body　272
- Part 6　Completing the Composition　274

Chapter 20 Writing a Story — 277

- Part 1   What Is a Story?   278
- Part 2   Planning a Story   281
- Part 3   Writing a Story   285

Chapter 21 Group Discussion — 289

- Part 1   Taking Part in a Discussion   289
- Part 2   Roles in a Group Discussion   293

Chapter 22 Telling Stories — 297

- Part 1   Choosing a Story   298
- Part 2   Studying the Story   300
- Part 3   Telling the Story   308

Chapter 23 Oral and Written Reports — 311

- Part 1   Finding a Subject   312
- Part 2   Gathering Information   314
- Part 3   Making a Plan   317
- Part 4   Writing Your Report   323
- Part 5   Giving an Oral Report   326

Chapter 24 Writing Letters — 331

- Part 1   Writing a Friendly Letter   331
- Part 2   Writing Social Notes   335
- Part 3   Writing Business Letters   338
- Part 4   Addressing Envelopes   344

Handbook: The Mechanics of Writing

Chapter 25 **Capitalization** 347

    Part 1 Capitalizing Proper Nouns, Proper Adjectives, and *I*   347

    Part 2 Some Kinds of Proper Nouns   349

    Part 3 More About Proper Nouns   352

    Part 4 First Words   355

    Part 5 Capitalizing Titles   358

    Additional Exercises   359

Chapter 26 **Punctuation** 363

    Part 1 Using the Period   363

    Part 2 Using the Question Mark   367

    Part 3 Using the Exclamation Point   368

    Part 4 Using the Comma   369

    Part 5 Using the Apostrophe   371

    Part 6 Using the Hyphen   374

    Part 7 Using Quotation Marks   375

    Part 8 Underlining   379

    Additional Exercises   381

Chapter 27 **Improving Your Spelling** 385

    Part 1 Plan Your Study of Spelling   386

    Part 2 Rules for Spelling   389

    Additional Exercises   395

Chapter 1

Learning New Words

Your vocabulary grows when you learn new words. Sometimes the meaning of a new word is clear right away. Often, however, you may hear or read a new word that is difficult.

Many words that seem long and difficult can be broken into parts. Very often you know the meanings of these smaller parts.

Look at the word *worker*. What is the base word in *worker*? Yes, it is *work*.

The word *unworkable* can also be broken into parts. The parts are the base word (*work*), a beginning (*un*), and an ending (*able*). There are many words that you can take apart in this same way to find their meanings.

This chapter will teach you how to find the base word in new long words. It will teach you the meanings of some common word beginnings and word endings. With this information, you will be able to unlock many new words for yourself.

Chapter Objectives

1. To find base words in words that include prefixes or suffixes or both

2. To recognize and use common prefixes to discover meanings of unfamiliar words

3. To recognize and use common suffixes to discover meanings of unfamiliar words

Preparing the Students

Write these words on the chalkboard: *preheated, nonfattening*. Ask students if they are able to identify parts of each word that can be removed from the beginning or ending, and still leave a meaningful word. Cross off or erase those parts until only *heat* and *fat* are left. Point out that the parts added to the beginning and ending changed the meanings of the words *heat* and *fat*. Explain that this first chapter of the book will help them use word parts to understand new words.

Read and discuss page 1.

Additional Resources

Mastery Test—pages 438 and 439 in this T.E. Recommended for use after teaching the chapter.

Additional Mastery Test—Recommended for use after any necessary reteaching. (In separate booklet, *Mastery Tests, Silver Level*, pages 1 and 2.)

Skills Practice Book—pages 1–4
Duplicating Masters—pages 1–4

Part 1

Objective

To find base words in words that include prefixes or suffixes or both

Presenting the Lesson

1. Read and discuss page 2. Make sure students understand the meaning of the term *base word,* and can interpret the chart on page 2.
2. Examine the illustration at the top of page 3. On the board, write the base word from which each word in the picture is formed. Point out that the final *e* in *believe* and *freeze* has been dropped, but that this change does not affect the meaning. Ask students to supply additional examples of words with added parts that would fit in the picture.
3. It is strongly recommended that, before assigning any Exercise throughout this text, the teacher should read over the directions with the class and resolve any difficulties or misunderstandings. Often it is advisable that the class do part of the Exercise together. In all cases, after the students have completed the assignment, it is important that the answers be discussed. Students need to know how to improve incorrect answers, and will benefit from reinforcement of correct responses. The phrase "assign and discuss" is used throughout the Teacher's Edition to refer to this development and use of each Exercise.

It is suggested that Exercise A on page 3 be done as a class activity. Assign and discuss Exercise B.

4. Use Exercise A on page 11 for additional practice or review.

Part 1 Base Words

Some new words are built. That is, a beginning or an ending is added to a word you already know. For example, the beginning *un-* is added to the word *tie* to make a new word. The new word is *untie.* Also, the ending *-ment* is added to the word *move* to make *movement.* The words *tie* and *move* are examples of base words. A **base word** is the word to which a beginning or ending is added.

Beginning	Base Word	Ending	New Word
un +	tie		= untie
	move	+ ment	= movement

What base word is in these three words?

> reader
> misread
> readable

The base word is *read.* The ending *-er* was added to make *reader.* The beginning *mis-* was added to make *misread.* The ending *-able* was added to make *readable.* These three new words were built. They all have the same base word.

What Is the Base Word?

pre**view**   **sense**less
viewer   non**sense**
re**view**   **sens**ible

Exercises Base Words

A. Copy each of the following words on a sheet of paper. Find the base word in each. Write the base word after each word.

1. rebuild
2. unthinkable
3. nonspeaker
4. laborer
5. precooked
6. joyous
7. misspell
8. hopeless
9. thoughtful
10. unfit

B. Follow the directions for Exercise A.

1. careless
2. misbehave
3. untouchable
4. caller
5. unhelpful
6. hazardous
7. unwanted
8. preview
9. remake
10. harmless

Optional Practice

1. Make a set of flash cards from the following list:

Base Words	Beginnings	Endings
work	count	mis	er
use	make	non	or
pay	name	pre	ous
stop	call	un	able
place	help	re	ible
zip	wash		less
print	turn		ful
play			

Have drills and contests using these cards. Students identify cards as base words, beginnings, or endings.

2. Another activity is to combine flash cards. Shuffle each group separately, and have a student select one card from each set. The student earns a point for each new word he or she can make by combining the cards. Variations of this activity can be devised for team contests.

3. Have students draw a chart like the one on page 2. Ask them to search through books, newspapers, and advertisements for words that have added beginnings, endings, or both. Give them a few days to fill up their chart.

Part 2

Objective

To recognize and use common prefixes to discover meanings of unfamiliar words

Presenting the Lesson

1. Explain that the word *prefix* has the base word *fix* plus a beginning *pre*. This beginning means "before." The total word *prefix* means "to fix before" a word. Give examples of words changed by having prefixes added, such as cook, precook; heat, preheat; test, pretest.

2. Read and discuss pages 4 and 5 including the illustration. Put the headings *Prefix, Base Word,* and *New Word* on the chalkboard. Ask students to build additional words by using the prefix *mis* plus a base word, and to write their examples on the board. Do the same for each of the five common prefixes listed on page 5.

3. Emphasize that when words begin with the letters found in these prefixes, the letters are not necessarily a prefix. Besides the words *unit, real,* and *miser* discussed in the text, test the words *under* and *unhealthy* for prefixes.

4. Assign and discuss Exercises A and B on page 6.

5. You may prefer to do Exercise C as a class activity.

6. Use Exercise B on page 11 for additional practice.

Part 2 Prefixes

A **prefix** is a word part added at the beginning of a word. When a prefix is added to a word, it changes the meaning of the word. It makes a new word. If *mis-* is added to *use*, a new word is made. The new word is *misuse*. The base word is *use*. The prefix is *mis-*.

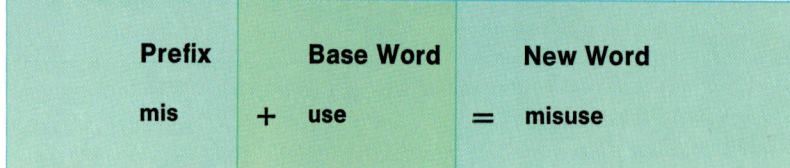

Prefix	Base Word	New Word
mis	+ use	= misuse

Five Useful Prefixes

Here are five prefixes that are often used in English. Each prefix has one or two meanings. Learn the meanings of these five prefixes. You will then be better able to understand hundreds of English words.

> **mis-** This prefix means "wrong" or "wrongly." A *misstep* is a step in the wrong place. To *mistreat* is to treat wrongly.
>
> **non-** This prefix always means "not." *Nonliving* means "not alive." *Nonstop* means "having no stops, continuous."
>
> **pre-** This prefix always means "before." *Preschool* is the school before elementary school. *Presoak* means "to soak clothes before they are washed."
>
> **un-** This prefix may mean "not." *Unnamed* means not named. The prefix may also mean "the reverse of." *Unzip* means the reverse of *zip*. Therefore, it means "to open or unfasten."
>
> **re-** This prefix also has two meanings. It may mean "back." *Repay* means "to pay back." The prefix may also mean "again." *Reappear* means "to appear again."

Sometimes you may come across a word that looks as if it has a prefix but really doesn't. For example, the letters *un-* are not a prefix in *unit*. The letters *re-* are not a prefix in *real*.

How can you tell when a group of letters is a prefix and when it is not? Decide whether the word makes sense when you take off the prefix. Is *mis-* a prefix in *miser*? Take off *mis-* and test what is left. There is no such word as *er*. Then *mis-* is not a prefix in *miser*.

Optional Practice

1. Ask students to create their own list of base words and to follow the directions for Exercise B on page 6.

2. Have small groups of students examine various parts of a newspaper for prefixes. Good sections are: sports, classified, fashions, recipes, politics, weather, and tv and movie reviews. Have students list the words they find in two categories: *Prefixes studied*, and *Prefixes not studied*.

Have students research the following prefixes:

ex- uni- sub- super-
bi- multi- post- trans-

Students should do the following:
  a. Find the meaning of each new prefix
  b. Write two example words with each new prefix

Exercises Prefixes

A. One word in each of the following pairs has a prefix discussed in this chapter. The other does not. Write only the words with prefixes. Draw a circle around each prefix.

1. nonviolent, none   (non) violent
2. pressure, prewar   (pre) war
3. reckless, replace   (re) place
4. unkind, unite   (un) kind
5. misty, misprint   (mis) print

B. Here are a list of prefixes and a list of base words. Build as many new words as you can. Use any of the prefixes with any of the base words. For example, from the base word *pay* you could make *repay* and *prepay*. Not all of the base words and prefixes will go together. Use your dictionary to check your new words. *These are suggested answers.*

	Prefixes	Base Words
misnamed, miscalled	mis-	named
nonsmoking	non-	called
preheated	pre-	smoking
unnamed, unmade, unheated	un-	made
renamed, recalled, remade, reheated	re-	heated

mismatch

C. Answer these questions.

1. If a *conception* is an idea, what is a *misconception*?   *wrong idea*
2. If *compliance* is giving in to the wishes of others, what is *noncompliance*?   *not giving in*
3. If *dawn* is the beginning of daylight, what is *predawn*?   *before the beginning of daylight*
4. If a *grateful* person is thankful, what is an *ungrateful* person?   *not grateful*
5. What do these mean?
   a. to *redo* a project   *do a project again*
   b. to *replay* a tape   *play a tape again*

Part 3 Suffixes

A **suffix** is a word part added at the end of a base word. A suffix changes the meaning of the base word. The word part *-less* is a suffix in *breathless* and *helpless*. The base words are *breath* and *help*.

Base Word	Suffix	New Word
breath	+ less	= breathless
help	+ less	= helpless

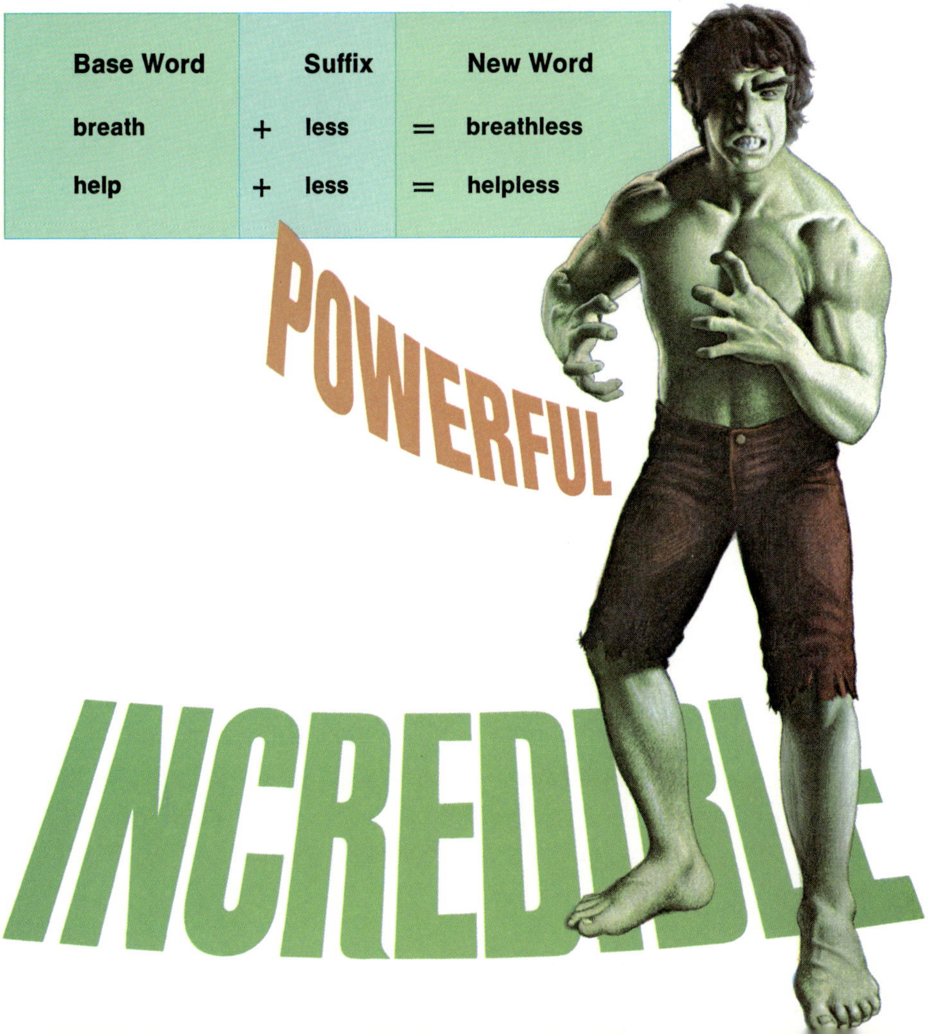

Part 3

Objective

To recognize and use common suffixes to discover meanings of unfamiliar words

Presenting the Lesson

1. Read and discuss pages 7 and 8, including the illustration on page 7. Note that the text covers relevant spelling changes in Chapter 27, Improving Your Spelling.

2. Put on the chalkboard the suffixes listed on page 8. Ask students to recall words they know using these suffixes. List the students' examples under each suffix.

3. It is suggested that Exercise A on page 9 be done as a class activity. Assign and discuss Exercises B and C.

4. Use Exercise C on page 11 for additional practice or review.

5. Assign and discuss the Review Exercises on page 10.

Optional Practice

1. Have students search a newspaper for common suffixes.

2. Have students prepare an exercise similar to Exercise B on page 6, using suffixes listed on page 8 and common base words.

Extending the Lesson

1. Have students research these suffixes and answer the following questions:

-age   -fold   -ship
-hood   -word

1. From what language did each suffix originate?
2. What does each of them mean?
3. Can you use each one to form at least two new words?

2. Play Build-A-Word Rummy. Have groups of two to four students use a deck of fifty-two 3x5 index cards made up of base words, prefixes, and suffixes. The deck consists of the following: fifteen common base words, such as those used in the text examples and exercises; the five prefixes studied; the five suffixes studied; and two wild cards.

Five Useful Suffixes

Here are five common suffixes. These suffixes have one or two clear meanings.

-er or **-or**	These suffixes mean "a person or thing that does something." For example, a *traveler* travels, and a *collector* collects. The suffix *-er* may also mean "more." *Colder* means "more cold."
-less	This suffix means "without." For example, a *speechless* person is a person without speech.
-able or **-ible**	These suffixes have two meanings. They can mean "can be." For example, a *divisible* number can be divided. A *crushable* box can be crushed. The suffixes can also mean "having this feature." For example, a *comfortable* chair has the feature of comfort. A *sensible* question has the feature of good sense.
-ful	This suffix has two meanings. It can mean "full of." A *handful* of dirt means a hand that is full of dirt. The suffix can also mean "having." A *beautiful* person has beauty.
-ous	This suffix also means "full of" or "having." A *vigorous* person is full of vigor or energy.

When a suffix is added to some base words, the spelling of the base word changes. Notice how these words are changed:

beauty, beautiful   sense, sensible   flip, flipper

For more information on these spelling changes, refer to Chapter 27, pages 390 to 392.

beauty	erase	flip
beauti**ful**	eras**able**	flipp**er**

Exercises Suffixes

A. Copy these words on a piece of paper. After each word, write the base word. Then write the suffix that was added.

Examples: dipper = dip + er   ridiculous = ridicule + ous

1. carrier *carry + er*
2. eventful *event + ful*
3. thoughtless *thought + less*
4. continuous *continue + ous*
5. pitiful *pity + ful*
6. famous *fame + ous*
7. breakable *break + able*
8. actor *act + or*
9. lovable *love + able*
10. fearless *fear + less*

B. Put the following base words and suffixes together. Check the spelling in a dictionary.

1. warm + er *warmer*
2. spoon + ful *spoonful*
3. drink + able *drinkable*
4. conduct + or *conductor*
5. convert + ible *convertible*
6. play + er *player*
7. control + able *controllable*
8. danger + ous *dangerous*
9. hope + less *hopeless*
10. joy + ful *joyful*

C. Answer these questions.

1. If *pacify* means "to bring peace," what is a *pacifier*? *a person or thing that brings peace*
2. If *decipher* means "to change a code into plain language," what does *decipherable* mean? *able to be changed into plain language*
3. If worth means "value," what does *worthless* mean? *without value*
4. If *glee* means "joy," what does *gleeful* mean? *full of joy*
5. If *advantage* means "benefit or favor," what does *advantageous* mean? *having an advantage*

The object of the game is to build words by combining the base word cards with the prefixes and/or suffixes. Words are then allowed to be placed, face up, in front of the student until he or she has used up all the cards in hand.

The cards are shuffled and dealt, seven to each player, starting at the dealer's left. The remaining cards are laid in a pile, face down, in the center of the playing surface. One card is turned over to start a discard pile. The player to the left of the dealer either chooses the turned-up card or the first face-down card. This player may form one or more words with the cards he or she holds, placing them on the playing surface. The player then discards one card. The next player can choose the discard or draw a new one.

Play continues until someone uses all his or her cards and yells, "Rummy." That player is the winner.

Review Exercises

Assign and discuss the Review Exercises on page 10.

Review Exercises **Learning Word Parts**

A. Copy the following words. Find the base word. Write the base word. Then write any prefix or suffix used with it.

Example: unhappy
happy, un

1. miscast cast, mis
2. returnable turn, re, able
3. joyous joy, ous
4. predate date, pre
5. unlawful law, un, ful
6. nonfiction fiction, non
7. mislead lead, mis
8. react act, re
9. marker mark, er
10. heartless heart, less

B. Follow the directions for Exercise A. Do not be confused by spelling changes: some final *e*'s have been dropped; final *y*'s have been changed to *i;* and final consonants have been doubled.

Example: maker
make, er

1. unspeakable speak, un, able
2. nonsmoker smoke, non, er
3. worrier worry, er
4. nonconductor conduct, non, or
5. endless end, less
6. runner run, er
7. reusable use, re
8. presoak soak, pre
9. carrier carry, er
10. nonpoisonous poison, non, ous

C. Answer these questions.

1. If *force* means strength, what does *forcible* mean? having strength
2. If *fancy* means imagination, what does *fanciful* mean? full of imagination
3. If *fortune* means luck, what does *misfortune* mean? bad luck
4. If *relenting* means becoming easy or letting up, what does *unrelenting* mean? not becoming easy, not letting up
5. If *aggression* means violence, what does *nonaggression* mean? not violent

Additional Exercises

Learning New Words

A. Base Words (Use after page 3.)

Copy each of the following words on a sheet of paper. Find the base word in each. Write the base word after each word.

1. un*fold*
2. *noise*less
3. pre*school*
4. re*place*
5. *wonder*ful
6. mis*judge*
7. *paint*er
8. un*sink*able
9. un*believe*able

B. Prefixes (Use after page 5.)

Answer these questions.

1. If an *informed* person is one who knows things, what is a *misinformed* person?   <small>a person who has the wrong information</small>
2. If something *flammable* is something that will burn, what is something *nonflammable*?   <small>something that will not burn</small>
3. If *fabricate* means "make," what does *prefabricate* mean?   <small>to make before</small>
4. Something *remarkable* is something unusual enough to be noticed. What is something *unremarkable*?   <small>something not unusual enough to be noticed</small>
5. If *construct* means "build," what does *reconstruct* mean?   <small>to build again</small>

C. Suffixes (Use after page 8.)

Answer these questions.

1. If *purify* means "to make clean," what is a water *purifier*?   <small>a water cleaner</small>
2. If *excuse* means "to forgive," what is an *excusable* act?   <small>an act that can be forgiven</small>
3. If a *defense* is a way of protecting something, what is a *defenseless* animal?   <small>an animal without defense</small>
4. If *fret* means "to worry," what is a *fretful* person?   <small>a person who is full of or has worry</small>
5. If *thunder* is a loud sound, what is *thunderous* applause?   <small>very loud applause (full of thunder)</small>

Additional Exercises

If these Exercises were not used with each lesson, they may now be assigned for chapter review.

Chapter 2

Learning Word Meaning from Context

Often, in your reading, you will find a totally new word, or a word with two possible meanings. The rest of the sentence can give you a clue to its correct meaning. The words and sentences around a specific word are called its **context.**

How do you use context to discover the meaning of a new word? This example shows you how. Notice how the word *light* is used in each of these sentences.

> The boys on their shoulders are small and *light*.
> The *light* on their faces is bright.

In the first sentence, *light* means "not heavy." In the second sentence, it means "the light from the sun." You can tell the meanings from the other words in the sentences.

In this chapter, you will learn how to examine the context of a new word. The context may reveal its meaning.

Chapter Objectives

1. To find definitions in context, signaled by certain key words
2. To find and use restatement in context to discover word meanings
3. To recognize examples in context that suggest meanings of unfamiliar words

Preparing the Students

Review with the students the different methods they use for discovering the meaning of unfamiliar words. They should be able to suggest such approaches as breaking the word down to base word plus prefix or suffix, asking someone else, and consulting the dictionary. List the approaches on the board. If nobody suggests it, add the method of examining the passage in which the word appears. Remind the students that this last method will often reveal the meaning of the word, without the use of any outside source.

Read and discuss the introduction to the chapter on page 13.

Additional Resources

Mastery Test—pages 440 and 441 in this T. E. Recommended for use after teaching the chapter.

Additional Mastery Test—Recommended for use after any necessary reteaching. (In separate booklet, *Mastery Tests, Silver Level,* pages 3 and 4.)

Skills Practice Book—pages 5–8
Duplicating Masters—pages 5–8

Part 1

Objective

To find definitions in context, signaled by certain key words

Presenting the Lesson

1. Put the words *horseshoe crab, arid, philatelist,* and *key* on the chalkboard. Ask how many students could tell the meaning of each word.

2. Read the first paragraph and the examples at the top of page 14. Again ask how many students could tell the meaning of each word. Point out that many of the students learned the meanings simply from the examples. They found the definitions in context.

3. Read and discuss the rest of pages 14 and 15. Emphasize the role of the key words *which is, that is, in other words,* and *is,* as signals to definitions. Go over the steps to finding a definition in context.

4. Assign and discuss the Exercise on page 15. It may be helpful to have students put their answers on the chalkboard.

5. For extra practice, assign Exercise A on page 21.

Optional Practice

1. Put the word *pass* on the chalkboard. Ask students to give you as many meanings as possible for the word *pass*. List them on the chalkboard. Now guide students to construct sentences using the key words explained on page 14. Put this example on the chalkboard.

> He threw a touchdown pass, which is a scoring throw, to his favorite receiver.

Part 1   A Definition in Context

Sometimes a writer knows that a certain word will be new to many readers. Therefore, the writer may include a **definition** of the word in a sentence.

Read these examples:

> He caught a *horseshoe crab*, which is a sea animal with a large oval shell.
>
> It was an *arid* desert. That is, it was dry and hot.
>
> She is a *philatelist*. In other words, she collects stamps.
>
> He sailed his boat near the *key*. A key is a low-lying island or reef.

In the first example, the writer tells you that the horseshoe crab is a certain kind of sea animal. In the second example, the writer tells you that *arid* means hot and dry. In the third example, the writer tells you that a philatelist is a person who collects stamps. In the fourth example, the writer gives you the definition of *key* in a sentence of its own. In these examples, the key words *which is, that is, in other words,* and *is* signal definitions.

Definitions are easy to spot. The context of the word tells you exactly what the word means.

Finding a Definition in Context

When you read a word you don't recognize, follow these steps:

1. Examine the words following the new word. Look for these key words: *which is, who is, that is, in other words, is*.

2. If you find one of these keys, carefully read the words following the key. These words give the definition of the new word.

3. Reread the sentence or paragraph with the new word. Be sure the meaning of the new word is clear to you.

Elicit examples for different meanings of *pass* using *which is, that is, in other words*, and *is*. Write the students' sentences on the board. Examine these and discuss their use of the keys.

2. This exercise may be assigned to your more advanced students, for a small group game. Before the group session, provide a list of interesting unfamiliar words, such as those suggested below. Each student is to find the meaning of one of the words in a dictionary, and to prepare a sentence that will explain the meaning by using one of the key words. In the group session, each student has a turn reading his or her sentence. The first classmate able to identify the word being defined, and the definition, earns a point. Play continues until each student has had a turn.

Suggested words:

tycoon	bedlam	yawl
aardvark	deluge	zither
apex	defunct	xyster
adieu	ibex	gourmet
beacon	zebu	egress

Exercise   A Definition in Context

Each of these sentences contains a definition. Write the word that is defined. Write the definition. Then write any key words that helped you find the definition.

Example: Benjamin Franklin published an almanac, which is a yearly calendar.
almanac—a yearly calendar—which is

1. He is a philanthropist. That is, he devotes time and money to helping others.
philanthropist—a person who devotes time and money to helping others—that is

2. The clown rode a dromedary, which is a camel having only one hump.
dromedary—a camel having only one hump—which is

3. You should not prevaricate. In other words, you should not tell a lie.
prevaricate—to tell a lie—in other words

4. For breakfast, I ate a scone with butter. A scone is a round, flat cake or biscuit.
scone—a round, flat cake or biscuit—is

5. In Mexico he saw an iguana, which is a large, climbing lizard.
iguana—a large climbing lizard—which is

Part 2

Objective

To find and use restatement in context to discover word meanings

Presenting the Lesson

1. Read and discuss pages 16 and 17. Pay particular attention to the guidelines on page 17.

2. Make it clear that the four keys discussed in this Part do not always signal a restatement. Present the following sentences to the students and ask them to identify which sentence in each pair presents a restatement.

or: Either Bob or Annie will help you.
    The rotund, or round, man played Santa Claus.

dashes: She was squeamish—easily made sick—after the roller coaster ride.
    My money—have you seen my money?

commas: He ordered squab, a pigeon used for food, for dinner.
    Clinton, Massachusetts, is north of Worcester.

parentheses: The first story (about a mermaid) is the saddest one in the book.
    That shirt is chartreuse (a light yellowish green).

3. Assign and discuss the Exercise on page 17.

4. For additional practice, assign Exercise B on page 21.

16

Part 2   A Restatement in Context

A writer will not always give an obvious definition for a new word, with key words to signal the definition. More often, he or she will tell you the meaning indirectly in a **restatement.**

A restatement tells you almost as much as a definition. However, it is not as easy to spot. Look at the following examples.

Rotting leaves put *fertilizer*, or plant food, on the roses.

She saw a colony of *gannets*—large, white sea birds—on the rocks by the sea.

Her eyes were like *limpid* pools of water, perfectly clear.

I'd like some *pâté* (chopped liver).

In the first example, the writer restates *fertilizer* as "plant food." There are two keys that a restatement comes next. The first key is the word *or*. The second key is the use of commas. They separate the restatement from the rest of the sentence.

In the second example, *gannets* is restated. They are "large, white sea birds." Dashes separate the words *large, white sea birds* from the rest of the sentence. These dashes are a key that a restatement comes next.

The words *perfectly clear* restate *limpid* in the third example. There is only one small key. It is the comma that separates the words *perfectly clear* from the rest of the sentence.

The writer uses parentheses in the fourth example. The words *chopped liver* restate *pâté*. The parentheses are the key.

These four examples show four different keys for restatement. The keys are as follows:

1. the word *or*
2. dashes
3. commas
4. parentheses

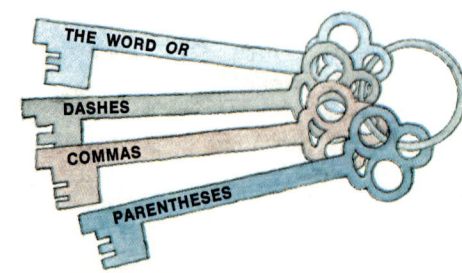

Finding a Restatement in Context

When you read a word you don't recognize, follow these steps:

1. Examine the sentence containing the new word. Look for the four keys for restatement: the word *or*, dashes, commas, or parentheses.

2. If you find *or* or a comma, carefully read the words following that key. They may give the meaning of the new word. If you find dashes or parentheses, read the words between those marks for the meaning.

3. Reread the sentence until you understand the meaning of the new word.

Optional Practice

Find and reproduce a newspaper article, or other short reading selection, that has examples of restatement keys. Students are to circle the word whose meaning is defined through context keys. They are to underline the surrounding words and sentences that help give the meaning. Give bonus credit to students finding all the examples in the passage.

Exercise A Restatement in Context

Number a sheet of paper from 1 to 5. Each of these sentences includes a restatement of the underlined word or words. Write the meaning of the underlined word. Then write which key helped you find the restatement.

1. The sound of a bell reverberated, or echoed, through the town.

echoed—the word or

2. We were trying to learn the mambo, a Latin American dance.

a Latin American dance—comma

3. The river was lined by levees (raised banks of earth or concrete to keep the river from flooding).

raised banks of earth or concrete to keep a river from flooding—parentheses

4. The smelt, a small fish, has a delicate taste.

a small fish—commas

5. A vista—distant view—of pine forests and lakes opened before us.

distant view—dashes

Part 3

Objective

To recognize examples in context that suggest meanings of unfamiliar words.

Presenting the Lesson

1. Read and discuss page 18. Stress the fact that using examples to find meaning requires both imagination and logical thinking. The reader must be able to identify the category to which the given example or examples belong, before being able to place the new word in that category. For example, one sentence tells about ''implements like screwdrivers and pliers.'' This can be helpful only if the reader knows what screwdrivers and pliers are. Then the reader must correctly put them in the category ''small tools used in repair work.'' Only then can the reader define *implements* as ''small tools.''

2. Assign and discuss the Exercise at the top of page 19. Some students may find it difficult to find the terms in the dictionary. Give them individual assistance at this time; they will improve dictionary skills when studying Chapter 15, Using the Dictionary.

3. For additional practice, assign Exercise C on page 21.

Optional Practice

1. Divide students into groups of six. Provide each group with a different list of six unknown words and simple meanings. Here is a sample list.

1. adios—goodbye in Spanish
2. adze—a carpenter's tool for chipping

Part 3 An Example in Context

A writer may use an **example** to give a clue to the meaning of a new word. Look at these sentences.

> The children were dressed as hobgoblins and other scary characters.
>
> Most kinds of spooky creatures, like hobgoblins, are not real.

Neither sentence tells what a hobgoblin is. But both sentences give clues. The first sentence tells that a hobgoblin is an example of a scary character. The second sentence tells you that a hobgoblin is an example of a spooky creature. Therefore, you have a good idea of what *hobgoblin* means. You have received context clues in the form of examples.

Watch for the following key words. They will often tell you that the context gives an example:

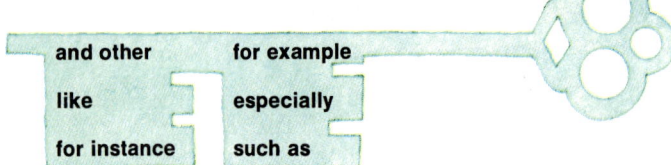

and other   for example
like   especially
for instance such as

Here are some sentences that use these key words. Can you find the context clues that suggest the meaning of the underlined words?

> Mary likes schnauzers and other kinds of dogs. and other
>
> Implements like screwdrivers and pliers are handy. like
>
> Diane can do some difficult dives—the half gainer, for instance. for instance
>
> The buffet included some sausages I had never tasted before —knockwurst, for example. for example
>
> I don't like bugs, especially locusts. especially
>
> Stay away from such toxic substances as poison ivy. such...as

A Guide to Examining BUILDING ENGLISH SKILLS

This book is one of a series of English texts for grades 1–12. Each level is color-coded.*

Pink Level	Grade 1	Silver Level	Grade 5
Plum Level	Grade 2	Gold Level	Grade 6
Brown Level	Grade 3	Red Level	Grade 7
Aqua Level	Grade 4	Green Level	Grade 8

As you examine this text, note the following distinctive features:

1. Clear organization. BUILDING ENGLISH SKILLS makes the structure of language clear by developing each topic or skill completely in one chapter, rather than on pages scattered throughout the text. Research shows that students learn more successfully if they understand the structure of what they are learning.

2. More composition. The series contains far more material on fundamental writing skills than other leading series. It contains more writing models and many more writing exercises... both important tools by which students learn to write clearly and effectively.

3. Better grammar. The text features an exceptionally clear, developmental approach to basic grammar, usage, and the support skills of capitalization, punctuation, and spelling.

4. More exercises. The series provides a wealth of exercises in the student texts, in the accompanying workbooks, in duplicating masters, and in the Teacher's Editions.

5. Easy-to-use Teacher's Editions. The Teacher's Edition for each level contains:
- The entire student text, not reduced in size
- Answers to all exercises, printed in blue
- Marginal notations giving lesson objectives, preparatory lessons, additional exercises for enrichment

The Teacher's Editions for grades 1–6 also contain:
- Reproducible copy masters at the end of the book providing additional exercises, diagnostic tests, and mastery tests
- Class record sheets and letters to parents

For more information write or call TOLL FREE and ask for an area customer representative.

McDougal, Littell & Company

P.O. Box 1667-X
Evanston, IL 60204

(800) 323-5435

Call between 9:00 a.m. and 4:00 p.m. Central Time.
Illinois residents call collect (312) 967-0900.

*Write for details about books for grades 9–12.

Exercise An Example in Context

Number a sheet of paper from 1 to 5. Read the following sentences. Each sentence contains a context clue for the underlined word. Use the context clue to write a general definition for the word. Then check your definition in a dictionary.

1. Please pass the salt, pepper, and other <u>condiments</u>. *things used to flavor food*
2. In my garden I grew such vegetables as <u>kohlrabi</u>. *a kind of vegetable*
3. I enjoy Japanese meals—<u>sukiyaki</u>, for example. *a Japanese meal*
4. The museum collects Lincoln <u>memorabilia</u>, especially things Mr. Lincoln used when he lived in the White House. *things worth remembering*
5. Old pottery, like <u>majolica</u>, is hard to find. *old pottery*

Review Exercises Learning Word Meanings from Context

A. Find the meaning of each underlined word in these sentences. Write a definition for each word. Then write the kind of clue that helped you (definition, restatement, or example).

Example: John planted several kinds of <u>cucurbits</u>, or gourds.

gourds, restatement

1. You should get shots to prevent such diseases as <u>pertussis</u>. *disease, example*
2. How do they make <u>napoleons</u>, rich pastries filled with cream? *rich pastries filled with cream, restatement*
3. Stock up on <u>gherkins</u> and other kinds of pickles. *kind of pickle, example*
4. Mario took a course in <u>linguistics</u>, which is the study of languages. *study of languages, definition*
5. We saw a picture of a <u>unicorn</u> (an animal that looks like a horse, with one long horn growing out of its forehead). *horse-like animal with one horn on its forehead, restatement*
6. The hunters put the sugar in a <u>cache</u>—a hiding place—to keep it away from the bears. *hiding place, restatement*
7. This machine <u>extrudes</u>, that is, forces out, the melted plastic. *forces out, definition*

3. aloe—a bitter plant used in medicine
4. albino—a person or animal with extremely white skin
5. apex—the top of something high
6. azure—a sky blue color

Each group is to compose one sentence for each word, using each context example listed on page 18.

2. Have an example key search. Provide students with mimeographed forms listing down the left side the six example keys discussed in Part 2. Allow them to use newspapers, magazines, textbooks, or popular reading material to find examples of the six keys. After each key, they are to write a sentence they find using the key. They are to underline the word being defined, and identify the source of their find. A brief time limit may add competition to the exercise.

Review Exercises

It is suggested that you assign Review Exercises A and B on pages 19 and 20 for chapter review.

8. Do you know how to play percussion instruments like drums and chimes? *instruments played by being struck, example*

9. Roger wanted some fruit—for example, mangoes. *fruit, example*

10. A straw vote, or unofficial poll, showed that Mae was ahead in the race. *unofficial poll, restatement*

11. Valerie asked the librarian for a story of intrigue, secret plotting or scheming. *secret plotting or scheming, restatement*

12. Mark has a regal manner. That is, he acts like a king. *kingly, definition*

13. Penny's favorite color was red, and she especially liked vermilion. *shade of red, example*

14. The mural, or wall painting, showed George Washington at Valley Forge. *wall painting, restatement*

15. Wear something around your neck, such as a cravat. *something worn around neck, example*

B. In each of the following sentences, the underlined word has more than one meaning. Two definitions follow each sentence. Number your paper from 1 to 5. Write the correct definition. Use context clues to help you.

1. The waitress served us corn bread, sticky buns, and other breads and rolls.

    a. piece of baked dough   b. list of names

2. The new house was built on the crown of the hill.

    a. a circlet of gold worn by a monarch   b. the highest point

3. The pilot thought that the weather was too bad for flying, and he was especially worried about the low ceiling.

    a. roof of a room   b. height of the lowest layer of clouds

4. We were slow getting home because of heavy traffic.

    a. of great weight   b. of great quantity

5. Shall we paint the bathroom turquoise?

    a. light greenish blue   b. a jewel

Additional Exercises

Learning Word Meanings from Context

A. A Definition in Context (Use after page 14.)

Each of these sentences contains a definition. Write the word that is defined. Then write the definition.

1. Ed is a <u>herpetologist</u>. That is, he studies reptiles.
   herpetologist—person who studies reptiles
2. I used an <u>adze</u>, which is a kind of flat-bladed ax.
   adze—a kind of flat-bladed ax
3. Sometimes the plane will <u>yaw</u>. In other words, it will swing to the right or left.
   yaw—to swing to the right or left
4. These hedges form a <u>labyrinth</u>. A labyrinth is a maze.
   labyrinth—a maze

B. A Restatement in Context (Use after page 16.)

Number a sheet of paper from 1 to 4. Write the meaning of the underlined word in each sentence.

1. Our plans <u>fluctuated</u>, or changed, with the weather.
   fluctuated—changed
2. For lunch we'll have <u>souvlaki</u>, a Greek lamb dish.
   souvlaki—a Greek lamb dish
3. The harbor is protected by a <u>jetty</u> (a long pier of stones or concrete to stop the force of waves).
   jetty—long pier of stone or concrete to stop the force of waves
4. A <u>buttress</u>—outside support—keeps the wall solid.
   buttress—outside support

C. An Example in Context (Use after page 18.)

Number a sheet of paper from 1 to 4. Use the context clue to write a definition for the underlined word.

1. Herons, <u>terns</u>, and other water birds nest here.
   tern—a water bird
2. I like the flavor of most herbs—<u>fennel</u>, for example.
   fennel—an herb
3. Nora read about <u>marsupials</u>, especially kangaroos.
   marsupial—a pouched mammal
4. Today some old musical instruments, like the <u>serpent</u>, are almost forgotten.
   serpent—an old musical instrument

Additional Exercises

If these Exercises were not used with each lesson, they may now be assigned for chapter review.

Chapter 3

Improving Your Reading and Study Skills

Chapter Objectives

1. To recognize the importance of a good study environment, and to discover ways of creating one
2. To understand the concept of reading rate
3. To learn to adjust reading rate to the type of material and to the purpose for reading
4. To develop the skill of study-type reading

Preparing the Students

Discuss various ways of acquiring knowledge. Encourage the students to think beyond obvious sources such as textbooks, television programs, and explanations by parents and teachers. Direct attention to the photograph on page 22. Discuss briefly the method of acquiring knowledge that it illustrates.

Additional Resources

Skills Practice Book—pages 9–13
Duplicating Masters—pages 9–13

You spend most of your time learning. Think of all the time you spend every day doing these things:

Observing what is happening around you

Sharing ideas with your classmates and friends

Practicing your skills

These are all ways of learning. Studying is another way of learning. Because you are in school, you spend much time studying. That is why it is important to know *how* to study.

This chapter will help you to use your study time well. The first part of the chapter gives suggestions for studying at home. The second part teaches you how to read different kinds of materials.

Part 1

Objective

To recognize the importance of a good study environment, and to discover ways of creating one

Presenting the Lesson

1. Read page 24. Ask the students to form a mental picture of their own study spaces and to consider whether they meet the three basic requirements outlined in the lesson.

2. Read the first three paragraphs on page 25. Discuss the meaning of *distraction*. Ask for additional examples from the group or direct the students to make personal lists of those distractions common in their homes.

3. Read and discuss the remaining sections in Part 1. Explain that the lesson provides general guidelines, which should be adapted to each student's particular needs and circumstances.

4. Assign the Exercise on page 26. Ask the students to describe their study plans in sentences or in a short paragraph.

5. Use Exercise A on page 36 for additional practice.

Extending the Lesson

Work with those students who have difficulty applying the suggestions in the lesson because of unusual home situations. If it is obvious that a home is not at all conducive to quiet study, urge the student to develop the habit of regular library study.

Part 1 Getting Ready To Study

In school you usually do not have much choice about where to study. It is either in the classroom or in the library. Outside of school, however, you may choose your own place. Some of you may prefer the neighborhood library. Most of you, however, probably do most of your studying at home.

Find a Place

The first thing to do is to find a place to study. It can be any place in the house. It may be your bedroom. It may be the dining room or kitchen. Wherever it is, it should have the following:

1. A place to write and a place to sit. A desk is nice, but a table and chair work just as well.

2. A good light. A window is fine for daytime study. However, you will need a lamp in the evening.

3. A comfortable temperature. If it is too hot, you will get sleepy. If it is too cold, you will be thinking about how uncomfortable you are rather than what you are studying.

Eliminate Distractions

Your study place should have no distractions. A *distraction* is anything that takes your mind away from what you are doing. A television program, a telephone call from your best friend, or your playful dog can all be distractions.

Distractions for some people are not always distractions for others. For example, some people find radio music distracting. Others think it helps to drown out noises. Some people find that being near a refrigerator is distracting. They keep wanting to get snacks. Others are not interested in food.

Think about what might take your mind away from studying. Then choose a study place away from these distractions.

Gather Supplies

You have decided on a place. Next you will need to put all your supplies there. Then you won't have to waste time looking for things you need.

Your basic supplies will include the following:

1. Paper
2. Sharpened pencils
3. One or two pens
4. An eraser
5. Books you use often, such as a dictionary

Get into the habit of keeping your school books in your study place, too. In that way, you will have them there when you are ready to use them.

Your study place may be a place that your family uses for other things. If so, put your supplies into a box. Keep the box in an out-of-the-way place. Take it out when you are ready to study.

Decide on a Time

Decide when you are going to study. Try to study at the same time each day. Some people like to study right after school. Others like to study after a break and some play time. Still other people like to study early in the morning when everyone else is still asleep.

It's a good idea to set aside the same amount of time to study each day. Your regular homework may not keep you busy the entire time. However, you can use the rest of the time to read a library book or to write a letter.

Tell Your Family

Tell everyone in your house about your study place. You might even help your brothers and sisters find their special places, too. In that way, they will be less likely to use yours. Show your family, by concentrating on your work, that you do not want to be interrupted.

Exercise   Preparing To Study

Get ready to study by following the suggestions given here. Decide on a place away from distractions. Get your supplies together. Decide on a time to study. Share what you are doing with the rest of your family.

Part 2 Improving Your Reading

Think about all the kinds of things you read. They include things as different as directions for making soup, your favorite comic strip, the sports pages of the newspaper, street signs, school assignments, and books that you choose from the library. You don't read all of these in the same way. You read some very quickly. You *scan* or *skim* them. You read others carefully. In other words, you adjust your reading rate to what you are reading.

The following pages describe ways to read different kinds of things. They will help you to improve your reading.

Scanning

Consider the following situations.

1. Your teacher has made a list of everyone's birthday. Everyone gets a copy. The first thing you do when you get the list is to look for your own name.

2. All day you have been looking forward to a big, juicy cheeseburger for dinner. You go to a restaurant with your family. You look at the menu above the order counter. Right away the word *cheeseburger* catches your eye.

3. You are doing a report on chicken pox. You turn to the index of the book *Lumps, Bumps, and Rashes*. You glance at the entries under *c* and spot *chicken pox*.

In each case, you were looking for specific information. You used a type of fast reading called **scanning.** When scanning, you don't read every word. You skip words until you find what you want.

Part 2

Objectives

1. To understand the concept of reading rate
2. To learn to adjust reading rate to the type of material and to the purpose for reading
3. To develop the skill of study-type reading

Presenting the Lesson

1. Read the introduction to Part 2 on page 27. Explain that *rate* means *amount,* then ask the students to define *reading rate.* Emphasize that adjustment of reading rate usually occurs automatically, but that for some materials, such as difficult school assignments, reading rate should be slowed consciously.
2. Read the section concerning scanning on page 27. Emphasize that the purpose of scanning is to locate specific information.
3. Assign the Exercise on page 28. Be certain the students understand that they are seeking one item of information: the points scored by Baker in the game against the Chargers. For a class of facile readers, do the exercise as a group, setting a time limit to encourage students to increase their speed.
4. Read the description of skimming on page 28. Emphasize that the purpose of skimming is to identify the main ideas and important details in a piece of writing.
5. Assign the Exercise on page 29. Guide the class in identifying the title and the four main headings in the article. Point out that the title

and headings alone give a good idea of the article's content.

6. Read and discuss the steps for study-type reading listed on page 30. Emphasize that students should first look over an entire article quickly (step 1) before beginning to read carefully.

7. Assign the Exercise on pages 30 to 32. Set a limit of one or two sentences for reporting the main ideas of each section to aid students in focusing their attention on these ideas.

8. Discuss the content of Reading for Enjoyment on page 33.

9. Discuss the Exercise on pages 33 to 35. The reading rates for Selection 1 will be slower than those for Selection 2 because of the denseness of copy, complex sentences, difficult vocabulary, and many descriptive details.

It is recommended that the classroom library include materials requiring a variety of reading rates, to provide students with individual practice in adjusting their rates. The books used in the exercise are *Miss Hickory* by Carolyn Sherwin Bailey (Viking Press), and *Rosie and Michael* by Judith Viorst (Atheneum Publishers).

10. Use Exercise B on page 37 for additional practice.

Extending the Lesson

During the next several weeks, encourage students to do study-type reading in subjects other than language arts, for example, in science and social studies. When introducing new material, such as a new chapter or lesson, take the class through the process described in step 1 on page 30. Refer to steps 2 and 3 in making assignments.

Exercise Scanning an Article

Imagine that you are a fan of the basketball player Alvin Baker. You have followed his career closely. Scan the following article to learn how many points Baker scored in the game against the Chargers. 36 points

BEARCATS SQUEAK BY CHARGERS

Guards Alvin Baker and Pete Layton combined for 60 points as the Chicago Bearcats beat the Iowa City Chargers 121–120. The Chicago win on its home court ended a six-game losing streak.

Baker matched his season high with 36 points. Layton, who scored an astonishing 20 points in the final period, led the Bearcats' fourth quarter drive to victory.

Skimming

Skimming is another way of reading fast. You skim to get a general idea of what something is about. You look for the main ideas. You look for important details.

When skimming, you do not read every word. You do pay special attention to the following:

Titles
Headings
Topic sentences
Key words

Exercise   Practicing Skimming

Skim the following article on lightning. Keep these questions in mind. They will help you to pick out the main ideas.

1. What are the different kinds of lightning?   forked, zigzag, or chain; sheet or heat; ball
2. What is forked lightning?
3. How are sheet lightning and heat lightning different?
4. What is ball lightning?

Kinds of Lightning

All lightning strokes are basically about the same. However, they appear to have different forms, depending on the position of the observer.

₂ **Forked, zigzag, or chain lightning** is a chain of brilliant light that appears to zigzag. It actually follows a winding path, like that of a river. The single streak of lightning often breaks into several branches or forks.

Sheet lightning has no particular form. It is usually a bright flash that spreads all over the horizon and lights up the sky. Sheet lightning is really light from a flash of chain lightning that takes place beyond the horizon.

₃ **Heat lightning,** often seen on summer evenings, is the same as sheet lightning, but the flashes are fainter.

₄ **Ball lightning** seems to consist of balls of fire, as small as walnuts or as large as balloons, that last about three to five seconds. They fall swiftly from the clouds until they strike the ground and explode. Sometimes they roll slowly along the ground and do not explode until they hit an obstacle. Ball lightning is the least understood of all forms of lightning. Many meteorologists even doubt that it exists. They think it may be an optical illusion. However, so many reliable witnesses have seen it that scientists have begun to study it. They have produced ball lightning in the laboratory. This kind of lightning does not appear to be dangerous.
—*World Book Encyclopedia*

Study-Type Reading

Sometimes it is important to learn material. You can't scan or skim it because you need to learn the details, too. You need to do **study-type reading**.

Here are the steps to follow for study-type reading. They will help you to remember what you read.

1. **First, get a general idea of what the entire article or chapter is about.** Read the title. It gives the topic. Read the headings. They tell more about what is included. Look at the pictures. Read any questions at the end of the chapter. They will cover most of the main ideas. Read the introduction or the first few paragraphs. Read the summary or the last few paragraphs.

2. **Next, read the article or chapter carefully and slowly.** Stop at new words and ideas. Make sure you understand their meanings. Reread them. For each main idea, ask yourself: What does this add to the topic? Stop after each section. Review the main ideas from that section.

3. **Then, review the main ideas covered in the article or chapter.** Write them in your own words. Save your list for later reviews.

4. **Once in a while, review the article or chapter again.** Read the headings. Recall the main ideas from each section. Refer to your own list of ideas. See if you can still answer the end-of-chapter questions.

Exercise Using Study-Type Reading

The following paragraphs explain where energy comes from and how it goes from one living thing to another. Do a study-type reading of these paragraphs. First, get a general idea of what the paragraphs are about. Next, read the four sections carefully. Then write the main ideas in your own words.

These are possible answers.

THE FLOW OF ENERGY IN NATURE

The *energy* of life flows from one living thing to others. As it does so, more and more of it *seems* to disappear. Actually it only changes into a form that is no longer useful for maintaining life. Thus more energy is needed. Plants and animals can live only because new supplies of energy constantly come from the sun. To trace the pathways of life's energy, you must begin at the sun.

Supplying Energy

A small amount of the sun's energy is used by the leaves of green plants to produce food energy.

Our sun is ninety-three million miles away. It gives off great amounts of energy. Only a small part of this energy reaches the earth. Near the earth, 50 percent of the sun's energy is reflected by clouds and dust back into space. Another 20 percent is absorbed by the atmosphere. About 30 percent heats the land and water. Some of it strikes the leaves of green plants. Of all the sunlight that shines on the earth, only about 2 percent is used by the leaves of green plants. Within these leaves something extraordinary happens. The sun energy is changed to food energy.

Turning Sun Energy into Food Energy

Only green plants are able to change sun energy into food energy, combining carbon dioxide, water, and sun energy to form simple sugars.

Food energy is the fuel that supports all life on earth. The sun powers the hop of a toad, the flight of an eagle, and the growth of a blade of grass—or of a person.

The process of changing sun energy into food energy is called *photosynthesis*, which means "putting together with light." That is what happens within green plants. A gas called carbon dioxide and water are "put together" with sun energy, forming simple sugars such as glucose. Later, these simple sugars change to other forms of food energy within the plants. Now the energy is in a form that can be used by animals, including people.

Only green plants are able to trap the sun's energy and change it into food energy. Some of this energy is used by the plants as they grow and produce seeds. The rest is stored in the plant, and can be used by other living things.

Forming Food Chains

Energy flows from one living thing to another in a series of steps called a food chain.

When an animal eats a plant, it receives some of the plant's stored energy. That animal may be eaten by another animal. Energy flows from one living thing to another in a series of steps called a food chain.

Since no animal can make its own food, all food chains begin with green plants, the food producers. Some food chains have only two steps or links, such as corn→ human. Whenever you eat corn, a cookie (made from wheat flour), an apple, or any other food that came from a green plant, you are part of a simple food chain.

Losing Energy

A great deal of heat is lost every time energy changes.

Some food chains have several links: grass→ mouse→ snake→ hawk. Food chains sometimes have as many as five links, but most have only three or four. There is a good reason for this. As energy flows through a food chain it seems to disappear. Actually, energy can be changed but not destroyed or created. However, every time energy changes, some of it becomes heat energy which is given off into the air or water. So far as living things are concerned, this energy is useless.

A great deal of energy is lost in this way at each link in a food chain. Whenever an animal eats and digests part of a plant or animal, some of the energy it receives is lost as heat. Animals use large amounts of energy for moving about. Even while you are eating, you use energy to chew, swallow, and digest your food. As you sleep, energy is needed to keep your heart, lungs, and other organs working. Whenever stored energy is changed to working energy, some energy is lost as heat. —LAURENCE PRINGLE

Questions for Review

1. What is the source of all the energy on earth? *sun*
2. What is photosynthesis? *process of changing sun energy into food energy*
3. What is a food chain? *series of steps whereby energy flows from one living thing to another*
4. How is energy lost? *as heat—passing through food chain, in process of eating and in keeping organs working*

Reading for Enjoyment

Sometimes you can read exactly what you want to read. You choose the material yourself. Therefore, you do not have to worry about learning it.

You do not have to worry about how fast or how slowly you are reading, either. Your reading rate will adjust automatically. You will read books with short sentences and easy words much more quickly than books with long sentences and hard words. You may even read different parts of books at different rates. Where you read has something to do with reading rate, too. For example, if you try to read on a crowded bus, you may slow down because of the distractions.

Exercise   Timing Your Reading Rate

You can see how your reading rate changes. Use the following selections. They are about the same length. Read each one at a comfortable rate. Have someone time you with a second hand or a stop watch. Compare your reading times.

Selection 1

   Miss Hickory heard heavy footsteps, clump, clumping along the stones of the pasture, then approaching her lilac bush. Out of the corner of one sharp little black eye she could see a pair of large yellow feet but she did not turn her head. As a matter of fact, Miss Hickory had difficulty in turning her head. It was a hickory nut that had grown with an especially sharp and pointed nose. Her eyes and mouth were inked on. Her body was an applewood twig formed like a body with two arms and two legs, hands and feet, as twigs sometimes grow. To this body Miss Hickory's nut head was glued. She wore a blue-and-white checked gingham dress. A white cap with ruffles was tied in a smart bow beneath her chin. Many persons, looking first at Miss Hickory, would have said that she was a country doll, made by Miss Keturah who kept the notions store in Hillsborough, and given to Ann. But not you or I. The tilt of her sharp little nose, her pursed mouth, and her keen eyes were not those of a doll. You and I would have known Miss Hickory as the real person she was.   —CAROLYN SHERWIN BAILEY

Selection 2

Rosie is my friend.

She likes me when I'm dopey and not just when I'm smart.
I worry a lot about pythons and she understands.

My toes point in,
and my shoulders droop,
and there's hair growing out of my ears.

But Rosie says I look good.
She is my friend.

Michael is my friend.

He likes me when I'm grouchy
and not just when I'm nice.

I worry a lot about were-
wolves, and he understands.
There are freckles growing all
over me, except on my eye-
balls and teeth.

But Michael says I look good.
He is my friend.

**When I said that my nickname was Mickey, Rosie said
Mickey. When I said that my nickname was Ace, Rosie
said Ace. And when I was Tiger, and Lefty, and Ringo,
Rosie always remembered.**

That's how friends are.

When I wrote my name with a *y,* Michael wrote Rosey.
And when I wrote my name with an *i,* Michael wrote Rosi.
And when I wrote Rosee, and Rozi, and Wrosie,
Michael always did too.

That's how friends are.

**Just because I dug a hole and covered it with leaves and
told her to jump on the leaves, and she fell into the
hole, doesn't mean that Rosie's not my friend.**

Just because I put a worm in his tuna salad sandwich,
doesn't mean that Michael's not my friend.

—JUDITH VIORST

Additional Exercises

If these Exercises were not used with each lesson, they may now be assigned for chapter review.

Additional Exercises

Improving Your Reading and Study Skills

A. Preparing To Study (Use after page 26.)

1. Choose the things that will help you study at home.

    ✓ A good study lamp
    Your favorite television program
    ✓ A place to put books and supplies
    A dictionary that you keep at school
    ✓ A study place
    A different time for study each day
    Telephone calls from your friends
    ✓ A desk or table and chair

2. Bruce Bailey had ten math problems to do for homework. Read this description of what Bruce did. Then tell what he should have done.

    Bruce planned to do his homework right after school. On the way home, though, he met his friend Carlos. Carlos was going to the park to shoot baskets. Bruce joined him. He stayed there until 4:30. Then he rushed home.

    Bruce threw his books and jacket on the couch. He ran upstairs to check his fish. "Boy, is this water dirty!" he said. "I think I'll change it now." He worked on his fish tank until dinner.

    After dinner Bruce looked for a good place to study. His desk was heaped with dirty clothes. His sister was using the kitchen table. He finally decided on a chair in the corner of the living room. "Having the TV on won't be so bad," he said. "I might even get to see part of 'Star Chase.'"

    Bruce hunted for a pencil and a sheet of paper. He searched for his math book. At last he was ready to begin.

B. Using Study-Type Reading (Use after page 32.)

The following short chapter describes the climate of Puerto Rico. Do a study-type reading of the chapter.

The Climate of Puerto Rico

Puerto Rico has a mildly tropical climate. It is summer all the time. The sun shines every day. In some parts of Puerto Rico it rains almost every day, too. The rain lasts only a little while and then the sun is out again. Puerto Rico has no real rainy season.

Trade winds blow across Puerto Rico. These winds dry up moisture in the air and give the coastal areas an ideal climate. Inland there is less wind and it is warmer.

Hurricanes. From late June to the end of November is hurricane season. A hurricane is a storm with high winds, which can reach up to 150 miles per hour, and heavy rains.

Hurricanes are dangerous. They can cause houses and crops to be blown away. People can drown in the floods that are caused by the heavy rains.

The worst hurricane to hit Puerto Rico was in 1899. Over 1,000 people died. In 1928, 1932, 1956, and 1960 destructive hurricanes hit Puerto Rico. —NATALIE NELSON

Choose the three sentences that give the main ideas in the chapter.

1. Puerto Rico is a beautiful island to visit.
2. Puerto Rico has a mild tropical climate.
3. Trade winds blow across Puerto Rico.
4. Many people from Puerto Rico live in New York City.
5. Dangerous hurricanes sometimes hit Puerto Rico.

Chapter 4

Learning About Sentences

In the photograph on the opposite page the girls are having fun.

Look at the photograph. What are the girls doing? Do you enjoy doing this?

Imagine that you had been the photographer. Would you have taken a picture of the same activity? What other activity or game would you have photographed?

When you talk about the photograph, or about other things, you use sentences. Sentences express ideas.

Chapter Objectives

1. To identify a sentence and to differentiate between fragments and sentences

2. To distinguish the four kinds of sentences—declarative, interrogative, imperative, and exclamatory—and to understand their purposes

3. To use proper end punctuation for the four kinds of sentences

4. To identify the two parts of the sentence: subject and predicate

5. To identify the simple predicate, or verb

6. To identify the simple subject, or subject of the verb

7. To identify the subject in unusual positions

8. To identify the subject in imperative sentences

Preparing the Students

Discuss the importance of communication in everyday life. Ask students to name both written and spoken situations where clear communication is necessary.

Read page 39 and discuss the questions about the picture. You may wish to point out to students that they are communicating ideas when they talk about what is happening in the picture.

Additional Resources

Diagnostic Test—page 428 in this T.E. Recommended for use before teaching the chapter.

Mastery Test—pages 442 to 445 in this T.E. Recommended for use after teaching the chapter.

Additional Mastery Test—Recommended for use after any necessary reteaching. (In separate booklet, *Mastery Tests, Silver Level,* pages 5 to 8.)

Skills Practice Book—pages 14–22

Duplicating Masters—pages 14–22

Part 1

Objective

To identify a sentence and to differentiate between fragments and sentences

Presenting the Lesson

1. Read and discuss page 40 and the first two paragraphs of page 41. Ask students to define the word *fragment.* Point out that a fragment of any kind is always a piece or a part of something else. It is not whole or entire in itself. Relate the discussion to the words *complete* and *incomplete.* You may wish to put the headings *Fragments* and *Complete Things* on the board and ask students to give examples. Have them complete the sentence "A _____ is part of a _____" to verify their examples.

Examples:

Fragments	Complete Things
nose	face
player	team
fragment	sentence
shoelace	shoe

2. The box on page 40 does not introduce rules about punctuation at the end of the sentence, so that at this time students may concentrate on the need for a complete thought. End punctuation is discussed thoroughly in Parts 2 and 3.

3. Read and discuss pages 41 and 42.

4. Assign and discuss Exercises A, B, and C on page 43. You may want to have students change the fragments in Exercise C to sentences.

5. Use Exercise A on page 64 for additional practice.

Part 1 What Is a Sentence?

Read the three groups of words below. Each group of words expresses a complete thought or idea. Each group of words is a **sentence.**

1. Laura made a skirt by herself.
2. Richard plays the bongos.
3. The gym class practiced tumbling stunts.

> A **sentence** is a group of words that expresses a complete thought.
>
> When you write a sentence, begin it with a capital letter.

Not All Groups of Words Are Sentences

Read these groups of words. Can you tell whether each of the groups expresses a complete thought?

> Example 1. The children went to the pool.
>
> Example 2. Dominic and his brother.
>
> Example 3. Played in the snow.

Perhaps you were not sure how to answer the question about the groups of words. Here are two basic questions to help you decide whether a group of words expresses a complete thought.

1. Who or what did something?
2. What happened?

If a group of words answers these two questions, it expresses a complete thought. The group of words is a sentence.

If a group of words does not answer the questions, it does not express a complete thought. It is a **fragment**.

Making Sure Sentences Are Complete

Now let's return to the three groups of words shown earlier. Let's test them for complete thoughts.

> Example 1. The children went to the pool.

Who or *what* did something?	What happened?
The children	went to the pool.

This group of words answers both questions. We know, then, that it is a sentence. It expresses a complete thought.

> Example 2. Dominic and his brother.

Who or *what* did something?	What happened?
Dominic and his brother	

Does this group of words answer both questions? No, it does not. We can see that it is not a sentence. It is a fragment. It tells only part of a thought.

We can change this fragment into a whole sentence. Which of the questions needs an answer? The fragment did not answer *What happened*. Here are three different ways we could answer that question and complete the sentence.

Who or *what* did something?	What happened?
Dominic and his brother	played checkers.
Dominic and his brother	planted a garden.
Dominic and his brother	won the three-legged race.

Optional Practice

List the fragments below on the board or make up a worksheet. Instruct students to match a fragment from Column A with one in Column B to make a complete sentence. If you wish, have them write out the entire sentence.

Column A
1. The policeman
2. uses a calculator.
3. The acrobat
4. honked his horn.
5. Our guinea pig

Column B
1. stopped the traffic.
2. runs around his cage.
3. The angry driver
4. My father
5. performed for the audience.

Extending the Lesson

Put the fragments list below on the board. (You may wish to add more.) Have students complete them orally or as a written assignment. Ask for two completions for each fragment.

The students
eats worms
The bell
opens easily

> Example 3.　Played in the snow.

Who or what did something?	What happened?
	Played in the snow.

Does this group of words answer both questions? No, it does not. Like Example 2, it is not a sentence. It is a fragment.

How can we change this fragment into a sentence? Which question needs an answer? Think of some ways to answer the question *Who or what did something*. Here are two possible answers. You may have thought of others.

Who or what did something?	What happened?
Dorothy	played in the snow.
The black kitten	played in the snow.

Exercises   **Making Sure That Sentences Are Complete**

A. The following groups of words answer the question *Who or what did something.* Study each group of words. Think of an answer for the question *What happened.* On your paper, write the complete sentence you have thought of.   Answers will vary.

Example: The neighbor's cat

Possible Answer 1:   The neighbor's cat fights our dog.

Possible Answer 2:   The neighbor's cat had kittens.

1. The boy with the sled
2. An angry dog
3. My two sisters
4. The TV set
5. Most birds

B. The following groups of words answer the question *What happened.* Study each group of words. Think of an answer for the question *Who or what did something.* On your paper, write the complete sentence you have thought of.   Answers will vary.

1. talked on the phone
2. made brownies
3. found a good pencil
4. likes football
5. told a secret

C. Study the following groups of words. Some of them answer both of these questions: *Who or what did something? What happened?* These groups of words are sentences. Others answer only one of the questions. They are fragments.

Number your paper from 1 to 10. Write *Sentence* after each number that stands before a sentence. Write *Fragment* after each number that stands before a fragment.   S = Sentence
F = Fragment

1. We built a snowman **S**
2. The lifeguard **F**
3. An anthill in the yard **F**
4. Our class took a field trip **S**
5. Carved the turkey **F**
6. Rides a bike to school **F**
7. Our hamster is loose **S**
8. Alice dived into the lake **S**
9. Makes jewelry out of tabs from pop cans **F**
10. The cattle rancher **F**

Part 2

Objective

To distinguish the four kinds of sentences—declarative, interrogative, imperative, and exclamatory—and to understand their purposes

Presenting the Lesson

1. Have students follow the directions on page 44. Ask them to explain why they read the sentences as they do.
2. Read and discuss pages 45 and 46. Ask students to supply additional examples for each type of sentence and to explain when they would be used. Here are some examples: declarative, to tell someone where I am going; interrogative, to ask my mother if I can visit a friend after school; imperative, to tell my brother to leave me alone; and exclamatory, to show pain when I pinch my finger. If students know any of the four types of sentences by other names (statement for declarative, exclamation for exclamatory), show the relationship of those names to the ones in the text.
3. Assign and discuss Exercises A and B on page 47.
4. It may be helpful to divide the class into three groups. Assign Exercise C on page 47 to one (average students), Exercise D on page

Part 2 Different Kinds of Sentences

Read the sentences in the picture the way you think the children said them at the talent show.

I will announce the acts.

Is it your turn?

Begin your act now.

I won the prize!

In the sentence that goes with the first picture, Jack says that he will announce the acts.

In the second picture, Maria asks Eddie a question.

In the third picture, Jack tells Maria to do something.

Notice the excitement in the last picture. Imagine the feeling with which the sentence is said.

Every sentence that you read or write is one of these four different kinds.

The Declarative Sentence

Jack used this sentence to tell Tonya something: *I will announce the acts.* This sentence is a **declarative sentence.** The word *declarative* comes from *declare,* which means "to make known" or "to announce." A declarative sentence makes something known to the person who reads or hears it.

A declarative sentence tells or states something.

Use a period (.) at the end of a declarative sentence.

We practiced our act last night.

The Interrogative Sentence

Maria used this sentence to ask Eddie a question: *Is it your turn?* This sentence is an **interrogative sentence.** The word *interrogative* comes from *interrogate,* which means "to ask."

An interrogative sentence asks a question.

Use a question mark (?) at the end of an interrogative sentence.

Did you bring your costume?

48 to the second (more advanced students) and Exercise B on pages 64 and 65 to the third (those who need more basic practice). Have students be prepared to read at least one original sentence to the rest of the class.

Optional Practice

Put the sentences below on the board. Have students divide a paper into four columns. Head the columns *Declarative, Interrogative, Imperative,* and *Exclamatory.* Have them decide which group each sentence belongs to, and put the number of that sentence in the proper column.

1. Are you going out after dinner?
2. Put the boxes in the back of the car.
3. What a great movie that was!
4. I need to buy some notebook paper.
5. Be quiet.
6. Will you help me carry the packages?
7. My sister works after school.
8. Does your brother have a job?
9. I like ice cream for dessert.
10. What a sunny day this is!

Extending the Lesson

Ask the students to find an example of each of the four kinds of sentences used outside of class. Have them choose from a family conversation or a favorite TV program.

The Imperative Sentence

In the sentence that goes with the third picture, Jack gives this direction to Maria: *Begin your act now.* This sentence is an **imperative sentence.** The word *imperative* comes from the Latin word *imperare*, which means "to order."

An imperative sentence makes a request, or gives directions or orders.

Use a period (.) at the end of most imperative sentences.

Turn on the record player.

The Exclamatory Sentence

Maria was excited when she won the prize. She called out: *I won the prize!* This sentence is an **exclamatory sentence.** The word *exclamatory* comes from the same word as *exclaim*, which means "to cry out or say suddenly."

An exclamatory sentence shows excitement and strong feeling.

Use this mark (!), called an exclamation point, at the end of every exclamatory sentence.

I liked all of the acts!

---

1. A **declarative sentence** tells something.
2. An **interrogative sentence** asks something.
3. An **imperative sentence** requests, directs, or orders.
4. An **exclamatory sentence** expresses joy, surprise, anger, excitement, or other strong feeling.

Exercises   Finding Four Kinds of Sentences

A. Number your paper from 1 to 10. Tell what kind of sentence each is. Tell what punctuation mark is used at the end of the sentence.

   Example: Are you going shopping Saturday?
   interrogative, question mark

1. What luck you have! exclamatory, exclamation point
2. Do you have a skateboard? interrogative, question mark
3. Tom takes piano lessons. declarative, period
4. When will the train arrive? interrogative, question mark
5. Aim for the target. imperative, period
6. Tomorrow is my birthday. declarative, period
7. Are you telling the truth? interrogative, question mark
8. Guess the right number. imperative, period
9. I heard a scream! exclamatory, exclamation point
10. Hurry up. imperative, period

B. Follow the directions for Exercise A.

1. The rocket took off. declarative, period
2. Have you seen the circus? interrogative, question mark
3. Please stay with me. imperative, period
4. Ken erased the chalkboards. declarative, period
5. Something in the shadows moved! exclamatory, exclamation point
6. Our family took a vacation in Virginia. declarative, period
7. What a mess we made! exclamatory, exclamation point
8. Have another piece of cake. imperative, period
9. Where does the trail end? interrogative, question mark
10. Those fireworks are noisy! exclamatory, exclamation point

C. Look in some of your other books. Find and copy two sentences of each kind to read in class. Answers will vary.

D. Imagine that you and your family are watching television. The year is 1903. The TV crew is on location on a beach at Kitty Hawk, North Carolina. You see Orville and Wilbur Wright prepare their first airplane for a test flight. You watch as Orville takes off on the first successful flight, lasting twelve seconds.

Write sentences that you or other members of your family might say as you watch this historic event. Use at least one sentence of each kind. Answers may vary.

Part 3 Punctuating Sentences

Punctuation marks are important signals in reading and writing. Use the correct signals in your writing. Follow the signals when you read.

Remember these rules:

1. **Use a period after a declarative sentence.**

   You may have milk or hot chocolate with your snack.

2. **Use a question mark after an interrogative sentence.**

   Do you want milk?

3. **Use a period after most imperative sentences. If the imperative sentence expresses strong feelings, use an exclamation point.**

   Give me the hot chocolate, please. Don't spill it!

4. **Use an exclamation point after an exclamatory sentence.**

   This chocolate is too hot!

Exercises — Punctuating Sentences Correctly

A. Copy these sentences. Use the correct punctuation mark at the end of each sentence.

1. How funny the monkey looks !
2. What is the name of that movie ?
3. Turn on the radio, please .
4. Are you going on the bike hike ?
5. Henry read a story to the class .
6. Marcia hit a home run .
7. What a game it was !
8. What time is it ?
9. Our class went to the museum .
10. Please open the window .

B. Follow the directions for Exercise A.

1. We went to a carnival .
2. Can you answer the question ?
3. Stop it !
4. Do you have a pen pal ?
5. I found a gift for Mother .
6. Try the vanilla milkshake .
7. Please come to my house .
8. Does Ector wear glasses ?
9. What a surprise this is !
10. I watched the baseball game .

C. Write two declarative sentences, two interrogative sentences, two imperative sentences, and two exclamatory sentences. Capitalize and punctuate each sentence correctly.
Answers will vary.

D. Write a story, with at least four sentences, about something exciting, funny, or different that has happened to you. Use the four kinds of sentences. *Answers will vary.*

---

them list nine examples (three for each) and after the sentence write what type of sentence it is. Tell students they should be ready to explain why the end marks were used. You may also use this exercise with the punctuation cards suggested for Extending the Lesson.

Extending the Lesson

Using notebook-size heavy paper or cardboard, draw a period, a question mark, and an exclamation point. Draw each on a separate sheet, large enough to cover almost the entire sheet. Color the shapes so they can be seen from a distance. Show your samples to the students and have them do the same. While they are doing that, put the following ten sentences on the board without end punctuation.

1. The bear growled
2. I like guitar music
3. Watch out for that dangerous car
4. Does your friend live near you
5. That girl has two older brothers
6. Can you play ball after school
7. What a colorful picture
8. My neighbor works at the grocery store
9. We saw a good movie last night
10. The mailman had a lot of mail

Ask different students to read each sentence they way they think it should sound. Have the rest of the students hold up the correct end punctuation card to match the student's reading. Discuss the results. Point out how intonation affects the meaning of the sentence.

You can extend this exercise further by having students use the cards with the additional practice sentences on page 65 or any of the other appropriate exercises in the chapter. You may wish to use the cards themselves later for a bulletin board display.

Part 4

Objective

To identify the two parts of the sentence: subject and predicate

Presenting the Lesson

1. You might want to discuss how the two parts of a sentence that fit together are like two pieces of a puzzle that fit together. One part without the other is incomplete. Both parts are needed to make a sentence. Build on what the students have already learned. If necessary, review the discussion in Part 1 concerning what a complete sentence is and how it is different from a fragment. Review especially the two basic questions (page 40) used to decide whether or not a sentence is complete.

2. Read and discuss pages 50 to 52.

3. Assign and discuss Exercises A and B on pages 52 and 53. For each sentence, ask students to tell who or what did something and what that person or thing did. Make sure the students understand what subjects and predicates are.

4. Use Exercise D on pages 65 and 66 for additional practice.

Part 4   Parts of the Sentence

Every sentence has two parts. One part of the sentence is the **subject.** The subject answers the question *Who or what did something*.

Let's take another look at the sentences from Part 1.

1. Laura made a skirt by herself.
2. Richard plays the bongos.
3. The gym class practiced tumbling stunts.

Can you find the subject in each of these sentences? Find the answer to the question *Who or what did something*.

Here are the subjects:

1. Laura
2. Richard
3. The gym class

The other part of the sentence is the **predicate.** The predicate tells something about the subject. The predicate tells the following:

What the subject does
What the subject did
What happened

First, see if you can find the predicates in the sample sentences by yourself. Then look at the following chart to find out if you were right.

	Subject	Predicate
1.	Laura	made a skirt by herself.
	(who)	(what the subject did)
2.	Richard	plays the bongos.
	(who)	(what the subject does)
3.	The gym class	practiced tumbling stunts.
	(what)	(what the subject did)

1. The **subject** of a sentence tells who or what did something, or what the sentence is about.
2. The **predicate** of a sentence tells what the subject does, what the subject did, or what happened.
3. A group of words is not a sentence unless it has a subject and a predicate.

Here are three new sentences. Decide by yourself which words belong in the subject. Decide which words belong in the predicate. Then check yourself against the chart on the next page.

1. That big dog barks loudly.
2. My older sister went to the movie.
3. Dave's book of cartoons fell into a puddle.

Optional Practice

On a worksheet, list five subjects on the left and five predicates on the right. Have the students draw a line from each subject to a predicate that will complete the thought. They then should write each complete sentence.

Example:

Subject	Predicate
1. The little girl	barked loudly.
2. The dog	sat on the swing.
3. My baby brother	ate leaves from the tree.
4. The tall giraffe	jog every day.
5. Some of our neighbors	cried.

Extending the Lesson

Discuss some of the students' favorite sports. Ask them to write five sentences expressing five things that happen during the playing of a particular sport. Have them draw one line under the subject of each sentence and two lines under the predicate.

	Subject	Predicate
1.	**That big dog**	**barks loudly.**
	(what)	(what the subject does)
2.	**My older sister**	**went to the movie.**
	(who)	(what the subject did)
3.	**Dave's book of cartoons**	**fell into a puddle.**
	(what)	(what happened)

Exercises Finding Subjects and Predicates

A. Copy these sentences. Draw one line under the subject of each sentence. Draw two lines under the predicate.

Example: The red wagon makes squeaky noises.

1. My friends went to the beach.
2. The fierce tiger growled in his cage.
3. Two boys raced on roller skates.
4. The plants in the yard need water.
5. Aunt Beth has many plants.
6. The baby reached for her bottle.
7. The first show begins soon.
8. Some of our neighbors built a tree house.
9. A baby bird flew from the nest.
10. Susan told a good joke.

B. Follow the directions for Exercise A.

1. The small airplane landed in a field.
2. A team of horses pulled the wagon.
3. Dark clouds moved swiftly overhead.
4. The runners lined up.
5. We watched the fireworks.

6. The gymnast did a backflip.
7. The old fisherman uses no bait.
8. That little girl found a dollar.
9. The people of Mexico speak Spanish.
10. A magician performed many tricks.

Part 5 The Simple Predicate, or Verb

In Part 4 of this chapter, you learned about the two parts of the sentences. When we divide a sentence into these two parts, we call the subject part the **complete subject.** We call the predicate part the **complete predicate.**

The complete subject may be short or long. It includes all the words that tell who or what did something.

The complete predicate may be short or long. It includes all the words that tell what happened.

Here are some examples:

Complete Subject	Complete Predicate
A cat	howled.
A black cat	howled loudly.
A black cat in the alley	howled loudly all night.
The girl	played.
The tall girl with glasses	played basketball at the Y.

In each complete predicate, there is one part that is more important than the rest. This part is the **verb.** The first three sentences above have the same verb: *howled.* The last two sentences have the same verb: *played.*

The verb is sometimes called the **simple predicate.** In the rest of this book, we will speak of it as the *verb.*

Part 5

Objective

To identify the simple predicate, or verb

Presenting the Lesson

1. Read pages 53 to 55 and discuss the different kinds of verbs. Ask students to give further examples of the two types of action verbs. Emphasize that usually the verb follows the subject. Point out that verbs are not really anything new. Stress that in Part 1 of this chapter, when they answered the question, *What happened?* in a sentence, they were talking about the verb. If necessary, review Part 1.

2. Assign and discuss Exercise A on page 55. You might remind students to use the questions on page 50 to help them locate the action verbs and the list on the bottom of page 54 to find state-of-being verbs. Assign and discuss Exercise B on page 55.

3. Use Exercise E on page 66 for additional practice or review.

Optional Practice

Put the following list of verbs on the board. Have students make two columns on a sheet of paper, one headed *Action,* the other *State-of-Being.* Tell them to decide what kind of verb each one is and write it in the correct column. Verbs: grabbed, saw, is, laughed, raced, signaled, were, has been, repair, broke, seemed, expressed, awoke, are, bounced, appeared, collected, am, spill, will be.

Extending the Lesson

The following game of Action Charades will help students understand the concept of action in an action verb. Remind students that a subject must always do the action.

Write each of the following verbs on a separate slip of paper:

paint, pop, fly, drive, stare, clean, laugh, pour, listen, trap, wait, search, jog, cry, escape, jerk, pull, sing, write, grow.

Fold the papers and put them into a container. Divide the class into two teams. Each team chooses five to ten papers (depending on how much time you wish to allow), and spends a few minutes discussing what pantomime actions they can use to show what the verb is. Have one student keep time (preferably with a stopwatch) and another write the times on the board. Timekeeping begins as soon as a student begins to pantomime. Set a limit of one minute.

Put each team's slips of paper into separate containers. Have a student from Team 1 pick a slip from the Team 1 container, think about an action, and perform it for the other team. Anyone on Team 2

Finding the Verb

The underlined words in these sentences are the verbs.

The children slid on the ice.
The children skated on the ice.
The children fell on the ice.

Some verbs tell of an action you can see.

The trained lion jumped through a hoop.
Robert rode his bike to school.

Other verbs tell of action you cannot see.

My mother heard the baby's cry.
I remember all the words of that song.

These two kinds of verbs are called **action verbs.**

Another kind of verb tells that something is.

Your desk is there.
Books of jokes and riddles are in the library.

This kind of verb is called a **state-of-being verb.**

Here are some of the verbs we often use as state-of-being verbs:

is	was	has been	seem
are	were	have been	appear
am	will be	had been	look

> A **verb** is a word that tells of an action, or that tells what the subject is.

Exercises Finding the Verb

A. Copy these sentences. Draw two lines under the verb only.

   Example: Valerie <u>bought</u> a pet snake.

1. Miss Morgan <u>writes</u> with a quill pen.
2. My uncle <u>is</u> a test pilot.
3. The Apollo rockets <u>went</u> to the moon.
4. Margie <u>rested</u> before the race.
5. Three penguins <u>waddled</u> to the water.
6. The sky <u>looked</u> pink and orange.
7. At noon the zookeeper <u>feeds</u> the lions.
8. The truck <u>took</u> garbage to the dump.
9. Our class <u>made</u> dolls from cornhusks.
10. Adam <u>hoped</u> for better luck.

B. Number your paper from 1 to 10. Write down the verb in each of the following sentences. After the verb, write *Action* or *State-of-being* to tell what kind of verb it is.

1. That flag <u>is</u>^{SB} colorful.
2. Valerie's dog <u>performed</u>^A a new trick.
3. Two girls <u>paddled</u>^A the canoe.
4. The lizard <u>darted</u>^A up a tree.
5. Our class <u>wrote</u>^A a newspaper.
6. Father <u>seems</u>^{SB} impatient.
7. Eli <u>used</u>^A the microphone.
8. The Girl Scouts <u>are</u>^{SB} at camp.
9. Indians <u>made</u>^A these beaded necklaces.
10. The fans <u>were</u>^{SB} happy about the victory.

A = Action
SB = State-of-being

Part 6

Objective

To identify the subject of the verb

Presenting the Lesson

1. Read and discuss pages 56 and 57. You might remind students that they are familiar with subjects of sentences (Part 4). Now they are to look more closely and pick out the one word that tells *who* or *what*. Point out that in most sentences the subject comes before the verb, but other words may come between them.

2. It may be helpful to do Exercise A on page 58 with the students. Then assign and discuss Exercise B. You may want to review the purpose of a subject in a sentence during the discussion.

3. Use Exercise F on page 66 as additional practice or review.

Optional Practice

You may wish to put this exercise on the board or make up a worksheet for the students. Tell them that each of the sentences has the same verb. They are to find it and write it inside the triangle. Then they should find the subject of each sentence, and write the subject in the blank at the left.

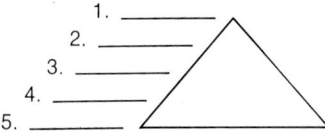

1. The choir sang at the concert.
2. My older sister sang in a musical.
3. The Muppets sang their theme song.
4. The soloist sang softly.
5. The children in the class sang the National Anthem.

Part 6 The Simple Subject, or Subject of the Verb

In each complete subject, there is one part that is more important than the rest. This is sometimes called the **simple subject.** Another name for it is the **subject of the verb.** In this book, we will call it the *subject of the verb*.

In the examples below, the subject of the verb is printed in italics.

Complete Subject	Verb
The *clock*	stopped.
The old *clock*	stopped.
The old *clock* on the shelf	stopped.

Finding the Subject of the Verb

To find the subject of the verb, first find the verb. Then ask *who?* or *what?* before the verb.

Examples:

1. Monkeys escaped from the zoo.

   Verb: *escaped*

   Who or what *escaped?*   *Monkeys*

   Monkeys is the subject of *escaped*.

2. Three young monkeys escaped from the zoo.

   Verb: *escaped*

   Who or what *escaped?*   *Monkeys*

   Monkeys is still the subject of the verb.

> 3. Three young monkeys from South America escaped from the zoo.

Verb: *escaped*

Who or what *escaped*?   *monkeys*

Monkeys is still the subject of the verb.

See if you can find the verb, and then the subject of the verb, in this example.

The cake in the oven burned.

Did you find the action verb *burned?* The subject tells you *what* burned. What is the subject?

Did you say the *cake burned? Cake* is the subject of the verb *burned*.

In the next example, look for a state-of-being verb. Then find the subject of the verb.

Victor's blue jacket is here.

Did you find the state-of-being verb *is?* The subject tells you *what* is. Did you say the *jacket is? Jacket* is the subject of the verb *is*.

Exercises Finding the Verb and Its Subject

A. Copy each sentence. Draw two lines under the verb. Then draw one line under the subject of the verb.

1. High waves tipped the sailboat.
2. Juanita added three books to her library.
3. Three jugglers in the main ring tossed balls and pins.
4. My new gloves are waterproof.
5. Tom Sawyer found a secret hideout.
6. Jocelyn was her sister's bridesmaid.
7. A large group sang carols.
8. Six climbers from Nevada reached the mountaintop.
9. The desert seems endless.
10. Which camel has two humps?

B. Follow the directions for Exercise A.

1. Outside, hailstones fell.
2. Melinda leaped over the fence.
3. Our parrot speaks Spanish.
4. The American flag now has fifty stars.
5. The pickers handled the fruit gently.
6. Dr. Mendez taped my wrist.
7. One unusual vegetable in my garden is the rutabaga.
8. Today we had a fire drill.
9. A stray dog slept on our steps.
10. That lollipop with yellow and orange stripes is the size of a pumpkin!

Part 7 The Subject in Unusual Positions

In most sentences the subject comes before the predicate, but not in all sentences. Where is the subject placed in each of the sentences below?

> 1. The rocket soared toward the planet Venus.

Verb: *soared*
Who or what *soared*?   the *rocket*

Rocket is the subject of the verb. It is placed before the verb near the beginning of the sentence.

> 2. Toward the planet Venus the rocket soared.

Rocket is still the subject of the verb. It is still placed before the verb. It is now near the end of the sentence.

> 3. Toward the planet Venus soared the rocket.

In this sentence, the subject is still *rocket*, but it has been moved again. Now it is placed after the verb.

When you are looking for the subject in sentences like examples 2 and 3, follow the usual steps. First, find the verb. Then ask *who* or *what* before the verb.

Example: Over the river to Grandmother's house we go.

Verb: *go*
Who or what *goes*?   *we* go

Part 7

Objective

To identify the subject in unusual positions

Presenting the Lesson

1. Read and discuss page 59. Emphasize that even when the subject and verb change positions in a sentence, the students should still use the same procedure for finding verbs and subjects that they learned earlier in the chapter.

2. It may be helpful to do Exercise A on page 60 with the students. Assign and discuss Exercise B on page 60.

3. Use Exercise G on page 67 as additional practice or review.

Optional Practice

You may wish to have more advanced students work on this exercise and those who need more basic practice do Exercise G on page 67.

Have students make sentences out of each group of phrases below. They should place the subject in three different positions, as in the example. Have them identify the subject in each sentence.

Example:
  sketched, the artist, on his pad

(subject + verb + phrase)
The artist sketched on his pad.

(phrase + subject + verb)
On his pad the artist sketched.

(phrase + verb + subject)
On his pad sketched the artist.

1. the racers, up the hill, ran
2. marched, the robot, into the spaceship
3. splashed, a dolphin, in the pool
4. the choir, in the auditorium, sang
5. into the air, roared, the rocket
6. in the garden, grew, many plants

> The **lobster crawled** over the rocks.
> Over the rocks the **lobster crawled.**
> Over the rocks **crawled** the **lobster.**

Exercises   Finding the Subject in Unusual Positions

A. Copy each sentence. Draw two lines under the verb. Then draw one line under the subject of the verb.

1. Down the hill ran José.
2. In the early evening, fireflies appeared.
3. On the top branch sat a bird.
4. From the trees fell the colored leaves.
5. Down came the rain.
6. Into the hall the band marched.
7. Up into the tree sailed the balloon.
8. Into the water fell our money.
9. Out of the dark came a strange sound.
10. Across the range the cowboys rode.

B. Follow the directions for Exercise A.

1. Around the barnyard waddled a goose.
2. Out went the cat.
3. After the storm a rainbow appeared.
4. Into the water jumped a frog.
5. Over the trees my kite sailed.
6. In front of the store Mom waited.
7. Through the gate came a large wagon.
8. Across the snow whisked a shiny sled.
9. Above the clouds the plane soared.
10. At the front of the parade was a loud band.

Part 8 The Subject in Imperative Sentences

An imperative sentence makes a request, or gives directions or orders. Study these examples of imperative sentences. Look for the subjects.

> Switch off the light.
> Turn left at the gas station.
> Don't wake the baby.

In each of these sentences, the subject is not expressed. The subject is understood to be *you.*

> (You) Switch off the light.
> (You) Turn left at the gas station.
> (You) Don't wake the baby.

Exercises Finding the Subject

A. Copy the following sentences. Some are imperative sentences. Draw two lines under the verb in each sentence. Draw one line under the subject of the verb. If the subject is not given in the sentence, write it in parentheses in the place where it is understood.

> Example: Wait here for me.
>
> (You) Wait here for me.

1. Try it again.   (You) try
2. Deliver the papers before school.   (You) deliver
3. Karen took the message.
4. Have a second helping.   (You) have
5. Stay in your seats.   (You) stay
6. Who wants chocolate ice cream?
7. Look at that fancy car.   (You) look
8. Add one cup of flour.   (You) add

Part 8

Objective

To identify the simple subject, or subject of the verb

Presenting the Lesson

1. If necessary, review the definition of an imperative sentence. Read and discuss page 61. Ask students for further examples. Ask them how many different subjects there are for imperative sentences. Point out that knowing that *you* is the only subject makes it much easier to find.

2. You may want to do Exercise A on pages 61 and 62 with the students. Assign and discuss Exercise B on page 62.

3. Use Exercise H on page 67 for additional practice or review.

Optional Practice

Give the following directions to your students:

Imagine you are the adult leader of a scout troop (or other social organization). You are going to take your group to a play. Write six imperative sentences telling them how you want them to behave. Leave a space before each sentence. After you finish, go back and write the understood subject *you* in parentheses in that space. Be ready to read one of your sentences aloud.

Extending the Lesson

Have each student write three imperative sentences which tell another student to do something in the classroom. (Examples: Write your name on the board. Stand up next to your desk.) Call on two students. The first student reads one of his sentences, and the second student follows the direction. With an advanced group, call on two more students. The third student asks a question concerning what the second student is doing, and the fourth student replies with a statement that describes the action. Example: Student 1—"Throw a piece of paper into the wastebasket." Student 2 performs the action. Student 3—"What is (student's name) throwing into the wastebasket?" Student 4—"(Student's name) is throwing a piece of paper into the wastebasket."

You may want to discuss how imperative, interrogative and declarative sentences can be used to express different parts of a situation.

9. Read Chapter 2 for tomorrow. (You) read
10. Those boys need help.

B. Follow the directions for Exercise A.

1. Astronomers watch for shooting stars.
2. Bait your hook this way. (You) bait
3. Speak a little louder. (You) speak
4. Hold the noise down. (You) hold
5. Keep up the good work. (You) keep
6. Careful shoppers compare prices.
7. Clap along with the music. (You) clap
8. Rosa's friends go to McDonald's often.
9. Use fine sandpaper for this job. (You) use
10. Buy your tickets at the box office. (You) buy

Sentence Patterns — Word Order and Meaning

A sentence is a group of words. However, not every group of words is a sentence. For example, read these word groups. Which one makes sense?

Pete fast ran.

Pete ran fast.

Ran Pete fast.

The only group that sounds right is the second group. Its words are in the order we are used to. We would say its words are in the right order for a sentence. A good sentence needs the right word order.

Sometimes a group of words has more than one right order. Read these two sentences. They have the same words. The words are simply in different orders.

Carrie tagged Brad.

Brad tagged Carrie.

Each word order sounds right. Each tells an idea. However, changing the word order changes the idea. The difference in word order makes an important difference in meaning.

Exercise Word Order and Meaning

Read each sentence. Then change the order of the words to change the meaning. Write each new sentence on your paper.

1. Herb called Sylvia.
2. Some girls are cooks.
3. The rug hid the dirt.
4. Some dogs chase cats.
5. Pam is in front of Vic.
6. Bob introduced my sister.
7. Jeanne saw a puppy.
8. Tom cheered the team.

Sentence Patterns

Objective

To recognize the usual word order of sentences

Presenting the Lesson

1. Ask the class to listen carefully and follow the instructions below. Read them no more than twice, and wait for the students to figure them out.

1. Book your hold up.
2. Hand raise your other.

Discuss why they had difficulty understanding the directions.

2. Read and discuss page 63.

3. Assign and discuss the Exercise on page 63.

Optional Practice

Put the list below on a worksheet. Tell students to unscramble the words in each, and to write them in two different orders for two correct sentences. You may wish to set a time limit, and have students work in groups to see which group can finish first.

1. Pencil the on the book is.
2. Introduced the magician his assistant.
3. Fights the bull the matador the.
4. Protected dog the the boy.
5. Is friend my Sally.

Additional Exercises

If these Exercises were not used with each lesson, they may now be assigned for chapter review.

Additional Exercises

Using Sentences

A. Making Sure That Sentences Are Complete
(Use after page 42.)

Study the following groups of words. Some of them answer both of these questions: *Who or what did something* and *What happened.* These groups of words are sentences. Other groups of words answer only one of the questions. They are fragments.

Number your paper from 1 to 10. Write *Sentence* after each number that stands before a sentence. Write *Fragment* after each number that stands before a fragment.

S = Sentence
F = Fragment

1. Were skateboarding in the parking lot **F**
2. A frisky young mare **F**
3. Took the train downtown **F**
4. We fed the polar bear **S**
5. A map of the United States **F**
6. My brother plays the flute **S**
7. The large coal mine **F**
8. Watched an exciting magic show **F**
9. The children on the bus sang **S**
10. The giant balloon popped **S**

B. Finding Four Kinds of Sentences (Use after page 46.)

Number your paper from 1 to 10. Tell what kind of sentence each is. Tell what punctuation mark is used at the end of the sentence.

1. Listen to this song. *imperative, period*
2. We won! *exclamatory, exclamation point*

3. Where is the subway? *interrogative, question mark*
4. The airplane taxied down the runway. *declarative, period*
5. Olga has a pet rabbit. *declarative, period*
6. Can you put this puzzle together? *interrogative, question mark*
7. Turn to page 80. *imperative, period*
8. Look out! *exclamatory, exclamation point*
9. Would you like some popcorn? *interrogative, question mark*
10. I read the Peanuts comic strip every day. *declarative, period*

C. Punctuating Sentences Correctly (Use after page 48.)

Copy these sentences. Use the correct punctuation mark at the end of each sentence.

1. Russell wrote a poem .
2. Turn off the TV, please .
3. The rancher saddled his horse .
4. Did you finish the book ?
5. Susan takes ballet lessons .
6. Where is your camp ?
7. How hot it is today !
8. Jump over this log .
9. Hurry up !
10. What is a salamander ?

D. Finding Subjects and Predicates (Use after page 52.)

Copy these sentences. Draw one line under the subject of each sentence. Draw two lines under the predicate.

1. Our family stayed on a farm.
2. A small snake slid away.
3. Walter's cat had kittens.
4. A fire truck sped past.
5. The sheriff's deputy arrived.
6. Tracey picked a bushel of apples.

7. Two girls joined the baseball team.
8. A librarian answered our question.
9. Planets revolve around the sun.
10. The drum and bugle corps marched up the street.

E. Finding the Verb (Use after page 54.)

Copy these sentences. Draw two lines under the verb only.

1. Our art class drew self-portraits.
2. The runners raced for the finish line.
3. Ronnie lives in a trailer.
4. The bikers followed the trail.
5. R2D2 is a robot.
6. Tyrone ate a bunch of grapes.
7. A hockey player scored a goal.
8. Your backpack seems heavier than mine.
9. Jenny has a strong volleyball serve.
10. A reporter interviewed the President.

F. Finding the Verb and Its Subject (Use after page 57.)

Copy each sentence. Draw two lines under the verb. Then draw one line under the subject of the verb.

1. A seaplane landed nearby.
2. The smallest package was best.
3. The pen on my desk writes with purple ink.
4. Spencer read a book about whales.
5. The cactus in that flowerpot is very prickly.
6. A huge iceberg floated on the sea.
7. Two red lobsters topped the platter.
8. Slowly, Nina crawled through the tunnel.
9. My older sister camped at Yellowstone.
10. Vendors at the stadium sell hot dogs.

G. **Finding the Subject in Unusual Positions**
   (Use after page 59.)

Copy each sentence. Draw two lines under the verb. Then draw one line under the subject of the verb.

1. During the fourth inning the rain started.
2. Close by a helicopter hovered.
3. Around the corner came a motorcycle.
4. In the bleachers sat my parents.
5. Out of the water splashed a seal.
6. Under our porch some squirrels nested.
7. Toward its target flew the arrow.
8. On the tape my voice sounded strange.
9. High in the air the tower swayed.
10. On Ann's T-shirt was a map.

H. **Finding the Subject in Imperative Sentences**
   (Use after page 61.)

Copy the following sentences. Some are imperative sentences. Draw two lines under the verb in each sentence. Draw one line under the subject of the verb. If the subject is not given in the sentence, write it in parentheses in the place where it is understood.

1. Hold onto the railing. (You) hold
2. Plant these seeds in the dirt. (You) plant
3. Stop at the corner. (You) stop
4. Good cooks watch the oven temperature.
5. Trick-or-treaters go out on Halloween.
6. Tell your favorite riddle. (You) tell
7. Use the big beach towel. (You) use
8. Make room for the groceries. (You) make
9. The singers practice in Room 213.
10. Help me with this problem. (You) help

Chapter 5

Writing Good Sentences

Part 1 Avoiding Run-on Sentences

What's wrong with this sentence?

Evan is sitting at the window he is waiting for his friend.

How many ideas can you find in the example? Is there just one complete thought? Can you find more than one?

If you read the example carefully, you will see that it should be broken into two separate sentences:

Subject	Predicate
Evan	is sitting at the window.
He	is waiting for his friend.

Chapter Objectives

1. To recognize and avoid run-on sentences
2. To recognize and avoid stringy sentences

Preparing the Students

Review how our voices show the beginnings and endings of ideas. Have the students say these sentences with expression:

Come to the movie with me. Everyone is going.

Then ask the students to say the same sentences in a monotone, with no pause between the thoughts. Point out that in writing, punctuation must tell what our voices show about idea beginnings and endings. This chapter will help the students become aware of common errors in punctuation that mix up ideas and confuse readers.

Additional Resources

Diagnostic Test—page 429 in this T.E. Recommended for use before teaching the chapter.
Mastery Test—pages 446 and 447 in this T.E. Recommended for use after teaching the chapter.
Additional Mastery Test—Recommended for use after any necessary reteaching. (In separate booklet, *Mastery Tests, Silver Level*, pages 9 and 10.)
Skills Practice Book—pages 23–25
Duplicating Masters—pages 23–25

Part 1

Objective

To recognize and avoid run-on sentences

Presenting the Lesson

1. You may wish to review what a good sentence does: it expresses one complete idea. Stress particularly that it is important to write clear sentences because a writer is not present to explain anything to a reader. Have different students give one sentence each about the picture on page 68, describing it to someone who cannot see it. Use this experience as an example of how much care is needed to express thoughts clearly.
2. Read and discuss pages 69 and 70. Stress the importance of avoiding run-ons by thinking of each idea separately and using end marks to show the separations.
3. You may wish to do part of Exercises A and B on page 71 with students to check their understanding, and then assign and discuss the rest.
4. Use Exercise A on page 74 as additional practice or review.

Optional Practice

Put the following sentences on the board or a worksheet. Tell the students that eight sentences are run-ons and two are correct. They are to find the run-on sentences and draw a line separating the two ideas.

1. Did you find a glove I lost mine.
2. The baseball went over the fence it landed in the garden.
3. Those books are due at the library I want to get some more.
4. The dog is barking the cat is howling.
5. I need to buy a birthday present for my friend.

In the example, two sentences were run together. There was no period to mark the end of the first idea, and no capital letter to mark the beginning of the second idea. This kind of sentence is called a **run-on sentence.** If you write run-on sentences, your reader can become confused.

Study this paragraph. It has three good sentences and one run-on sentence. Find the run-on sentence. You should be able to break it into two shorter sentences.

> Martha has a garden. She grows vegetables in it. Last week she found a tomato worm on a tomato it looked like a big green caterpillar. On its back were white stripes.

This run-on sentence shows you why you should avoid run-ons. You probably had to read it more than once to decide what it was saying. Here is the way it should have been written.

> Martha has a garden. She grows vegetables in it. Last week she found a tomato worm on a tomato. It looked like a big green caterpillar. On its back were white stripes.

When you are writing, follow these rules:

1. Express only one complete thought in each sentence.
2. Mark the beginning of every new idea with a capital letter.
3. Mark the ending of every idea with a period, or a question mark, or an exclamation point.

Exercises **Avoiding Run-on Sentences**

A. Number your paper from 1 to 10. If the sentence is correct, write *Correct*. If it is a run-on, write *Run-on Sentence*.   C = Correct
R = Run-on

1. Three clowns were riding on one donkey they pushed each other off. R

2. Lillian and Darren raced on the playground at recess. C

3. I had a piano lesson for one hour then my teacher played a piece for me. R

4. We played baseball yesterday Judy scored three runs. R

5. At the beginning of the program, everyone recited the Pledge of Allegiance. C

6. Mel had tomato soup and a cheese sandwich for lunch. C

7. It rained on the Fourth of July we had our picnic inside. R

8. Jeff answered an ad in the paper he got a furry puppy. R

9. Adelle played checkers with her father every night last week. C

10. The 4-H Club met Tuesday after school a speaker told about a contest. R

6. My aunt is going to school she is learning to fix her car.
7. The little baby is crying he wants a bottle of milk.
8. The television is broken we can't watch it.
9. There were a lot of dirty dishes in the sink.
10. Can you roller skate it's fun.

B. Number your paper from 1 to 10. If the sentence is correct, write *Correct*. If it is a run-on, rewrite the sentence as two sentences, with correct capitalization and punctuation.

1. I have two younger brothers. T they are twins.
2. Janet has a paper route each morning. Correct
3. My friends from camp exchange letters. Correct
4. Keith catches fireflies. H he keeps them in a jar.
5. Last year, we planted a maple tree. I it's in the back yard.
6. Sally rode a horse. S she followed a trail guide.
7. Aunt Meg knits sweaters for everyone in the family. Correct
8. Rick knows the capital city of every state. Correct
9. Luis likes corn. H he doesn't like broccoli.
10. Cassie filled the bookcase with Nancy Drew mysteries. Correct

Part 2

Objective

To recognize and avoid stringy sentences

Presenting the Lesson

1. Discuss the meaning of stringy and examples of things that are stringy (spaghetti, ball of yarn, string, etc.). Ask students to tell you what has to be done to make them usable (cutting off, shortening, using part at a time). Explain that some sentences, too, are stringy and have to be cut apart to be useful.

2. Read and discuss page 72. Make sure students notice the use of the comma in the examples of related sentences joined by *and*.

3. You may wish to do part of Exercises A and B on page 73 with the students to check their understanding, and then assign and discuss the rest. Use of commas in these sentences is optional.

4. Use Exercise B on pages 74 and 75 as additional practice or review.

Optional Practice

Have students rewrite the stringy sentences in Exercise A on page 73 as correct sentences.

Extending the Lesson

Discuss the similarities and differences between run-on and stringy sentences. Review good sentences and their two main parts, subject and predicate. Then present the following long sentence, which combines run-on and stringy

Part 2 Avoiding Stringy Sentences

>Last week I bought a sweater and a new skateboard and I tried out my skateboard on the big hill and I fell down and I tore my sweater.

Almost everyone would agree that this is not a good sentence. It has too many ideas in it. It uses *and* too many times.

However, not everyone would agree on how to correct it. There are several different ways that are satisfactory.

This kind of sentence is called a **stringy sentence.** It strings together several different sentences by using the word *and*.

Here are some examples of places where you should use *and*:

>Mother *and* I went downtown.
>I bought a sweater *and* a new skateboard.
>Howard practiced *and* learned several card tricks.

You may use *and* now and then to connect related sentences, as in these examples:

>The audience waited patiently, *and* soon the show began.
>This pen has black ink, *and* that one has red ink.
>Jackie read this book, *and* she liked it.

However, you should not use *and* to connect sentences too often. Most sentences should stand alone. When you use *and* to connect sentences, connect only two related sentences.

Now let's return to the stringy sentence at the top of the page. Here are two satisfactory ways of dividing it.

>Last week I bought a sweater and a new skateboard. I tried out my skateboard on the big hill. I fell down. I tore my sweater.

>Last week I bought a sweater and a new skateboard. I tried out my skateboard on the big hill. I fell down, and I tore my sweater.

Exercises   Avoiding stringy sentences

A. Number your paper from 1 to 10. If the sentence is correct, write *Correct*. If it is a stringy sentence, write *Stringy Sentence*.   C = Correct   S = Stringy

1. We built a fire and we cooked hot dogs and then we ate. **s**
2. Kristin and Brett are crossing guards and members of the student council. **c**
3. Sue and I played Ping-Pong with Chee, and he beat us. **c**
4. My sister water-skis and she belongs to a club and they put on shows. **s**
5. We went to the Hancock Building and to Sears Tower in downtown Chicago. **c**
6. The porpoises jumped and they did tricks and the audience clapped. **s**
7. Terry ice skates well and he leaps and twirls and he does figure eights. **s**
8. Lisa's pets are a chicken and a monkey and they live in her back yard and she takes care of them. **s**
9. A repairman fixed both the radio and the TV at the school media center. **c**
10. Geese fly south for the winter and they fly in formation and they return in the springtime. **s**

B. Number your paper from 1 to 10. If the sentence is correct, write *Correct*. If it is a stringy sentence, rewrite the sentence as two or three sentences.   Answers will vary for all but item 1. Possible answers are at right.

1. Our class visited the Museum of Natural History and the Historical Society Museum. *Correct*
2. We learned soccer in gym class and we formed a team and we play other schools.
3. John went to Disney World and he loved it and he wants to go back.
4. Darla bought a ticket and she knocked over three pins and she won a teddy bear.

> 4. Darla bought a ticket. She knocked over three pins. She won a teddy bear.
> Darla bought a ticket, and she knocked over three pins. She won a teddy bear.
> Darla bought a ticket. She knocked over three pins, and she won a teddy bear.

thoughts, either on the board or on a worksheet. Have the students circle every complete idea. Then they should list every verb and the subject of that verb. They must find a subject/verb combination in every circle. You may wish to use the exercise as a contest. Challenge the students to be the first to find all eight ideas and list all eight subjects and verbs.

Last summer the older kids on my block organized a circus parade and we all wore costumes and I was a lion and my two brothers were clowns the little kids watched our parade we marched down the street and then rain poured down and everyone ran home.

> 2. We learned soccer in gym class. We formed a team. We play other schools.
> We learned soccer in gym class, and we formed a team. We play other schools.
> We learned soccer in gym class. We formed a team, and we play other schools.
>
> 3. John went to Disney World. He loved it. He wants to go back.
> John went to Disney World, and he loved it. He wants to go back.
> John went to Disney World. He loved it, and he wants to go back.

Additional Exercises

If these Exercises were not used with each lesson, they may now be assigned for chapter review.

Additional Exercises

Writing Good Sentences

A. Avoiding Run-on Sentences (Use after page 70.)

Number your paper from 1 to 10. If the sentence is correct as it is, write *Correct*. If it is a run-on, rewrite the sentence as two sentences, with correct capitalization and punctuation.

1. At night my brother and I played Clue or Probe. *Correct*
2. My sister is twelve years old. I'm ten.
3. One day, we hiked through Blueberry Woods. *Correct*
4. The firefighters came. They put out the blaze.
5. The classroom gerbil escaped from its cage. *Correct*
6. The dog barks fiercely. He frightens strangers.
7. That pitcher throws fast curve balls. *Correct*
8. I added two fish to the aquarium. Both are goldfish.
9. There are nine planets in the solar system. *Correct*
10. Carmen looked through a telescope. She saw the stars.

B. Avoiding Stringy Sentences (Use after page 72.)

Number your paper from 1 to 10. If the sentence is correct as it is, write *Correct*. If it is a stringy sentence, rewrite the sentence as two or three sentences, with correct capitalization and punctuation. *Answers will vary for items 2, 3, 6, 9 and 10. Possible answers are on the next page.*

1. The boy in the apartment down the hall and my best friend Juan have the measles. *Correct*
2. Dolores broke her leg and she has a cast and everyone signs it.

3. Bob read a book and he liked it and it was called *A Very Young Rider*.

4. The plane landed, and the passengers and crew got off.

5. Two of my favorite programs on TV are "Zoom" and "Big Blue Marble."

6. Marla drew plans and she built a birdhouse and now it's outside.

7. We went to the children's zoo, and I petted the sheep there.

8. The snow covered the ground and drifted high against houses.

9. Tony had a Halloween party and everybody wore costumes and I was Darth Vader.

10. Amy painted a picture and she gave it to Dad and he hung it in his office.

---

2. Dolores broke her leg. She has a cast. Everyone signs it.
   Dolores broke her leg, and she has a cast. Everyone signs it.
   Dolores broke her leg. She has a cast, and everyone signs it.

3. Bob read a book. He liked it. It was called *A Very Young Rider*.
   Bob read a book, and he liked it. It was called *A Very Young Rider*.

4. Correct

5. Correct

6. Marla drew plans. She built a birdhouse. Now it's outside.
   Marla drew plans, and she built a birdhouse. Now it's outside.
   Marla drew plans. She built a birdhouse, and now it's outside.

7. Correct

8. Correct

9. Tony had a Halloween party. Everybody wore costumes. I was Darth Vader.
   Tony had a Halloween party, and everybody wore costumes. I was Darth Vader.

10. Amy painted a picture. She gave it to Dad. He hung it in his office.
    Amy painted a picture, and she gave it to Dad. He hung it in his office.
    Amy painted a picture. She gave it to Dad, and he hung it in his office.

Chapter 6

Writing Good Paragraphs

Chapter Objectives

1. To understand the meaning of the term *paragraph*
2. To identify the topic sentence in a paragraph
3. To write good topic sentences

Preparing the Students

Ask several students to make up sentences describing selected objects on your desk, for example: *The blotter is green.* Then ask a student to give several sentences that describe the desk as a whole. Point out that some ideas are simple and can be expressed in one sentence, while others are more complex and must be expressed in several sentences.

Read the introduction to the chapter on page 77.

Additional Resources

Mastery Test—pages 448 and 449 in this T.E. Recommended for use after teaching the chapter.

Additional Mastery Test—Recommended for use after any necessary reteaching. (In separate booklet, *Mastery Tests, Silver Level*, pages 11 and 12.)

Skills Practice Book—pages 26–29
Duplicating Masters—pages 26–29

A good sentence helps you express an idea. A good paragraph also helps you express an idea.

In this chapter you are going to study paragraphs. This is what you will learn:

1. What a paragraph is
2. What makes a good paragraph
3. How to write good paragraphs of your own

Part 1

Objective

To understand the meaning of the term *paragraph*

Presenting the Lesson

1. The composition chapters in this book present a highly structured type of paragraph, a basic model that consists of a topic sentence developed by several additional sentences. This model is useful in getting students to discipline their thinking and their writing. However, it should not be presented as the only way to organize a paragraph. Therefore, you may want to mention occasionally that the sample paragraphs represent one way to write a paragraph.

2. Read page 78 and the first paragraph on page 79. Explain that the main idea of a paragraph is the answer to this question: What is the paragraph about? Point out additional examples of indented paragraphs, selecting from sample paragraphs and from explanatory material.

3. Read the introduction to Finding the Main Idea, on page 79. Then ask a student to read the sample paragraph and to answer the questions: What is the paragraph about? Which sentence presents the main idea? Read the remainder of the page. As you read the four-point description of paragraph content, ask students to read the sentences in which these ideas are given.

4. Read and discuss page 80. Emphasize the importance of sticking to the one main idea of a paragraph.

Part 1 What Is a Paragraph?

1. A paragraph is a group of sentences.
2. A paragraph has a main idea.
3. All the sentences in a paragraph work together to tell about the main idea.

A paragraph is a group of sentences. Here's an example of a paragraph with six sentences. Read the paragraph.

> Elmer Allthumbs is the world's worst housekeeper. One day he burned the breakfast to a crisp and then broke all his dishes. He dissolved the kitchen floor and killed the entire front lawn. He vacuumed a hole in the living room rug and knocked over all the lamps. He turned the laundry the color of mud and then ironed it to shreds. And that was an ordinary day!

Notice that the first line of a paragraph begins a little to the right. The first line is **indented.**

A paragraph has a main idea. The main idea of the paragraph above is told in the first sentence. The main idea is that Elmer Allthumbs is the world's worst housekeeper.

All the sentences in a paragraph work together to tell about the main idea. In the paragraph above, all the sentences after the first one give examples of Elmer's bad housekeeping. This is what Elmer did:

1. He burned the breakfast.
2. He broke all the dishes.

3. He dissolved the kitchen floor.
4. He killed the front lawn.
5. He vacuumed a hole in the living room rug.
6. He knocked over all the lamps.
7. He turned the laundry the color of mud.
8. He ironed the laundry to shreds.

The last sentence says that Elmer did all this on an ordinary day.

Finding the Main Idea

The next paragraph has eight sentences. They all work together to tell about the main idea. Try to find the sentence that tells the main idea.

> After a baby kangaroo is born, it must go from outside its mother's body to a pocket, or pouch, on her belly. The new baby is hairless and blind. It would fit easily into a teaspoon. Even so, it must climb into the pouch by itself. Its mother bends over and licks her belly, making a wet pathway through her fur. The baby crawls up this pathway to the pouch. It swings its tiny head back and forth until it finds a place to hold on. Then it clamps with its mouth and doesn't let go.
>
> —RUSSELL FREEDMAN

The main idea of the paragraph is that a baby kangaroo must get to a pouch on its mother's belly. The rest of the sentences tell about the main idea:

1. That the tiny baby must climb into the pouch by itself
2. How the mother makes a path to the pouch
3. How the baby crawls to the pouch
4. What the baby does when it gets to the pouch

The eight sentences form a paragraph. They work together to tell about the main idea.

the second sentence because it does not describe something Buffy has done to help young Native Americans.

6. Use Exercise A on page 89 for additional practice.

Optional Practice

Direct each student to find one example of a paragraph from a source outside the classroom. Suggest that students copy paragraphs from encyclopedias and books, and cut paragraphs from magazines and newspapers. Group the students according to either the content or the source of their paragraphs. Have each group put together a montage of paragraphs to hang in the classroom.

Sticking to the Main Idea

Sometimes a paragraph contains a sentence that does not tell about the main idea. This next paragraph has such a sentence. See if you can pick it out.

> The taste of hot cooked cereal can be improved in many ways. Raisins, dates, or other fruit can be mixed in with the cereal. Wheat germ, cooked soygrits, or powdered milk can be added. Cereal boxes give information about the cereal. Honey or brown sugar can be used to sweeten the cereal.

The first sentence tells you that the taste of hot cooked cereal can be improved in many ways. That is the main idea. The second sentence gives suggestions for doing this. The third and fifth sentences give other suggestions. The fourth sentence, though, does not give suggestions. It tells about cereal boxes. This is a brand new idea. It does not work with the main idea of the paragraph.

Now read the paragraph again. This time skip the fourth sentence. See how the sentences that are left all stick to the main idea.

Guide for Writing Paragraphs

When you write paragraphs of your own, check them by asking yourself these three questions:

1. Is each sentence a complete sentence?

2. Does the paragraph have one main idea?

3. Do all the sentences tell about that one idea?

Exercise **Studying Paragraphs**

Find the main idea in each of the following paragraphs. Then check the sentences to make sure that they help to explain the main idea. In two of the paragraphs there is an extra sentence. This sentence does not work with the others to explain the main idea. See if you can find these two sentences.

1

My biggest problem is my two-year-old brother Skippy. He's always in my way. He messes up the whole house, including my room. ~~He likes ice cream~~. Once in a while he doesn't get his own way. Then he screams and kicks and bangs his head on the floor.

2

One day a change came over the woods and the pond. Warm air, soft and kind, blew through the trees. The ice, which had softened during the night, began to melt. Patches of open water appeared. All the creatures that lived in the pond and in the woods were glad to feel the warmth. They heard and felt the breath of spring, and they stirred with new life and hope. There was a good, new smell in the air. It was a smell of earth waking after its long sleep.

3

The largest kite ever to fly was made in Japan in 1906. It was round in shape and sixty feet across. The kite flew a tail four hundred and eighty feet long. It weighed more than five thousand pounds. It was heavier than the biggest car made today. —JOHN PETERSON

4

Folksinger Buffy Saint Marie, a member of the Cree tribe, has done many things to help young Native Americans. ~~Buffy's favorite songwriter is Mick Jagger~~. She has worked to change the way Native Americans are presented in school books. She has also written a school book in the Cree language. She has worked with groups who train Native Americans for jobs. She has also tried to start a theater run completely by Native Americans.

Part 2

Objective

To identify the topic sentence in a paragraph

Presenting the Lesson

1. Read the examples and explanations on pages 82 and 83. Emphasize that the topic sentence tells the main idea of a paragraph and that the other sentences in the paragraph add to the idea in the topic sentence. For additional examples of well-written paragraphs, review page 81, paragraphs 2 and 3. For examples of paragraphs in which a sentence does not add to the main idea, see paragraphs 1 and 4 on that page.

2. It is recommended that Exercise A on page 83 be done as a class activity. Sentence 3 names the topic that is explained by the other three sentences. To clarify this concept, ask a student to read the sentences in the following order: 3, 1, 2, 4.

3. It is suggested that you do Exercise B on page 84 with the class. In paragraph 2, the third sentence is the extra sentence because it does not describe the television program, but rather focuses on swimming in general. In paragraph 4, the final sentence does not belong because it does not describe Lisa Vance as a football player. Ask two volunteers to reread paragraphs 2 and 4 without these extra sentences.

4. Use Exercise B on page 89 for practice in developing topic sentences into paragraphs.

Part 2   The Topic Sentence

You have learned that a paragraph is a group of sentences. You will now learn that in each paragraph one sentence is special. This is the topic sentence. It usually comes first. It tells the main idea. It tells what the entire paragraph is going to be about.

Example 1

Here's an example of a topic sentence:

Owls sound different to almost everyone who hears them.

It is the first sentence in the paragraph. It tells you that the rest of the sentence will explain how owls sound to different people. This is the main idea.
Now let's look at the whole paragraph. Notice how each sentence adds something to the main idea.

Owls sound different to almost everyone who hears them. If several people hear the same owl at the same time, it still may sound different to each of them. Even experts on birds cannot agree on how to describe owl calls. Some scientists think, for example, that the call of the great horned owl sounds like this: *hoo, hoohoo, hoo, hoo*. Others describe the call this way: *oot-too-hoo, hoo-hoo*. Still other bird experts say the call is *hoo, hoo-hoo-oo, hoot, hoot*. —EDWARD R. RICCIUTI

The second sentence tells what happens when people hear the same owl. The third sentence tells that even experts disagree on how to describe owl calls. The fourth, fifth, and sixth sentences give three ways of describing the call of the great horned owl. Each of these sentences adds to the idea in the topic sentence.

Example 2

The next paragraph starts out with the topic sentence, "Lizards move around in many different ways." This tells you that the rest of the sentences are about the ways lizards move. Check each sentence to see if this is so.

> Lizards move around in many different ways. One type of giant lizard swims between islands. A type of lizard called a *flying dragon* flies from tree to tree. Chameleons use their long tongues to catch insects. Some lizards are able to climb straight up on rough or smooth surfaces. That's because they have claws and brush-like hooks. Some lizards raise the front parts of their bodies and walk on their hind legs. Others get along without any legs at all.

One sentence does not describe ways that lizards move around. It tells how chameleons catch insects. This has nothing to do with the main idea of the paragraph. The sentence should be taken out of the paragraph.

Exercises Studying Topic Sentences

A. Following are four sentences. They make up a paragraph. One of the sentences is the topic sentence. It tells what all of the sentences are about. See if you can pick out the topic sentence.

1. The worm is the larva of a small moth.
2. When the larva moves, the bean "jumps."
3. A Mexican jumping bean is a seed that contains a tiny worm. Topic
4. The warmer the bean, the faster the larva moves.

Optional Practice

Work in a small group with those students who had difficulty with Exercise B. For each paragraph do the following:

a. Read the first sentence.
b. Ask: What is the paragraph going to be about?
c. Write the main idea on the chalkboard, summarizing it in a word or phrase.
d. Read the next sentence.
e. Ask: Does this sentence tell you something about the main idea?
f. Do the same with each remaining sentence.

This activity will help students develop the habit of checking the ideas in a paragraph against the main idea in the topic sentence.

B. Each of the following paragraphs begins with a topic sentence. The main idea is presented in that sentence. Read the topic sentence. Then check the rest of the sentences to make sure that they stick to the main idea. In two of the paragraphs one sentence does *not* belong. Pick out that sentence.

1

My dog Storm is a big English setter. He weighs ninety pounds. He is mainly white, with dark red shadings. His coat is long and wavy. He has long, silky ears and a long tail. His eyes are large and dark brown in color. He is a friendly, loving dog.

2

The smash hit of the new TV season is *Splash!* It stars a family of champion swimmers. Swimming is a healthy sport. They develop an act and entertain people all over the world. In one episode, the youngest member of the family is kidnapped by a performer from another act. The kidnapper demands that the family give up its act.

3

One day Big Roy and Baggie Maggie and Scooter and little Barnaby played Marching Band. Big Roy came first, twirling a mop handle. Then came Baggie Maggie, playing tissue paper on a comb. Then came Scooter, tooting on a funnel. Last came little Barnaby, banging a spoon on a pan. Past the pawn shop, past the shoeshine, past the newsstand, past the delicatessen they marched. Past the empty store and the other empty store and the fruit stand and Tiny's Spaghetti Place they paraded.   —BARBARA KLIMOWICZ

4

Lisa Vance was the first girl to play football in Peoria's Junior Football League. In 1978 the eleven-year-old sixth-grader at Pioneer Junior High School joined a lightweight division team. This was her first chance to play a contact sport. The other players were asked about having a girl on the team. They agreed that it didn't matter one bit. The professional football season ended with the Super Bowl.

Part 3 Writing Good Topic Sentences

You know some important things about paragraphs. Here they are.

> 1. A paragraph is a group of sentences.
> 2. A paragraph has a main idea.
> 3. All the sentences in a paragraph work together to tell about the main idea.
> 4. The main idea is presented in a topic sentence.
> 5. The topic sentence is usually the first sentence in a paragraph.
> 6. The topic sentence tells what the paragraph is going to be about.

What Is a Good Topic Sentence?

In this lesson you will practice writing good topic sentences. Before you begin, let's look at an example.

A spider web is one of nature's wonders.

After reading this sentence, you know what the rest of the paragraph is going to be about. It is going to describe a spider web. The topic sentence does something else, too. It makes you want to read the rest of the paragraph.

Part 3

Objective

To write good topic sentences

Presenting the Lesson

1. Read and discuss the six characteristics of a paragraph, listed on page 85.
2. Read and discuss What Is a Good Topic Sentence?, on pages 85 and 86. Emphasize the two purposes of a topic sentence: to state the main idea of a paragraph and to catch the reader's attention.
3. Read and discuss Writing a Topic Sentence on pages 86 and 87. Stress that each sentence in a paragraph must relate in some way to the topic sentence.
4. Before assigning the Exercise on pages 87 and 88, suggest these four steps for use in doing the Exercise:

   1. Decide what all the sentences are about.
   2. Write a sentence that states the general idea of the paragraph.
   3. Test the sentence by checking each sentence in the paragraph against the proposed topic sentence.
   4. Revise and write a final topic sentence.

Demonstrate these four steps with the first paragraph in the Exercise. It may also be necessary to make sure the students are familiar with landmarks in Washington, D.C. (the subject of paragraph 2) and with the story of Tarzan (the subject of paragraph 4). Then have the students complete the Exercise independently.

5. Assign the final Exercise on page 88. Encourage the students to check their paragraphs by using the questions on page 80 and the list of characteristics on page 85. You may prefer to develop the checklist described in Extending the Lesson before directing the students to revise their paragraphs.

6. Use Exercise C on page 89 for practice in writing topic sentences.

Extending the Lesson

As a class, make up a checklist to use in revising completed paragraphs. Include the three questions at the bottom of page 80, questions based on the characteristics given on page 85, and any other points, such as rules of punctuation and capitalization, about which many students need frequent reminders. Transfer the checklist to a large sheet of poster paper and hang it in the classroom.

Here are three more examples of good topic sentences. They tell what the paragraphs are about. They also make you want to read the paragraphs.

1. The old man put down the basket and took off the cover.
2. When Jim Gary has an idea for a new sculpture, he heads for the junkyard.
3. Golden lion marmosets are little monkeys with big problems.

Notice what happens when you read these sentences. Questions begin to pop into your mind. What did the man find in the basket? What does Jim Gary look for in a junkyard? What kinds of problems do the marmosets have? The topic sentences have made you want to read more.

Writing a Topic Sentence

Now let's take a look at a paragraph. It needs a topic sentence. Read the paragraph. Try to decide what all of the sentences are about.

_____(topic sentence)_____. Marcie heads for the city pool every morning. Dolores doesn't have a pool near her house. She does have a backyard sprinkler. Sometimes she turns it on and runs through it. Other times she puts a lawn chair right in the sprinkler's path and sits there for hours. When it's very hot, Reymondo lives on his shaded porch. He even moves a mattress out there for sleeping. Shannon always visits his cousin Craig on the hottest days. Craig's house is air conditioned.

These sentences describe ways that people cool off on hot days. This is the main idea of the paragraph. It must be stated in the topic sentence. The topic sentence for this paragraph might be something like this:

On hot days my friends have their own special ways to cool off.

Notice how the topic sentence ties together the entire paragraph. It gives the main idea. All the other sentences work together to explain the main idea.

Exercise   Writing Good Topic Sentences

Here are five paragraphs. They need topic sentences. Read each paragraph. Decide what each group of sentences is about. Then write a topic sentence that gives the main idea.

These are suggested answers.

1

At night the children in our neighborhood played games.
_____(topic sentence)_____. Some nights we'd play "Red Light." Other nights we'd play "Kick the Can." The game we played most often, though, was "Hide-and-Seek." We'd use the entire block for hiding. No one wanted to be "it" because it was almost impossible to find people before they reached home.

2

Washington, D.C. has many interesting places to visit.
_____(topic sentence)_____. The city has famous buildings, like the White House and Capitol Hill. It has the Smithsonian Institution. There visitors can see things like rocks from the moon, important inventions, dinosaur bones, and paintings of famous Americans. The city has a zoo with the only giant pandas in America. It has the National Archives Building where people can see the Declaration of Independence and the Constitution.

3

Signs of a coming storm were everywhere.
_____(topic sentence)_____. Dark clouds were moving in from the west. The air was heavy and still. Thunder rumbled in the distance. Animals were scurrying for shelter. Parents were gathering their children and heading for home.

4
His life story was most unusual.

_____ *(topic sentence)* _____. He was the son of an English lord. As a boy he was lost in the African jungle. Apes taught him to survive in the jungle. They showed him how to get from place to place by swinging on trees and vines. As he grew up he learned to communicate with all the animals. He learned to call them with his special "jungle cry." Eventually he met and married Jane. They had a child named Boy.

5
There were only five minutes until the show began.

_____ *(topic sentence)* _____. Raul and Maria, the stars of the show, paced nervously behind the drawn curtain. The narrator read and reread the script. The nervous director gave last-minute instructions. The lighting engineer made her final adjustments. So did the people in charge of make-up and costumes.

Exercise   Writing a Good Paragraph

You have learned how to write a good paragraph and a good topic sentence. You are now ready to write a paragraph of your own. Choose a topic that interests you, and write a paragraph about it. You may choose one of the following topics if you can't think of one of your own. *Answers will vary.*

your pet	a rainy day
a sport	a holiday
a place	something you like
a hobby	something you dislike

Additional Exercises

Writing Good Paragraphs

A. Studying Paragraphs (Use after page 81.)

Read the following paragraph. Then answer the questions.

    Redwoods are the tallest trees in the world. The oak tree in front of our house is very tall, too. Redwoods grow to about 90 meters, or over 300 feet, high. The trunk of a full-grown redwood is about three meters, or ten feet, across. Its bark can be 30 centimeters, or nearly a foot, thick. Some redwoods have enough wood to build four houses.

1. What is the main idea of the paragraph? *The size of redwood trees*
2. What sentence does not help to explain the main idea? *Sentence 2*

B. Studying Topic Sentences (Use after page 84.)

Choose one of the following topic sentences. Write a four- or five-sentence paragraph.

1. Thanksgiving dinner at our house is always the same.
2. Our family album has some funny pictures.
3. Roller skating is easy if you remember a few important things.
4. Many people carry good luck charms.

C. Writing Good Topic Sentences (Use after page 88.)

Choose one of the following topics. Write a topic sentence. Then explain what the rest of the paragraph would be about.

    your favorite meal   a time you were surprised
    an insect   a friend
    a time you were sad   an outdoor game

Additional Exercises

If these Exercises were not used with each lesson, they may now be assigned for chapter review.

Chapter 7

Ways of Developing Paragraphs

Chapter Objectives

1. To recognize details and to understand their use in a paragraph
2. To develop a paragraph by using details
3. To develop a paragraph by using an example

Preparing the Students

Ask the students to recall the definition of a paragraph:

1. A paragraph is a group of sentences.
2. A paragraph has a main idea.
3. All the sentences in a paragraph work together to tell about the main idea.

Explain that, while Chapter 6 examined the function and characteristics of a topic sentence in some detail, this chaper will focus on the sentences that develop, or tell about, the main idea of the paragraph.

Read and discuss page 91.

Additional Resources

Mastery Test—pages 450 and 451 in this T.E. Recommended for use after teaching the chapter.

Additional Mastery Test—Recommended for use after any necessary reteaching. (In separate booklet, *Mastery Tests, Silver Level*, pages 13 and 14.)

Skills Practice Book—pages 30–34
Duplicating Masters—pages 30–34

You have learned what a good paragraph is. You have also learned how important the topic sentence is. You will now learn about ways to develop paragraphs.

There are many ways to develop a paragraph. In this lesson you will study two ways of developing paragraphs:

1. By using details
2. By using an example

Part 1

Objectives

1. To recognize details and to understand their use in a paragraph
2. To develop a paragraph by using details

Presenting the Lesson

1. Read and discuss page 92. Use the examples to illustrate three ways of adding details to noun phrases: adding words that tell what kind or how many (*golden, two, rain-slicked*), adding phrases that tell what kind (*of sunflowers*); and adding modifiers to words that tell what kind (*brilliant* added to *blue*). (The terms *adjective* and *adverb* will be introduced in Chapters 16 and 17.)
2. Direct the class's attention to the photograph on page 90. Ask the students to name three or four things shown in the picture (flowers, ring, hair, tree). Then guide them in adding details and in substituting specific words for general ones.
3. Assign the Exercise on page 92. In correcting the Exercise, bring out the different ways that each phrase was modified and changed.
4. Read pages 93 and 94. Ask the students to identify the one detail that describes how the building smelled. Outline for the class the steps to follow in developing a paragraph with details:
   1. Choose a subject.
   2. Picture the subject in your mind.
   3. Write a topic sentence.
   4. List details.
   5. Write the paragraph.

Part 1 Developing a Paragraph by Using Details

Learning About Details

Before you can use details to develop a paragraph, you must know something about them. Details are the "little things" a writer tells about someone or something. Details help to make a person or a place more interesting for the reader. They help to create a strong mental picture.

Here are some pairs of phrases. First is a phrase without details. Following it is the same phrase with details added. Sometimes a word has been changed to make it more specific. For instance, the general word "flower" has been changed to the specific word "cornflower." The general word "child" has been changed to the specific "six-year-old." As you read the phrases, notice how details and specific words help to sharpen your mental picture.

the field	the golden field of sunflowers
two frogs	two green bullfrogs
a road	a rain-slicked highway
a flower	a brilliant blue cornflower
the woman	the bent old woman
the child	the happy six-year-old

Exercise Working with Details

Below is a list of phrases without details. Add details to each. You may want to change some words to more specific ones.

1. the cat
2. the horse
3. a bush
4. a shirt
5. a cold day
6. a leaf
7. a toy
8. a food
9. a boy
10. a floor
11. a girl
12. the moon

Studying a Paragraph with Details

The following paragraph describes a city building. Notice the details the writer uses in her description.

> New House was as old as any of the other brownstone buildings on West 94th Street. In fact, for a time it had looked even sadder than the rest of the rundown rooming-houses. That was after the fire. All the people had moved out. The broken windows stared like blind eyes. The boys on the block climbed inside the building. They hoped to find a place for a clubhouse, but they saw that floorboards had been burned through. Ceiling beams were charred and blackened. The stinging smell of smoke still hung about the empty rooms. —PEGGY MANN

The topic sentence tells you that the paragraph is about an old brownstone building called New House. The sentences that follow give details about New House.

1. The second sentence tells you that New House looked sad. It also suggests that New House was a rundown rooming-house.

2. The third sentence tells you that there had been a fire.

3. The fourth sentence tells you that all the people had moved out.

4. The fifth sentence tells you that the building had broken windows.

5. The seventh sentence tells you that the floorboards had been burned through.

6. The eighth sentence tells you that the ceiling beams were charred and blackened.

7. The last sentence tells you that the empty rooms smelled of smoke.

5. Assign the Exercise on page 95. Remind the students to picture the subject and to make a list of details before beginning to write the paragraph.

6. Use Exercises A and B on page 97 for additional practice.

Optional Practice

Cut pictures of simple objects from magazines. Use parts of pictures, if necessary; for example, select one plant from a garden scene or one house on a block. Distribute the pictures among the students. Have each student write a four- or five-sentence paragraph that gives details about what is shown in his or her picture.

The writer has developed the paragraph by using details. She has included details about how the old building looked. She also has included a detail about how it smelled.

As you read each sentence, your mental picture of the building becomes clearer and clearer. You end up knowing a great deal about the old building.

Developing Your Paragraph

When you want to develop a paragraph by using details, first decide what you want to write about. Let's say you decide to write about a littered river bank. You might begin with this topic sentence: *The river bank needed a good clean-up.* You would then list details about the river bank. Your list might look like this:

> 6 old tires
> 10 feet of frayed rope
> broken bottles
> a tennis shoe
> a T-shirt
> a rusted sink

After making your list, you would be ready to develop the paragraph. You would try to use details from your list in each sentence. Your final paragraph might be something like this one:

> The river bank needed a good clean-up. It was littered with things that had been forgotten or thrown away. Six old tires and ten feet of frayed rope were scattered along the river's edge. A tennis shoe, a T-shirt, and dozens of broken bottles were stuck in the shoreline mud. There was even a rusted old sink half-buried in the muck.

All the details work together to explain the main idea.

Exercise   Developing a Paragraph by Using Details

Here are ten topic sentences. Choose one and develop a paragraph by adding details. Make sure that each sentence adds one or more details to the main idea.

1. The room was a disaster.
2. The tall grass bent under the weight of a huge insect.
3. My birthday present was an exciting surprise.
4. I opened the door and there stood _____.
5. My super special dinner was just about ready.
6. The city sky was beautiful that night.
7. The five cousins had decorated the holiday table.
8. Fred was the strangest looking animal I'd ever seen.
9. The ornate mask had been worn by a great hunter.
10. The final burst of fireworks was breathtaking.

Part 2   Developing a Paragraph by Using an Example

Another way to develop a paragraph is by using an example. In this kind of paragraph, the topic sentence states the main idea. The rest of the sentences give an example. The example explains the main idea.

Let's say you start with a topic sentence like this one:

Some animals aren't as fierce as people think they are.

You might then tell about an animal that is supposed to be fierce but is really not. You would be developing the paragraph by giving an example.

the paragraph. Point out that the sample paragraph about dolphins describes an incident, or something that happened. This is the most common approach to development by example.

3. Assign the Exercise on page 96. Before the students begin to write, check to be sure that they understand the meaning of example, as it applies to paragraph development. Do this by asking each student to describe briefly the intended content of his or her paragraph. The paragraphs developed from topic sentences 5, 6, 8, and 9 will probably not present incidents, but rather explanations and descriptions of the example.

4. Use Exercise C on page 97 for additional practice.

Optional Practice

Work in a group with those students who had difficulty writing a paragraph. Guide them through the following steps:

1. Write the name of a person that you know.
2. Begin a sentence: *(name of person)* is _____.
3. Complete the sentence with a word or phrase. (Suggest *smart, kind, a good friend, a great baseball player.*)
4. Think of something that happened that illustrates this quality.
5. Write a paragraph using the sentence you wrote for Step 3 as a topic sentence and the incident from Step 4 as the example treated in the rest of the paragraph.

Studying a Paragraph with an Example

The following paragraph is developed by using an example.

Dolphins can solve simple problems. At Marineland of Florida, gates separate the dolphins' small pools from the big show pool. One night, some dolphins must have wanted to play in the big pool. They figured out how to use their snouts to open the gates. —*National Geographic World*

The topic sentence states that dolphins can solve simple problems. The rest of the paragraph tells how the dolphins at Marineland of Florida solved a problem. This is an example of the main idea.

Exercise **Developing a Paragraph by Using an Example**

Here are ten topic sentences. Choose one and write a paragraph using an example. You can write about something that actually happened to you, or you can make something up. Be sure that your example illustrates the main idea in the topic sentence.

1. Sometimes dreams can be frightening.
2. Sometimes your best friend can hurt your feelings.
3. You can learn a lot from a book.
4. Good things always seem to happen on Saturdays.
5. Recycling makes a lot of sense.
6. Our town has interesting places to visit.
7. I made some important discoveries last summer.
8. My brother has a favorite hiding place.
9. Many different combinations of things can be added to a hamburger.
10. Vacations aren't always fun.

Additional Exercises

Ways of Developing Paragraphs

A. Working with Details (Use after page 92.)

Below is a list of words that could apply to any person. Choose a specific kind of person. Add details that describe that person. Answers will vary.

1. hair   3. nose   5. hands   7. clothes
2. eyes   4. teeth   6. skin   8. shoes

B. Developing a Paragraph by Using Details (Use after page 95.)

Make a list of details in this paragraph.

    We pushed open the creaky iron gate and there was Blake House. It was built of gray stones that looked pale in the moonlight. Dead vines clung to the walls. The long front porch was covered with wild thorn bushes. The wind sighed in the bare tree branches. A loose shutter banged. The only sign of life was a jack-o'-lantern glowing in a downstairs window.

C. Developing a Paragraph by Using an Example
(Use after page 96.)

Below is a topic sentence. Develop a paragraph using an example from your own experience. Answers will vary.

Many interesting people live in my neighborhood. One of the most interesting is . . .

Additional Exercises

If these Exercises were not used with each lesson, they may now be assigned for chapter review.

Chapter 8

Kinds of Paragraphs

Some paragraphs tell what happened. These are called **narrative paragraphs.** Others paint pictures in your mind. These are **descriptive paragraphs.** Some explain how to do something. These are **explanatory paragraphs.** In this lesson you will study the three main types of paragraphs:

1. Narrative
2. Descriptive
3. Explanatory

Chapter Objectives

1. To understand the term *narrative paragraph*
2. To recognize and use time sequence in the organization of narrative paragraphs
3. To understand the term *descriptive paragraph*
4. To recognize and use natural order in the organization of descriptive paragraphs
5. To understand one type of explanatory paragraph: the "how" paragraph
6. To recognize and use time sequence in the organization of "how" paragraphs

Preparing the Students

Ask the students to recall the subjects of some of the paragraphs they wrote for Chapters 6 and 7. Write the subjects on the chalkboard. Using this list, suggest that different subjects require different kinds of paragraphs.

Read the chapter introduction on page 99.

Additional Resources

Mastery Test—pages 452 and 453 in this T.E. Recommended for use after teaching the chapter.

Additional Mastery Test—Recommended for use after any necessary reteaching. (In separate booklet, *Mastery Tests, Silver Level*, pages 15 and 16.)

Skills Practice Book—pages 35–41

Duplicating Masters—pages 35–41

Part 1

Objectives

1. To understand the term *narrative paragraph*
2. To recognize and use time sequence in the organization of narrative paragraphs

Presenting the Lesson

1. Read and discuss the introduction to Part 1 on page 100. Review the twofold function of a topic sentence: to state the main idea of the paragraph and to catch the reader's attention.
2. Read Paragraphs About Yourself on pages 100 and 101. Ask volunteers to read the sentences in the sample paragraph in which the pronoun *I* appears. Ask the students to explain in their own words the main events described in the paragraph. Write the events on the chalkboard in chronological order.
3. Read Order in a Narrative Paragraph on page 101. Direct the class to check their list on the blackboard against the list of events on page 101.
4. Read Paragraphs About Other People on page 102. After reading each sample paragraph, ask the students to identify the topic sentence and to describe the five or six main events. Make sure the students are aware of the time sequence in which the events are presented.
5. Point out that narrative paragraphs, such as the second example on page 102, contain many details. Review the ways to add details to nouns (adding words and phrases that tell what kind or how

Part 1 The Narrative Paragraph

A narrative paragraph tells about something that happened. Its topic sentence presents the main idea. Here's an example of a topic sentence that begins a narrative paragraph.

> One day we were all sitting on the stoop and along came Robin and two other boys from 118th Street.

After reading the sentence, you expect the paragraph to tell you what is going to happen. The sentence has probably made you curious, too. It has made you want to read the rest of the paragraph.

The next three topic sentences do the same thing. They let you know that the paragraphs are about things that happened. They also make you want to read further.

1. I glanced nervously over my shoulder and saw a shadow back into the bushes.
2. There once lived an old landlord in a small village in Japan.
3. Long ago the Lord of the Sun sent the spark of life to earth.

Paragraphs About Yourself

The following paragraph was written by Joy Adamson. It describes an experience with Elsa, a lion she raised. The topic sentence lets you know what the paragraph is about. It describes what happened when the writer sat down to read some letters. The word *I* lets you know that the paragraph is about something that happened to her personally.

> Whenever I sat down, Elsa wanted to play. One day I sat with my back against a tree and started reading a huge bundle of letters. Suddenly I was squashed by Elsa. As I tried to free myself from her three hundred pounds, the letters were scattered all over. I finally got to my feet and

began to collect them. Elsa bounced onto me every time I bent down to pick one up, and we rolled together on the ground. Elsa's cubs thought this was great fun. They dashed around after the fluttering paper. I thought that the writers would have enjoyed seeing how much their letters were appreciated.

Order in a Narrative Paragraph

You can list the things that happen in a narrative paragraph. Your list would include the following for the paragraph about Elsa:

1. The writer sat down and started reading letters.
2. Elsa jumped on the writer.
3. The writer struggled and the letters were scattered.
4. The writer tried to collect the letters, but Elsa kept jumping on her.
5. Elsa's cubs chased the letters.

These events are described in the order that they happened. This is the way most narrative paragraphs are arranged. The writers tell what happened first, what happened next, and so on.

Paragraphs About Other People

The writer of this next paragraph also tells events in the order that they happened. However, he has not described something that happened to him. He has described something that happened to a boy named Davie.

> Davie picked up a sack of clover. As he lugged it to the rabbit hutch it seemed to feel warm and damp in his hands. There was a queer, sweet, hot smell that seemed to come from the sack. He untied the knot and poked his hand inside. The clover was hot inside the sack. His hand came out sticky–smelly hot. He hurried to the other sacks and ripped them open. His brother had said the clover would be one rotten mess. It was! All the clover had spoiled. All three bags! —MEINDERT DEJONG

In the following paragraph, too, the writer tells about something that happened to someone else. As you read the paragraph, notice the way she makes the scene real for the reader.

> The wolf glanced at his paw and slowly turned his head Julie's way without lifting his eyes. He licked his shoulder. A few matted hairs sprang apart and twinkled individually. Then his eyes sped to each of the three adult wolves that made up his pack. Finally he looked at the five pups who were sleeping in a fuzzy mass near the den entrance. The great wolf's eyes softened at the sight of the little wolves. Then they quickly hardened into brittle yellow jewels as he looked out at the frozen land. —JEAN CRAIGHEAD GEORGE

The writer has used words in interesting ways. You can almost see the wolf's "matted hairs," the "fuzzy mass" of pups, the wolf's eyes harden into "brittle yellow jewels," and the "frozen land." These words help you to picture the scene in your mind. In the next lesson you are going to learn more about how writers paint vivid pictures with words.

Things To Remember About Narrative Paragraphs

1. They are paragraphs that tell what happened.

2. They tell what happened either to the writer or to someone else.

3. They describe events in the order that they happened.

4. They make experiences real for readers.

Exercises Writing Narrative Paragraphs

A. Following are five topic sentences. Choose one, or make up a topic sentence of your own. Then write a narrative paragraph. It should be about something that happened to you.

1. I never knew I was afraid of heights until _____.
2. When I was _____ years old, I decided to run away from home.
3. I once tried to wash my favorite _____.
4. Our class assignment was to _____.
5. One birthday I got the present of my dreams.

B. Here are five more topic sentences. Each could be developed into a paragraph about something that happened to someone else. Choose a sentence, or make up a topic sentence of your own. Use your imagination to write a paragraph.

1. Virginia decided to write a letter.
2. Kit stopped her frantic barking and stood absolutely still.
3. The dripping faucet was driving Elmer crazy.
4. Bugs and Sam were on the porch playing checkers when a big, shiny car pulled up.
5. One day Joshua announced that he had given up eating.

Part 2

Objectives

1. To understand the term *descriptive paragraph*
2. To recognize and use natural order in the organization of descriptive paragraphs

Presenting the Lesson

1. Read the introduction to Part 2 and Using Details on page 104. As you read the sample paragraph, tell the students to close their eyes and to try to picture the scene in their minds.
2. Read and discuss Arranging Details and Natural Order on pages 105 and 106. After reading the sample paragraph on page 105, ask the students to identify the topic sentence and several of the many details included by the writer. Emphasize that natural order is the order in which a person would describe something without consciously thinking about arranging details.
3. If students have difficulty with the concept of natural order, refer them to Exercise B on page 111, and do the Exercise as a class or group activity.
4. Assign the Exercise on page 107. After the students have completed their paragraphs, discuss the use of details, using several of their paragraphs as examples. Then have the students revise their paragraphs, adding details wherever possible.
5. If Exercise B on page 111 was not used as a group activity, it may be assigned now for individual practice.

Part 2   The Descriptive Paragraph

Descriptive paragraphs are like narrative paragraphs in many ways. They are different, though, in one important way. Narrative paragraphs tell what happened. Descriptive paragraphs have very little happening in them. That's because the purpose of a descriptive paragraph is to paint a picture with words.

The picture that is painted often appeals to one or more of the senses. This lesson has examples that appeal to the sense of sight. The writers use words to help you "see" in your mind what they see in theirs.

Using Details

The most important way that writers create word pictures is by using details. You have learned that details are the words and phrases that help the reader get a clear picture.

Here is a paragraph that describes a hot day in the country. The writer has used many details that appeal to the sense of sight. As you read the paragraph, make a list of the words and phrases that help you form a vivid mental picture of the scene.

> It is a day in the country, and everything is hot. The grass looks dry and parched. The buttercups are sticky with dust. The daisies' white petals look gray. All the flowers, the rambler roses climbing up the gate, the hollyhocks leaning against the house, hang limply on their stems.
> —CHARLOTTE ZOLOTOW

You can see from your list how well the writer has used words. She has used descriptive words such as "hot," "dry," and "parched." She has used specific words like "buttercups" and "hollyhocks." She has used phrases like "sticky with dust" and "hang limply." Together, these words help you to see in your mind what the writer saw in hers.

Arranging Details

This next paragraph is also filled with details. They appeal to your sense of sight. They help you to see the room in your mind.

> It was a warm, comfortable room of doors and wood and pictures. From it a person could reach the front or the side porch, the kitchen, and the two other bedrooms. Its walls were made of smooth oak. On them hung gigantic photographs of Grandpa and Big Ma, Papa and Uncle Hammer when they were boys, Papa's two eldest brothers, and pictures of Mama's family. The furniture was a mixture of walnut and oak. It included a walnut bed whose fancy headboard rose halfway up the wall toward the high ceiling and a cabinet with a floor-length mirror. It also included a large rolltop desk and four oak chairs. Two of them were rockers, which Grandpa had made for Big Ma as a wedding present. —MILDRED D. TAYLOR

An interesting thing about this paragraph is the way the writer has arranged the details. She first gives an overall idea of the room. She describes it as warm and comfortable. She next describes the location of the room. She then tells about the walls of the room. Finally she gives details about the main pieces of furniture. She has arranged the details in the order you'd probably notice things. This is called **natural order.**

Optional Practice

Direct each student to choose one piece of playground or athletic equipment and to write a paragraph describing its physical characteristics. Ask volunteers to read their paragraphs aloud. Have the rest of the class try to name the equipment being described.

Natural Order

The writer of this next paragraph also begins with an overall impression. He then gives details about the lumberjack. He begins from the top of the man's head and moves down. The details are also arranged in the order you'd probably notice them.

> The lumberjack stood six feet, six inches in his stockinged feet. Everything about him, from the top of his head to the tips of his toes, was big. His flowing hair and beard were flaming red. Even his skin was a reddish color. His bright blue eyes twinkled beneath bushy brows. His eyes could easily have been those of a carefree wanderer. His hands, though, marked him as a working man. They were hard and blunt-fingered and strong.

There are many different ways to arrange details. It depends on what you are describing. For example, you would most likely describe a tall tree from bottom to top. You would probably describe a wall of pictures from left to right. These are natural orders. They follow the way you would ordinarily look at something.

Things To Remember About Descriptive Paragraphs

1. Have a clear picture in your mind of what you want to describe.

2. Examine your mental picture.
   Decide in what order you will describe things.
   Try to find the most natural order.

3. As you examine your mental picture, make a list of details.

4. Write the paragraph, using as many of the details as you can.

Exercise   Writing Descriptive Paragraphs

Here are ten topic sentences. Choose one and write a descriptive paragraph. Follow the four steps given in this lesson. Be sure that all of your sentences work together to explain the main idea.

1. The sand sculpture was carefully done.
2. The tree house rested on the lower branches of a huge oak tree.
3. The totem pole traced the history of the family.
4. The view from the tower was breathtaking.
5. The first float in the parade came into view.
6. _____ sits next to me in _____ class.
7. The street in front of our house was ready for the block party.
8. _____ is an outstanding breed of dog.
9. The Nutty Crunch is a special snack bar.
10. The morning sun sparkled on ten inches of new snow.

Part 3

Objectives

1. To understand one type of explanatory paragraph: the "how" paragraph
2. To recognize and use time sequence in the organization of "how" paragraphs

Presenting the Lesson

1. Read and discuss page 108. Remind the class that narrative paragraphs are also arranged in time sequence.
2. Read Being Specific on page 109. To clarify the concept, give the class the following general directions and ask the students to make directions that are more specific.
    1. Move your hand.
    2. Mix the paints together.
    3. Turn one knob, then turn the other one.
    4. Clean your shoes, then shine them.
3. Read Giving Specific Directions on pages 109 and 110. Have each student try out the directions given in the sample paragraph. Stress the reminders listed in the box on page 110.
4. Assign and discuss the Exercise on page 110.
5. Use Exercise C on page 111 for additional practice.

Extending the Lesson

Create a bulletin board on which are displayed examples of the three kinds of paragraphs studied in Chapter 8. Include the definition of each kind of paragraph. Students may also wish to illustrate these paragraphs.

Part 3 The Explanatory Paragraph

The explanatory paragraph explains something. The type of explanatory paragraph you will meet most often is one that gives directions. Many times this is called a "how to" paragraph. It explains how to do something.

Arranging Ideas

Think of all the times you have read directions. You have read them on tests and on worksheets. You have read them on game boxes and in recipes. These directions have something very important in common. They explain what to do in the order that it should be done. They tell what to do first, what to do next, and so on. They are arranged in **time sequence.**

Here is a paragraph that explains how to steam a hot dog. The directions are easy to follow because they are in time sequence. A person reading them knows exactly what to do first, what to do next, and so on.

> Steaming a hot dog is a simple way to cook one. First, fill a pan with about two inches of water. Be sure the pan is a little wider than the length of the hot dog. Next, boil the water. Then put the hot dog into the water. Finally, turn off the heat and cover the pan. After seven minutes remove the cooked hot dog from the water.

Notice that the writer has used words like "first," "next," "then," and "finally." These words help a person follow the directions in the right order.

Words That Help the Reader Follow Directions				
First	Next	Before	When	Then
Second	Now	While	After	Finally

Being Specific

Directions must be in the right order. They must also be specific. For example, one person giving directions might say, "Go a few blocks. Then turn right." Another person might say, "Go three blocks. Then make a right turn at 12th Street. That's the corner with two gas stations, a drug store, and a laundry." You would have a much easier time following the second person's directions. That's because they're more specific.

It is often hard to write specific directions. This is especially true when you are explaining something you yourself know how to do well. When you are giving directions, put yourself in your reader's place. Think of exactly what you would need to know. Put your directions into the right order.

Giving Specific Directions

The writer of this next paragraph has been very specific.

> You can learn to undo a knotted hair. First, pluck a hair out of your head. Tie it in a simple knot. Draw the knot as tight as possible without breaking the hair. It should be impossible to untie with the fingers. Next, place the hair in the top crease of your right palm. The knot should be near the left edge of the palm. The tail of the knot should hang over the edge. Wet the knot with saliva. Then close your fist over the knot. Finally, pound the tail of the knot against the palm of your left hand. Keep pounding. In a few minutes the knot will be open enough to untie with your fingers.

These directions are specific. They tell you exactly what to do:

Where to get the hair
How to tie it

How tight to tie it
Where to place it on your hand
What to wet it with
Where to pound your hands together
How long to pound
What happens to the knot when you pound

Things To Remember About Explanatory Paragraphs

1. Be specific. Tell exactly what should be done.
2. Arrange the steps in time sequence.
3. Use words like *first*, *next*, *then*, and *finally*.

Exercise   Writing an Explanatory Paragraph

Here are some ideas for explanatory paragraphs. Choose one or use an idea of your own. Then write a "how to" paragraph. Remember to be clear and specific.

How to:
- wash a dog
- name a baby
- carve a pumpkin
- make paste
- blow up a balloon
- wrap a present
- make popcorn
- fix a sandwich
- hang a poster
- brush your teeth
- pack a suitcase
- kick a football
- clean your room
- build a fire
- make magic freckle juice
- clean a fish bowl
- cover a book
- wash a car

Additional Exercises

Kinds of Paragraphs

A. Writing Narrative Paragraphs (Use after page 103.)

Tell whether or not the following paragraph is about something that happened to the writer. Then list what happened. *It is about something that happened to the writer. Events are numbered.*

^{1}We followed the stranger deeper and deeper into the woods. ^{2}We were doing well until I stepped on a dry twig. ^{3}It snapped. ^{4}We froze. ^{5}The stranger stopped. ^{6}He turned and searched the darkening woods. ^{7}He took a step toward us. ^{8}Our hearts were pounding. ^{9}We scarcely dared to breathe.

B. Writing Descriptive Paragraphs (Use after page 107.)

Explain how you would arrange the details in each paragraph. *Answers will vary.*

1. My New Bicycle
2. My Closet
3. My Best Outfit
4. Count Dracula
5. My Garden
6. Bald Mountain
7. The School Band
8. A Perfect Pizza

C. Writing an Explanatory Paragraph (Use after page 110.)

Here are the directions for making a bird feeder from a milk carton. First arrange the directions in the right order. Then write the paragraph.

- 1   1. Rinse the milk carton with water.
- 5   2. Fill the bird feeder with seed.
- 4 or 3   3. Run yarn or string through the holes in the top.
- 2 or 4   4. Cut a feeding window on one side near the bottom.
- 6   5. Hang the feeder from a tree branch in a sheltered place.
- 3 or 2   6. Punch two holes in the top.

Additional Exercises

If these Exercises were not used with each lesson, they may now be assigned for chapter review.

Chapter 9

Using Nouns

Part 1 What Are Nouns?

Look at the photograph. It shows an Indian boy holding a lamb. How many things in the picture can you name? The words you use to name these things are called **nouns.**

Look around you. Think of things you use every day. The words you use to name all of these things are called nouns. The words that name people and places are nouns.

>Who sits in front of you or behind you?
>
>What is the name of your school?
>
>What street or road is it on?
>
>What city or town do you live in?

Chapter Objectives

1. To understand the concept of a noun and to identify nouns in sentences

2. To differentiate between common nouns and proper nouns

3. To differentiate between singular and plural nouns, and to form plurals correctly

4. To form and use possessive nouns correctly

5. To recognize the basic word order in the N V sentence pattern

Preparing the Students

Review the term *verb*. Remind students that verbs may tell action or they may say that something is. However, verbs do not not name the person or thing that does the action or that is being talked about. Students will now learn about another group of words. These words name *who* or *what*.

Additional Resources

Diagnostic Test—page 430 in this T.E. Recommended for use before teaching the chapter.

Mastery Test—pages 454 and 455 in this T.E. Recommended for use after teaching the chapter.

Additional Mastery Test—Recommended for use after any necessary reteaching. (In separate booklet, *Mastery Tests, Silver Level*, pages 17 and 18.)

Skills Practice Book—pages 42–46

Duplicating Masters—pages 42–46

Part 1

Objective

To understand the concept of a noun and to identify nouns in sentences

Presenting the Lesson

1. Read and discuss pages 113 and 114. Point out that sometimes one noun can fit into two classes. For example, *ranch* is listed as a place; it could also be considered a thing.

2. In addition to the definition of a noun given in this Chapter, there are other ways to identify a noun. The following chart, Ways To Identify Nouns, is based on what linguists have discovered about the structure of a word and the order of words in a sentence. It is suggested that the information in the chart be used to point out additional ways in which nouns function.

Ways To Identify Nouns

1. Look for words that have a singular, plural, or possessive form.

Singular	Plural	Possessive
clown	clowns	clown's

2. Look for words that follow *a, an,* or *the*.

3. Look for words that fit the blanks in one of these test sentences:

I am talking about _____.
_____ are important.
See the _____.
That is a _____.

3. Assign and discuss the Exercise on page 114. Suggest that students use one of the test sentences when they are unsure of whether or not a word is a noun.

4. Use Exercise A on page 124 for additional practice or review.

Optional Practice

Have students divide a piece of paper into two columns headed *persons* and *things*. Have them list at least ten things in each column.

Nouns are words that name persons, places, or things.

Persons	Places	Things
Luke Skywalker	frontier	tree
firefighter	Milwaukee	robot
pilot	ranch	food
Diana Ross	playground	Frisbee

Some nouns, like all those listed above, are names of things you can see. Other nouns are names of things you cannot see. Here are some examples of things you cannot see:

| idea | courage | loneliness | peace |
| hope | friendship | hunger | interest |

Exercise   Finding Nouns

Number your paper from 1 to 10. Find the nouns in each sentence below. Write them down.

1. Stacy saw the fireworks last July.
2. A surfer rode a huge wave.
3. Clowns and puppets performed at the fair.
4. My brother has excellent eyesight.
5. My cousin lives on a farm in Iowa.
6. Jason plays the piano and the trombone.
7. The Dodgers will play in the World Series.
8. Keith has a picture of the Incredible Hulk on his notebook.
9. Ms. Mason told the story behind Thanksgiving.
10. Many students do chores and earn an allowance.

Part 2 Common Nouns and Proper Nouns

The word *child* is the name for a whole group of persons. Your own name stands for one particular person.

The word *city* is the name for a whole group of places. The name *San Francisco* stands for one particular city.

The word *candy* is the name for a whole group of things. The name *Baby Ruth* names one particular candy.

> A **common noun** names a whole group of persons, places, or things.
>
> Examples are *child, city,* and *candy.*
>
> A common noun begins with a small letter.
>
> A **proper noun** names a particular person, place, or thing.
>
> Examples are your own name, *San Francisco,* or *Baby Ruth.*
>
> A proper noun always begins with a capital letter.

Many proper nouns are made up of two or more words. Your own name is made up of two or more words. So are *Atlantic Ocean* and *Grand Canyon National Park.* When the proper noun has several words, capitalize all the important words. You do not have to capitalize *of, on,* or *the.*

Look at the map on page 116 to find other proper nouns.

Part 2

Objective

To differentiate between common nouns and proper nouns

Presenting the Lesson

1. Read and discuss page 115. Ask students for further examples of common and proper nouns, including some with more than one word. Ask them whether the noun *map* is common or proper, and the reason for their decision.
2. Do Exercise A on page 116 together. You may wish to discuss why proper nouns need to be capitalized and common nouns do not. Assign and discuss Exercise B on page 116.
3. Use Exercise B on pages 124 and 125 for additional practice or review.

Optional Practice

1. Have students list five examples each of common and proper nouns. They are to challenge the rest of the class with their lists. Each student gets a turn to read his items and have the rest of the class tell whether each is common or proper.
2. On the board, list several common nouns, such as *city, student, explorer,* and *planet.* On separate slips of paper, write matching proper nouns, such as *Omaha,* a student's name, *Christopher Columbus,* and *Mars.* Put the slips in a container. Each student gets a turn to draw a slip and match the proper noun with the appropriate common noun. You might want to use some proper nouns from their other studies.

Exercises Finding Common Nouns and Proper Nouns

A. On your paper, label two columns *Common Nouns* and *Proper Nouns*. Number from 1 to 12 down the left-hand margin. After each number, write the noun on the list below in the proper column. Begin every proper noun with a capital letter.

CN = Common Noun
PN = Proper Noun

1. person CN
2. city CN
3. washington PN (W)
4. ms. steele PN (M, S)
5. paper CN
6. albert PN (A)
7. maria PN (M)
8. post office CN
9. england PN (E)
10. building CN
11. mr. ruiz PN (M, R)
12. elm street PN (E, S)

B. Copy the following common nouns in a list. After each one, write the name of a particular person, place, or thing that the noun makes you think of. *Answers will vary.*

1. girl
2. boy
3. planet
4. restaurant
5. company
6. store
7. automobile
8. street
9. soap
10. building
11. singer
12. actress

Part 3 Singular and Plural Nouns

What is the difference between these columns of words?

cake   cakes
person   persons
thought   thoughts
planet   planets

You probably noticed immediately that the words are almost the same. However, they have different endings. Each word in the second column has an *s* added.

What difference does that *s* make in the meaning of the words?

Did you say that the *s* changes the number of things? *Cake* refers to one thing but *cakes* refers to more than one thing. *Person* refers to one person, but *persons* refers to more than one. Does *thoughts* refer to one, or more than one? Does *streets* refer to one, or more than one? Adding *s* to the nouns *thought* and *street* made them refer to more than one.

A noun that names one person, place, or thing is called a **singular noun.** A noun that names more than one person, place, or thing is called a **plural noun.** All the nouns in the first column above are *singular*. All nouns in the second column are *plural*. Changing a word from singular to plural is called forming the plural of the noun.

Here are seven rules for forming the plurals of nouns:

1. To form the plural of most nouns, just add an *s*.

sticks   cows   bikes   drinks
stones   dogs   skates   snacks

2. When the singular ends in *s*, *sh*, *ch*, *x*, or *z*, add *es*.

buses   ashes   foxes
classes   lunches buzzes

Optional Practice

1. After students have studied all the rules on pages 117 and 118, have a spelling bee using only plural nouns. Divide the class into teams, and have each team stand in a line. Dictate words from the text, or the word list below, or the students' other work. If a student misspells a word, that student must sit down. Alternate teams. The winning team will be the one with the most students standing at the end.

If you wish to make the game more difficult, use singular nouns and have the students say the plural form and spell it.

Rule 2—crosses, boxes, churches, catches, benches, crashes, wishes, dishes, splashes, dresses, patches, glasses, guesses, mixes, passes, circuses, bunches, porches, watches, inches, peaches, scratches, sandwiches, expresses, kisses, riches.
Rule 3—zoos, buffalos/buffaloes/buffalo (All three are acceptable).
Rule 4—armies, countries, cries, families, histories, parties, stories, babies, industries, puppies, cookies, bakeries, daddies, enemies, replies.
Rule 5—hoofs, scarfs/scarves.

2. You may wish to put the paragraph below on a worksheet. Have students fill in each blank with the correct plural form of the noun underneath. Tell them to check the rules on page 117 and 118 if they are unsure of the correct spelling.

When our class visited the zoo, we saw many different _____.
                                            animal
We went to the farm section first. In one of the _____ we saw _____.
                  pen   sheep
There were six _____ in another.
               goose
We saw some _____ too. In one
             mouse
pen there two mother _____ and
                         cow
three _____. We could even pet
       calf

3. When the singular ends in *o*, add *s*.

    studios   radios   stereos   banjos

Exceptions: For the following nouns ending in *o*, add *es*:

    echoes   heroes   tomatoes   potatoes

4. When the singular noun ends in *y* with a consonant before it, change the *y* to *i*, and add *es*.

    fly—flies   penny—pennies
    pony—ponies   candy—candies

5. For most nouns ending in *f* or *fe*, add *s*. For some nouns ending in *f* or *fe*, however, change the *f* to *v* and add *es* or *s*.

    belief—beliefs   elf—elves   loaf—loaves
    chief—chiefs   self—selves   calf—calves
    roof—roofs   wife—wives   knife—knives
    dwarf—dwarfs   life—lives   wolf—wolves
    cuff—cuffs   leaf—leaves   shelf—shelves
    hoof—hoofs   half—halves   thief—thieves

6. Some nouns are the same for both singular and plural.

    deer   trout   sheep   moose   salmon

7. Some nouns form their plurals in special ways.

    mouse—mice   man—men   tooth—teeth
    goose—geese   woman—women   foot—feet
                          child—children

A **singular noun** names one person, place, or thing.

A **plural noun** names more than one person, place, or thing.

Exercises **Forming Plurals**

A. Number your paper from 1 to 16. Copy each pair of nouns below. Then write the number of the rule that tells how the plural was formed. *denotes exception to rule

Example: brush—brushes 2

1. bench—benches ₂
2. party—parties ₄
3. tax—taxes ₂
4. pencil—pencils ₁
5. lady—ladies ₄
6. tomato—tomatoes ₃*
7. man—men ₇
8. thief—thieves ₅
9. turkey—turkeys ₁
10. tooth—teeth ₇
11. shelf—shelves ₅
12. cat—cats ₁
13. box—boxes ₂
14. cameo—cameos ₃
15. baby—babies ₄
16. roof—roofs ₅

B. Write the plural form of each of these nouns.

1. woman — women
2. knife — knives
3. sheep — sheep
4. girl — girls
5. candy — candies
6. dwarf — dwarfs
7. radio — radios
8. watch — watches
9. child — children
10. boy — boys
11. trout — trout
12. noise — noises
13. half — halves
14. potato — potatoes
15. gas — gases
16. copy — copies
17. mouse — mice
18. team — teams
19. sandwich — sandwiches
20. leaf — leaves

C. Study this picture. List as many nouns as you see pictured. Then write the plural for each noun you have written.
Some possible answers are at right.

some of the animal _____ baby. There were _____ bunny, _____ deer, and _____ lamb. One of the _____ goat tried to eat my _____ shoelace. When some _____ man fed the _____ pig, we heard a lot of _____ squeal. We ate our _____ lunch at picnic _____ table under _____ tree. Everyone brought peanut butter _____ sandwich. All the _____ child enjoyed the zoo.

fishing pole—fishing poles
ax—axes
hoe—hoes
rake—rakes
shovel—shovels
hammer—hammers
pliers—pliers
screwdriver—screwdrivers
scissors—scissors
clamp—clamps
shelf—shelves
tire—tires
saw—saws
toolbox—toolboxes
trunk—trunks
ladder—ladders
window—windows
sprayer—sprayers
hose—hoses
*shears—shears
trash can—trash cans
watering can—watering cans
wheelbarrow—wheelbarrows
ball—balls
bottle—bottles
skateboard—skateboards
bicycle—bicycles
air pump—air pumps

Part 4

Objective

To form and use possessive nouns correctly

Presenting the Lesson

1. Discuss the meaning of the word *possess*. Show that besides indicating ownership (the car of my brother), it can also refer to a relationship (the sister of Bob) or other connection (the friend of my uncle). *Possess* could also mean "to use" (the crib of the baby), or simply "to have" (the collar of the dog). Ask students for the shorter way of saying each phrase in parentheses, and discuss the idea of possession in each.
2. Read and discuss page 120. Ask students to write on the board the possessive forms they gave for the five phrases in step 1.
3. Read and discuss pages 121 and 122. Stress that a possessive form is made by adding to a noun which is *already* singular or plural. An apostrophe is added at the end of the original word; the word is not changed for the apostrophe.
4. You may want to do Exercise A on page 122 with the students. Have them read each sentence aloud with the possessive form, then spell that form correctly. Assign and discuss Exercise B.
5. Use Exercise D on page 125 for additional practice or review.

Part 4 Making Nouns Show Possession

Study these examples.

1. These are my sister's skates.
   Who owns the skates? my *sister*

2. Sally's mother called.
   Whose mother called? the mother of *Sally*

3. This is the boy's cap.
   Who owns the cap? The *boy*

What has been added to the nouns *sister*, *Sally*, and *boy*? Adding 's makes the nouns show ownership, or possession. We call *sister's*, *Sally's*, and *boy's* **possessive nouns**.

> A **possessive noun** shows possession of the noun that follows.

Making Singular Nouns Show Possession

To make a singular noun show possession, add an apostrophe and *s*.

Singular Noun	Possessive Noun
mechanic	mechanic's
James	James's
Ms. Roberts	Ms. Roberts's

Making Plural Nouns Show Possession

There are two rules to remember for making a plural noun show possession.

1. If the plural noun ends in *s*, simply add an apostrophe after the *s*.

Plural Noun	Possessive Noun
workers	workers'
nurses	nurses'
dentists	dentists'

2. If the plural noun does not end in *s*, add an apostrophe and an *s* after the apostrophe.

Plural Noun	Possessive Form
men	men's
women	women's
children	children's

Adding the Apostrophe

Look carefully at these words. See where the apostrophe is added.

the athlete's shoes	This means shoes belonging to one athlete.
the athletes' shoes	This means shoes belong to more than one athlete.

If you are not sure where to add the apostrophe, write the word by itself first. Then follow the rules.

When writing 's in cursive handwriting, you should not connect the *s* following the apostrophe to the last letter before

Optional Practice

1. Have students rewrite each of the following phrases, using the possessive form.

Example: the growl of the bear
 the bear's growl

1. the daughter of the woman
2. the chattering of the birds
3. the coat of the person
4. the stunts of the acrobats
5. the wild pitch of the pitcher

2. Put the phrases below on the board or on a worksheet. Have students identify the noun in possessive form, and its base noun. Then have them divide a paper into two columns, headed *singular* and *plural*. Ask them to write the base noun of the phrase in the correct column. You may also want to review the rules for forming plural nouns (pages 117 and 118).

Examples: a. my grandmother's hat
 b. the horses' hoofs

	Singular	Plural
a.	grandmother	
b.		horses

1. the thieves' getaway car
2. the chiefs' fire helmets
3. the fox's footprints
4. the class's play
5. the women's coats

the apostrophe. The apostrophe should separate the two letters.

the cook's recipe

Charles's skateboard

Exercises Making Nouns Show Possession

A. In each sentence one word is underlined. Write this word so that it shows possession. Write the word first. Then add the apostrophe or apostrophe and *s*.

1. We found Ramon bike in the basement. Ramon's
2. There are two girls coats in the closet. girls'
3. One man hat blew into the street. man's
4. It was "Ladies Day" at Yankee Stadium. Ladies'
5. The children library closes at five o'clock. children's
6. We found George mittens. George's
7. Which department sells babies cribs? babies'
8. Where are the women tickets? women's
9. I lost my father knife. father's
10. The girls were wearing their mothers dresses. mothers'

B. Copy the following sentences. Make the underlined words show possession.

1. Rosa team beat Dwayne team yesterday. Rosa's Dwayne's
2. In my uncle shop they sell men and ladies clothes. uncle's men's ladies'
3. The boys team won the spelling match. boys'
4. Tammy little sister got lost in the store. Tammy's
5. Where are the children toys? children's
6. My two brothers clothes were all over the floor. brothers'
7. The girl book fell out of the car. girl's
8. The doctor felt the dog paw gently. dog's
9. I left my sweater at the dentist office. dentist's
10. Richard hobby is collecting ballplayers autographs. Richard's ballplayers'

Sentence Patterns — The N V Pattern

Every sentence has a subject and a verb. The subject is usually a noun. In this chart, N stands for the noun in the complete subject. V stands for the verb in the complete predicate.

N	V
Diana	stumbled.
My brother	waited.
This camera	works easily.
The gray cat	purred softly.

The word order in these sentences follows a pattern. That pattern is noun-verb, or N V. It is called the **N V pattern.**

Exercises — The N V Pattern

A. Make a chart like the one above. Label one column *N.* Label the other *V.* Write these sentences on the chart.

1. Rain fell.
2. Birds fly.
3. Katy bats next.
4. Scott laughed.
5. The bus stopped.
6. Red ink spilled.

(Each sentence labeled N V)

B. Copy this chart. Complete each sentence in the N V pattern.

Answers will vary.

N	V
1. _____	listened.
2. _____	worked carefully.
3. The sun	_____.
4. _____	turned around.
5. Harry	_____.

C. Make a chart of your own for the N V pattern. Write five sentences in the N V pattern. Answers will vary.

Sentence Patterns

Objective

To recognize the basic word order in the N V sentence pattern

Presenting the Lesson

1. Read and discuss page 123. As the chart indicates, the noun-part of each sentence includes not only the noun identified as the subject, but also all the modifiers of that noun (as in *The gray cat*). The verb-part includes the verb and its modifiers, if any (as in *purred softly*). The students should be able to identify the point at which a sentence can be divided into these two parts.

2. Assign and discuss Exercise A. It is suggested that the class do Exercises B and C together.

Extending the Lesson

The following lengthy sentences are basic N V pattern sentences. Ask students to identify the break between the noun-part and the verb-part.

1. That old rusty car in the junk yard can still run.
2. The creamy frosting on the cake oozed down the sides and onto the plate.
3. All the fire engines rushed quickly to the scene of the explosion.

Additional Exercises

If these Exercises were not used with each lesson, they may now be assigned for chapter review.

Additional Exercises

Using Nouns

A. Finding Nouns (Use after page 114.)

Number your paper from 1 to 10. Find the nouns in each sentence below. Write them.

1. The girls tried their new skateboards.
2. A truckdriver asked for directions.
3. Children played on the slide and swings.
4. Thomas Jefferson drew the plans for his new home.
5. Emeralds and diamonds are precious gems.
6. My birthday is in August.
7. Practice will begin on Friday.
8. Colorado has beautiful mountains.
9. Vanessa put the change in her pocket.
10. The two poodles wore identical sweaters.

B. Finding Common Nouns and Proper Nouns
(Use after page 116.)

On your paper label two columns, *Common Nouns* and *Proper Nouns*. Number from 1 to 20 down the left-hand margin. After each number, write the noun in the proper column. Begin each proper noun with a capital letter. CN = Common Noun PN = Proper Noun

1. utah PN
2. bird CN
3. buick PN
4. gum CN
5. shaun cassidy PN
6. glasses CN
7. pacific ocean PN
8. pretzel CN
9. cadillac PN
10. garbage CN
11. mrs. thorpe PN
12. fifth-grader CN
13. people CN
14. statue of liberty PN

15. basketball CN 18. camera CN
16. oven CN 19. movie CN
17. ᴰdenver PN 20. ᴰdisneyland PN

C. Forming Plurals (Use after page 118.)

Write the plural form of each of these nouns.

1. shoe — shoes
2. ax — axes
3. lion — lions
4. loaf — loaves
5. crutch — crutches
6. navy — navies
7. fish — fish
8. story — stories
9. hero — heroes
10. chief — chiefs
11. boss — bosses
12. foot — feet
13. lunch — lunches
14. calf — calves
15. salmon — salmon
16. goose — geese
17. brush — brushes
18. bath — baths
19. factory — factories
20. tomato — tomatoes

D. Writing the Possessive Form (Use after page 122.)

In each sentence one word is underlined. Write this word so that it shows possession. Write the word first. Then add the apostrophe or apostrophe and *s*.

1. In the story, <u>Beth</u> death is very sad. — Beth's
2. <u>Alonzo</u> coach gave the team a pep talk. — Alonzo's
3. The nurse took the <u>man</u> pulse. — man's
4. Leslie borrowed <u>Carla</u> ruler. — Carla's
5. I clean my <u>birds</u> cages every day. — birds'
6. <u>Archie</u> car is second-hand. — Archie's
7. <u>Pamela</u> winning streak at checkers is over. — Pamela's
8. Our club is selling <u>children</u> T-shirts. — children's
9. The <u>boys</u> locker room is filled with steam. — boys'
10. An <u>ant</u> strength is amazing. — ant's

Chapter 10

Using Verbs

Chapter Objectives

1. To identify verbs as either action or state-of-being verbs
2. To differentiate between main verbs and helping verbs and to recognize and use them correctly in sentences
3. To understand the function of direct objects and to identify them in sentences
4. To use the correct forms of the verb *be*
5. To use the correct form of *be* after *there*, *here*, and *where*
6. To choose the correct verb from verb pairs that are often confused
7. To identify contractions and to use them correctly
8. To identify negatives (no-words and not-words) and to use them correctly
9. To recognize the basic word order in the N V N sentence pattern
10. To recognize the basic word order in the N LV N sentence pattern

Preparing the Students

Explain that in this chapter students will review what they have already learned about verbs. This will help them use verbs correctly.

Additional Resources

Diagnostic Test—page 431 in this T.E. Recommended for use before teaching the chapter.

Mastery Test—pages 456 to 459 in this T.E. Recommended for use after teaching the chapter.

Additional Mastery Test—Recommended for use after any necessary reteaching. (In separate booklet, *Mastery Tests, Silver Level*, pages 19 to 22.)

Skills Practice Book—pages 47–58

Duplicating Masters—pages 47–58

Part 1 What Are Verbs?

Read these sentences. What do the underlined words tell you?

Marilyn <u>ran</u> very fast.

She <u>jumped</u> over the stick.

She <u>landed</u> on both feet.

The underlined words tell what Marilyn did. They tell about action. Words that tell about action are called **verbs**.

Part 1

Objective

To identify verbs as either action or state-of-being verbs

Presenting the Lesson

1. Read and discuss pages 127 and 128. Ask students for examples of both types of action verbs.

2. Assign and discuss Exercises A and B on pages 128 and 129.

3. Read and discuss page 129. Ask students to find the state-of-being verbs in these sentences.

1. This art project is difficult.
2. My scissors are not sharp.
3. I am very careful with paints.
4. The directions were clear.
5. The final product will be a mobile.

4. In addition to the general definition of a verb given in the text, there are other ways to identify a verb. These ways, listed in the following chart, are based on what linguists have discovered about the structure of a word and the order of words in a sentence. It is suggested that the information in the chart be used to point out additional ways in which verbs function.

Ways To Identify Verbs

1. Look for words that change their forms to show past time.

Present	Past
touch	touched
see	saw

2. Look for words that follow helping verbs (forms of *be*, *do*, *have*, and helping verbs like *can*, *could*, *shall*, *will*, *may*, *might*, and *must*).

3. Look for words with the following endings or suffixes:
 -ify (*identify*)   -ize (*hypnotize*)

4. Look for words that fit the blank in this test sentence:
 Please _____.

Action Verbs

Some verbs tell about action you can see, such as *hit*, *ran*, and *rode*. Other verbs tell about action you cannot see, as in these examples:

Sarah <u>worried</u> about the test.

Tony <u>wanted</u> a new green jacket.

Linus <u>believes</u> in the Great Pumpkin.

Exercises   Using Action Verbs

A. Copy each sentence. Underline the action verb twice.

1. The hikers <u>lost</u> their way.
2. Jennifer <u>agreed</u> with Mother.
3. Marty <u>ordered</u> a cheeseburger.
4. Jim <u>wished</u> for a sunny day.
5. Senators <u>make</u> laws.
6. Linda <u>climbed</u> the maple tree.
7. The child <u>expected</u> a visit from Santa.
8. The band <u>marched</u> onto the field.
9. Jessica <u>wondered</u> about her new school.
10. The cast <u>painted</u> their faces with makeup.

B. Think of an action verb that will complete each sentence. Copy the sentences, filling in the blanks with your verbs. Many correct answers are possible for each sentence.

Answers will vary.

Example: Toby _____ the ball.

Some possible answers: Toby caught the ball. Toby threw the ball. Toby held the ball. Toby hit the ball.

1. The class _____ at the joke.
2. Aunt Suzanne _____ a present.
3. Several children _____ on the beach.
4. A fox _____ over the fence.
5. Gina _____ her pen.
6. Anita _____ down the hall.
7. The two brothers _____.
8. The conductor _____ tickets.
9. We _____ for the signal.
10. The scientist _____ an Arctic expedition.

State-of-Being Verbs

Not all verbs tell about action. Some verbs just state that something is. The underlined verbs in these sentences are often used just to say that something is. They are called **state-of-being verbs.**

1. I <u>am</u> here.
2. John <u>is</u> sick.
3. We <u>are</u> late.
4. The storm <u>was</u> over.
5. The girls <u>were</u> happy.
6. The weather <u>has been</u> bad.
7. We <u>had been</u> at the show.
8. We <u>will be</u> on time.

The most common state-of-being verbs are these:

is	was	be
are	were	being
am		been

5. It is suggested that Exercise A on page 130 be done as a class activity. Then assign and discuss Exercises B and C.

6. Use Exercise A on page 152 as additional practice or review.

Optional Practice

You may wish to put this exercise on a worksheet or on the board. Tell students there are 6 action verbs and 6 state-of-being verbs in the list. Have them write the action verbs on the spokes of the action wheel, and the state-of-being verbs on the state-of-being line. One action verb and one state-of-being verb from the list have been provided as examples.

Verb List: will be, called, watch, was being, be, are, unlock, worked, is, wrap, arrive, am, were.

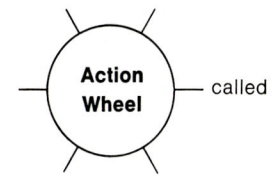

State-of-Being Line

will be, _____

> **Verbs** are words that tell action or state that something is.

Exercises **Using Action Verbs and State-of-being Verbs**

A. Copy each of these sentences. Underline each verb twice. Some are action verbs, and some are state-of-being verbs.

1. The Dodgers are her heroes.
2. The boys were hungry.
3. Aaron bought his ticket.
4. Pam argued with her sister.
5. The store opens tomorrow.
6. Evel Knievel is a stunt driver.
7. Donny and Marie Osmond sang together.
8. Lisa climbed the spiral staircase.

B. Number your paper from 1 to 8. Write the verb in each of the following sentences. After the verb, write *Action* or *State-of-being* to tell what kind of verb it is. A = Action Verb
SB = State-of-being Verb

1. Wes plays (A) the drums.
2. Gino's parents own (A) a toy store.
3. Gloria is (SB) the class clown.
4. I am (SB) in love with the Muppets.
5. The sparrow injured (A) its wing.
6. "Studio See" is (SB) a children's news show.
7. Gail hid (A) in the basement.
8. The tulips were (SB) in bloom.

C. On your paper write complete sentences to answer these questions. The verbs you use will state that something is. They should not tell any action. Answers will vary.

1. How old are you?
2. What is your teacher's name?
3. How many children are in your class?
4. In what grade will you be next year?
5. Where were you yesterday?

Part 2 Main Verbs and Helping Verbs

Many of the verbs you have studied so far have been just one word: *hit, is, ran, climbed*.

A great many verbs are made up of two or three words. Notice the verbs in these sentences. The verbs are underlined.

Betsy walked home.   Steven called you.
Betsy is walking home.   Steven was calling you.
Betsy has been walking home. Steven might have called you.

When a verb is made up of two or more words, the last word is the main verb. The other words are called **helping verbs**.

Helping Verb	Main Verb	Verb
	walked	walked
is	walking	is walking
has been	walking	has been walking
	called	called
was	calling	was calling
might have	called	might have called

The most common of the helping verbs are the forms of *be*, *have*, and *do*:

be—am, is, are, was, were
have—has, have, had
do—does, do, did

These words can also be used by themselves as main verbs.

Used as Helping Verb	Used as Main Verb
Janet *was* visiting.	Janet *was* in Indiana.
Ralph *does* like math.	Ralph *does* his work.

131

5. You might wish to do Exercise A on pages 133 and 134 with the class. Make it clear that more than one helping verb may be used with each main verb. Then assign and discuss Exercise B on page 134.

6. Read and discuss page 134. Stress that separation of the helping verb from the main verb does not change the meaning of the whole verb.

7. Assign and discuss Exercises A and B on page 135.

8. Use Exercise B on pages 152 and 153 as additional practice or review.

Optional Practice

Have the students follow the directions for the Exercises on page 135, using these sentences. Let the students know that verbs that are used as helping verbs in some sentences are used as main verbs in other sentences.

1. Did the baby crawl up the stairs?
2. The racer has run many times before.
3. The carpenter did a good job on the repairs.
4. We are members of the school choir.
5. My friend has two dogs.
6. The dogs are swimming in the water.
7. The lions have locks on their cages.
8. The seals have been fed already.

Extending the Lesson

Ask students to bring in a short newspaper or magazine article. Have them underline the main verbs twice and put a box around the helping verbs.

There are several other helping verbs that can be used with main verbs.

can	could	may
shall	should	might
will	would	must

> A verb may be a single word or a group of words, made up of a **main verb** and one or more **helping verbs.**

Exercise   Finding Main Verbs and Helping Verbs

Number your paper from 1 to 10. Make two columns. Head the first column *Helping Verbs.* Head the second *Main Verb.* Write the parts of the verbs in the right columns.

Example: That car should have stopped for the school bus.

Helping Verbs	Main Verb	
should have	stopped	HV = Helping Verb
		MV = Main Verb

1. Ernest **had**[HV] **eaten**[MV] some fudge.
2. Tomorrow we **will**[HV] be **holding**[HV MV] a field day.
3. One horse **was**[HV] **leading**[MV] the parade.
4. Laraine **is**[HV] **wearing**[MV] her catcher's mitt.
5. The trip **should**[HV] **have**[HV] **ended**[MV] sooner.
6. Stephanie **does**[HV] **like**[MV] the new apartment.
7. We **may**[HV] **wash**[MV] the car today.
8. They **could**[HV] **have**[HV] **arrived**[MV] on time.
9. Julio **has**[HV] **been**[HV] **painting**[MV] with poster paints.
10. Our teacher **had**[HV] **explained**[MV] the experiment.

Some Verbs Need Helping Verbs

Look at these three sentences.

1. We *ate* the cookies.
2. We *eaten* all of them.
3. We *eating* crackers now.

Something is wrong with the last two sentences. What can you add to make them sound right? You will add helping verbs.

2. We *have* eaten all of them.
3. We *are* eating crackers now.

Four of the verbs you use very frequently must be used with helping verbs. They are *been, done, gone,* and *seen.* Verbs with the *-en* ending, like *chosen* or *ridden,* must be used with helping verbs. Verbs with the *-ing* ending, like *sitting* and *talking,* must be used with helping verbs. There are many other verbs that must be used with helping verbs. You will learn more about them in Chapter 12.

Exercises Supplying the Helping Verbs

A. Number your paper from 1 to 10. If the sentence is correct, write *Correct.* If the verb needs a helping verb, write a helping verb and the main verb.

These are suggested answers. Answers will vary for all but items 2, 5, 6, and 8.

Example: Ms. Lorne waiting at the bus stop.

was waiting

1. The groundhog seen his shadow. has seen, had seen
2. A huge truck had swept the streets. Correct
3. We playing concentration. are playing, were playing
4. The vase broken by accident. was broken, has been broken
5. Superman rescued the trapped miners. Correct

6. Babe Didrikson was a great athlete. *Correct*
7. A lady walking the tightrope. *is walking, will be walking*
8. The child was sitting on Santa's lap. *Correct*
9. We been listening to a Bee Gees album. *have been listening, had been listening*
10. I using your ruler. *am using, was using, have been using*

B. Follow the directions for Exercise A. *Answers will vary for all but items 2, 4, and 8.*
1. Barb ridden a bronco. *has ridden, had ridden*
2. Millions of years ago, dinosaurs lived. *Correct*
3. The class learning about government. *is learning, was learning*
4. Alec had a haircut. *Correct*
5. My sister Carmen chosen the records. *has chosen, had chosen*
6. A children's theater opening soon. *is opening*
7. We leaving for Boston tomorrow. *are leaving, will be leaving*
8. Costumes were stored in a trunk. *Correct*
9. That dog bitten our mail carrier. *has bitten, had bitten*
10. Listeners guessing the punch line. *were guessing, may be guessing*

Separated Parts of the Verb

Sometimes another part of the sentence comes between the helping verb and the main verb.

> Ezra **may** not **pitch** today.
> Joanne **will** probably **stay** for dinner.
> The gate **should**n't **have been locked** last night.

Notice that *not* and the ending *n't* are not verbs.

In questions, we very often use one or more words between the helping verb and the main verb.

> **Does** this bicycle **need** oil?
> **Were** you **looking** for me?
> **Have** you ever **seen** a meteor shower?

Exercises **Finding Separated Parts of the Verb**

A. Number your paper from 1 to 10. Make two columns. Head the first column *Helping Verb*. Head the second *Main Verb*. Write the verbs for each of these sentences in the proper column.

    Example: Joseph didn't see the curb.

Helping Verb	Main Verb
did	see

HV = Helping Verb
MV = Main Verb

1. Our goalie **has** (HV) not **blocked** (MV) any shots.
2. Vicky **had** (HV) never **missed** (MV) a Sox game.
3. **Would** (HV) you **repeat** (MV) your answer?
4. The floats **were** (HV) usually **awarded** (MV) prizes.
5. Devonna **will** (HV) probably **break** (MV) the school record in the 100-yard dash.
6. The champ **was** (HV) peacefully **resting** (MV).
7. We **couldn't** (HV) **cross** (MV) the railroad tracks.
8. The queen **did** (HV) not **order** (MV) this entertainment.
9. Prisoners **had** (HV) often **escaped** (MV) from that jail.
10. **Didn't** (HV) immigrants **come** (MV) to Ellis Island?

B. Follow the directions for Exercise A.

1. I **was** (HV) only **joking** (MV).
2. **Will** (HV) winter ever **end** (MV)?
3. Grandma **has** (HV) never **missed** (MV) my birthday party.
4. Winona **could** (HV) barely **reach** (MV) the rings.
5. Barry **has** (HV) almost **finished** (MV) his homework.
6. The children **were** (HV) impatiently **waiting** (MV) for Christmas.
7. When **does** (HV) your library card **expire** (MV)?
8. The smell of cookies **was** (HV) quickly **spreading** (MV).
9. I **can't** (HV) **understand** (MV) this language.
10. **Shouldn't** (HV) the cartoon **start** (MV) now?

Part 3

Objective

To understand the function of direct objects and to identify them in sentences

Presenting the Lesson

1. Read and discuss pages 136 and 137. Ask students what kind of word a direct object must be if it is a person or thing. If necessary, review the definition of a noun. Avoid mentioning pronouns at this time. They will be introduced in Chapter 11.

2. Assign and discuss Exercises A and B on page 137. Remind students to ask the question *What?* after the verb to find the direct object.

3. Use Exercise C on page 153 for additional practice or review.

Optional Practice

Direct students to write complete sentences that answer these questions. In their sentences, they should underline the verb twice and circle the direct object.

Example: What does the football player receive?
The football player <u>receives</u> the (ball).

1. What does the artist paint?
2. What do seals eat?
3. What does the musician play?
4. What does a doctor use?
5. Whom does the salesperson meet?
6. What do people read?

Part 3   Direct Objects of Verbs

In many sentences, a subject and a verb are enough to express a complete thought.

Subject	Verb
The child	fell.
The telephone	rang.

In other sentences the thought is not complete until other words have been added.

Kirk spilled the *glue.*
Jeannie dialed the *number.*

The word that is needed after the verb to complete the action of the verb is the **direct object of the verb.** *Glue* tells what Kirk spilled. *Number* tells what Jeannie dialed. *Glue* and *number* are the direct objects in the sample sentences.

The **direct object** tells what receives the action of the verb.

Jack ate _____ .

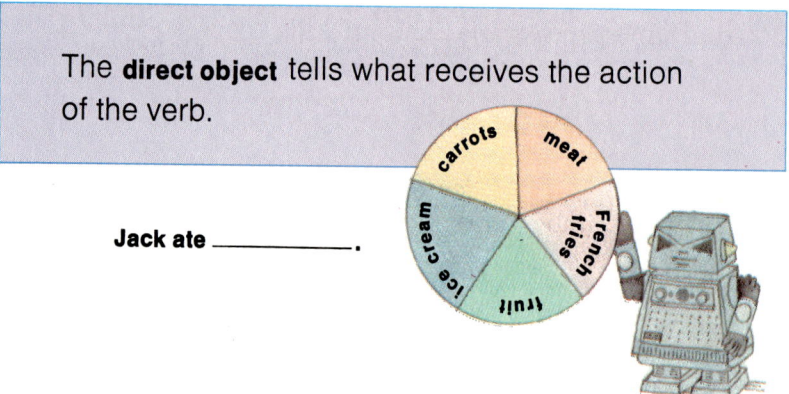

Recognizing Direct Objects

To find the direct object in a sentence, first find the verb. Then ask *what?* after the verb. If a word answers *what?* after the verb, it is the direct object.

Examples:

John sharpened his pencil.
John sharpened *what?* his *pencil*
The direct object is *pencil*.

Laura was watching TV.
Laura was watching *what?* TV
The direct object is *TV*.

Exercises **Using Direct Objects**

A. Copy the following sentences. Underline the verb twice. Draw a circle around the direct object.

Example: Della was riding her (bicycle.)

1. Teresa broke her (ruler.)
2. Tim borrowed my (book.)
3. The fielder should have caught that (ball.)
4. The conductor will collect (tickets.)
5. This computer will solve (mysteries.)
6. Sally rolled the (ball) down the bowling alley.
7. My little brothers made a (snowman.)
8. Phyllis and Marni were doing a (puzzle.)
9. Long ago, Indians hunted (buffalo) here.
10. Lyndon cut the (cake) into small pieces.

B. On a sheet of paper, write sentences using the following verbs. Put a direct object in each sentence. Draw a circle around the direct object that you have added.

1. lost
2. was building
3. dropped
4. will fill
5. likes
6. was writing
7. covered
8. should have read
9. will eat
10. touched

Extending the Lesson

This exercise is provided for students who confuse subjects and direct objects.

Point out that all verbs have subjects, but not all have direct objects. Have students list the differences in position and purpose. (They should mention that the subject usually comes before the verb, but the direct object after; the subject tells who or what did something, while the object tells who or what completes the action of the verb.)

Using the following sentences, ask students to underline the verb twice, underline the subject noun once, and circle the direct object noun.

1. The gym teacher blew her whistle.
2. The movers carried the furniture.
3. Dale bought groceries at the store.
4. O. J. Simpson made a touchdown.
5. Some pillows have feathers.
6. My father vacuumed the rug.
7. The girls played Red Rover during recess.
8. The scissors cut the string easily.
9. The mail carrier delivered a package.
10. The guests brought gifts to the party.

Part 4

Objective

To use the correct forms of the verb *be*

Presenting the Lesson

1. Read and discuss pages 138 and 139. Ask students for further examples for each rule. Point out that the students are probably familiar with most, if not all, of the rules.
2. Assign and discuss Exercises A and B on page 139.
3. Use Exercise D on page 153 for additional practice or review.

Optional Practice

Most students are usually aware of rules 1 to 4, so you may find it useful to concentrate on rule 5. You may wish to use this exercise for your more advanced students and have those who need more basic practice do Exercise D on page 153.

Review rule 5. Put these sentences on a worksheet or on the board. Have the students rewrite the sentences correctly by adding a helping verb to the verb in parentheses. They should then underline the whole verb.

Example: That boy (being) good.
That boy <u>is being</u> good.

1. Those students (been) working hard.
2. The brown pony (being) difficult.
3. I (been) hungry for the last two hours.
4. The car (be) in the garage until this afternoon.
5. The movie *Superman* (been) at the theater a long time.

Part 4 Using the Right Form of *Be*

You have already learned that the verb *be* has many forms:

is	was	be
are	were	being
am		been

Some of these forms may be used alone or as helping verbs. Others may be used only with helping verbs. There are also rules about the subjects that can be used with some of these forms.

Here are five important rules to remember in using the forms of the verb *be*:

1. If the subject names one person, place, or thing, use the forms *is* and *was*.

Christine *is* here. She *is sitting* near me.
Teddy *was* here. He *was called* away.

2. If the subject names more than one person, place, or thing, use the forms *are* and *were*.

The children *are* late. They *are riding* their bikes.
The cookies *were* on that plate. They *were eaten* at lunch.

3. When the subject is *you*, use the forms *are* and *were*.

You *are* my best friend. Are you *coming* with me?
You three *were* the best swimmers. You *were doing* the strokes correctly.

4. When the subject is *I*, use the forms *am* or *was*.

I *am* here. I *am studying* English.
I *was* at home. I *was sleeping* in bed.

5. Use a helping verb before the forms *be*, *being*, and *been*.

Do not use one of these forms alone or as the only helping verb before a main verb.

Karen *will be* here later.
The patient *was being taken* to surgery.
Jeff *has been looking* for you.
These questions *have been* too hard!

Exercises Using the Right Form of *Be*

A. Number your paper from 1 to 10. Choose the right form of *be* from the parentheses. Write it down.

1. George and Eileen (is, are) my neighbors.
2. I (is, am, are) a loyal friend.
3. You (is, are) the team captain.
4. The TV (been, has been) on for hours.
5. You (was, were) blocking my view.
6. Craig and Ilona (was, were) tossing the beachball.
7. The Great Dane (being, was being) mean.
8. Your backpack (is, are) loaded with books.
9. Nancy (be, is) ten years old.
10. The boys (been, were) jumping over puddles.

6. That bus driver (been) driving a bus for ten years.
7. The library (be) open until noon.
8. The building on the corner (being) torn down.
9. Fozzie Bear (been) a popular Muppet.
10. Perhaps someday spaceships (be) common.

B. Follow the directions for Exercise A.

1. Tammy and I (is, are) building a fort.
2. I (am, is, are) guessing his age.
3. You (is, are) a good sport.
4. Jorge (be, is) feeding the fish.
5. I (am, be) helping Mother.
6. Eric and Sam (been, have been) wearing suspenders.
7. The haunted house (was, were) scary.
8. They (was, were) throwing snowballs.
9. You (being, was being, were being) silly.
10. The passengers (is, are) boarding the plane.

There is the _____.

There are the _____.

Here is the _____.

Here are the _____.

Part 5 Using the Right Verb After *There, Here,* and *Where*

Many sentences begin with the words *There is* or *There are*. How can you tell which of these to use?

You must find the subject of the verb in order to tell. The word *there* is never the subject. When a sentence begins with *there*, the subject usually comes after the verb.

    verb subject
There *is* a squirrel in the tree. (*squirrel* is the subject)

    verb   subject
There *are* the boats. (*boats* is the subject)

Can you decide which form to use in each of these sentences?

1. There (is, are) a *leak* in that boat.

2. There (was, were) *papers* on the floor.

First, find out whether the subject names one person, place, or thing, or more than one. Then follow the rules for the forms of the verb *be*.

The subject in sentence 1 is *leak*. This names one thing. You probably chose *is*.

The subject in sentence 2 is *papers*. Since this names more than one thing, you probably chose *were*.

The words *here* and *where* are also used to begin sentences. They cause the same problem as *there*. When should you say *Here is* or *Where is*? When should you say *Here are* or *Where are*?

You can tell by finding the subject. *Where* and *here* are never the subject. In sentences beginning *Where is* or *Here is*, the subject comes after the verb.

    Here *is* the *trail*. (*trail* is the subject)
    Where *is* the *door*? (*door* is the subject)
    Here *are* the *sandwiches*. (*sandwiches* is the subject)
    Where *are* the *books*? (*books* is the subject)

When the subject names one person, place, or thing, use one of these forms:

There is	**Here is**	**Where is**
There was	**Here was**	**Where was**

When the subject names more than one person, place, or thing, or is the word *you*,
use one of these forms:

There are	**Here are**	**Where are**
There were	**Here were**	**Where were**

Optional Practice

1. Make up a worksheet with a circle at the center and eight long spokes projecting out at regular intervals. Write the word *There* inside the circle.

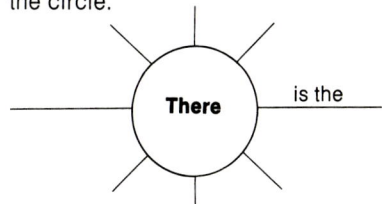

On each spoke, write one of these phrases:

is the	is a
are	are
was the	was a
were	were

Have the students add a subject on each spoke to complete a *There* sentence.

Do the same for *Here* and *Where*. (Add a question mark to the end of *Where* spokes.)

2. Use the same basic pattern as for the first exercise, but leave space for the verb and write a subject at the far end of each spoke. Have the students fill in a verb for each subject, choosing from *is*, *are*, *was*, and *were*. Be sure to use both singular and plural nouns, and *I* and *you* for subjects.

Where is the 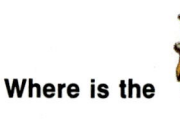 **Where are the**    **?**

Exercises Using the Right Verb After *There*, *Here*, and *Where*

A. Number your paper from 1 to 10. Find the subject of each of the sentences below. Write it down. Then choose the correct form of the verb *be* from the parentheses. Write it after the subject.

1. Where (is, are) your friends?
2. There (is, are) five pears on the plate.
3. Where (is, are) the two broken cups?
4. There (is, are) a strong wind from the west.
5. Here (is, are) the oldest trees in the park.
6. There (was, were) a letter in the mailbox.
7. Here (is, are) several children that you've met.
8. Where (is, are) the Big Dipper?
9. (Was, Were) there any more plums on the tree?
10. Here (is, are) the box of crayons.

B. Copy each of the following sentences, using the correct form of the verb *be*.

1. Where (is, are) my book?
2. There (is, are) six cookies left.
3. Here (is, are) several old magazines.
4. Where (is, are) the keys for the car?
5. Here (is, are) a box of your old toys.
6. There (is, are) a good reason for my mistake.
7. Here (is, are) the tracks of a big animal.
8. Where (is, are) my old blue jeans?
9. Here (is, are) the pencils you lost.
10. There (is, are) my two best friends.

Part 6 Some Confusing Verbs

There are several pairs of verbs that cause trouble because they look alike. Others have meanings that people confuse. In this section you will learn how to use these verbs.

Set and Sit

Set means "to place something somewhere."
Sit means "to rest in one place."

Say these sentences over and over to yourself until they sound right and natural.

Set the vase of flowers on the table.

Sit where you can see it.

Set the packages on the bed.

Don't *sit* on them.

Let and Leave

Let means "to permit."
Leave means "to go away from."

Say these sentences over until they sound natural.

Will you please *let* me use your book?
Let me go!
Please *leave* your book on the table.
The bus will *leave* in five minutes.

Part 6

Objective

To choose the correct verb from verb pairs that are often confused

Presenting the Lesson

1. Read page 143. Ask students to explain the difference in meaning and use between the two sets of verbs. Have them give other examples using the words in sentences. You may want to take more time with *let* and *leave* since they are sometimes more difficult to differentiate.

2. Assign and discuss Exercises A and B on page 144. When correcting Exercise A, you may want to ask students to act out the action of each sentence.

3. Read page 145. Discuss the same questions as for page 143.

4. If the distinctions appear to be understood, assign and discuss Exercises A and B on page 146. Otherwise, you may want to do part of each Exercise with the class first.

5. Use Exercise F on page 154 as additional practice or review.

Optional Practice

Direct the students to fill in the blanks with one of the verbs written above each group of sentences.

sit—set
1. _____ on the ground.
2. _____ the glass down.
3. _____ in the bleachers.
4. _____ on the curb.
5. _____ the cup on the tray.

may—can
1. _____ I borrow your crayons?
2. My uncle _____ tune up his car.
3. Everyone _____ have more dessert.
4. _____ you ride a horse?
5. _____ I use your bike?

let—leave
1. _____ the baby bird go when it can fly.
2. _____ the mail next door.
3. _____ the money in the bank.
4. _____ me walk with you.
5. _____ me enough cereal for breakfast.

teach—taught—learn
1. _____ me how to play the guitar.
2. The sailor will _____ to tie knots.
3. The tailor _____ his assistant to sew.
4. I had to _____ to be patient.
5. Will the champion _____ us to throw the Frisbee?

sit   set

Exercises   Using the Right Verb

A. Number your paper from 1 to 10. Choose the right verb from the parentheses. Write it down.

1. I will (set, sit) the lemonade on the table.
2. Please (set, sit) on this stool.
3. We can (set, sit) in the front row.
4. (Set, Sit) that candy bar on the counter.
5. In music class we (set, sit) on the floor.
6. The vase should (set, sit) on the piano.
7. My dog will (set, sit) by my side.
8. Don't (set, sit) the ice cream on the stove.
9. Anne will (set, sit) under the hairdryer.
10. Did the old man (set, sit) his hat down?

B. Follow the directions for Exercise A.

1. Don't (let, leave) the parakeet get out.
2. The guests will (let, leave) soon.
3. Dad (lets, leaves) me win at cards.
4. (Let, Leave) your suggestions in the box.
5. Did you (let, leave) your gym shoes at school?
6. (Let, Leave) me choose the music.
7. Will you (let, leave) your hair grow?
8. (Let, Leave) my kite alone.
9. Will Mom (let, leave) you come with us?
10. The students (let, leave) their bikes in the yard.

May and *Can*

May asks or gives permission.
Can means "to be able to do something."

Look at the sentences below. Study the difference between *may* and *can* in them.

You *may* have more cake. May I ride your bike?
Nina *can* walk on stilts. You *may* ride it if you *can*.

Teach, *Taught*, and *Learn*

Teach means "to show how" or "to explain."
Taught means "showed how" or "explained."
Learn means "to understand" or "to gain knowledge."

Study these sentences to see how to use the verbs.

It's easy to *teach* a dog to carry a newspaper.
My dog *learned* to do it in five lessons.
The lifeguard *taught* me to swim in one week.
You should *learn* to swim under water.

teach

learn

Exercises   Using the Right Verb

Number your paper from 1 to 10. Choose the right verb from the parentheses. Write it down.

1. (May, Can) I borrow your sled?
2. The child (may, can) tell time.
3. A magician (may, can) make things disappear.
4. Lionel (may, can) run very fast.
5. Yes, you (may, can) have some candy.
6. Cats (may, can) see in the dark.
7. Magnets (may, can) attract metals.
8. You (may, can) try my new bike.
9. No one (may, can) shout in the library.
10. (May, Can) we please feed the animals?

Follow the directions for Exercise A.

1. Will you (teach, learn) me checkers?
2. Ms. Casey (teaches, learns) first-graders.
3. I (taught, learned) to fish.
4. Mr. Dior (teaches, learns) ballet classes.
5. My sister (taught, learned) me to ride a horse.
6. Beginners (teach, learn) a lot by watching.
7. By reading, Elena (taught, learned) about other countries.
8. Your parents (taught, learned) you good manners.
9. Miss Fairbanks (taught, learned) our class about the planets.
10. These students (taught, learned) their multiplication tables.
11. Beth (taught, learned) me the words to the song.
12. Nobody (teaches, learns) babies to talk.
13. Henry (taught, learned) us the rules.
14. (Teach, Learn) me that trick, Raoul.
15. People (teach, learn) from their mistakes.

Part 7 Using Contractions

Sometimes a verb is combined with another word to make one word. Here are some examples:

I'll = I will	here's = here is
I'm = I am	there's = there is, there has
I've = I have	they're = they are
she'd = she would	they've = they have
he's = he is	isn't = is not
we'll = we will	aren't = are not
we're = we are	weren't = were not
you're = you are	hasn't = has not
it's = it is, it has	can't = can not
that's = that is, that has	don't = do not
what's = what is, what has	won't = will not
where's = where is, where has	shouldn't = should not

These shortened forms are called **contractions.** Whenever we write a contraction, we use an **apostrophe** (') to show where letters are left out.

Exercises Making Contractions Correctly

A. Copy the contractions below. Place the apostrophe where it belongs.

1. I've
2. well
3. they've
4. can't
5. there's
6. aren't
7. don't
8. he's
9. that's
10. I'm
11. here's
12. isn't

B. Copy the following sentences. Make a contraction of the underlined words in each sentence.

1. <u>You are</u> the first to arrive. *You're*
2. Francis <u>has not</u> eaten lunch yet. *hasn't*
3. <u>They are</u> all ready. *They're*

Part 7

Objective

To identify contractions and to use them correctly

Presenting the Lesson

1. Read and discuss page 147. You may find it helpful to talk about possible meanings for the base word *contract* (agreement, pull together). Point out that most definitions of this word mean some form of coming together. A word contraction is a coming together of a verb and another word to make a shortened form. There is no change of meaning. Ask students to tell what the missing letters are in the examples.
2. Assign and discuss Exercises A and B on pages 147 and 148.
3. Use Exercise G on page 155 as additional practice or review.

Extending the Lesson

Have each student write a question using a contraction with *n't*. Then ask each student to read the question to the class. The class must answer in complete sentences, using the words the contractions stand for.

Examples:
1. Don't you want to go?
   I do not want to go.
2. Won't you jog to the corner with me?
   I will not jog to the corner with you.

4. We are on Debra's team. **We're**
5. I will help you with these books. **I'll**
6. What has happened here? **What's**
7. I think she would like to go. **she'd**
8. Bethina will not go near snakes. **won't**
9. Where is the bike pump? **Where's**
10. It is Bill's football. **It's**

Part 8 — Objective

To identify negatives (*no*-words and *not*-words) and to use them correctly

Presenting the Lesson

1. Discuss the meaning of the word *negative*. Ask students to give you examples of things they consider to be negative (things that should *not* be done). Read and discuss pages 148 and 149.

2. You may find it helpful to do Exercise A on page 149 with the students. Discuss the reasons for the answers and have students point out *no*-words and *not*-words. Have them check each sentence to be sure it has only one negative. Assign and discuss Exercise B.

3. Use Exercise H on page 155 as additional practice or review.

Part 8 Using Negatives Correctly

Some contractions are made by joining *not* with certain verbs, like this: *is + not = isn't*. The **apostrophe** (') takes the place of the *o* in *not*. Words made in this way are called *not*-words.

have + not = haven't   is + not = isn't
were + not = weren't   do + not = don't
would + not = wouldn't   could + not = couldn't

The *no*-words are different. You can see *no* in all but one:

no   nobody   none   never
no one   nothing   nowhere

Together, the *not*-words and the *no*-words are called **negatives.** Two negatives used together make what is called a **double negative.** Avoid double negatives.

Wrong: Melvin does**n't** do **no**thing.

The sentences below show the right way to use *no*-words and *not*-words. Read them aloud. Then study the rule.

1. Melvin does**n't** do anything.
   Melvin does **no**thing.

2. We have**n't** gone anywhere.
   We have gone **no**where.

3. There is**n't** any flour left.
   There is **no** flour left.

4. **Don't** ever do that again.
   Never do that again.

> Do not use a *no*-word and a *not*-word together.

Exercises   Keeping *No*-words and *Not*-words Apart

A. Choose the right word from the parentheses. Write it.

1. Doesn't (nobody, anybody) want to skip rope?
2. Don't those boys have (anything, nothing) to do?
3. Haven't you (never, ever) been downtown?
4. There isn't (none, any) of the pie left for us.
5. Adam doesn't go (nowhere, anywhere).
6. Isn't there (no one, anyone) we could ask?
7. There weren't (any, no) prizes left for June and her.
8. I guess no one (is, isn't) coming.
9. (Does, Doesn't) nobody want to sing along?
10. (Weren't, Were) none of you at the picnic?

B. Follow the directions for Exercise A.

1. There won't be (anything, nothing) left for lunch.
2. Those girls don't do (nothing, anything) wrong.
3. Nothing was (never, ever) said about the lawn.
4. We didn't hear (anybody, nobody) crying.
5. Doesn't (nothing, anything) ever go wrong at camp?
6. We don't want (any, no) trouble.
7. I couldn't see (nothing, anything) on the stage.
8. These scissors won't cut (any, no) cardboard.
9. The bus didn't have (no, any) empty seats.
10. Manuel's glasses (were, weren't) nowhere to be found.

Optional Practice

Put the 10 sentences below on a worksheet or on the board. Tell students that 5 of them are correct and 5 contain double negatives. If the sentence is correct, they should put a *C* to the right of it; if it is not, they should write an *X*. You might want to have the more advanced students rewrite the double negative sentences correctly.

1. Paul won't never eat so much again.
2. No one is allowed to go into that room.
3. I don't think anyone knows my secret.
4. My pen doesn't have no ink left.
5. There aren't any basketballs in the gym.
6. We didn't see anything better on the menu.
7. No one couldn't hit a home run.
8. My brother can't drive a car yet.
9. Why wouldn't nobody go on the trip?
10. There wasn't no orange juice left.

Extending the Lesson

Point out that sentences containing a *not*-word may also contain these words:

any   anybody   anywhere
anyone   anything   ever

Have students write a sentence for each of these words, using a *not*-word in each sentence, also.

Examples: I don't want any more dinner.
Jean didn't ask anyone for help.

Sentence Patterns

Objective

To recognize the basic word order in the N V N sentence pattern.

Presenting the Lesson

1. Read and discuss page 150. Make it clear that each of the three parts in the N V N pattern may have one or more than one word. Any words that describe the subject noun are grouped in the first noun-part. Any words that describe the verb are grouped in the verb-part. Any words that describe the object are grouped in the second noun-part.

2. Assign and discuss Exercises A and C on page 150. It might be helpful to do Exercise B with the class.

Optional Practice

Have students make a chart for the N V N pattern and fill in the chart with the following sentence parts. They must match the parts to make sensible sentences. Remind them to capitalize and punctuate where necessary.

N (First Noun-part)
1. the football player
2. the soccer player
3. the baseball player
4. the hockey player
5. the basketball player
6. the tennis player

V (Verb-part)	N (Second Noun-part)
scores	the football
serves	the soccer ball
kicks	a home run
passess	a goal
hits	the basketball
dunks	the tennis ball

Sentence Patterns — The N V N Pattern

A sentence in the **N V N pattern** has three parts. The first N stands for the subject noun. The V stands for the verb. The second N stands for the direct object noun. Read the sentences in the following chart. They are in the N V N pattern.

N	V	N
Cora	writes	songs.
Snakes	lay	eggs.
My friends	planned	a party.
The plumber	fixed	the sink.
Donald	likes	his new bike.

Exercises — The N V N Pattern

A. Make a chart like the one above. Label the three columns *N*, *V*, and *N*. Write these sentences on the chart.

1. Therese plays the flute.
2. Phyllis copied Terry.
3. My dog watches TV.
4. Andy took a deep breath.
5. We cheered our goalie.
6. Saturn has ten moons.
7. Both arrows hit the target.
8. Martin rode the train.

B. Copy this chart. Complete each sentence in the N V N pattern. *Answers will vary.*

N	V	N
1. Angela	pushed	_____.
2. _____	measured	_____.
3. Don	_____	carrots.
4. _____	answered	the phone.
5. This kitten	chases	_____.

C. Make a chart of your own for the N V N pattern. Write five sentences in the N V N pattern. *Answers will vary.*

Sentence Patterns — The N LV N Pattern

A sentence in the **N LV N pattern** has three parts. The first N stands for the subject noun. LV stands for a linking verb. *Linking verb* is another name for *state-of-being verb*. The second N stands for the noun that follows the linking verb.

N	LV	N
Janet	is	an artist.
Ralph	is	her brother.
The best speller	was	Linn.
Pine	is	a soft wood.
My skates	were	a birthday present.

Exercises — The N LV N Pattern

A. Make a chart like the one above. Label the three columns *N, LV,* and *N.* Write these sentences on the chart.

1. Tomatoes are fruits.
2. This game is a challenge.
3. Africa is a continent.
4. My partner was Reba.
5. The boys were friends.
6. Larry is a joker.
7. Nutmeg is a spice.
8. These dogs are poodles.

B. Make a chart like the one below. Complete each sentence in the N LV N pattern. *Answers will vary.*

N	LV	N
1. The last batter	was	_____.
2. _____	are	insects.
3. Juan	_____	a good swimmer.
4. _____	was	_____.
5. _____	is	a new invention.

C. Make a chart of your own. Write five sentences in the N LV N pattern. *Answers will vary.*

Sentence Patterns

Objective

To recognize the basic word order in the N LV N sentence pattern

Presenting the Lesson

1. Read and discuss page 151. You might find it helpful to talk about the meaning and use of something that *links* (joins, brings together) and relate it to the *linking verb.* Make it clear that, as with the N V and N V N patterns, each part of an N LV N sentence may have one or more than one word.

2. Assign and discuss Exercises A, B, and C on page 151.

Optional Practice

Have students make a chart for the N LV N pattern. Tell them to fill in a subject noun from the following list. They should choose a matching linking verb and a noun to follow it and fill in the entire sentence. Remind them to capitalize and punctuate where necessary.

N (subject)	LV	N (after LV)
1. flowers	is	fish
2. cauliflower	are	cookies
3. hamburgers		a vegetable
4. rolls		candies
5. tuna		plants
6. peppermints		bread
7. vanilla wafers		a dessert
8. ice cream		meat

Additional Exercises

If these Exercises were not used with each lesson, they may now be assigned for chapter review.

Additional Exercises

Using Verbs

A. Using Verbs (Use after page 129.)

Number your paper from 1 to 10. Write the verb in each of the following sentences. After the verb, write *Action* or *State-of-being* to tell what kind of verb it is.

A = Action Verb
SB = State-of-being Verb

1. Spiderman climbed (A) the building.
2. Roberta is (SB) a Hula-Hoop champion.
3. Fozzie Bear wore (A) a top hat.
4. The runners were (SB) thirsty.
5. I am (SB) a doughnut lover.
6. The tadpole changed (A) into a frog.
7. Janice wiggled (A) her ears.
8. Carolyn is (SB) an aunt now.
9. Tom and Sheila waded (A) in the fountain.
10. You are (SB) good at checkers.

B. Finding Main Verbs and Helping Verbs (Use after page 134.)

Number your paper from 1 to 10. Make two columns. Head the first column *Helping Verbs*. Head the second *Main Verbs*. Write the verbs for each of these sentences in the proper column.

HV = Helping Verb
MV = Main Verb

1. Did (HV) you see (MV) Princess Leia?
2. Pete and Michelle are (HV) not watching (MV) TV.
3. Where does (HV) the eagle build (MV) its nest?
4. Dennis has (HV) never played (MV) in left field.
5. Claire will (HV) always be (MV) my friend.
6. The weather has (HV) suddenly become (MV) warm.
7. Have (HV) you taken (MV) the bus to school?

8. The Tigers could probably beat the Rangers. [HV: could, MV: beat]
9. Buddy wouldn't pose for a picture. [HV: wouldn't, MV: pose]
10. Ms. Drew had carefully printed the list. [HV: had, MV: printed]

C. Using Direct Objects (Use after page 137.)

Copy the following sentences. Underline the verb twice. Draw a circle around the direct object.

1. The movers packed the (truck).
2. Angela served (sandwiches) at her party.
3. Bert will frame this (picture).
4. At the movie, we bought (popcorn).
5. The police officer was directing (traffic).
6. Scientists have measured (distances) between stars.
7. Fire destroyed the (hotel).
8. Danielle was carrying her (books).
9. I can climb any (tree).
10. Sherman might have seen this (movie) before.

D. Using the Right Form of *Be* (Use after page 139.)

Number your paper from 1 to 10. Choose the right form of *be* from the parentheses. Write it down.

1. Paul Simon (**is**, are) singing.
2. I (is, **am**, are) in charge of clean-up.
3. Carlos and Heather (was, **were**) teammates.
4. We (**will be**, be) playing kickball.
5. You (was, **were**) making me laugh.
6. I (been, **have been**) thinking of a better plan.
7. Snoopy (be, **is**) Charlie Brown's dog.
8. (Was, **Were**) I talking too fast?
9. Hurry up! You (is, **are**) taking too long.
10. The girls (is, **are**) jumping rope.

E. Using the Right Verb after *There, Here,* and *Where*
(Use after page 141.)

Number your paper from 1 to 10. Find the subject of each of the sentences below. Write it down. Then choose the correct form of the verb *be* from the parentheses. Write it after the subject.

1. There (is, are) the caboose.
2. Here (is, are) your badminton racket.
3. Where (was, were) the first settlements?
4. There (was, were) enough taffy apples.
5. Where (was, were) the ski slope?
6. Here (is, are) the fire trucks.
7. There (was, were) many stars on that show.
8. Here (is, are) my allowance.
9. Where (is, are) Sanibel Island?
10. There (is, are) fifty states in the United States.

F. Using the Right Verb (Use after page 145.)

Number your paper from 1 to 10. Choose the right verb from the parentheses. Write it down.

1. Does your dog (set, sit) on command?
2. The guards won't (let, leave) us past.
3. (May, Can) I please read that comic book?
4. Mom (taught, learned) a class in yoga.
5. (Set, Sit) the cookie jar here.
6. Did you (let, leave) some dessert for Dad?
7. Marka (may, can) punt farther than Sherry.
8. My class will (teach, learn) Spanish.
9. The jury (sets, sits) in a special room.
10. (Let, Leave) Tommy open the mail.

G. Making Contractions Correctly (Use after page 147.)

Copy the following sentences. Make a contraction of the underlined words in each sentence.

1. He will introduce you to Benjie.   He'll
2. She has eaten three cupcakes.   She's
3. My friends have not arrived yet.   haven't
4. They are ice skating at the park.   They're
5. What is your answer?   What's
6. It is too cold for a picnic.   It's
7. Marguerite does not like crossword puzzles.   doesn't
8. Where is the storage room?   Where's
9. The broken door would not budge.   wouldn't
10. He would like to run a steam shovel.   He'd

H. Using Negatives Correctly (Use after page 149.)

Copy these sentences. Choose the right word from the parentheses.

1. Milton (has, hasn't) never missed "Happy Days."
2. The police can't find (any, no) clues.
3. Isabella didn't like (anything, nothing) on the menu.
4. Nobody (will, won't) miss recess.
5. This maze doesn't lead (nowhere, anywhere).
6. Aren't (any, none) of the actors ready?
7. Can't (no one, anyone) pitch a curve?
8. Most of us haven't (ever, never) seen a jungle.
9. That tire (has, doesn't have) no air.
10. Nobody (wasn't, was) watching the robot.

Chapter 11

Using Pronouns

Chapter Objectives

1. To understand the function of the pronoun, and to identify pronouns in sentences
2. To use pronouns correctly as subjects of sentences, particularly in compound subjects
3. To use pronouns correctly after state-of-being verbs
4. To use pronouns correctly as objects in sentences, particularly in compound objects
5. To use *we* and *us* correctly
6. To identify and use the possessive pronouns correctly

Preparing the Students

Ask students to tell you about the picture on page 157. Perhaps write some of the sentences or noun phrases they use on the board. Then say those same sentences or phrases, using pronouns to substitute for the nouns. Ask students what the difference is. Ask how they know what the pronouns refer to. Stress that they need to know the noun referred to in order to understand the meaning of the pronoun.

Additional Resources

Diagnostic Test—page 432 in this T.E. Recommended for use before teaching the chapter.
Mastery Test—pages 460 and 461 in this T.E. Recommended for use after teaching the chapter.
Additional Mastery Test—Recommended for use after any necessary reteaching. (In separate booklet, *Mastery Tests, Silver Level*, pages 23 and 24.)
Skills Practice Book—pages 59–65
Duplicating Masters—pages 59–65

Part 1 Substituting Pronouns for Nouns

Read the two paragraphs that follow. Which paragraph sounds more natural?

1

Pam and *Carla* wanted to earn money to go to the movie. *Pam* and *Carla* asked *Pam's* and *Carla's* mothers for a job. *Pam's* and *Carla's* mothers told *Pam* and *Carla* that *Pam* and *Carla* could wash the family cars. *Pam* and *Carla* worked hard. *Pam* and *Carla* earned enough money for the movie.

Part 1

Objective

To understand the function of the pronoun, and to identify pronouns in sentences

Presenting the Lesson

1. Read and discuss pages 157 to 159. Point out that the second sample paragraph on page 158 not only sounds better, but is easier to write and say. Ask students for sentences using the pronouns listed on page 159.

2. Assign and discuss Exercises A, B, and C on pages 159 and 160. It might be helpful to discuss Exercises A and B before assigning C. Ask students to work the arithmetic problem given in Exercise C. (The answer is 22 feet.)

3. Use Exercise A on page 171 for additional practice or review.

Extending the Lesson

Have students list five people they know (such as family members, friends, or neighbors), five things in their house or apartment, and five animals. Next to each noun they should write every pronoun listed on page 159 that could refer to it.

Example: My aunt Cleo—she, her, hers, you, your, yours

2

Pam and *Carla* wanted to earn money to go to the movie. *They* asked *their* mothers for a job. *Their* mothers told *them* that *they* could wash the family cars. *Pam* and *Carla* worked hard. *They* earned enough money for the movie.

Did you decide that the second paragraph sounds more natural? What sounded strange about the first paragraph?

You were probably tired of hearing *Pam* and *Carla* over and over again. In the third sentence alone, *Pam* and *Carla* appeared three times.

How did the second paragraph avoid using the names *Pam* and *Carla* too often? Try to find the places where the following words were used instead of the girls' names: *They, their, them.*

The words *they, their,* and *them* are **pronouns.** Use of the pronouns in the second paragraph did not change the meaning of the paragraph, but it improved the sound.

> A **pronoun** is a word used in place of a noun.

You use pronouns to do three things.

1. To refer to yourself:

   I asked *my* mother to give *me* a ride.

2. To refer to the person you are talking to:

   Did *you* bring *your* camera?

3. To refer to other persons, places, or things:

   The people ran from the lion. *They* were afraid of *it.*

Like nouns, pronouns can be singular or plural. Usually, the whole word changes to make different forms.

Singular Pronouns			
Person Speaking:	I	my, mine	me
Person Spoken To:	you	your, yours	you
Other Persons, Places, and Things:	he	his	him
	she	her, hers	her
	it	its	it

Plural Pronouns			
Person Speaking:	we	our, ours	us
Persons Spoken To:	you	your, yours	you
Other Persons, Places, and Things:	they	their, theirs	them

Exercises **Using Pronouns for Nouns**

A. Copy the following sentences. Underline the pronouns.

1. I wore my new boots today.
2. Katy displayed her model ships.
3. Steve, do you read comic books?
4. Dad brought me to the roller rink.
5. The horse tugged at its reins.
6. Roger told us a secret.
7. She took the rock and skipped it across the water.
8. The waitress asked them for their order.
9. Carrie threw snowballs at him and me.
10. We rubbed our fingers to keep them warm.

B. Copy the sentences below. Use pronouns instead of nouns where they will make the sentences sound better.

1. Ted ran in the 50-yard dash. ~~Ted~~ *He* was the winner.
2. Maria likes baseball. ~~Maria~~ *She* plays every Saturday.
3. The dog has rabies. ~~The dog~~ *It* is dangerous.
4. The men saw Jim walking down the road. ~~The men~~ *They* waited for ~~Jim~~ *him*.
5. Betty brought ~~Betty's~~ *her* new book to school.
6. Tom and I are neighbors. ~~Tom and I~~ *We* walk to school together.
7. The boys wore ~~the boys'~~ *their* best suits for the school program.
8. Sam is Lisa's brother. ~~Sam~~ *He* is two years older than ~~Lisa~~ *she* is.
9. The puppy played with ~~the puppy's~~ *its* bone.
10. Toni, would ~~Toni~~ *you* lend me ~~Toni's~~ *your* pencil, please?

C. Number your paper from 1 to 5. In the following arithmetic problem, the pronouns are underlined. Copy each pronoun. After each pronoun, write the noun or nouns it stands for.

1. Cathy and Larry made a wire pen. <u>They</u> *[Cathy and Larry]* made <u>it</u> *[pen]* for some rabbits.
2. First, <u>they</u> *[Cathy and Larry]* drew a plan for <u>it</u> *[pen]*.
3. Larry said, "<u>We</u> *[Cathy and Larry]* will make <u>it</u> *[pen]* five feet wide and six feet long."
4. Cathy said, "<u>We</u> *[Cathy and Larry]* need ten feet of wire for the short sides."
5. How much wire did <u>they</u> *[Cathy and Larry]* need for all the sides?

Part 2 Using Pronouns as Subjects

The subject of a sentence tells who or what does something. Find the subject of each of these sentences:

1. I visited my uncle.
2. He gave me a ride on his motorcycle.
3. We drove along River Road.

Did you find that the subjects were the pronouns *I*, *He*, and *We*? These are three of the pronouns we use often as subjects. Four others are *you*, *she*, *it*, and *they*.

Usually we have no trouble using these pronouns as subjects. However, when there are two parts in a subject, we sometimes get confused.

Which of these sentences is correct?

Rita and she played together.
Rita and her played together.

The first sentence is correct.
To figure out which pronoun to use, try each part separately.

Rita played.
She played.

Then put the two parts together, using the same pronoun.
Follow the same plan when there are two pronouns in the subject.

(She, her) and (I, me) took piano lessons.
She took piano lessons. I took piano lessons.
She and I took piano lessons.

Part 2

Objective

To use pronouns correctly as subjects of sentences, particularly in compound subjects

Presenting the Lesson

1. Read and discuss pages 161 and 162. Ask students for other examples of sentences using pronouns as subjects.
2. You may find it helpful to do Exercise A on page 163 with the students. Have them try each part of the subject in each example separately, as the text suggests. Assign and discuss Exercise B.
3. Use Exercise B on page 171 as additional practice or review.

Optional Practice

Put the following sentences on the board or a worksheet. Have students insert a subject pronoun that makes sense in the blank in each sentence.

1. My brother looked for his watch. _____ was under the chair.
2. Those are library books. _____ are on the top shelf.
3. My sister sews. _____ made a dress for herself.
4. My father likes to barbecue. _____ does a good job.
5. _____ asked my friend to go with me.
6. _____ won our baseball game yesterday.

Here are two important rules for you to study about using pronouns as the subject of a sentence.

1. These pronouns may be used as the subject:

   I   we   you   he   she   it   they

   These pronouns may *not* be used as the subject:

   me   us   him   her   them

2. If the pronoun *I* is used with another noun or pronoun as the subject of a sentence, put *I* last.

   Rafael and I were there. He and I bought a present.

Pick a Subject Pronoun.

Nancy and _____ are friends.

Exercises **Using Pronouns in the Subject**

A. Copy the sentences below. Choose the right pronoun from the two in parentheses.

1. Frances and (I, me) are going to a party.
2. Jane and (her, she) will be there.
3. Donald and (them, they) often visit me.
4. Philip and (he, him) went to the circus.
5. (Juan and I, I and Juan) ate the cookies.
6. (I and Donna, Donna and I) watched the parade.
7. Ms. Coburn and (we, us) saw a movie yesterday.
8. Eva and (me, I) will finish the work.
9. (He, Him) and his mother painted his room.
10. You and (I, me) make a good team.

B. Choose the right pronoun from the two in parentheses. Write the correct pronoun on your paper.

1. Lydia and (I, me) started quarreling.
2. Rusty and (them, they) don't play fairly.
3. Elena and (she, her) demonstrated a roundoff.
4. Someday you and (me, I) will play first string.
5. (I and Joanne, Joanne and I) apologized to Kim.
6. My parents and (I, me) had a conference.
7. Uncle Jerry and (we, us) ate dinner at Pizza Hut.
8. Alex and (he, him) are best friends.
9. Julena and (they, them) raced for the front seat.
10. (She, Her) and Carl caught two trout.
11. (Calvin and I, I and Calvin) left early.
12. Josh and (him, he) shared the reward.
13. The teachers and (they, them) boarded the bus.
14. Mary Ann and (she, her) built a model ship.
15. Dad and (us, we) take hikes on weekends.

Part 3

Objective

To use pronouns correctly after state-of-being verbs.

Presenting the Lesson

1. Read and discuss page 164.
2. Assign and discuss the Exercise on page 164.
3. Use Exercise C on page 172 as additional practice or review.

Optional Practice

Write the sentences below on the board. Have students rewrite them putting the pronoun *before* the state-of-being verb.

Example: The boy is he.
He is the boy.

1. The fastest swimmers are they.
2. The best singer is she.
3. The contest winners were she and I.
4. The crossing guards are Mr. Jones and she.
5. The clerks at the grocery are Mrs. Allan and he.

Part 3 Using Pronouns After State-of-Being Verbs

Read these two sentences.

The doctor is she.
She is the doctor.

The sentences mean the same thing. As you see, the pronoun following *is* can be made the subject without changing the meaning of the sentence. The same is true with pronouns that follow the other state-of-being verbs *are, was, were,* and *will be*.

Change these sentences without changing their meaning.

The best player was he.
The semi-finalists were Dan and I.
The teams in the playoffs will be the Jays and we.

After the state-of-being verbs, use these pronouns:

I   we   you   he   she   it   they

Exercise **Choosing the Right Pronoun**

Choose the right pronoun. Write it on your paper.

1. The new library aides are Darla and (he, him).
2. Tim's closest neighbors are Lee and (I, me).
3. The family's biggest eaters are Dad and (her, she).
4. The only shoppers left were (them, they).
5. Your biggest fans are Deena and (me, I).
6. The lifeguards are Molly and (I, me).
7. The cooks for the banquet are Candy and (him, he).
8. The co-captains are Sandra and (I, me).

Part 4 Using Pronouns as Objects

Which pronoun should be used in each of these sentences?

1. The cat scratched (they, them).
2. Eddie asked Rani and (she, her) a question.
3. Divide the candy among (we, us) now.

If you are not sure which pronoun to use in a sentence, first decide if the missing pronoun is in the subject or follows a state-of-being verb. You know that if the pronoun is in the subject or follows a state-of-being verb, you use *I, we, he, she,* and *they.* If the missing pronoun is not in either of those two places, you use *me, us, him, her,* or *them.*

> If a pronoun is not in the subject and does not follow a state-of-being verb, use these pronouns:
>
> **me   us   him   her   them**
>
> Use these pronouns in any part of the sentence:
>
> **you   it**

In Example 1 above, the subject is *cat*. Since the missing pronoun is not in the subject, we cannot use *they*. The correct sentence is *The cat scratched them.*

In Example 2, what is the subject? Is the missing pronoun in the subject? Since the missing pronoun is not in the subject, we cannot use *she*. The correct sentence is *Eddie asked Rani and her a question.*

In Example 3, there is an understood subject, *you*. The missing pronoun is not in that subject. The correct sentence is *Divide the candy among us now.*

2. Make two large signs: *action verb & object pronoun* and *state-of-being verb & subject pronoun*. Use different colors (red for "action verb" and blue for "state-of-being verb") to help distinguish the two. Put the signs at the front of the room.

Make flashcards, each card showing a sentence from the Exercises on pages 164 and 166, or similar sentences. Make sure both types of sentences are represented on the flashcards. Divide the class into two or more equal teams, and then distribute the flashcards so that each member has a sentence. Call on individual students to read each sentence aloud with a pronoun choice, state what the verb is and which kind it is, and stand to the side of the correct sign. The team with the greatest number of correct choices wins.

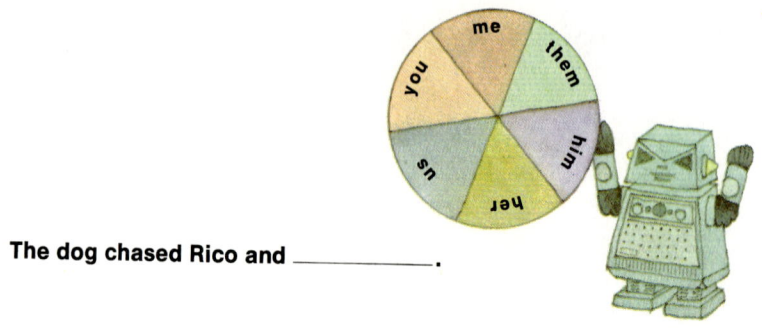

The dog chased Rico and _____.

Exercises   Using Pronouns as Objects

A. Choose the right pronoun. Write it on your paper.

1. Mildred put makeup on Hal and (she, her).
2. The car almost hit Bill and (I, me).
3. Would you like to visit Peter and (we, us)?
3. Sue chose Brian and (she, her) for the team.
5. Eduardo's mother called (him, he) and his brother.
6. Louella finally found Marion and (they, them).
7. Telephone Mike and (I, me) after the game.
8. Mary Lou and (me, I) went to the shore.
9. Dad gave June and (I, me) a ride.
10. Can you give Arlene and (she, her) your address?

B. Follow the directions for Exercise A.

1. Lightning struck near Frank and (us, we).
2. Jody's father sent his mother and (he, him) a postcard from Kansas City.
3. The little poodle greeted Anna and (she, her).
4. Did you meet Valerie and (she, her) at the park?
5. I made chocolate sundaes for (them, they) and me.
6. A loud crash frightened Angelo and (we, us).
7. The officer handcuffed Mills and (he, him).
8. Hit some fly balls to Emily and (me, I).
9. Mrs. Kee settled the argument between Josh and (I, me).
10. Take Roberto and (she, her) to their seats.

Part 5 Using *We* and *Us*

Read each pair of sentences. Which sentence is correct?

1. We boys are going hiking.
   Us boys are going hiking.

2. Have you ever seen us girls in a hockey game?
   Have you ever seen we girls in a hockey game?

Try the sentences above without the word *boys* or the word *girls*. You will see that in the first example the pronoun is in the subject. *We* is the correct pronoun. In the second example, the pronoun is in the object. *Us* is the correct choice.

Exercises Choosing the Right Pronoun

A. Copy these sentences, using the right pronoun in each.

1. (We, Us) boys went on a hike.
2. Mother sent (we, us) girls to the store.
3. (We, Us) cyclists took our lunch with us.
4. In the woods (we, us) hikers saw a deer.
5. The dragon costume is for (we, us) two.
6. After lunch, (we, us) gardeners rested for a long time.
7. Nora played for (we, us) campers on her harmonica.
8. Terence told (we, us) Scouts a ghost story.
9. The food was divided among (we, us) four.
10. This present is from (we, us) students.

B. Choose the right pronoun from the two in parentheses. Write it down.

1. (We, Us) girls took the bus downtown.
2. The tame pony nuzzled (we, us) visitors.
3. (We, Us) boys had a tug-of-war.

4. Finally, Jamie spotted (we, <u>us</u>) wanderers.
5. (<u>We</u>, Us) six planned a farewell party.
6. A net fell on top of (we, <u>us</u>) girls.
7. The child asked (we, <u>us</u>) bystanders for help.
8. The sixth-graders challenged (we, <u>us</u>) fifth-graders.
9. Together (<u>we</u>, us) swimmers pulled the boat to shore.
10. An acrobat performed for (we, <u>us</u>) boys.

Part 6 Possessive Pronouns

To make the possessive form of a noun, you add an apostrophe or an apostrophe and *s* to the noun. Pronouns have special possessive forms. These do not use apostrophes at all.

> These are the possessive forms of pronouns:
>
> **my, mine**   **our, ours**
>
> **your, yours**
>
> **his, her, hers, its**   **their, theirs**

Some possessive pronouns may be used before a noun. They identify ownership of that noun. Others may be used by themselves. They identify ownership of the nouns they follow.

Examples:

This is **my** coat.	The coat is **mine**.
That is **your** hat.	The hat is **yours**.
We have **our** clothes.	These clothes are **ours**.
Here is **his** dog.	The dog is **his**.
Here is **her** cat.	The cat is **hers**.
Here are **their** pets.	The pets are **theirs**.

Using *Its* and *It's*

The major problem most people have with possessive pronouns is confusing the possessive *its* with the contraction *it's*. *Its* (without an apostrophe) is the possessive form of *it*. *It's* (with an apostrophe) means *it is* or *it has*.

> That book is missing *its* cover. (The cover belongs to the book).
>
> *It's* a library book. (*It is* a library book.)

Exercises **Using Possessive Pronouns and *It's***

A. Copy each of the following sentences. Where there is a blank, write a possessive pronoun according to the information in the parentheses.

> Examples: I found _____ notebook. (The notebook belongs to you.)
>
> I found your notebook.
>
> That jacket is _____. (The jacket belongs to him.)
>
> That jacket is his.

1. _Your_ handwriting can be read easily. (The handwriting belongs to you.)
2. Did you see _their_ faces? (The faces belong to them.)
3. Those keys are _yours_. (The keys belong to you.)
4. Next comes _his_ turn. (The turn belongs to him.)
5. The error is _hers_. (The error was made by her.)
6. The reward is _ours_. (The reward belongs to us.)
7. This is _our_ chance. (The chance belongs to us.)
8. The fingerprints are _his_. (The fingerprints belong to him.)

Extending the Lesson

Make sure students can explain the difference in meaning between *its* and *it's*. Then discuss the differences between *they're*, *their*, and *there*. Have the students find examples in their textbooks or independent reading of all five words used correctly. Ask them to keep a separate list of sentences or other instances (such as signs or labels) in which the words are used incorrectly.

9. That was _____ book. (The book belongs to me.)
10. The red car is _____. (The car belongs to them.)

B. Copy the following sentences. Insert apostrophes where they are needed.

1. It's a home run!
2. It's raining outside.
3. The leopard chased its prey.
4. What is its title?
5. The spaniel dropped its bone.
6. Mom makes candy, and it's great.
7. The railroad stopped its service to Clinton.
8. Our school has its own hockey team.
9. Grandpa has a beard. It's white and thick.
10. It's the championship game today.

C. Follow the directions for Exercise B.

1. The gum lost its flavor.
2. It's a wig, isn't it?
3. The cat licked its paws.
4. I have a Frisbee, and it's green.
5. It's the largest mountain in the United States.
6. I like this program and its stars.
7. It's an X-ray machine.
8. The hospital has a cafeteria for its staff.
9. I rode Thunder. It's a very patient horse.
10. The earth revolves on its axis.

Additional Exercises

Using Pronouns

Additional Exercises

If these Exercises were not used with each lesson, they may now be used for chapter review.

A. Using Pronouns for Nouns (Use after page 159.)

Copy the following sentences. Underline the pronouns.

1. We share a locker.
2. She framed her picture.
3. I forgot my lines.
4. He is a firefighter.
5. Dede, are you wearing jeans?
6. The crowds surprised us.
7. She watches too much television.
8. The teacher found it in her desk.
9. He checked our car's engine.
10. I went on the Ferris wheel with them.

B. Using Pronouns in the Subject (Use after page 162.)

Copy the sentences below. Choose the right pronoun.

1. The other campers and (us, we) miss our counselor.
2. The twins and (them, they) went on a hayride.
3. Wes and (I, me) mow lawns.
4. Lavonne and (he, him) talked to the teacher.
5. (She, Her) and her dad carved the pumpkin.
6. (Wilson and I, I and Wilson) traded cards.
7. My sister and (me, I) toured the White House.
8. Judy and (she, her) gathered firewood.
9. (Vincent and I, I and Vincent) wear the same shoe size.
10. Bonita and (them, they) work at an ice rink.

C. Using Pronouns after State-of-Being Verbs
(Use after page 164.)

Choose the right pronoun from the two in parentheses. Write it down.

1. The next batters will be Sammy and (she, her).
2. The dancers in that show are Fay and (me, I).
3. The finalists were Paula and (he, him).
4. My favorite singers are the Bee Gees and (them, they).
5. The youngest Eagle Scouts were Charley and (he, him).
6. The swimming instructors are Cleo and (me, I).
7. The judges of the contest are Mr. Parks and (she, her).
8. The owners of the model airplane are Joseph and (him, he).
9. Our family's dishwashers are my brother and (I, me).
10. The girls in the picture are Lila and (her, she).

D. Using Pronouns as Objects (Use after page 165.)

Choose the right pronoun from the two in parentheses. Write it down.

1. Bees stung both Beverly and (he, him).
2. Meg introduced Allan and (I, me).
3. Dad called Mom and (us, we) from Toledo.
4. The weaver showed Mr. Mohr and (we, us) her loom.
5. The gingerbread house was made by (him, he) and Sally.
6. A family of raccoons followed Lars and (he, him).
7. The leads are played by (she, her) and Chad.
8. Randi brought Andrea and (I, me) presents.
9. My friends went with my brother and (I, me).
10. The miniature railroad was constructed by Vinnie and (she, her).

E. **Using *We* and *Us*** (Use after page 167.)

Choose the right pronoun from the two in parentheses. Write it.

1. (<u>We</u>, Us) two shared a popsicle.
2. My uncle teases (we, <u>us</u>) boys.
3. Jesse and (<u>we</u>, us) helpers made ice cream.
4. The beekeeper showed (we, <u>us</u>) 4-H members a honeycomb.
5. (<u>We</u>, Us) dancers appreciated *The Nutcracker Suite*.
6. Dave sprayed (we, <u>us</u>) girls with the hose.
7. A jellyfish swam by (we, <u>us</u>) boys.
8. For dessert, (<u>we</u>, us) campers roasted marshmallows.
9. Miss Jones handed the trophy to (we, <u>us</u>) winners.
10. In the program (<u>we</u>, us) girls played Santa's elves.

F. **Using Possessive Pronouns** (Use after page 169.)

Copy each of the following sentences. Where there is a blank, write a possessive pronoun according to the information in the parentheses.

1. __His__ smile cheers me up. (The smile belongs to him.)
2. I changed __my__ clothes. (The clothes belong to me.)
3. One mitten is __yours__. (The mitten belongs to you.)
4. They bathed __their__ dog. (The dog belongs to them.)
5. This is __our__ lunchtime. (The lunchtime belongs to us.)
6. That locker is __hers__. (The locker belongs to her.)
7. That hammer is __theirs__. (The hammer belongs to them.)
8. The bird built __its__ nest. (The nest belongs to it.)
9. Do you bite __your__ nails? (The nails belong to you.)
10. The pleasure is __mine__. (The pleasure belongs to me.)

Chapter 12

Using Irregular Verbs Correctly

Part 1 Regular Verbs

When we use the basic form of a verb, as in *they dance*, we mean that the action is happening now. For subjects that are singular, we simply add an *s* to the basic form. All the following examples express actions that are happening in the **present.**

    he works   we play

    she paints   you carry

    it stops   they dance

The subjects *I* and *you* are exceptions. *I* always refers to one person, but it does not follow the rule for singular subjects. *You*

Chapter Objectives

1. To understand the function of the principal parts of the verb in forming the present and past tenses of regular verbs

2. To differentiate between regular and irregular verbs, and to become familiar with the principal parts of common irregular verbs

Preparing the Students

Discuss the meanings of the words *regular* (follows a certain order) and *irregular* (different from the normal). Explain that this chapter will give information about verbs that are regular or irregular.

Additional Resources

Mastery Test—pages 462 and 463 in this T.E. Recommended for use after teaching the chapter.

Additional Mastery Test—Recommended for use after any necessary reteaching. (In separate booklet, *Mastery Tests, Silver Level,* pages 25 and 26.)

Skills Practice Book—pages 66–70

Duplicating Masters—pages 66–70

Midyear Test—pages 464–467 in this T.E. Recommended for use after teaching this chapter, to review Chapters 1 through 12.

Additional Midyear Test—Recommended for use after any necessary reteaching. (In separate booklet, *Mastery Tests, Silver Level,* pages 27–30.)

Part 1

Objective

To understand the function of the principal parts of the verb in forming the present and past tenses of regular verbs

Presenting the Lesson

1. Read and discuss pages 175 and 176. Have students talk about the picture on page 175. Write on the board the regular verbs they use, in the present form. Have them tell the past form for each of these verbs. The spelling changes mentioned briefly at the bottom of page 176 are discussed in greater depth in Chapter 27.

2. Assign and discuss the Exercise on page 177.

3. Read and discuss pages 177 and 178. Refer once more to the picture on page 175 or use another picture. Again write on the board the regular verbs used to describe the picture (in present form). Have students change the verbs to the past form with helping verbs, using any of the helping verbs on pages 177 and 178.

4. Assign and discuss Exercises A and B on page 179.

Optional Practice

In each of the following sentences, have students underline the verb twice. Next to the sentence, they are to write whether the verb is in the *present, past,* or *past with helping verb* form.

Example: The train <u>roared</u> down the track. past

1. That clown laughs all the time.
2. The librarian had ordered the books.
3. Some flowers bloom early.
4. The boy zipped his jacket.
5. The Harlem Globetrotters have played hundreds of basketball games.
6. The juggler tossed the balls high.
7. I feed my fish every morning.
8. The puppets jump up and down.

may refer to one person, but it never follows the rule for singular subjects, either. For *I* and *you,* the verb form always stays the same.

    I talk   you call

Often we talk or write about an action that has already happened. We say it happened in the **past.** How can we change the basic form of the verb to show action in the past? If you are not sure of an answer, study the examples below to see how they were changed. Now they express action completed in the past. We call this form the **past form.**

I talked	we played
you called	you carried
he worked	they danced
she painted	
it stopped	

All the verbs in the examples follow the usual rule for expressing action in the past. They add the ending *-ed.* Most of our verbs follow this rule. All the verbs that add *-ed* to make the past form are called **regular verbs.**

> **Regular verbs** express action that happened in the past by adding the ending *-ed* to the basic form.

You probably noticed three examples that had to follow spelling rules as well as the rule about adding the *-ed* ending. When we change *stop* to *stopped,* we have to double the final consonant after the single vowel before adding the ending. When we change *carry* to *carried,* we change the *y* to *i* before adding *ed.* When we change *dance* to *danced,* we have to drop the final *e* before adding the ending.

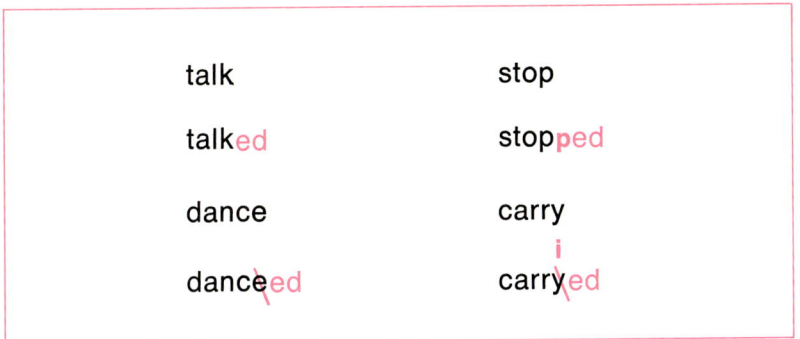

Exercise Changing Regular Verbs To Express the Past

Number your paper from 1 to 12. Change each of the following verbs to express the past by adding -ed. Follow the necessary spelling rules.

1. march — marched
2. number — numbered
3. order — ordered
4. hop — hopped
5. color — colored
6. slam — slammed
7. hammer — hammered
8. hope — hoped
9. finish — finished
10. hurry — hurried
11. gaze — gazed
12. walk — walked

Using the Helping Verbs *Has, Have,* and *Had*

There is a second way to express action that happened in the past. This way is by using the helping verbs *has*, *have*, or *had* with the past form. Here are examples of this second past form of verbs:

I have talked
we have played
you have called
he has worked
she has painted
it has stopped
they have danced

I had talked
we had played
you had called
he had worked
she had painted
it had stopped
they had danced

Extending the Lesson

Have students write ten sentences about things they do, using regular action verbs in the present form. They should underline the verb in each sentence twice. Then they should rewrite the sentences twice, first putting the verb in the past form, then putting it in the past with helping verb form (using *has* or *have*).

Example: I walk to school.
I walked to school.
I have walked to school.

Using Other Helping Verbs

We can use many other helping verbs with the past form. The verbs we make with these other helping verbs do not always express action in the past. Here are a few examples:

it is stopped	it will be stopped
it is being stopped	it should be stopped
it was stopped	it might have been stopped
it has been stopped	it will have been stopped

All this information in Part 1 can be put together in a simple chart, like the one below. The first column of the chart shows the basic form of the verb. The second column shows the past form that is used without helping verbs. The third column shows the past form that can be used with different helping verbs. For all regular verbs, the second and third columns are the same.

Present	Past	Past with Helping Verbs
talk	talked	talked
call	called	called
paint	painted	painted
work	worked	worked
play	played	played
stop	stopped	stopped
grab	grabbed	grabbed
carry	carried	carried
hurry	hurried	hurried
dance	danced	danced
save	saved	saved
trade	traded	traded

Exercises **Using Regular Verbs**

A. Number your paper from 1 to 10. Write the form asked for in the parentheses following each verb. Use *has* or *have* to make the Past Form with Helping Verbs.

Example: touch (past with helping verbs)

have touched

1. like (past) liked
2. crash (present) crash(es)
3. raise (past with helping verbs) has raised, have raised
4. add (past) added
5. cover (past) covered
6. fix (past with helping verbs) has fixed, have fixed
7. subtract (past with helping verbs) has subtracted, have subtracted
8. notice (present) notice(s)
9. move (past) moved
10. marry (past with helping verbs) has married, have married

B. Write a sentence for each verb below. Use the verb form asked for in the parentheses following the verb. Use *has* or *have* to make the Past Form with Helping Verbs.

Answers will vary.

Example: fill (past)

Nancy filled the thermos.

1. squeal (past) squealed
2. show (past) showed
3. park (present) park(s)
4. change (past with helping verbs) has changed, have changed
5. help (present) help(s)
6. use (past with helping verbs) has used, had used
7. remember (past with helping verbs) has remembered, had remembered
8. happen (present) happen(s)
9. bury (past with helping verbs) has buried, have buried
10. measure (past) measured

stopped

should have stopped

Part 2

Objective

To differentiate between regular and irregular verbs, and to become familiar with the principal parts of common irregular verbs

Presenting the Lesson

1. Read and discuss page 180.

2. You might find it helpful to read the list of irregular verbs on page 181 aloud in a rhythmical manner, having students repeat each set after you. If this is successful, you may wish to do it periodically until the students become more familiar with the correct forms of the irregular verbs.

3. Eighteen special pages on irregular verbs are located on pages 405 to 424 of this Teacher's Edition. The pages provide practice with these verbs:

begin	eat	run
break	fall	see
choose	give	sing
come	go	take
do	grow	throw
drink	know	write

Before assigning these pages, administer the diagnostic test (page 406). Assign only those practice pages a student demonstrates need for. Assign and discuss each of the practice pages individually. They should not be presented as an uninterrupted unit.

Part 2 Irregular Verbs

There are about sixty verbs that do not make the past form by adding *-ed* to the present. Some of them have a separate, third form to be used with helping verbs. Here are some examples:

Present	Past	Past with Helping Verbs
eat	ate	eaten
drink	drank	drunk
sleep	slept	slept
go	went	gone
run	ran	run

These verbs are not regular verbs. They are called **irregular verbs.**

Irregular verbs are important because many of them are verbs we use frequently. We cannot avoid them.

In order to use them properly, you must know the correct form that is used alone to mean past action. You must also know the correct form that is used with helping verbs. Since the irregular verbs do not follow rules, you must study and memorize as many of these verb forms as possible.

On the next page is a list of the most commonly used irregular verbs. Read through all of the verbs. Study the verbs that give you trouble. Refer to the list when you are unsure of the correct form.

When you are using irregular verbs, remember these rules:

1. The past form is used by itself, without a helping verb.

The dragon *ate* the knight.

2. The Past Form with Helping Verbs is always used with a helping verb.

It *has eaten* several brave knights.

Principal Parts of Common Irregular Verbs

Present	Past	Past with Helping Verb
begin	began	begun
break	broke	broken
bring	brought	brought
choose	chose	chosen
come	came	come
do	did	done
drink	drank	drunk
eat	ate	eaten
fall	fell	fallen
fly	flew	flown
freeze	froze	frozen
give	gave	given
go	went	gone
grow	grew	grown
have	had	had
know	knew	known
lay	laid	laid
lie	lay	lain
ride	rode	ridden
ring	rang	rung
rise	rose	risen
run	ran	run
say	said	said
see	saw	seen
sing	sang	sung
sit	sat	sat
speak	spoke	spoken
steal	stole	stolen
swim	swam	swum
take	took	taken
teach	taught	taught
throw	threw	thrown
wear	wore	worn
write	wrote	written

Optional Practice

Have students write ten sentences about what happened on a favorite TV show or in a favorite book. (They should note which one.) Have them underline the verb in each sentence twice. Under the sentence they should write the three principal parts of that verb. Lastly, they should write whether the verb is *regular* or *irregular*.

Example:
The detective <u>chased</u> the getaway car.
chase, chased, chased—regular
The car <u>drove</u> quickly through an alley.
drive, drove, driven—irregular

Chapter 13

Improving Your Handwriting

Part 1 Studying Handwriting

You use handwriting every day in your schoolwork. You will always do some handwriting. Even if your job does not require handwriting, you will write letters to friends and notes to yourself. You will fill out forms and sign receipts. Your handwriting will be important all your life.

On the next page are examples of the handwriting of two students. Look at the examples carefully. What does each example show about the student who wrote it?

Chapter Objectives

1. To develop habits that contribute to clear, readable handwriting
2. To recognize and use both manuscript and cursive writing
3. To write letters and numbers carefully and clearly

Preparing the Students

Challenge a right-handed student to write his or her name on the board left-handed, or *vice versa*. Challenge another to write with eyes closed or turned away. Point out that even though the students know the right way to form the letters, their writing is not clear. Stress that knowledge isn't enough, and that practice and careful looking are required for good handwriting. Tell students that this chapter will help them find their problems with their normal writing, and correct those problems.

Additional Resources

Skills Practice Book—page 71
Duplicating Masters—page 71

Part 1

Objective

To develop habits that contribute to clear, readable handwriting

Presenting the Lesson

1. Read and discuss pages 183 and 184. Ask the students to take out paper and pencil, write their names, and then judge themselves on the five guides listed on page 184.

2. Assign and discuss Exercises A and B on page 185.

3. Use Exercise A on page 189 for additional practice or review.

Optional Practice

1. Prepare the students as a class by following the guides on page 184. Write on the board a list of spelling words or vocabulary from another subject. Have students copy the words twice on their papers as carefully and clearly as they can. If they are not satisfied with how the words look, they should rewrite them.

2. Have students vote on the nicest looking practice papers (unsigned). Discuss the attractive features of the papers that received the most votes.

I started violin lessons last March.
I started Violin lessons last March.

Is it likely that the student who wrote the first sample of handwriting is more careful? Why do you think so? Look at the height of the letters and the spacing between letters and words.

Which handwriting is easier to read? Which student's handwriting makes a better impression on you? Why?

When you write, the position of your body and the way you hold your pen or pencil are important. Study the following Guides.

Guides for Good Handwriting

1. Clear the top of your desk of books, extra papers, rulers, and other things. Have on your desk only the materials you need for your writing.

2. Sit well back in your chair or seat. Lean your body slightly forward and face the desk squarely.

3. Rest both arms on the desk with your elbows extending just over the edge. Do not rest your weight on your arms.

4. Hold your pen firmly, but do not grip it tightly. Gripping your pen too tightly slows down your writing.

5. Hold your paper steady with your free hand. Move the paper upward as you go down the page.

Exercises Studying Handwriting

A. Write the sentence in the handwriting example. Compare your writing with the first sample. Circle every letter that you made with an irregular form or uneven shape. Then write the sentence again, giving special attention to those letters you circled.

B. Examine one complete line of handwriting on one of your papers from past assignments. As in Exercise A, circle those letters that are irregular, uneven, or formed incorrectly. Rewrite the line. Compare your second handwriting sample with your first. If you still find poorly made letters, practice those letters until you are satisfied with their shape.

Part 2 Learning Different Ways of Writing

You probably remember that there are two common ways of writing. One is called **manuscript writing.** It is very much like the printing in books. Manuscript writing is useful in making labels and signs. Here is the alphabet in manuscript writing.

Aa Bb Cc Dd Ee Ff Gg
Hh Ii Jj Kk Ll Mm Nn
Oo Pp Qq Rr Ss Tt Uu
Vv Ww Xx Yy Zz

Part 2

Objective

To recognize and use both manuscript and cursive writing

Presenting the Lesson

1. Read and discuss pages 185 and 186.
2. Assign and discuss Exercises A and B on page 186.
3. Use Exercise B on page 189 as additional practice or review.

Optional Practice

Ask students to write five sentences in manuscript about their favorite food or drink, and then rewrite them in cursive writing.

Extending the Lesson

If you feel students could use a review of irregular verbs, you might use some of the list on page 181 for writing practice.

The other style of writing is called **cursive writing.** This is the style that most people use.

Here are the alphabet and numbers in cursive writing.

Aa Bb Cc Dd Ee
Ff Gg Hh Ii Jj Kk
Ll Mm Nn Oo Pp
Qq Rr Ss Tt Uu
Vv Ww Xx Yy Zz

Exercises   Practicing Writing

A. On lined paper, practice writing the alphabet in both styles. Be sure to form each letter correctly. Write the alphabet several times. Give extra practice to those letters that you find are difficult for you. Then make a copy of the alphabet to keep in your notebook so that you can look at it later when you want to check your writing.

B. Write labels that you could use for things in a hobby or book exhibit. Practice writing them in manuscript. Write first on lined paper and then on unlined paper or cardboard. Then write the same label in cursive handwriting on lined and plain papers.

Examples:

Hobby Show   Puppets and Marionettes
Hobby Show   *Puppets and Marionettes*

Part 3 Shaping Letters Carefully

In order to have good handwriting, you must be careful about how you shape your letters. This will make your handwriting clear and attractive.

1. **Slant your letters correctly.** In cursive writing, all the letters should slant the same way. Which of these samples is easier to read?

   Flying squirrels do not really fly.

   Flying squirrels do not really fly.

2. **Space your words and letters evenly.** Crowded letters and words make writing difficult to read. Compare these two samples.

   Rubber trees grow in a warm climate.

   Rubber trees grow in a warm climate.

3. **Form letters and numbers correctly.** If letters and numbers are not formed correctly, they may be read wrong.

   Man first walked on the moon on July 21, 1969.

   Man first walked on the moon on July 21, 1969.

4. **Join your letters carefully.** The letters *u*, *v*, *o*, and *w* require particular care when joined to other words. The following samples show why.

Good	Poor	Good	Poor
level	level	woman	womon
loan	laan	favor	favor
awake	awake	hoed	hoed
young	young	lawyer	lawyer

Part 3

Objective

To write letters and numbers carefully and clearly

Presenting the Lesson

1. Read and discuss pages 187 and 188. You may wish to discuss the problems that can result from people misreading letters and numbers, such as mispronouncing names, sending something to the wrong address, or getting the wrong answer for a math problem.
2. Assign and discuss Exercises A and B on page 188.
3. Use Exercise C on page 189 as additional practice or review.

Optional Practice

You might find it helpful to have students practice writing in a different format to stimulate interest. You may wish to make up multiple worksheets using the step design as illustrated below. Students can practice manuscript or cursive writing of letters or short phrases. The list below contains short practice words beginning with letters from *a* to *z*. It is suggested that you use no more than five steps at once.

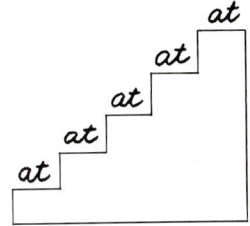

Practice Words: at, be, can, do, eat, fat, get, hit, it, jump, kite, lap, me, no, on, put, quit, red, sat, to, up, vase, will, x-ray, yard, zoo.

Extending the Lesson

Have students write a letter to the President, mayor, senator or representative telling him what they would do to make the country, state, or city better if they had his job.

5. **Keep your letters even in height.** This is easier to do if you keep your letters on the line. Capital letters and tall letters should be about the same height. The samples below show you how much difference height makes. Be particularly careful with *e* and *l*.

Balboa discovered the Pacific Ocean in 1513.

Balboa discovered the Pacific ocean in 1513.

Exercises   Shaping Letters Carefully

A. From old papers, select a story, report, or some other paper you have written. Look at it carefully. Which of the five ways of shaping letters did you do well? Which ones do you need to practice?

Mark the paper wherever you feel you could improve the handwriting. Then make a new copy of it.

B. In your best and neatest handwriting, copy the poem below. When you have finished, compare your handwriting with the handwritten samples.

Windy Nights

Whenever the moon and stars are set,
    Whenever the wind is high,
All night long in the dark and wet,
    A man goes riding by.
Late in the night when the fires are out,
    Why does he gallop and gallop about?

—ROBERT LOUIS STEVENSON

Additional Exercises

Improving Your Handwriting

A. Studying Handwriting (Use after page 184.)

Copy the sentence in the following handwriting sample. Compare your writing with the sample. Circle every letter that you made with an irregular form or uneven shape. Then write the sentence again, giving special attention to those letters you circled.

The quick brown fox jumped over the lazy dog.

B. Practicing Writing (Use after page 186.)

For each letter of the alphabet, think of a word beginning with that letter. Write each word first in manuscript writing and then in cursive handwriting.

C. Shaping Letters Carefully (Use after page 188.)

In your best and neatest handwriting, copy the poem below. When you have finished, compare your handwriting with the handwritten samples on pages 187 and 188.

The Witch of Willowby Wood

There once was a witch of Willowby Wood,
and a weird wild witch was she,
with her hair that was snarled
and hands that were gnarled,
and a kickety, rickety knee.
She could jump, they say
to the moon and back,
but this I never did see.

—ROWENA BENNETT

Additional Exercises

If these Exercises were not used with each lesson, they may now be assigned for chapter review.

Chapter 14

Using the Library

Originally, a library was a place where books were stored. Today, a library is much more. It holds books, magazines, records, picture files, and other materials.

More importantly, a library does not merely store these materials. The materials are there to be used. There are storybooks and records to entertain you. There are books to tell you how to cook, make kites, or do magic tricks. Whatever your hobby is, you are almost sure to find information about it at the library. If you make reports for school, the library is your most valuable aid.

Every library has librarians to help you find what you want. However, the librarians cannot help every person every time. To make good use of a library, you yourself must know how to find the materials you want.

Chapter Objectives

1. To distinguish between fiction and nonfiction books
2. To understand and be able to use the arrangement systems for fiction and nonfiction books
3. To understand and be able to use call numbers and the card catalog to locate books
4. To use the table of contents and index to locate information in a book

Preparing the Students

Call on students to give as many reasons as they can imagine for using the library. Also ask students what types of books are housed in a library. List responses on the chalkboard. Read page 191 and compare the students' list with the types of books mentioned in the text.

Emphasize that to make the best use of a library, a person should know what services a library offers and exactly where everything is located. This chapter explains ways to find books and information quickly and easily.

Additional Resources

Mastery Test—pages 468 and 469 in this T.E. Recommended for use after teaching the chapter.

Additional Mastery Test—Recommended for use after any necessary reteaching. (In separate booklet, *Mastery Tests, Silver Level,* pages 31 and 32.)

Skills Practice Book—pages 72–76
Duplicating Masters—pages 72–76

Part 1

Objectives

1. To distinguish between fiction and nonfiction books
2. To understand and be able to use the arrangements systems for fiction and nonfiction books

Presenting the Lesson

1. Read and discuss page 192. Emphasize the meaning of the term *fiction,* and test students' understanding by asking them to suggest some titles of fiction they have read. (At this point, folk tale and other story titles are acceptable answers.)
2. Examine the picture at the top of page 192. Discuss how it illustrates the rules for grouping and ordering presented in the text.
3. Before assigning Exercise A on page 193, make sure the students realize that all ten authors' names are to be alphabetized in one list. Assign and discuss Exercises A and B on page 193.
4. Read the section on nonfiction on pages 193 and 194. Emphasize the meaning of the term *nonfiction.* Discuss the chart on page 194. Ask students to suggest other subjects of nonfiction books, and to name the category each subject is likely to be found in. Point out that some subjects may be grouped in more than one category. For example, *plants* may be listed under Science, 500, or Useful Arts (gardening), 700.
5. Assign and discuss Exercise A on page 195. Explain that in Exercise B, students are to use their knowledge of the Dewey system to make a logical choice of categories. They are not to use research materials to complete the Exercise. Assign and discuss Exercise B.

Part 1 Two Kinds of Books

There are two kinds of books, **fiction** and **nonfiction.** Each group is arranged according to a different system.

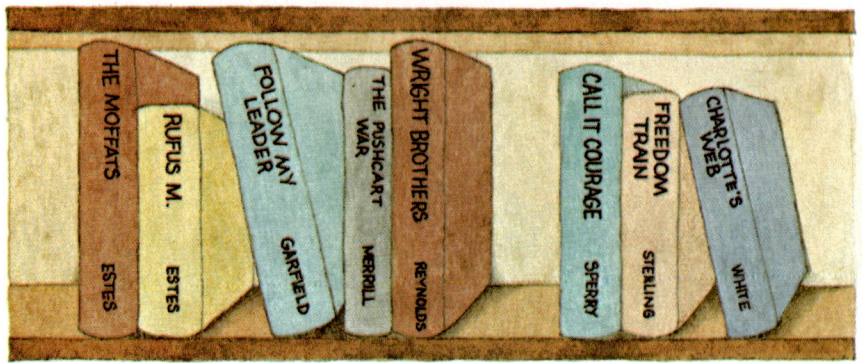

Fiction

Fiction books are stories that are made up by a writer, or **author.** They are not necessarily true, though there may be some real people or events in the book. The author has used his or her imagination to invent whatever was needed for a good story. In most libraries, all fiction books are shelved in the same area.

Fiction books are arranged on shelves alphabetically according to the author's last name.

For example, books by an author named Carol Brink are placed before books by an author named Scott O'Dell. Books by Scott O'Dell are placed before books by Donald Sobol.

All the books by one writer are shelved in one group. They are then arranged alphabetically, according to the first word in the title. First words like *a*, *an*, and *the* are not considered. If a title begins with *a*, *an*, or *the*, it is alphabetized according to its second word. For example, *The Children's War*, by Theodore Taylor, would be alphabetized under *C* rather than *T*.

Exercises Arranging Fiction Books

A. Number your paper from 1 to 10. Copy these authors' names in the order in which you would find their books on the shelves.

- 6 Eleanor Lattimore
- 5 Roald Dahl
- 1 Margaret E. Bell
- 8 Astrid Lindgren
- 9 Mary Norton
- 2 Hester Burton
- 10 Mary Rodgers
- 4 James L. Collier
- 7 Madeleine L'Engle
- 3 John Christopher

B. Number your paper from 1 to 5. List these books by Beverly Cleary in the order in which they would be arranged on the shelves.

- 5 *Socks*
- 4 *Runaway Ralph*
- 1 *Mitch and Amy*
- 3 *Ribsy*
- 2 *Ramona the Brave*

Nonfiction

Nonfiction books are books reporting facts or ideas. They tell about real people and happenings. There are books written on every subject you can imagine. In the library, nonfiction books are arranged according to their subjects. These subjects are grouped together in large categories. Most libraries use the categories of the **Dewey Decimal System.**

The Dewey Decimal System classifies all nonfiction books into ten major categories. Each category is assigned a number, counting by hundreds.

For example, the numbers from 600 to 699 are assigned to the category Useful Arts. This category includes books about gardening, cooking, sewing, radio, television, nursing, engineer-

Optional Practice

1. Have students tell the names of some favorite authors from fiction books they recently read. List these authors on the chalkboard. Have students arrange the authors alphabetically.

2. Using a favorite author, ask students for names of books they've read by that individual. List the titles under the author's name. Have students alphabetize the list. You might want to use the titles listed below, or supply titles if students don't know at least three.

Betsy Byars
The 18th Emergency
Trouble River
The Midnight Fox
The Summer of the Swans
The House of Wings

Matt Christopher
Stranded
Earthquake
Ice Magic
Devil Pony
Little Lefty

3. Ask each student to list three favorite hobbies, activities, or items of interest. Students then exchange lists and assign Dewey categories to their partner's listings.

4. Have a "Book Identification Bee." Ask the school librarian to supply lists of many titles of both fiction and nonfiction books. Be sure all nonfiction titles fit clearly into the ten Dewey Categories as described on page 194. Cut the lists into individual titles, and put them in a container. Call on students individually, or assign them to teams and call on the teams for answers.

To begin the game, pull out a book title and read it aloud. Ask the student if the book is fiction or nonfiction.

If the student answers this correctly and it is a nonfiction book, then the student must tell the correct category by name and/or number, such as, sports: 700–799.

If the students are playing as individuals, those who give wrong answers drop out until a winner is left. If they are playing as teams, award points for correct answers and compare scores at the end of the game.

Extending the Lesson

Have the students devise their own original systems of classifying and ordering books. This activity should make them more aware of the need for general categories such as the Dewey system uses.

ing, business, cars, and other subjects. Each of those books is given a number between 600 and 699, and placed in the shelves with the other 600's.

The numbers from 900 to 999 are assigned to History. This category includes books about real people, called **biographies.** It also includes books about historical happenings, and books about other countries.

The following chart lists all ten Dewey categories:

The Dewey Decimal System

000–099	General Works	(encyclopedias, almanacs, handbooks)
100–199	Philosophy	(conduct, psychology)
200–299	Religion	(the Bible, mythology, theology)
300–399	Social Science	(law, education, government, folklore)
400–499	Language	(languages, grammar, dictionaries)
500–599	Science	(mathematics, chemistry, physics, astronomy)
600–699	Useful Arts	(gardening, cooking, sewing, television, cars)
700–799	Fine Arts	(music, drawing, acting, games, sports)
800–899	Literature	(poetry, plays, essays)
900–999	History	(biography, travel, geography)

Exercises **Arranging Nonfiction Books**

A. Number your paper from 1 to 10. Decide whether each book listed is fiction or nonfiction. Write *Fiction* or *Nonfiction*.

Examples: A book about a boy's pet dragon *Fiction*
 The How and Why Book of Stars *Nonfiction*

1. *The White House: A History of Presidents* Nonfiction
2. *The Mathematical Princess and Other Stories* Fiction
3. A book about the search for new energy sources Nonfiction
4. *Bicycles: All About Them* Nonfiction
5. Encyclopedia Brown solves ten mysteries Fiction
6. A boy's adventures on earth one hundred years in the future Fiction
7. Biographies of four outstanding black women Nonfiction
8. *The House That Sailed Away* Fiction
9. *The Amateur Magician's Handbook* Nonfiction
10. An adventure tale set in ancient China Fiction

B. Using the categories of the Dewey Decimal System discussed in this chapter part, assign the correct category number to each of the following nonfiction books.

1. *Ginnie and Geneva Cookbook* by Catherine Woolley 600—699
2. *Jane Addams* by Gail Faithfull Keller 900—999
3. *The Backyard Astronomer* by Alan E. Nourse 500—599
4. *Double Fun: 100 Outdoor and Indoor Games* by Alma Heaton 700—799
5. *Guinness Book of Young Recordbreakers* by Norris and Ross McWhirter 000—099
6. *British Isles* by Robert Clayton 900—999
7. *Poetry of Earth* compiled by Adrienne Adams 800—899
8. *Fun with Growing Things* by Joan Eckstein and Joyce Gleit 600—699
9. *The Story of Folk Music* by Melvin Berger 700—799
10. *The I Hate Mathematics! Book* by Marilyn Burns 500—599

Part 2

Objective

To understand and be able to use call numbers and the card catalog to locate books

Presenting the Lesson

1. Read the introduction to Part 2 and Call Numbers on page 196. Have the students turn back to page 194 and examine the chart once more. Make sure they understand how the call number of a book depends on the category to which it belongs. Show a library nonfiction book to the class and point out its call number on its spine.
2. Read and discuss The Card Catalog on pages 196 and 197. It is suggested that the class as a group visit a school or local library to become familiar with the catalog, before the Exercises on page 201 are assigned.
3. Read and discuss the rest of the chapter, pages 197 to 201. Make sure the students can explain and recognize the differences between the four types of cards discussed. Have the students examine the cards and identify the items of information listed under Card Catalog Information on pages 199 and 200. Ask students why this information is valuable. (For example, the publication date of a book about space travel would indicate whether it reflects the latest developments.)
4. Assign and discuss Exercises A and B on page 201.

Part 2   Finding a Particular Book

If you are looking for a particular book of fiction and know the author's name, it is easy to locate the book. You simply find the area where fiction books are shelved, and then find the author's name according to alphabetical order. If the book is in the library, it will be with the other books by that author.

However, you may not know the author's name. You may be looking for information about a particular subject, and may not even know the title of the book that will help you.

In these cases, the **call numbers** of books and the **card catalog** will help you.

Call Numbers

In the Dewey Decimal System, every nonfiction book is assigned a specific identification number. For example, a book about cooking will get a number in the 600's, while a book about space exploration will get a number in the 500's. The specific number assigned to a book is its **call number.** The call number is printed on the spine of the book. The book is then shelved in numerical order according to its call number. You find the call number of a book in the card catalog.

The Card Catalog

The **card catalog** is a cabinet of small drawers filled with cards. Each card is printed with information about a book in the library. The cards are arranged alphabetically according to the top line of each card. In the upper left hand corner of each card in the catalog is the call number of the book listed on the card.

On the outside of each drawer there is a label that tells what letters of the alphabet are contained in that drawer. Inside each drawer there are **guide cards** that have tabs extending above the regular book cards. The tabs may have letters of the alphabet, complete words, or general subject headings printed on them. The guide cards separate the drawerful of cards into smaller groups. This makes it easier to find the exact card you are looking for.

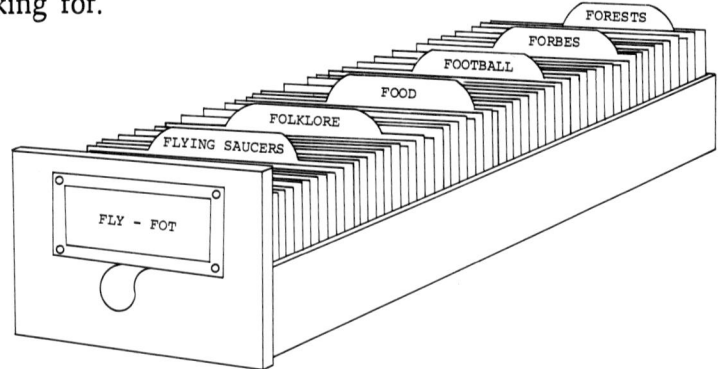

There are usually three cards for the same book in the card catalog: the **author card,** the **title card,** and the **subject card.** All three cards give you the same information about the book, but in slightly different order. An author card has the name of the author of the book on the top line. A title card has the title of the book on the top line. A subject card has the general subject or topic of the book on the top line. All three cards for one book have the same call number in the corner.

Look carefully at the following examples of card catalog cards for the book *Cherokee Chief: The Life of John Ross* by Electa Clark.

The Author Card

When you know the author of a book you want to read, use the card catalog to look up the author's name. There will be an author card for each book in the library written by that author. All the cards for one author will be together, filed alphabetically under the author's last name (on the top line of each card).

Optional Practice

1. Using an opaque projector and assorted catalog cards borrowed from the school librarian, show several cards to the class. For each one, ask the students to identify the type of card and to find the title, author, and call number listed on it.

2. Again using an opaque projector and several catalog cards, show the cards overlapping so that only the first line is seen. Have students copy the first lines in alphabetical order as they would be found in a catalog drawer.

Here is an example of an author card for the book *Cherokee Chief: The Life of John Ross*.

```
J921      Clark, Electa
Ro
              Cherokee chief; the life of John Ross.
          Illustrated by John Wagner. New York,
          Crowell-Collier Press      1970
              118 p.   Illus.
              Bibliog. pp. 115–116
              A biography of the Cherokee chief who
          struggled to maintain his tribe's indepen-
          dence and rights to its homeland.
              1. Cherokee Indians   2. Trail of Tears
                             O
```

The Title Card

When you know the title of a book, but not its author, look for the title card of the book in the card catalog. Title cards are filed alphabetically by the first word in the title, which is on the top line of each title card. Here is an example of a title card for *Cherokee Chief*.

```
J921      Cherokee chief; the life of John Ross
Ro
              Clark, Electa
                  Cherokee chief; the life of John Ross.
              Illus. by John Wagner. New York,
              Crowell-Collier Press      1970
                  118 p.   Illus.
                  Bibliog. pp. 115–116
                  1. Cherokee Indians   2. Trail of Tears
                                 O
```

The Subject Card

If you were writing a report on Cherokee Indians, you would want to know the names and authors of several books on that subject in the library. The best way to find books on your topic would be to look in the card catalog under the subject heading CHEROKEE INDIANS. The subject card for the book *Cherokee Chief: The Life of John Ross* would look like this.

```
J921      CHEROKEE INDIANS
Ro
             Clark, Electa
                Cherokee chief; the life of John Ross.
             Illus. by John Wagner. New York,
             Crowell-Collier Press        1970

                118 p.   Illus.
                Bibliog. pp. 115–116

                1. Cherokee Indians   2. Trail of Tears

                              o
```

The subject on every subject card is often printed completely in capital letters. This helps you tell the difference between it and an author or title card.

Card Catalog Information

Notice that all three types of catalog cards (author, title, and subject) give the same information. Make sure that you can identify the following information on the sample cards for the book *Cherokee Chief: The Life of John Ross.*

1. The call number
2. The title, author, publisher, and date of publication
3. The number of pages and a notation on whether the book has illustrations, maps, an index, or other features

The card catalog may also provide the following:

4. A brief description of the material in the book
5. A listing of other catalog cards for the book

Cross Reference Cards

Sometimes when you look up a subject you will find a card that reads *See* or *See also*. These cards will help you find the information you want. The "See" card refers you to another subject heading in the card catalog. For example, if you wanted a book on farm animals, you might see a card that reads as follows:

```
Farm animals
  see
Domestic animals
```

This "see" card means that the library catalogs all books on farm animals under the subject heading of "Domestic animals."

Notice that cross reference cards do not have call numbers. They do not refer to specific books. They tell you only where to look in the card catalog for more information.

Exercises **Using the Card Catalog**

A. Each of the five words or phrases below is the first line of a card in a card catalog. Copy the words or phrases in the order you would find them in the card catalog.

1. Haywood, Carolyn 1
   Hidden Heroines 4
   HELICOPTERS 2
   Hicks, Clifford 3
   HOCKEY 5

2. Sharp, Margery 4
   Sachs, Marilyn 1
   Science Fiction Trilogy One 2
   SKIING 5
   The Secret of the Seven Crows 3

3. Charlie and the Chocolate Factory 4
   Calhoun, Mary 1
   CAMPING 2
   Champions of the Little League 3
   CITIES AND TOWNS 5

B. Use the card catalog to find the title, author, call number, and publication date of a book on one of the following subjects: *Answers will vary*

1. A book about snakes
2. A book of fairy tales
3. A book about dinosaurs
4. A book of poems
5. A book about Abraham Lincoln
6. A book about China
7. A book of riddles
8. A book about pirates

Part 3

Objective

To use the table of contents and index to locate information in a book

Presenting the Lesson

1. Read and discuss pages 202 and 203. Using this or any other class textbook, give students practice in finding specific information in the table of contents and index as a group before assigning the Exercises.

2. Assign and discuss Exercises A and B on page 203. It is suggested that you do several items with the class first, and then assign completion of each exercise.

Optional Activities

1. Using any textbook, develop written and oral variations to Exercises A and B on page 203. Many reviews can be done with the tables of contents and indexes of math, science, and social studies books. Develop quizzes where students have books in front of them and search for answers, testing speed and accuracy.

2. Students can develop their own questions from their texts using the table of contents and index, and then form small groups to quiz each other.

Part 3 How To Find Information in a Book

If you are looking for specific information in a nonfiction book, you do not have to read the entire book to find out if the information is there. Almost every nonfiction book has two guides that make it easier for you to locate the facts you need. After you have found a book with the help of the library card catalog, you can examine the book for a few minutes. This fast examination will tell you if this is the book that will answer your questions.

The Table of Contents

At the front of every nonfiction book, there is a **table of contents.** The table of contents lists the title of every chapter and the page on which it begins. Some tables of contents list the more important topics discussed in each chapter, and the illustrations and graphs to be found there. By reading the table of contents, you will see immediately how much attention the book gives to your topic.

The Index

At the end of almost every nonfiction book, there is an **index.** The index is a list of topics that are discussed in the book. The topics are listed alphabetically and followed by the numbers of the pages on which they are found. Examine these entries:

Main verbs, 12, 48

Prefixes, 23–25
  defined, 23
  most commonly used, 24
    (list)

The first entry shows that the topic *Main Verbs* is mentioned on two different pages. The second entry shows that the topic *Prefixes* is discussed much more thoroughly, for three pages together. The subheadings under *Prefixes* tell you where to find a definition of the term and a list of prefixes.

If you are looking for specific information, such as definitions, lists, and dates, the index is the best place to look. You will quickly find out if the book includes this information.

Exercises Finding Information in a Book

A. Number your paper from 1 to 10. Examine the table of contents of this book. See if there is a chapter for each topic listed below. If there is, write the number of the chapter. If there is not a chapter on the topic, write *No*.

1. pronouns 11
2. telling stories 22
3. giving speeches No
4. spelling 27
5. rhyming No
6. the dictionary 15
7. the encyclopedia No
8. adverbs 17
9. letter writing 24
10. poetry writing No

B. Number your paper from 1 to 10. Look up the following topics in the index of this book. Write the topic and the numbers of all the pages on which it can be found.

1. suffixes 7–11, 390–394
2. accent mark 213–214
3. encyclopedia 312, 314–316
4. *it's* and *its* 169–170
5. word parts 1–11
6. reference books 312–314
7. initials 364–365; 350
8. subject cards in card catalogs 199, 201
9. commas in letters 370
10. dates, commas in 369–371, 382

Chapter 15

Using the Dictionary

Chapter Objectives

1. To develop alphabetizing skills

2. To use alphabetical order and guide words to find entry words in a dictionary

3. To use a dictionary entry to find syllabication, pronunciation, and the appropriate meaning of a word

Preparing the Students

Pass out dictionaries to the class. Have students try to find the word *range*. After a reasonable time, tell the proper page number. Ask students to look carefully at all the writing next to the word *range*.

Ask the students if they ever have been confused by all the writing, numbers, and symbols listed next to a word. Do they understand the strange spelling of *rānj*? Do they know why there are so many numbered phrases after the word?

Tell the students that the purpose of this chapter is to help them find and use all the information provided in a dictionary.

The dictionary used as a source for all examples in this chapter is *Webster's New World Dictionary for Young Readers* (William Collins & World Publishing Company, Inc.)

Additional Exercises

Mastery Test—pages 470 and 471 in this T.E. Recommended for use after teaching the chapter.

Additional Mastery Test—Recommended for use after any necessary reteaching. (In separate booklet, *Mastery Tests, Silver Level,* pages 33 and 34.)

Skills Practice Book—pages 77–81

Duplicating Masters—pages 77–81

Suppose you see or hear a new word. You want to know what the new word means. How can you find out? You can use a dictionary.

A dictionary will tell you even more than the meaning of the new word. It will tell you how to pronounce the new word. It will tell you what kind of word it is—a noun, a pronoun, a verb, and so on. A dictionary is a useful tool.

You have already seen how to use word parts and context clues to unlock word meanings. However, not every word meaning can be discovered by these methods. This chapter will show you how to use a dictionary to learn more about words.

Page 209 shows a sample page from a dictionary. In this chapter, we will talk about the many things that appear on that sample page.

Part 1

Objective

To develop alphabetizing skills

Presenting the Lesson

1. Read and discuss page 206. Emphasize the meaning of the term *entry word*.
2. Assign and discuss the Exercise on page 206.

Optional Practice

1. Provide students with a list of the first names of the boys and another list of the girls in the class. Students are to alphabetize each list. To add interest, have students time themselves.
2. Provide lists of words relating to certain subjects, such as those given below. Students are to alphabetize each list. You might encourage competition by challenging students to complete the task in a certain time limit, or by having individuals compete against each other. Students might also be asked to make original lists and exchange them for more practice.

Baseball Teams	Foods I
Cubs	Tomatoes
Red Sox	Lettuce
Pirates	Pickles
Cardinals	Watermelon
Yankees	Oranges
Astros	Onions
White Sox	Apples
Dodgers	Squash
Basketball Teams	**Foods II**
Pistons	Hamburgers
Bulls	Pizza
Lakers	Catsup
Bucks	Mustard
Pacers	Relish
Celtics	Steak
Rockets	Hot Dogs
Nets	Tacos

Part 1 Using Alphabetical Order

The words that are listed on each page of the dictionary are called **entry words.** They are usually listed in two or three columns. They are in alphabetical order. The first part of the dictionary has words that begin with *a*. Then come words that begin with *b*, and so on.

Many words begin with the same letter. When that happens, they are alphabetized by the second letter. For example, the word *sand* is listed before the word *scale*. Many words have the same first and second letters. Then they are alphabetized by the third letter. For example, the word *stamp* is listed before the word *steel*.

Here are some groups of words listed in alphabetical order.

Group 1	Group 2	Group 3
autumn	sail	the
eel	scale	their
pigeon	soap	them
zebra	sweater	then

Exercise Using Alphabetical Order

Here are four groups of words. Copy each group in alphabetical order.

1	2	3	4
2 hoot	5 mountain	3 lunchbox	7 palace
6 whoop	6 ocean	2 fruit	2 cabin
3 howl	8 valley	6 sandwich	5 igloo
5 squeal	4 meadow	1 cookies	4 house
1 bellow	2 hill	5 napkin	6 motel
4 screech	3 lake	7 thermos	1 apartment
8 yell	1 beach	8 tray	3 castle
7 yap	7 river	4 milk	8 wigwam

Part 2 Finding the Word You Want

To find words quickly, you must know where to look for them. Learn to open the dictionary at the right place.

Opening a Dictionary at the Right Place

Open your dictionary at a place that seems close to the middle. You should be in the *l*'s or *m*'s. Suppose that the word you want begins with a letter from *a* through *l*. Look in the first half of the dictionary for your word. Suppose that the word you want begins with a letter *m* through *z*. Then look in the second half of the dictionary.

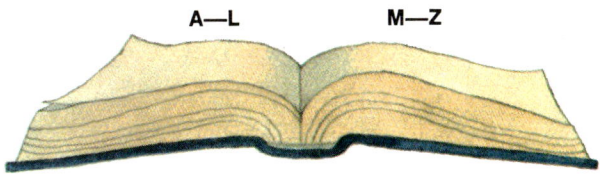

Exercises Opening a Dictionary at the Right Place

A. Work with a partner. Practice opening the dictionary as close as you can to a particular letter. Ask your partner to say a letter. Then try to open your dictionary as close as you can to that letter. Now switch. You choose a letter for your partner. Practice until you and your partner can open the dictionary to the right place most of the time.

Divide a sheet of paper into two columns. Label the first column *First Half, A-L*. Label the second column *Second Half, M-Z*. Write each of the following words in the correct column.

fang _{A—L} chain _{A—L} scissors ^{M—Z} bathtub _{A—L}
talon ^{M—Z} padlock _{M—Z} twine _{M—Z} towel _{M—Z}
claw _{A—L} strongbox ^{M—Z} parcel _{M—Z} sponge _{M—Z}

Part 2

Objective

To use alphabetical order and guide words to find entry words in a dictionary

Presenting the Lesson

1. Read and discuss page 207. Have the entire class work together to find a certain letter. Repeat until most of the students seem confident of the process.
2. Assign Exercise A on page 207. Allow as much time as the class appears to need.
3. Assign and discuss Exercise B on page 207.
4. Read and discuss page 208. Make sure students can define the terms *guide word* and *entry word*, and can find examples of each on the sample dictionary page on page 209.
5. Ask students to give fast responses as you dictate the following words, telling whether each word comes before the sample page, on it, or after it: *rolling pin, giraffe, snake, rodeo, mustard, roller, rusty, rod, door.*
6. It is suggested that you do part of Exercise A on page 210 with the class. When the majority of the class seems to understand the process, assign the rest of the Exercise. Give individual help to those that seem to need it. Correct the assignment together.
7. Assign and discuss Exercise B on page 210.

Optional Practice

1. Follow the directions for Exercise B on page 207, using these words:

tang	elf	victory
outlaw	costume	icicle
double	special	bargain
nature	house	rabbit

2. Have a "Guide Word Challenge." To play the game, each member of the class must have a copy of the same dictionary.

To prepare for the game, each student makes out five contest cards, heading each one with an entry word found in the dictionary. Under the entry word, the student is to note the guide words and the number of the page on which the entry word appears.

To play the game, form two teams. Collect the cards, mix them, and draw one at a time. Call out the entry word only. The students race to find the page on which the entry appears. Call on the first person to raise a hand. If that student can tell both the guide words and page number, that team gains a point. If the student is wrong, call on someone from the opposite team.

Using the Guide Words

Look at the sample dictionary page on page 209. In each of the top corners of the page, there is a word in heavy black type. This word is called a **guide word.** Guide words help you find the right page when you are looking for an entry word.

The guide words on the two sample pages are *rocky* and *Roman*. Now look at the entry words that are listed on the two dictionary pages. *Rocky* is the first entry word. *Roman* is the last entry word. Guide words tell you that all the entry words on these two facing pages will be between *rocky* and *Roman* in the alphabet.

When you use a dictionary, learn to use the guide words. They will help you find your word. First look for guide words that begin with the same letter as your word. Then look at the second and third letters of the guide words to find guide words that are as close as possible to your word in the alphabet. Sometimes your word may even be a guide word. Most of the time, however, your word will come between two guide words.

rock·y (räk′ē), *adj.* **1.** tending to rock or sway; not steady [a *rocky* desk]. **2.** weak or dizzy: *slang in this meaning*. —**rock′i·er,** *compar.*; **rock′i·est,** *superl.* —**rock′i·ness,** *n.*

Rocky Mountains, a mountain system in western North America. It stretches from Alaska to New Mexico. Also called *Rockies.*

rocking horse

ro·co·co (rə kō′kō), *adj.* having rich decoration and many fancy designs, such as leaves, scrolls, etc. [*Rococo* architecture was popular in the 18th century.]

rod (räd), *n.* **1.** a straight, thin bar of wood, metal, etc. [a fishing *rod*]. **2.** a stick for beating as punishment. **3.** punishment. **4.** a measure of length equal to 5½ yards. **5.** a staff carried as a symbol of position or rank, as by a king. —**spare the rod,** to keep from punishing.

rode (rōd), past tense of **ride.**

ro·dent (rō′d'nt), *n.* an animal having sharp front teeth for gnawing. Rats, mice, rabbits, and squirrels are rodents.

ro·de·o (rō′di ō *or* rō dā′ō), *n.* **1.** a contest or show in which cowboys match their skill in riding horses, roping and throwing cattle, etc. **2.** a roundup of cattle. —**ro′de·os,** *pl.*

roe (rō), *n.* fish eggs.

roe (rō), *n.* a small, graceful deer found in Asia and Europe. —**roe** or **roes,** *pl.*

roe·buck (rō′buk), *n.* the male of the roe.

Roent·gen rays (rent′gən), same as **X rays.**

rogue (rōg), *n.* **1.** a dishonest or tricky person; scoundrel; rascal. **2.** a person who likes to have fun and plays tricks. **3.** an elephant or other animal that wanders apart from the herd and is wild and fierce.

ro·guer·y (rō′gə rē), *n.* the actions of a rogue; trickery or playful mischief. —**ro′guer·ies,** *pl.*

ro·guish (rō′gish), *adj.* **1.** dishonest; tricky. **2.** playful; mischievous. —**ro′guish·ly,** *adv.*

roil (roil), *v.* **1.** to make muddy or cloudy, as by stirring up stuff at the bottom [to *roil* a pond]. **2.** to make angry; vex.

roist·er (rois′tər), *v.* **1.** to be noisy and lively; revel. **2.** to brag or show off. —**roist′er·er,** *n.*

role or **rôle** (rōl), *n.* **1.** the part that an actor takes in a play [the heroine's *role*]. **2.** a part that a person plays in life [his *role* as scoutmaster].

roll (rōl), *v.* **1.** to move by turning over and over [The dog *rolled* on the grass. Men *rolled* logs to the river.] **2.** to move on wheels or rollers [The wagons *rolled* by. *Roll* the cart over here.] **3.** to wrap up or wind into a ball or tube [*Roll* up the rug.] **4.** to move smoothly, one after the other [The waves *rolled* to the shore. The weeks *rolled* by.] **5.** to move or rock back and forth [The ship *rolled* in the heavy seas. Sally *rolled* her eyes.] **6.** to spread, make, or become flat under a roller [to *roll* steel]. **7.** to say with a trill [He *rolls* his "r's".] **8.** to make a loud, echoing sound [The thunder *rolled.*] **9.** to beat with light, rapid blows [to *roll* a drum]. —*n.* **1.** the act of rolling [the *roll* of a ball]. **2.** a list of names for checking who is present. **3.** something rolled up into a ball or tube [a *roll* of wallpaper]. **4.** bread baked in a small, shaped piece. **5.** a roller. **6.** a rolling motion [the *roll* of a boat]. **7.** a loud, echoing sound [a *roll* of thunder]. **8.** a number of light, rapid blows on a drum. —**roll in, 1.** to arrive or come in large numbers. **2.** to have much of: *used only in everyday talk* [*rolling in* wealth]. —**roll out, 1.** to make flat by using a roller on. **2.** to spread out by unrolling. —**roll up,** to get or become more; increase [to *roll up* a big score].

roll call, the reading aloud of a list of names, as in a classroom, to find out who is absent.

roll·er (rōl′ər), *n.* **1.** a tube or cylinder on which something is rolled [the *roller* of a window shade]. **2.** a heavy rolling cylinder used to crush, smooth, or spread [A steam *roller* crushed the gravel on the road.] **3.** a long, heavy wave that breaks on the shore line. **4.** a canary that trills its notes. **5.** anything that rolls.

roller coaster, an amusement ride in which cars move on tracks that curve and dip sharply.

roller skate, a skate having wheels instead of a runner, for skating on floors, walks, etc.

roll·er-skate (rōl′ər-skāt′), *v.* to move on roller skates. —**roll′er-skat′ed,** *p.t.* & *p.p.*; **roll′er-skat′ing,** *pr.p.*

rol·lick (räl′ik), *v.* to play in a gay, lively way; romp; frolic. —**rol′lick·ing,** *adj.*

rolling mill, a factory or machine for rolling metal into sheets and bars.

rolling pin, a heavy, smooth cylinder of wood, glass, etc., used to roll out dough.

rolling stock, all the locomotives and cars of a railroad.

ro·ly-po·ly (rō′lē pō′lē), *adj.* short and plump; pudgy [a *roly-poly* boy].

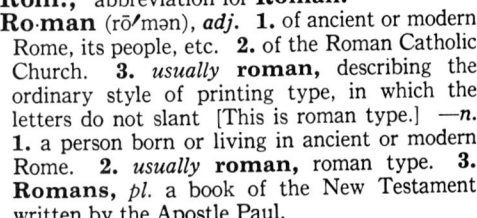
roller skates

rolling pin

Rom., abbreviation for **Roman.**

Ro·man (rō′mən), *adj.* **1.** of ancient or modern Rome, its people, etc. **2.** of the Roman Catholic Church. **3.** *usually* **roman,** describing the ordinary style of printing type, in which the letters do not slant [This is roman type.] —*n.* **1.** a person born or living in ancient or modern Rome. **2.** *usually* **roman,** roman type. **3.** **Romans,** *pl.* a book of the New Testament written by the Apostle Paul.

---

fat, āpe, cär, ten, ēven, hit, bīte, gō, hôrn, tōol, book, up, fûr;
get, joy, yet, chin, she, thin, then; zh = s in pleasure; ' as in able (ā′b'l)
ə = a in ago, e in agent, i in sanity, o in confess, u in focus.

Exercises   Using Guide Words

A. Number your paper from 1 to 10. In the list below are ten sets of guide words. After each set of guide words is another word. Decide whether you would find that word on a page *before* the guide words, on the page *with* the guide words, or on a page *after* the guide words. Write *before, with,* or *after* beside each number on your paper. Here is an example.

Guide words		Other words
able	animal	action

Action comes between *able* and *animal* in the alphabet. Therefore you would find *action* on the page with the guide words *able* and *animal.* So *with* is the right answer.

Guide words		Other words	
1. batter	bearing	bead	with
2. root	round	route	after
3. trillion	tropical	trouble	after
4. may	mechanic	mattress	before
5. baker	banana	balance	with
6. luggage	lying	lunch	with
7. home	hoof	hole	before
8. fan	fat	fascinate	with
9. burr	buzz	bystander	after
10. top	touch	tooth	before

B. See how quickly you can find the following words in your dictionary. Write each word. After the word, copy the two guide words from the pages where you find it.

Answers depend on dictionary used.

1. buffalo
2. shark
3. elk
4. walrus
5. butterscotch
6. raspberry
7. chocolate
8. vanilla
9. wood
10. plastic
11. glass
12. metal

Part 3 The Dictionary Entry

As you have already learned, the words that are listed in the dictionary are called **entry words.**

The information a dictionary gives about each word is called an **entry.** The dictionary gives several kinds of information in each entry. This part of the chapter will tell about three kinds of information in an entry.

Syllables

A dictionary entry shows how to divide each entry word into parts. Each word part pronounced with a single uninterrupted sound is called a **syllable.** In the sample dictionary page shown on page 209, there is a dot between syllables. For example, the word *roller* is shown as **roll · er.**

Why does an entry show how to divide the word into syllables? One reason is to help your spelling skills. If you can think of a word broken into little parts, it will probably be easier to remember how to spell it. For example, look at the hard word *roguery* on the sample dictionary page. It has been broken into syllables for you. Isn't it easier to sound out?

There's another reason why the dictionary breaks entry words into syllables. Sometimes a word will not fit at the end of a line you are writing. You may have to break the word into two parts. Part of the word will have to run on to the next line. When that happens, always divide the word between syllables. At least two letters of the word must be on each line. Use a hyphen to show that the word runs to the next line. Use the dictionary when you need to find out where to separate syllables in a word.

Right	Wrong	
ro-dent	rod-ent	rode-nt

Part 3

Objective

To use a dictionary entry to find syllabication, pronunciation, and the appropriate meaning of a word

Presenting the Lesson

1. Read and discuss page 211. Refer to page 209 and ask students to identify syllable division of entry words on the sample dictionary page. If the dictionary used in the class uses a different system (spaces, hyphens), point this out to the students.

2. Examine the illustration at the top of page 212. Discuss how each word is divided into syllables. See the first activity in Extending the Lesson for further teaching suggestions.

3. Assign and discuss Exercises A and B on page 212.

4. Read and discuss pages 213 and 214. Make sure students understand the terms *pronunciation* and *respelling*, and can find respellings and the pronunciation key both on the sample dictionary page (page 209) of the text and in the class dictionary. It is recommended that you review with the class the symbols used in respellings and pronunciation keys, such as macrons and breves. It is not necessary for the students to know the technical terms for the various symbols, but they must be able to recognize them in order to make effective use of the key. It may be helpful to have the students read through the key on page 209; ask for other words that could have been used as samples for each vowel or consonant sound listed.

5. Have the students look up a few words as a class. Write each word on the board, and then have different students copy the respelling and the accents. Ask the students to interpret the respelling, and to pronounce the word. Suggested words: *acrobat, chariot, exodus, exotic, focus, invest, mosaic, parka, safari.*

6. Assign and discuss the Exercise on page 214.

7. Look at the illustration on page 215 and discuss how usually, like Sherlock Holmes, we are looking for clues in a dictionary. Often, we are looking for clues to the meaning of a passage by finding the definition of an unfamiliar word in the passage.

8. Read and discuss pages 215 and 216, stressing the variety of clues provided in a dictionary entry to the meaning of a word. Refer once more to page 209 and ask students to identify the meanings of several words listed there. After each dictionary meaning is read, ask students to restate the definition in their own words, and to provide an original example sentence.

9. Assign and discuss Exercise A on page 217.

10. You may wish to use Exercise B on page 217 as a review of the entire chapter. Assign and discuss it, and use the results as a basis for any further drill or reteaching of dictionary skills.

Exercises   Syllables

A. Rewrite each of the following words. Divide the word into syllables, leaving spaces between the syllables. Use your dictionary for help.

1. whirlpool
2. jewelry
3. overboard
4. potato
5. thirsty
6. unlimited
7. citizen
8. delivery
9. allowance

B. Imagine that each of the following words comes at the end of a line of writing. Copy each word, adding a hyphen to show where you could divide the word at the end of a line. Use your dictionary for help.

Example: romantic

ro-mantic or roman-tic

1. diamond
2. sapphire
3. amber
4. emerald
5. amethyst
6. jasper
7. ruby
8. aquamarine
9. turquoise

Pronunciation

A dictionary entry also gives the **pronunciation** of a word. That is, it tells you how to say the word. The pronunciation appears in parentheses just after each entry word. For example, find the entry word **roll** on the sample dictionary page. Just after the entry word, you'll see (rōl). This is the pronunciation of *roll*.

Notice that words are respelled in the pronunciation. For example, *roll* is respelled rōl. The respellings usually look different from the correct spellings. Some of the letters have strange marks and symbols near them. A few of the words have upside-down letters in them. What do they mean?

The sample dictionary page shown on page 209 has a **pronunciation key** at the bottom. Let's use the pronunciation key to find out how to pronounce *roll* (rōl). Look at the pronunciation key. Find a word that has ō in it. The word is *gō*. This tells you that the *o* in *roll* is pronounced like the *o* in *go*. It is not like the *o* in *confess*.

Notice that in the respelling, the word is again broken into syllables. Each part of the respelling shows the pronunciation of one syllable. In these examples, the respelling of *Roentgen* and of *rogue* are printed below the correct spellings. Compare the forms. Notice where they are different.

Roent gen	rogue
(rent′ gən)	(rōg)

There's something else that you should notice about the pronunciation. Words that have more than one syllable have **accent marks.** These accent marks look like this: ′. A dictionary uses accent marks to show how to pronounce the words. When you say a word with more than one syllable, you say one part more strongly than the rest of the word. For example, say the

Optional Practice

1. To promote dictionary facility, mastery of the pronunciation key, and accent mark expertise, try this contest.

Have each student select from the dictionary an interesting, unfamiliar word. On a 3 x 5 card, the student should list the word, correctly spelled, and the phonetic respelling with accent marks. Then have the students form four teams.

To begin play, a member of Team 1 writes the respelling of his or her word on the board. The first member of a competing team who can pronounce the word correctly wins a point for the team. If no one else can identify the word, the Team 1 student who put up the word must give the correct answer. Then Team 1 gets a point. If the student putting up the word doesn't know the answer, that team loses two points. The game continues, with teams alternating.

2. You might like to do this exercise as an oral activity, or to make up a worksheet. Use each of the words listed below in a sentence. The students must find the word in a dictionary and select the one meaning that best fits the use of the word in the sentence.

arrest	flat
bind	grip
carry	handle
develop	image
error	jack

Students might also be asked to supply sentences for different meanings of the same words.

Extending the Lesson

1. Suggest three ways students can detect syllable divisions prior to using a dictionary.
   a. Students firmly grasp their Adam's apple while saying a word. Each time it moves, there is a syllable.
   b. Students place the back of their hand firmly under their chin while saying a word. Each time the chin drops there is a syllable.
   c. Students clap out each sound in a word.

All these techniques assume words are able to be pronounced by the students. Practice each of these techniques with the students. Use the words listed for Exercises A and B on page 212. Confirm answers with the dictionary's syllable divisions.

2. Have students make their own Picture Dictionary. Students clip unusual and interesting words (with complete sentences) from magazines and newspapers. They paste the entire sentence and any appropriate pictures on a sheet of paper. The word to be defined is underlined. Then the student is to follow the directions for Exercise B on page 217. Have students add to this booklet throughout the year and watch the growth in vocabulary and spelling skills. Students enjoy adding their own illustrations to reinforce meanings.

---

word *roller*. You said *ROLLer*. Now say it incorrectly. Say *rollER*. Can you hear the difference? *Roller* has a stronger emphasis on the first syllable. *Roller* is printed on the sample dictionary page as the example below shows. Look at the pronunciation.

roll·er

(rōl′ ər)

The dictionary has put an accent mark on the first syllable. This tells you that the first syllable is said more strongly than the second syllable. Learn to look for accent marks when you use the dictionary to find new words. The accent marks will help you to sound out new words.

Exercise   Pronunciation

Here are nine groups of words. Use a dictionary to find the pronunciation of each word. First, write down each word. Next, write the correct pronunciation of each word. Then underline the words that rhyme in each group.

Some answers may vary, depending on dictionary used.

1. fluff (fluf)   4. drought (drout)   7. vein (vān)
   through (thrōō)   thought (thôt)   ensign (en′ sin)
   enough (i′ nuf)   clout (klout)   reign (rān)

2. dough (dō)   5. trough (trof)   8. bury (ber′ ē)
   though (thō)   dough (dō)   cherry (cher′ ē)
   rough (ruf)   scoff (skof)   flurry (flur′ ē)

3. freight (frāt)   6. sleight (slīt)   9. steak (stāk)
   height (hīt)   weight (wāt)   beak (bēk)
   site (sīt)   eight (āt)   weak (wēk)

Definitions

Definitions are the largest part of every dictionary entry. They explain the meanings of entry words. Sometimes they use a picture to help explain the meaning of the entry words. Many words have more than one definition. If a word has more than one definition, the definitions are numbered. For example, look at the definitions for *rod* on the sample dictionary page. There are five definitions for this word.

Definitions are usually not written in complete sentences. They may sound a little strange to you at first. You will soon get used to them.

Many definitions are followed by a sentence that uses italics. (Italics are slanted letters.) This sentence shows a particular meaning of the entry word. It uses the word in a way that makes the meaning clear. For example, look at the entry for *roll* on the sample page. Look at definition 2.

> to move on wheels or rollers

Now look at the sentences that use italics.

> The wagons *rolled* by.   *Roll* the cart over here.

The sentences give a good example of what *roll* means.

Definitions also tell what **part of speech** a word is. The parts of speech are eight large groups into which all words are sorted, according to what the words do in sentences. This textbook has separate chapters on five parts of speech: nouns, pronouns, verbs, adjectives, and adverbs.

Look again at the definitions on page 209. There are abbreviations before the definitions. Here are the meanings of some of these abbreviations:

n.	noun	*adj.*	adjective
v.	verb	*adv.*	adverb
pron.	pronoun		

For example, *v.* appears before the definition of *rollick*. The list shows us that *v.* means "verb." Therefore, you know that *rollick* is a verb. Some words can be used as more than one part of speech. These words have more than one abbreviation.

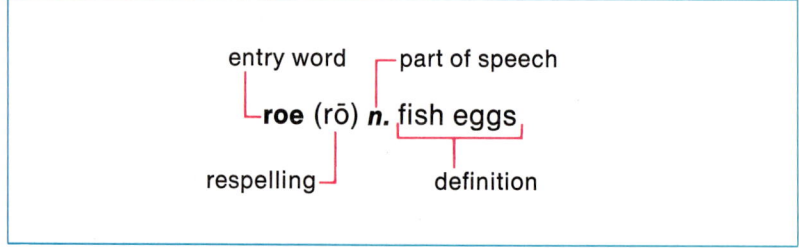

Exercises Finding Definitions

A. Each of the sentences below has a word that is underlined. Use your dictionary to find the meaning of the underlined word. Write down the definition that fits best in the sentence.

1. Derek learned to speak German abroad. outside one's country
2. At camp we told our favorite yarns. tale, story
3. Have you lived long enough to write your memoirs? autobiography
4. Our teacher primed us before we took our spelling test. to make ready
5. The outcome of the game hinges on how well we play. depends
6. Ellen leafed through the book to find her place. to turn the pages
7. Could the new medicine be a panacea? cure-all
8. The airplane began to yaw as the storm grew worse. to turn from its course
9. During practice our team trounced the other team. defeated soundly
10. He returned the missing wallet intact to its owner. with nothing missing

B. This exercise will make use of all you have learned about dictionary entries. Each of the sentences below has an underlined word. Look up each word in your dictionary. Write the word in syllables, with hyphens between syllables. Copy the respelling from the dictionary, including accent marks and all other marks that help in pronunciation. Then write the definition that best fits the use of the word in the sentence.

Some answers may vary, depending on dictionary used.

1. The silhouette of the old tree stood out against the winter sky. (sil´-ōō-et´) outline
2. The hunter wore a chamois jacket. (sham´-ē) soft, leather
3. The river is navigable only during the rainy season.
4. The bats looked like phantoms as they flew from the barn. (fan´-temz) ghosts
5. The sculler had trouble moving against the wind. (scull´-er) person who rows the oars

(nav´-i-gə-bəl) wide or deep enough to be traveled on by boats

Chapter 16

Using Adjectives

Chapter Objectives

1. To understand the function of adjectives and to identify them in sentences
2. To identify adjectives that tell *what kind*
3. To identify adjectives that tell *how many*
4. To identify the demonstrative adjectives *this, that, these,* and *those*
5. To identify articles and to use them correctly
6. To differentiate between *them* and *those,* and to use the demonstrative adjectives with the words *kind* and *kinds* correctly
7. To form the comparative and superlative forms of adjectives, and to use them correctly

Preparing the Students

Discuss the picture on page 219. Have students tell what people and things they see in the picture. Write those nouns on the board. Then ask for words that describe those people and things, and write them in front of the nouns. Point out that those descriptive words help us understand what someone is talking about.

Additional Resources

Diagnostic Test—page 433 in this T.E. Recommended for use before teaching the chapter.

Mastery Test—pages 472 and 473 in this T.E. Recommended for use after teaching the chapter.

Additional Mastery Test—Recommended for use after any necessary reteaching. (In separate booklet, *Mastery Tests, Silver Level,* pages 35 and 36.)

Skills Practice Book—pages 82–88
Duplicating Masters—pages 82–88

Part 1 What Are Adjectives?

What picture do you see in your mind when you read this sentence?

>I saw a dog.

Although the sentence expresses a complete idea, it does not make the idea clear. It needs words to describe *dog* more exactly. Here are a few ways the sentence could be improved:

>I saw a huge, furry dog.
>
>I saw a small, playful dog.
>
>I saw a vicious, wild dog.
>
>I saw four lovable, eager dogs.

Part 1

Objective

To understand the function of adjectives and to identify them in sentences

Presenting the Lesson

1. Read and discuss pages 219 and 220. At this time, the text does not discuss articles as adjectives. Articles will be introduced and discussed fully in Part 5.

2. In addition to the definition of an adjective presented in Chapter 16, there are other ways to identify an adjective. These ways, listed in the following chart, are based on what linguists have discovered about the structure of a word and the order of words in a sentence. It is suggested that the information in the chart be used to point out additional ways in which adjectives function.

Ways To Identify Adjectives

1. Adjectives have more than one form. They change form to show comparison. Adjectives of more than two syllables usually show comparison by using the words *more* and *most*.

tall	taller	tallest
bad	worse	worst
careful	more careful	most careful

2. Adjectives are often preceded by words such as *very*, *quite*, or *much*.

very tall   quite bad
much more careful

3. Adjectives usually occur before nouns.

Tommy has a *bad* cold.
Eva is a *careful* pitcher.

The words *huge*, *furry*, *small*, *playful*, *vicious*, *wild*, *four*, *lovable*, and *eager* tell you more about *dog* or *dogs*. They make the meaning of the word more exact. These words are called **adjectives.**

Adjectives are used with nouns and pronouns. They may come before the word they describe.

I saw *brown* and *black* dogs.

They may also come after the word they describe. Sometimes a state-of-being verb stands between a noun or pronoun and the adjective describing it.

The dogs were *friendly*. They were *restless*.

You probably noticed a big difference between these two sentences:

I saw a *huge, furry* dog.
I saw a *small, playful* dog.

The different adjectives changed, or *modified*, the meaning of the word they described. For this reason, adjectives are called **modifiers.**

> An **adjective** is a word that modifies a noun or pronoun.

Usually, when we use two or more adjectives together, we separate them with commas. Adjectives telling numbers do not have to follow this rule.

The *four lovable, eager* dogs belonged to *two young* children.
Several dangerous alligators lived in the *warm, murky* pond.

Exercises Finding Adjectives

A. In each of the following pairs of sentences, only the adjectives have been changed. Number your paper from 1 to 5. For each pair of sentences, list each noun that is modified. After the noun, write the adjectives that modify it.

> Example: a. The tall man lifted the heavy box.
> b. The strong man lifted the enormous box.
>
> man—tall, strong   box—heavy, enormous

1. a. The small girl ran through the grassy field.   girl—small, careless
   b. The careless girl ran through the muddy field.   field—grassy, muddy

2. a. Twenty clowns wore silly costumes.   clowns—twenty, wacky
   b. Wacky clowns wore huge costumes.   costumes—silly, huge

3. a. Many fairgoers won different prizes.   fairgoers—many, lucky
   b. Lucky fairgoers won valuable prizes.   prizes—different, valuable

4. a. Soft music played on an old radio.   music—soft, classical
   b. Classical music played on a nearby radio.   radio—old, nearby

5. a. A blue purse lay in the dusty hallway.   purse—blue, full
   b. A full purse lay in the busy hallway.   hallway—dusty, busy

B. Fold a paper into four squares and number the squares from 1 to 4. Follow these directions. Draw a different picture in each square.

1. Draw a building in the first square.
2. Draw a brick building in the second square.
3. Draw a tall brick building in the third square.
4. Draw a tall, narrow, brick building in the fourth square.

If possible, compare your drawings with your classmates' drawings. Which of the four did everyone make most alike? Why do you think this happened?

3. Assign and discuss Exercise A on page 221. It is suggested that Exercise B be done as a class activity.

4. Use Exercise A on page 235 for additional practice or review.

Optional Exercise

Have the students follow these directions: In each of the following pairs of sentences, only the adjectives have been changed. Write both sentences as one sentence, using all the adjectives. Use commas when needed.

> Example: a. The red book is on the top shelf.
> b. The small book is on the wooden shelf.
>
> The small, red book is on the top, wooden shelf.

1. a. The huge dog licked the tiny kitten.
   b. The furry dog licked the gray kitten.
2. a. The colorful fireworks filled the dark sky.
   b. The bright fireworks filled the summer sky.
3. a. The sidewalk sale attracted eager customers.
   b. The yearly sale attracted many customers.
4. a. The young man had good friends.
   b. The lonely man had few friends.
5. a. Little Tweety escaped from big Sylvester.
   b. Clever Tweety escaped from angry Sylvester.

Part 2

Objective

To identify adjectives that tell *what kind*

Presenting the Lesson

1. Read and discuss page 222. Ask students for other adjectives with the adjective endings pointed out in paragraph 2. Can they think of other adjective endings and at least two examples of each ending?

2. Assign and discuss Exercises A and B on pages 222 and 223.

3. Use Exercise B on page 235 as additional practice or review.

Optional Practice

To play "Adjective Riddles," first separate the class into two teams. Each team works together to make game cards, enough for each person on the opposing team. The name of an easily visible object in the room is written on each game card. The game cards are then folded or placed face down, and mixed together.

A player from Team A draws a card and tries to get the members of that team to guess the object. The only clues the player may give are adjectives. The player may say up to five adjectives describing the object. For example, to describe windows, the student might use *glass, large, open, clear,* and *rectangular.* If the team correctly guesses the object, it earns a point. Limit each turn to a minute or less. Teams A and B alternate turns until each student has drawn a card. The team with the greatest number of points wins.

Part 2 Some Adjectives Tell *What Kind*

Most of the adjectives used so far in this chapter describe what someone is talking about. Adjectives of this type tell *what kind.* Here are some adjectives we have used to tell *what kind:*

huge	brown	furry	vicious	playful
small	black	friendly	dangerous	lovable
wild		murky		restless
young				
eager				

In the last three columns, you can see these five endings often found on adjectives: *-y, -ous, -ful, -able,* and *-less.*

Exercises Using Adjectives That Tell *What Kind*

A. Copy these sentences. Draw a line under each adjective that tells *what kind.*

1. There were joyful shouts from the stands.
2. Mr. Chalmers is a capable carpenter.
3. Jed wore his warm red jacket.
4. We sang funny songs on the long trip.
5. Marguerite threw out an old, dirty folder.
6. Cecilia put a large poster on the blank wall.
7. The spare room is a hopeless mess.
8. Max imagined furry, monstrous creatures.
9. Long, colorful streamers hung from the ceiling.
10. A beautiful sunset lit the rosy sky.

B. In this exercise, you will write your own sentences using adjectives that tell *what kind.* The following list gives twelve nouns with an adjective modifying each noun. Write at least five sentences. Use two of the adjective-noun combinations in each of your sentences. You may add some adjective-noun combinations of your own in any of your sentences.

brave captain
fearless crew
comfortable spaceship
strange creatures
distant planet
dangerous journey
terrible adventure
purple skin
wiggly antennas
poisonous air
successful escape
rocky ground

Part 3 Some Adjectives Tell *How Many*

Some adjectives tell *how many* of the thing someone is talking about. Here are examples of adjectives that tell *how many*. The adjectives are in italics.

six animals   *many* birds   *several* people
three stores   *few* lions   *more* insects

Exercises Finding Adjectives That Tell *How Many*

A. Copy these sentences. Draw a line under each adjective that tells *how many*.

1. Two jets power the plane.
2. Eight children raced past.
3. A trainer groomed four horses.
4. We stayed for forty minutes.
5. Curt read several books.
6. Lucinda put nine roses in one vase.
7. The question has many answers.
8. Those girls threw a dozen snowballs.
9. The United States started as thirteen colonies.
10. Countless stars fill the sky.

Extending the Lesson

Have students write ten phrases using one adjective from Column A, one from Column B, and a noun from Column C in each one. Then they should write five sentences, using one or more of their phrases in each sentence.

A	B	C
several	fiery	houses
many	colossal	jeeps
few	busy	globe
more	rapid	earrings
some	narrow	shirts
one	round	robots
ten	broad	furnaces
thirty	tall	bicycles
fifty	violet	alleys
sixteen	shiny	ribbons

Part 4

Objective

To identify the demonstrative adjectives *this*, *that*, *these*, and *those*

Presenting the Lesson

1. Read and discuss page 224. Point out that those adjectives do not describe the nouns they modify, but serve to point them out. Make sure students recognize that *this* and *these* refer to objects close at hand, while *that* and *those* refer to objects at a distance. More information about demonstrative adjectives will be presented in Part 6 of this Chapter.

2. Assign and discuss Exercise A on page 225. It is suggested that Exercise B be done as a class activity.

3. Use Exercise D on page 236 as additional practice or review.

B. Number your paper from 1 to 10. For each sentence below, list the adjectives that tell *how many*.

1. Both eggs hatched.
2. This program lasts thirty minutes.
3. We picked three bushels of apples.
4. Mother bought a dozen glazed doughnuts.
5. Ken did twenty push-ups.
6. Seven cars were damaged in the accident.
7. Few children play chess.
8. I have six dollars in my wallet.
9. Dee had one scoop of chocolate ice cream.
10. There are thirty children and twenty-five desks.

Part 4 Some Adjectives Tell *Which Ones*

Some adjectives tell *which one* or *which ones* someone is talking about. Here are four adjectives in this group that we use often:

this koala   *these* squirrels
that kangaroo *those* rabbits

Adjectives that point to persons, places, and things always come before the word they point to.

224

Exercises Using Adjectives

A. Number your paper from 1 to 10. Make two columns. Head one column *Which Ones.* Head the other *How Many.* Find the adjectives in these sentences. Write them in the right column.

Example: This bush has seven roses.

WO = Which Ones
HM = How Many

    Which Ones   How Many

    this   seven

1. These four stones are quartz.
2. Those three colors are my favorites.
3. This rabbit has nine babies.
4. Does this piece serve six people?
5. This book has many torn pages.
6. Several sandwiches are in that bag.
7. This record player has three speeds.
8. That octopus in your picture has only seven arms.
9. We bought a dozen cookies at that bakery.
10. Some swans swam on that pond.

B. In this exercise, look for adjectives that tell *what kind.* Look for adjectives that tell *how many.* Also, look for adjectives that tell *which ones.* Number your paper from 1 to 15. Write each of the fifteen adjectives in these sentences. Then write the noun it tells about.

WK = What Kind
HM = How Many
WO = Which Ones

Example: The old, hollow tree fell.
        old tree, hollow tree

1. Put these three blue boxes on that empty shelf.
2. We had several sheets of green paper.
3. Many young people crowded into one tiny room.
4. Look at that silver tray of delicious chocolate cookies.

Optional Practice

Have students replace each *the* in the following sentences with *this, that, these,* or *those,* and rewrite the sentences. There are several possible revisions.

1. *The* gardener trimmed the high bushes on *the* corner.

2. *The* boxes of paper clips are in *the* top desk drawer under *the* package of file cards.

3. *The* magnificent lion stretched out in *the* cage and yawned at *the* people watching him.

4. *The* old building with *the* broken windows will be repaired by *the* new owners.

Part 5

Objective

To identify articles and to use them correctly

Presenting the Lesson

1. Read and discuss page 226. If students bring up the question, explain that the long *u* sound is grouped with the consonants. The article *a* is used before the long *u* sound (*a* uniform, not *an* uniform).

2. Hearing the article-noun combination may help students to remember the rules, so it is suggested that the class do Exercise A on pages 226 and 227 orally. Assign and discuss Exercise B.

3. Use Exercise E on pages 236 and 237 for additional practice or review.

Optional Practice

1. This Exercise is intended to help students associate the sounds of articles with the beginning sounds of the words that follow them. Make flash cards with the words and phrases listed below. Divide the class into two parts, one side representing the article *a*, the other, *an*. Show the cards, one at a time, to the class. Read the card to the class. If the word or phrase should have *a* before it, then that side of the room should stand and say *a* and the word or phrase. If it should be *an*, the *an* side of the room should answer.

airplane, old calendar, afternoon tour, additional problem, animal catcher, answer, arm, army, earthling, egg, engine, escape hatch, explanation, ice bucket, idea, inchworm, island, iron, handle, hat, head

Part 5 Articles

The words *a*, *an*, and *the* are called **articles**. Since they always modify nouns, they are also adjectives.

You may use the word *the* before singular or plural nouns beginning with any letter.

the alphabet   *the* sentences

You may use the words *a* and *an* before singular nouns only. Follow these rules in choosing the correct article:

1. Use *a* before words beginning with consonant sounds:

a person   *a* fresh egg
a story   *a* black olive
a cake   *a* good idea

2. Use *an* before words beginning with vowel sounds:

an average person   *an* egg
an impossible story   *an* olive
an upside-down cake   *an* idea

Some words begin with a silent *h*. In these words, you do not say the *h* sound. Instead, you begin the word with the sound of the vowel after the *h*. Therefore, you follow the second rule, and use *an*.

an honor   *an* hour   *an* honest child

Exercises Using Articles

A. Copy the following sentences. Fill in the blanks with *a* or *an*.

1. Do you keep __a__ diary?
2. Jones is __an__ honorable judge.
3. Sarah held __a__ brush and __a__ comb.

4. Gordon got __a__ haircut.
5. The train left __an__ hour ago.
6. __A__ dachshund has __a__ long body.
7. Diana tossed __a__ horseshoe.
8. __An__ old woman opened __an__ umbrella.
9. I had __a__ nightmare last night.
10. The woodsman carried __an__ ax and __a__ saw.

rest, heart shape, heat wave, hourly chime, human being, office worker, orange peel, uncle, hourly rate, angry bee, early bird, easy problem, empty basket, important lesson, inside curve, happy laugh, high note, open door, telephone call, window ledge, water wheel, wagon train, hot dog, long vacation, total surprise, summer sun, grocery bag, broken finger, large company, heavy book, hot air balloon

B. There are twelve nouns below. Write five sentences, using two of the nouns in each sentence. Place an article (*a, an,* or *the*) and another adjective before each noun. *Answers will vary.*

Example: A tall ringmaster greeted the eager audience.

1. circus
2. elephant
3. clown
4. tricks
5. act
6. ringmaster
7. acrobat
8. lions
9. man
10. woman
11. children
12. audience

2. Have students bring in a clipping of at least one paragraph from a newspaper or magazine, circle the articles, underline any other adjectives that follow the article and come before the noun, and put a box around the noun referred to.

Example: ⓘThe political ▢campaign is in full swing.

Part 6

Objective

To differentiate between *them* and *those*, and to use the demonstrative adjectives with the words *kind* and *kinds* correctly

Presenting the Lesson

1. Read and discuss page 228. Remind students that *them* is a plural pronoun and takes the place of plural nouns used as objects only. Ask students for sample sentences using *those*, *them*, *this kind*, *that kind*, *these kinds*, and *those kinds*.

2. Assign and discuss Exercise B. It is suggested that you do Exercise A on page 229 as a class activity.

3. Use Exercise F on page 237 as additional practice or review.

Optional Practice

Using the following sentences, have the students identify those sentences in which the underlined phrase can be replaced by *them*. They should revise those sentences, using the word *them* instead of the phrase.

    Example: a. We like <u>the red balloons</u> best.
                   We like them best.
           b. <u>Those groceries</u> are too heavy.
               (no revision possible)

1. I enjoy <u>this</u> kind of movie.
2. We bought <u>those new tennis balls</u> at this store.

Part 6   Using Adjectives Correctly

Four adjectives that tell which one, or which ones, are *this*, *that*, *these*, and *those*. When they modify nouns and pronouns, they point out specific things.

    This book is more interesting than *that* one.
    These pencils are sharper than *those* pencils.

Using *Them* and *Those*

Look at these sentences carefully.

1. I saw *those men* on the airplane.
2. Jeanie saw *them*, too.

The word *those* is an adjective. It tells which men. The word *them* is not an adjective. It is never used to point to a noun. *Them* is a pronoun. It is used in place of a noun.

3. We found *those books* in the pack.
4. Someone left *them* there.

This Kind and *That Kind*

The word *kind* sometimes causes trouble. It means just *one kind*. If we want to speak of more than one kind, we say *kinds*.

When we use an adjective to point to *kind*, we use *this* or *that*. We never say "these kind" or "them kind."

When we use an adjective to point to *kinds*, we use *these* or *those*.

Study the sentences below to see how these words are used.

1. I like *this kind* of ice cream.
2. I like *those kinds* of books.
3. I had *that kind* of hat last year.
4. *These kinds* of doughnuts are the best.

> Mike baked **those brownies.**
> We ate **them.**
> **Those brownies** were delicious.
> We liked **them.**

3. <u>These</u> kinds of puzzles confuse me.
4. The drugstore is having a sale on <u>that</u> kind of ice cream.
5. The young kitten clawed <u>the new drapes</u>.
6. The baby ate <u>ten</u> pieces of candy.
7. <u>These</u> kinds of books are difficult to read.
8. I enjoyed <u>those science fiction stories</u>.

Exercises   Choosing the Right Word

A. Choose the right word for each sentence. Write it on your paper.

1. We like (them, <u>those</u>) blue candies best.
2. Do you have any of (<u>those</u>, them) green caps?
3. (This, Them, <u>These</u>) kind of tire is safest.
4. (Them, <u>These</u>) kinds of problems are very hard.
5. I use (<u>that</u>, those, them) kind of pen at school.
6. We read (<u>those</u>, them) books last summer.
7. (This, Them, <u>These</u>) kind of story appeals to me.
8. Will you take (<u>those</u>, them) packages to the office?
9. Where can I see (them, <u>those</u>) kinds of monkeys?
10. (Them, <u>Those</u>) clothes must be washed.

B. Follow the directions for Exercise A.

1. (<u>Those</u>, Them) firecrackers exploded.
2. (<u>That</u>, Those) kind of candy is chewy.
3. Do (them, <u>those</u>) ski masks keep you warm?
4. Alethia always makes (<u>this</u>, these) kind of shot for the basket.
5. (That, Them, <u>Those</u>) kind of bug stings.
6. (<u>Those</u>, Them) reins control the horse.
7. A queen wore (them, <u>those</u>) jewels.
8. Terry likes (this, <u>these</u>) kinds of projects.
9. Many farmers grow (them, <u>those</u>) grains.
10. Marietta built (<u>that</u>, those) kind of model airplane.

Part 7

Objective

To form the comparative and superlative forms of adjectives, and to use them correctly

Presenting the Lesson

1. Read and discuss pages 230 to 232. If the students are familiar enough with the concept of syllables, you may find it helpful to define a *long* adjective as, usually, one with more than two syllables. Ask for more examples for each rule. Spelling changes will be discussed thoroughly in Chapter 27.

2. You may wish to do Exercises A and B on page 232 with the class. Assign and discuss Exercises C and D on page 233.

3. Use Exercise G on page 237 as additional practice or review.

Optional Practice

Direct students to complete the first five sentences below with *good*, *better*, or *best*, and the second five with *bad*, *worse*, or *worst*.

good—better—best
1. That camera is the _____ I've ever had.
2. The old car runs _____ than the new one.
3. That is the _____ record I've heard.
4. Clowns are _____ at making people laugh.
5. Those are _____ snacks.

Part 7 Making Comparisons with Adjectives

You often use adjectives to compare people, places, and things. The adjectives used to describe must be changed slightly when they are used to compare.

For example, you could describe two students with these sentences:

Jarilyn is *tall*.   Frank is *tall*.

What if you want to compare the two, and to say that they are not the same size? You would use one of these sentences:

Jarilyn is *taller* than Frank.
Frank is *taller* than Jarilyn.

Now, suppose you want to compare a third student with Frank and Jarilyn. César is taller than Frank, and taller than Jarilyn. What would you say?

You probably gave this sentence:

César is *tallest*.

tall   taller   tallest

Here are the rules we follow for using short adjectives in comparisons:

1. When you compare two people, places, or things, you usually add *-er* to the adjective.

 tall + er = taller happy + er = happier
 large + er = larger funny + er = funnier

(Note that if the adjective ends in *e*, you drop the *e* before adding *-er*. If the adjective ends in *y*, change the *y* to *i* before adding *-er*.)

2. When you compare three or more people, places, or things, you usually add *-est* to the adjective.

 tall + est = tallest happy + est = happiest
 large + est = largest funny + est = funniest

(If the adjective ends in *e*, drop the *e* before adding *-est*. If the adjective ends in *y*, change the *y* to *i* before adding *-est*.)

Using *More* and *Most* in Comparisons

We do not always add *-er* or *-est* to make comparisons. For example, if the adjective ends in *-ful*, like *hopeful*, we use *more* and *most* with it. If the adjective is a long one, we use *more* and *most* instead of adding *-er* and *-est*.

1. Ted has been *more careful* since the accident.
2. Barbara was the *most careful* of the three girls.
3. My puzzle is *more difficult* than yours.
4. This is the *most difficult* puzzle of all.

Here are the rules for using long adjectives in comparisons:

1. Use *more* when comparing two persons, places, or things.

 more careful more difficult
 more terrible more dangerous

bad—worse—worst
6. The careless driver was in a _____ accident.
7. That was the _____ candy I've ever had.
8. We were lucky the storm damage wasn't any _____ than it was.
9. The roads are in _____ shape than last year.
10. You had a _____ fall.

Extending the Lesson

Have students choose one or more of the sets of animals below and write six sentences comparing them, using *er* or *more* with adjective forms. Have them head their papers with the names of the animals they have chosen, then write three sentences comparing the first animal with the second, and three sentences comparing the second animal with the first.

 Example: a bear and a mouse
  a. A bear is bigger than a mouse.
  b. A mouse has a longer tail than a bear.

1. a kangaroo and an elephant
2. a giraffe and a snake
3. a skunk and a porcupine
4. a camel and a polar bear
5. a moose and a rabbit

2. Use *most* when comparing three persons, places, or things.

most careful   most difficult
most terrible   most dangerous

Use only one form of comparison at a time. If you use *-er* or *-est*, do not use *more* or *most* in the same comparison. You would not say, "My brother is more bigger than I am." You would not say, "My dog is the most smartest dog in our neighborhood."

The Forms of *Good* and *Bad*

A few adjectives change to completely new words when they are used in comparisons. Here are two important adjectives of this kind:

good   better   best
bad   worse   worst

Exercises   Making Comparisons with Adjectives

A. Some of the following adjectives add *-er* and *-est* when they are used in comparisons. Others are used with *more* and *most*. Number your paper from 1 to 12. Copy each adjective. Then write the two forms it uses in comparisons.

Example: slow
  slow, slower, slowest
colorful
  colorful, more colorful, most colorful

1. helpful — more helpful, most helpful
2. dark — darker, darkest
3. pretty — prettier, prettiest
4. handsome — more handsome, most handsome
5. dangerous — more dangerous, most dangerous
6. intelligent — more intelligent, most intelligent
7. wide — wider, widest
8. hard — harder, hardest
9. wonderful — more wonderful, most wonderful
10. great — greater, greatest
11. silly — sillier, silliest
12. curious — more curious, most curious

B. Number your paper from 1 to 10. Choose the correct adjective form for each sentence. Write it on your paper.

1. Jeff is (taller, more taller) than Lois.
2. Which of the two pails is (larger, largest)?
3. I picked the (thinner, thinnest) of the four books.
4. This piece of cloth is the (biggest, bigger) of the two.
5. Pat is (carefuler, more careful) than Tom.
6. Darren is the (fastest, most fast) runner of all.
7. The lake is (more deep, deeper, more deeper) than it was last year.
8. Your house is (more large, larger) than ours.
9. The last arithmetic example was also the (most hard, hardest).
10. This is the (most delicious, deliciousest) pie I have ever eaten.

C. Follow the directions for Exercise B.

1. Laura is the (most happy, happiest) baby I've seen.
2. This map is (more useful, usefuller) than the globe.
3. The (bigger, biggest) of the two packages was mine.
4. The cheetah is the (most fastest, fastest) animal of all.
5. A whale is (larger, more large) than an elephant.
6. That story was (sillier, more sillier) than the last one.
7. I read the (longer, longest) of the three books.
8. Of the thirty flavors, which is (better, best, bestest)?
9. Holcomb is the (accuratest, most accurate) passer.
10. Which of the two ponies is (gentler, gentlest?)

D. Choose five objects that are found both in classrooms and in homes. Make up sentences comparing the school objects with the home objects. Answers will vary.

Sentence Patterns

Objective

To recognize the use of adjectives in the N LV Adj sentence pattern

Presenting the Lesson

1. Read and discuss page 234. Remind students that an adjective following a linking verb describes the subject noun. If students raise the question, let them know that there may be more than one word in the adjective-part of an N LV Adj sentence.

N	LV	Adj
I	feel	very sleepy.

2. Assign and discuss Exercises A and C on page 237. You may prefer to do Exercise B as a class activity.

3. This may be a good time to review the four sentence patterns presented in this text: N V (page 123); N V N (page 150); N LV N (page 151); and now N LV Adj. Have the students examine a passage in their reading material and classify each sentence that fits one of the basic patterns.

Optional Practice

Have students make a chart for the N LV Adj pattern. Tell them to fill in the subject nouns from the following list. They should choose a linking verb and an adjective to follow it that matches each subject.

N	LV	Adj
1. rainbows	is	yellow
2. snow	are	spotted
3. stop lights	was	purple
4. pumpkin	were	white
5. the sun		colorful
6. some grapes		shiny
7. some buckles		orange
8. some cows		red

Sentence Patterns — The N LV Adj Pattern

Sentences in the **N LV Adj pattern** have three parts. The *N* stands for the subject noun. *LV* stands for linking verb. *Adj* stands for adjective that follows the linking verb. The sentences in the following chart are in the N LV Adj pattern.

N	LV	Adj
The classroom	is	quiet.
Lemons	taste	sour.
Chris	was	fearless.
This record	sounds	scratchy.
These new boots	look	large.

Exercises   The N LV Adj Pattern

A. Make a chart like the one above. Label the three columns N, LV, and Adj. Write these sentences on the chart.

1. Connie looks happy.
2. These roads are narrow.
3. Your sweater feels furry.
4. Tacos are tasty.
5. The radio sounds loud.
6. The mail was late.
7. The oranges were ripe.
8. This radish tastes bitter.

B. Make a chart like the one below. Complete each sentence in the N LV Adj pattern. Answers will vary.

N	LV	Adj
1. _____	is	funny.
2. _____	looks	sad.
3. Sandpaper	feels	_____.
4. The Haleys	_____	friendly.
5. _____	was	_____.

C. Make a chart of your own. Write five sentences in the N LV Adj pattern. Answers will vary.

Additional Exercises

Using Adjectives

A. Finding Adjectives (Use after page 220.)

In each of the following pairs of sentences, only the adjectives have been changed. Number your paper from 1 to 4. For each pair of sentences, list each noun that is modified. After the noun, write the adjectives that modify it.

1. a. We swam in a large, clear lake. lake—large, clear,
   b. We swam in a warm, shallow lake. warm, shallow
2. a. Tiny birds perched on the bare branches. birds—Tiny, White
   b. White birds perched on the dark branches. branches—bare, dark
3. a. The powerful speaker talked to a joyous crowd. speaker—powerful, fearful
   b. The fearful speaker talked to a rowdy crowd. crowd—joyous, rowdy
4. a. A hot, gusty wind swept the area. wind—hot, gusty,
   b. A fierce, cold wind swept the area. fierce, cold

B. Using Adjectives That Tell *What Kind* (Use after page 222.)

Copy these sentences. Draw a line under each adjective that tells *what kind*.

1. The nervous player bit his fingernails.
2. Stacey is a reliable friend.
3. Those mushrooms are poisonous.
4. This new restaurant has tasty hamburgers.
5. I like the cool, peaceful days of fall.
6. We ate crisp bacon and juicy tomatoes.
7. Martha brushed her beautiful white teeth.
8. The helpful boy erased the messy chalkboards.
9. A harmless snake slid across the narrow path.
10. The Cyclops was an evil, ugly monster.

Additional Exercises

If these Exercises were not used with each lesson, they may be assigned now for chapter review.

C. Finding Adjectives That Tell *How Many* (Use after page 223.)

Number your paper from 1 to 10. For each sentence below, list the adjectives that tell *how many*.

1. Stan hit four foul balls.
2. One girl stood alone in the dark.
3. The teacher broke up several fights.
4. Beth wore three new charms on her bracelet.
5. All games have rules.
6. The flood ruined ten homes.
7. Many houses have chimneys.
8. Some ski hats have pompoms.
9. Mickey Mouse is over fifty years old.
10. Two police officers ride in the squad car.

D. Using Adjectives (Use after page 225.)

In this exercise, look for adjectives that tell *what kind*. Look for adjectives that tell *how many*. Also, look for adjectives that tell *which ones*. Number your paper from 1 to 15. Write each of the fifteen adjectives in these sentences. Then write the noun it tells about.

WK = What Kind
HM = How Many
WO = Which Ones

1. These tiny mice have long, skinny tails.
2. Did you make this wonderful cake with four layers?
3. I'll buy these four colorful fish and that big fishbowl.
4. Several close neighbors visited the ill woman.

E. Using Articles (Use after page 226.)

Copy these sentences. Fill in the blanks with *a* or *an*.

1. Do you have __an__ extra oar?
2. The rock made __a__ loud splash.
3. I smelled __an__ odd odor.
4. Our town has __an__ outdoor pool.

5. Amy wore __a__ plaid skirt and __a__ yellow sweater.
6. It's __an__ honor to meet you.
7. Did you get __an__ answer to your letter?
8. __A__ lifeguard sat on __a__ high seat.

F. Choosing the Right Word (Use after page 228.)

Choose the right word for each sentence. Write it down.

1. A lumberjack cut down (them, __those__) trees.
2. (This, __These__) kinds of cereal are sugared.
3. Pam collects (this, them, __these__) kinds of stamps.
4. (__Those__, Them) scary stories are true.
5. What's in (them, __those__) boxcars?
6. Mom wears (__that__, those) kind of perfume.
7. (__That__, Those) kind of game takes too long.
8. Blacksmiths make (them, __those__) horseshoes.
9. We build fires with (that, them, __those__) kinds of wood.
10. I topped the sundae with (them, __those__) nuts.

G. Making Comparisons with Adjectives (Use after page 232.)

Number your paper from 1 to 10. Choose the correct adjective form for each sentence. Write it on your paper.

1. Angel's lunch is the (__biggest__, most biggest) of all.
2. Tammy told the (most silly, __silliest__) riddle.
3. Cats make the (wonderfullest, __most wonderful__) pets.
4. Hand me the (softer, __softest__) of the four pillows.
5. This plant is (__healthier__, healthiest) than that one.
6. Washing dishes is (__easier__, more easier) than drying them.
7. Popeye is (__funnier__, more funnier) than the Roadrunner.
8. One spy was (carefuller, __more careful__) than the others.
9. Of the two reports, Charla's is (__better__, best).
10. Saturday seems like the (shorter, __shortest__) day of the week.

Chapter 17

Using Adverbs

Chapter Objectives

1. To understand the function of adverbs and to identify them in sentences

2. To form the comparative forms of adverbs and to use them correctly

3. To differentiate between adverbs and adjectives, and to make the correct choice in sentences

Preparing the Students

Ask students for words that tell about the action in the picture on page 239. Write the verbs and related adverbs on the board. Point out that in these phrases the verbs are described. Tell students that the purpose of this chapter is to inform them about that group of words used to describe words other than nouns.

Additional Resources

Diagnostic Test—page 434 in this T.E. Recommended for use before teaching the chapter.

Mastery Test—pages 474–475 in this T.E. Recommended for use after teaching the chapter.

Additional Mastery Test—Recommended for use after any necessary reteaching. (In separate booklet, *Mastery Tests, Silver Level*, pages 37–38.)

Skills Practice Book—pages 89–94

Duplicating Masters—pages 89–94

Part 1 What Are Adverbs?

In Chapter 16, you learned that adjectives tell about nouns and pronouns.

We use another kind of word to tell about verbs and adjectives. These words are **adverbs.** Like adjectives, adverbs are called modifiers. Adverbs can also modify other adverbs.

Adverbs Modify Verbs

The girls worked.

How?   The girls worked *quickly.*

Where?   The girls worked *anywhere.*

When?   The girls *always* worked.

Part 1

Objective

To understand the function of adverbs and to identify them in sentences

Presenting the Lesson

1. Read and discuss pages 239 and 240. Ask for other adverbs belonging to each of the four groups. Have the students change the sample sentences by substituting their adverbs for those given.

2. In addition to the definition of an adverb given in this chapter, there are other ways to identify an adverb, based on what linguists have discovered about the structure of a word and the order of words in a sentence. The following chart lists these ways. It is suggested that the information in the chart be used to point out additional ways in which adverbs function.

Ways To Identify Adverbs

1. Adverbs are often difficult to separate from adjectives. One of the best ways to identify adverbs is by their positions in sentences. They are most often found at the end of a sentence.

>Don called *loudly*.
>Jana sang *softly*.

2. Adverbs can also be found in other places in a sentence.

At the Beginning
Now the race begins.

Between Subject and Verb
The vegetables *here* are fresh.

Within Verb Phrases
I can *always* eat dessert.

Before an Adjective
The box is *extremely* heavy.

3. Look for words that fit the blank in this test sentence:
>She did it _____.

4. Look for words with the ending -ly:
>adjective + ly = adverb
>calm + ly = calmly

Adverbs Modify Adjectives

	That box is heavy.
How heavy?	That box is *terribly* heavy.
	This is an interesting book.
How interesting?	This is an *extremely* interesting book.

Adverbs Modify Other Adverbs

	Dale goes to Burger King often.
How often?	Dale goes to Burger King *very* often.
	He always orders cheeseburgers.
To what extent?	He *almost* always orders cheeseburgers.

Here is a list of words frequently used as adverbs:

How	Where	When	To What Extent
well	here	now	quite
hard	there	never	almost
fast	inside	often	very
much	outside	always	too

Many more adverbs are formed by adding -ly to an adjective, as in these examples:

quick—quickly	happy—happily
slow—slowly	sad—sadly
tight—tightly	powerful—powerfully
loose—loosely	careless—carelessly

If you are not sure whether a word is an adverb, ask yourself two questions. Does the word modify a verb, an adjective, or another adverb? Does it tell *how*, *when*, or *where*? If you can answer *yes* to these questions, the word is an adverb.

> An **adverb** adds to the meaning of a verb, an adjective, or another adverb.
>
> It tells *how, where, when,* or *to what extent.*
>
> Many adverbs end in *ly.*

Exercises   Using Adverbs

A. In these sentences the words in italics are adverbs. Find the verb that each adverb tells more about.

1. Trigger whined *sadly*, but Luke left him behind.
2. Luke started *slowly* up the mountain.
3. He *carefully* watched where to put his feet.
4. One of the rocks slipped *suddenly*.
5. Luke scrambled *wildly* for a footing.
6. Then blackness surrounded him *completely*.
7. When he awoke, his head throbbed *painfully*.
8. He moved *slowly* in the darkness.
9. A cold nose touched his cheek *lightly*. It was Trigger!
10. Trigger barked *joyously*.

B. Number your paper from 1 to 10. Write every adverb used in each sentence.

1. The bikers were hopelessly lost.   *hopelessly*
2. The hunters never found the deer.   *never*
3. This watch is always wrong.   *always*
4. A shaft led down into the mine.   *down*
5. The teacher quickly turned around.   *quickly, around*
6. Debbie tugged very hard on the rope.   *very, hard*
7. Leroy outgrew his clothes too quickly.   *too, quickly*
8. My canteen is almost empty.   *almost*
9. The arrow nearly hit the horse.   *nearly*
10. Monica usually peers timidly around the corner.   *usually, timidly*

3. Assign and discuss Exercises A, B, and C on pages 241 and 242. In Exercises A and C, every adverb modifies a verb. In Exercise B, adverbs modify verbs, adjectives, and other adverbs. When checking Exercise B, you might have the students identify each word modified by adverbs, and tell which of the three types it is.

4. Use Exercise A on page 248 as additional practice or review.

Optional Practice

Have students divide their papers into four columns: *How, When, Where, To What Extent*. Ask students to list each of the following adverbs in the correct column:

almost, peacefully, seldom, correctly, fast, up, suddenly, too, outside, never, hard, loudly, much, easily, cheerfully, painlessly, very, there, silently, often, quite, down, inside, continuously, well, sometimes, outdoors, here, early, actively, yearly, late, tightly, always, weekly, briefly, now

Extending the Lesson

Have students imagine a "supermachine" that they would like to invent, give it a name, and write at least five sentences, each telling something different that it does. Students should use an adverb in each sentence to describe the action.

C. Here is a list of verbs. After each verb is an adverb that can be used with that verb in a sentence. Write a sentence using each verb-adverb combination.

Example: spoke softly   The lion tamer spoke softly to the big cats.

1. slipped   often
2. ran   quickly
3. barked   furiously
4. rushed   angrily
5. waited   there
6. flew   swiftly
7. trudged   sadly
8. danced   well

Part 2 Making Comparisons with Adverbs

Part 2

Objective

To form the comparative forms of adverbs and to use them correctly

Presenting the Lesson

1. Read and discuss pages 242 and 243. Point out that the rules for making the comparative forms of adverbs are the same as for adjectives. Ask for sentences using the sample adverbs correctly in all three forms.
2. Assign and discuss Exercises A and B on page 243.
3. Use Exercise B on pages 248 and 249 as additional practice or review.

Adverbs, like adjectives, can be used in comparisons.

John Henry worked *harder* than the steam engine.
He worked the *hardest* of all the drillers.

There are three ways adverbs are changed to show comparisons.

1. Some short adverbs add *-er* when two persons or things are being compared. They add *-est* when three or more are compared.

| hard | harder | hardest |
| fast | faster | fastest |

2. Most adverbs that end in *-ly* use the word *more* in comparing two persons or things. They use *most* in comparing three or more.

carelessly	more carelessly	most carelessly
quickly	more quickly	most quickly
strongly	more strongly	most strongly

3. Some adverbs change their forms completely when they are used in comparisons.

well	better	best
badly	worse	worst
much	more	most
little	less	least

Exercises **Making Comparisons with Adverbs**

A. The following adverbs are examples of all three groups discussed in this chapter part. Number your paper from 1 to 12. Copy each adverb. Then write the two forms it uses in comparisons.

Example: much

much, more, most

1. rapidly — more rapidly, most rapidly
2. little — less, least
3. happily — more happily, most happily
4. hopelessly — more hopelessly, most hopelessly
5. fast — faster, fastest
6. carefully — more carefully, most carefully
7. brightly — more brightly, most brightly
8. badly — worse, worst
9. loudly — more loudly, most loudly
10. well — better, best
11. slowly — more slowly, most slowly
12. hard — harder, hardest

B. Number your paper from 1 to 10. Choose the correct adverb form from the parentheses. Write it on your paper.

1. Please waken me (earlier, more early) tomorrow.
2. Louise pushed (hardest, harder) than Dan.
3. The squirrel came (more near, nearer) to us.
4. The new toaster works (more well, weller, better) than the old one.
5. Of the two girls, Anna jumped (higher, highest).
6. Colin runs (faster, more fast) than I can.
7. Jess swam (more evenly, evenlier) today.
8. The team played (best, wellest, bestest) in the finals.
9. Of the three cereals, I like Applepuffs (least, littlest).
10. The black fish ate (most greedily, more greedily) of all.

Optional Practice

Make copies of the sentences below or put them on the board. Have students copy the sentences putting an adverb in the blank. Next to the sentence, they should write the verb it describes.

Example: The cat meowed louder at night.   meowed

1. The thin greyhound ran _____ of all the dogs.
2. The huge elephant trumpeted _____ than the baby elephant.
3. The chattering monkeys swung _____ on the ropes than before.
4. The large opossum waddled _____ across the cage than the little mouse.
5. The old hippopotamus wallowed _____ in the mud than the young one.
6. The sleek jaguar leaped _____ than its prey.

Part 3

Objective

To differentiate between adverbs and adjectives, and to make the correct choice in sentences

Presenting the Lesson

1. Read and discuss pages 244 and 245.

2. It is suggested that you do Exercise A on page 245 with the class. Assign and discuss Exercise B on page 246.

3. Read and discuss page 246. Ask students for other sentences using *good*, *bad*, *well*, and *badly*.

4. It may be helpful to do Exercise A on page 247 with the class. Assign and discuss Exercise B.

5. Use Exercise C on page 249 as additional practice or review.

Optional Practice

Present the following lists of words on the board or on a worksheet. Students are to identify each word in the first column as either a noun or a verb, and each word in the second as an adjective or an adverb. Then they should choose a word from column 2 that can describe a word in column 1, and write the combination phrase either by itself or in a sentence. (If you ask students for complete sentences, have them underline the phrases they formed.)

1	2
1. hamburger	a. helpful
2. runs	b. narrow
3. searched	c. easily
4. behaves	d. raw
5. advice	e. solid
6. walked	f. closely
7. sat	g. oddly
8. stereo	h. comfortably
	i. fat
	j. seriously

Part 3   Adjective or Adverb?

Adjectives tell about nouns. Adverbs tell about verbs. Sometimes it is hard to tell whether to use an adjective or an adverb. This happens because many adverbs and adjectives look alike.

Many adverbs are made by adding *-ly* to an adjective. See how this works:

wise—wisely   slow—slowly
loud—loudly   honest—honestly
happy—happily   quick—quickly

Is Alan neat?

Does he paint neatly?

Now look at this sentence:

Joan watched (careful, carefully) where she put her feet.

Would you use *careful* or *carefully* in the sentence?

To find the answer, ask what you are trying to say. Are you trying to say

how many Joan watched?
which one Joan watched?
what kind Joan watched?

Or are you trying to say

how Joan watched?

You are try to say *how*. The kind of word that tells how something happened or how something was done is an adverb. This adverb modifies the verb *watched*. You would use the adverb *carefully* in this sentence.

Next, consider this sentence:

Carlos's mother makes (real, really) good tacos.

Would you use *real* or *really*?

Decide first which word is being modified. Is the modifier describing the noun *tacos*? Does it tell *what kind, how many*, or *which one*? Is it describing the adjective *good*? Does it tell *how good*?

If you were reading carefully, you probably gave the correct answer, that the modifier tells *how good*. Since it tells *how* and modifies an adjective, it must be an adverb. The correct word to use is *really*.

Exercises Choosing the Right Word

A. Number your paper from 1 to 10. Choose the right modifier. Write it on your paper. Next, write the word it modifies. Then write *Adjective* or *Adverb* to show how the word is used.

> Examples: The batter hit the ball (solid, solidly).
>
> solidly, hit, adverb
>
> Carol was (hopeful, hopefully) about the test.
>
> hopeful, Carol, adjective

1. I can see (perfect, perfectly) without glasses.   **Adv.**
2. Ramon ran (quick, quickly) to the corner.   **Adv.**
3. Janet was (eager, eagerly) for the play to begin.   **Adj.**
4. My father handles his tools (careful, carefully).   **Adv.**
5. Harriet won the game (fair, fairly).   **Adv.**
6. The light can be seen (clear, clearly).   **Adv.**
7. Faith decorated the room (colorful, colorfully).   **Adv.**
8. The old turtle moved (slow, slowly) through the grass.   **Adv.**
9. The sun shone (bright, brightly).   **Adv.**
10. Gregory is a (real, really) fast swimmer.   **Adv.**

Extending the Lesson

Have students think of an occupation: fireman, policeman, baseball player, secretary, etc. Tell them to write six sentences: three sentences using adjectives to describe different things a person in that occupation needs or uses; and three sentences using adverbs to describe actions a person in that occupation does. Students should underline the adjectives and adverbs they use, and be able to tell what word each modifies.

> Example: A fireman wears a <u>big</u>, <u>red</u> hat.
>
> He rides <u>rapidly</u> to a fire.

B. Follow the directions for Exercise A.

1. The children ran (noisy, noisily) to the lunchroom. Adv.
2. I carried a (real, really) heavy suitcase. Adv.
3. The tractor moved (slowly, slow) across the field. Adv.
4. Angela spoke (soft, softly) on the phone. Adv.
5. The racer turned the corner (sharp, sharply). Adv.
6. The guard made a (careful, carefully) search of the area. Adj.
7. Your serve is (near, nearly) perfect. Adv.
8. Division is my only (real, really) difficulty in math. Adj.
9. Paul was (shy, shyly) with the strangers. Adj.
10. Karen stitched the seam (perfect, perfectly). Adv.

Using *Good* and *Bad,* and *Well* and *Badly*

You will have no trouble with the words *good* and *bad* if you follow this rule.

> Use *good* and *bad* to describe nouns or pronouns. These words are adjectives.
>
> Jane has a *good* clarinet. (what kind)
> Jim has a *bad* cold. (what kind)

Follow this rule for using *well* and *badly*.

> Use *well* and *badly* with verbs to tell how something is done.
> These words are adverbs.
>
> Jane plays the clarinet *well*. (*how* she plays)
> Jim behaved *badly*. (*how* he behaved)

Exercises Using *Good* and *Bad,* and *Well* and *Badly*

A. Number your paper from 1 to 10. Write *Adjective* or *Adverb* to tell how each underlined word is used. Then write the word or words that the underlined word modifies.

Example: You are good at spelling.

adjective, modifies *you*

1. Dark clouds are a bad sign. Adj.
2. Tina has good news. Adj.
3. Hank draws very well. Adv.
4. The ferris wheel is a good ride. Adj.
5. Rosalie skates better than anyone else in the class. Adv.
6. That bike is badly dented. Adv.
7. The fashion model dresses well. Adv.
8. The new pencil sharpener is much better than the old one. Adj.
9. Last spring Matt had the worst cold ever. Adj.
10. Of all my friends, Gabe keeps a secret best. Adv.

B. Follow the directions for Exercise A.

1. The other team is badly coached. Adv.
2. Did you eat a good breakfast? Adj.
3. We planned the party well. Adv.
4. Tony has a bad temper. Adj.
5. My pen pal writes good letters. Adj.
6. The old car rattles badly. Adv.
7. The worst storm of the decade hit the county. Adj.
8. Tracy sees better with her glasses than without them. Adv.
9. This radio works best during the first ten minutes of operation. Adv.
10. Fried eggs upset Mona's stomach worse than scrambled eggs. Adv.

Additional Exercises

If these Exercises were not used with each lesson, they may now be assigned for chapter review.

Additional Exercises

Using Adverbs

A. Using Adverbs (Use after page 241.)

Number your paper from 1 to 10. Write down every adverb used in each sentence.

1. Otters slid swiftly into the water. *swiftly*
2. My dream almost happened. *almost*
3. This mystery is quite enjoyable. *quite*
4. The dog is terribly thirsty. *terribly*
5. Ruthie never rides after dark. *never*
6. The wet paint rubbed off on my sleeve. *off*
7. We took the bus too far. *too, far*
8. Dennis raked the leaves very thoroughly. *very, thoroughly*
9. The raft drifted lazily downstream. *lazily, downstream*
10. Those twins are totally different. *totally*

B. Making Comparisons with Adverbs (Use after page 243.)

Number your paper from 1 to 10. Choose the correct adverb form from the parentheses. Write it on your paper.

1. Emily drank her cocoa (most fast, <u>fastest</u>).
2. Hard candy lasts (<u>longer</u>, more long).
3. Julie hung the decorations (more well, <u>better</u>) than Kim did.
4. Of all the girls, Jenny swims (more strongly, <u>most strongly</u>).
5. We laughed (most hard, <u>hardest</u>) at that joke.
6. Albert works (<u>more quickly</u>, quicklier) than you.

7. Of all the children, Drew cares (most deeply, deepest) for the family farm.

8. This castle is guarded (more closely, most closely) than that one.

9. Van plays the piano (best, better) than Bill.

10. Now the dog limps (badder, worse, worst) than before.

C. Choosing the Right Word (Use after page 246.)

Number your paper from 1 to 10. Choose the right modifier, and write it on your paper. Next, write the word it modifies. Then write *Adjective* or *Adverb* to show how the word is used.

1. Water gushed (wild, wildly) from the pipe.   Adv.
2. Mr. Otis was (gruffly, gruff) with the children.   Adj.
3. Simon answered the phone (quick, quickly).   Adv.
4. Drive (safe, safely) on the highway.   Adv.
5. Ilona dresses (sloppy, sloppily).   Adv.
6. The prisoner escaped (easy, easily).   Adv.
7. Carlotta plays charades (good, well).   Adv.
8. Skip acted (badly, bad) on the trip.   Adv.
9. Ms. Rossi is (real, really) patient with her class.   Adv.
10. The soloist sang (sweet, sweetly).   Adv.

Chapter 18

Making Language Lively

Using lively language will sharpen your speaking and writing. Notice the difference between these two sentences.

    Mary jumped up and threw the basketball into the net.

    Mary leaped up and shot the basketball into the net.

Which sentence describes the action more vividly? Can you tell why?

The next few pages will show you how to write with lively language.

Chapter Objectives

1. To increase awareness and use of strong verbs
2. To recognize and compose similes
3. To learn to avoid clichés
4. To recognize and compose metaphors
5. To distinguish between similes and metaphors

Preparing the Students

Read and discuss page 251. Have the students examine the picture on page 250. Ask them to describe the picture to you. Encourage them to look for details, especially for those that show movement.

These questions will help students examine the picture closely:

(a) What sound does the ball make when it hits the backboard?
(b) How would you describe the hair of the girl on the left?
(c) What is the girl on the right doing with her feet?

Write students' observations on the chalkboard. When they use language that is not strong and to the point, ask them to rephrase their observations. Your main goal at this point is to have students recognize the difference between language that is interesting and that which is dull.

Additional Resources

Mastery Test—pages 476 and 477 in this T.E. Recommended for use after teaching the chapter.

Additional Mastery Test—Recommended for use after any necessary reteaching. (In separate booklet, *Mastery Tests, Silver Level*, pages 39 and 40.)

Skills Practice Book—pages 95–98

Duplicating Masters—pages 95–98

Part 1

Objective

To increase awareness and use of strong verbs

Presenting the Lesson

1. In Chapter 10, Part 1 introduced the action verb. If much time has passed since the study of Chapter 10, you may wish to review it before beginning the lesson on strong verbs.

2. Read page 252, through the list of "Weak Verbs—Strong Verbs." Write the examples of weak verbs on the chalkboard. Read and discuss the strong verbs suggested in the text. Ask students to add to the list by thinking of other strong verbs that could replace *go, put,* and *say.* Help the students see that the strong verbs tell much more than the weak verbs.

3. Read the rest of page 252. Point out that *am, is, are, was,* and *were* are state-of-being verbs. Their purpose is to state that something is. They are not intended to show action.

4. Do Exercise A on page 253 in class. Encourage students to suggest several different strong verbs to replace each weak verb. Ask them to explain the differences in meaning between the various suggestions.

5. For Exercise B, you may want to divide the class into small groups. Students may then work together on the sentences. Appoint one student in each group to write down the sentences.

6. Assign Exercise C. When discussing the answers, make sure that the students realize there are many good ways to improve each sentence.

Part 1 Using Strong Verbs

Look at the sentences below:

Jack *jogged* to the corner.
Jack *raced* to the corner.
Jack *skated* to the corner.

These sentences tell what Jack did. They show action. The action words are verbs.

Now look at this sentence:

Jack *went* to the corner.

Here the action is not clear. The sentence is flat and dull. "Went" is a weak verb.

Strong verbs show vivid action. They are never dull. Here are some examples of weak and strong verbs.

Weak Verbs	Strong Verbs
go	skate, race, amble, jog
put	throw, toss, pass, place
say	whisper, scream, beg, whine

The verbs *am, is, are, was,* and *were* are also weak. Use them as little as possible.

Strong verbs will make your writing lively. Choose them when you can. The following exercises will give you practice.

Exercises **Using Strong Verbs**

A. Read each sentence out loud. Find the verb. Is the verb strong? Discuss each sentence in class. Change it if it needs a stronger verb. Answers will vary for items 2, 6, 9, and 10.

1. The wounded kitten moaned. strong
2. Carol put her purse on the stairs. weak—tossed
3. Sue hops off the bus each morning. strong
4. Kate begged her mother for another cookie. strong
5. Slice my apple into thin pieces, please. strong
6. Sid came through the door. weak—raced
7. Jake stuffed his pockets with pebbles. strong
8. The spotted snake slithered across the grass. strong
9. The huge tractor moved down the field. weak—lumbered
10. The butterfly flew over the garden. weak—floated

B. Make a list of eight strong verbs. Then use each verb in a sentence. Answers will vary.

C. In each sentence below, make the verb stronger. You may need to rewrite the sentence. Write the new sentence on your paper. Your new sentences should be lively and colorful.

Answers will vary.

1. The sun was in the sky.
2. My sled went down the hill.
3. The horse moved out the barn door.
4. The bacon is on the stove.
5. Alice put her finger into the chocolate sauce.
6. The airplane went across the sky.
7. The cat lay on the bed.
8. Karen held the cord of the parachute.
9. The frightened dog made a noise.
10. I said my name in a low voice.

Extending the Lesson

Ask the students for various words that could be substituted for the verb *walked*. Some answers might be *sauntered*, *strolled*, and *glided*. Have the students demonstrate each method of "walking" to show that each word has its own distinct meaning.

Optional Practice

Ask students to write a paragraph describing something that happened to them. Encourage them to use specific details and strong verbs.

Part 2

Objectives

1. To recognize and compose similes
2. To learn to avoid clichés

Presenting the Lesson

1. Read pages 254 and 255. Discuss these questions in class:
   (a) How is Santa's belly like a bowl full of jelly?
   (b) In what way is Mary like the rose?

   Emphasize that a simile cannot be a comparison of two similar things, such as "He looks like his brother." The things compared must be different in almost every way, but comparable in the way brought out by the simile. Also, a good simile gives a fresh view of the things being compared. The statement "The moon looks like a half-circle" is a simple description. The simile "The moon looks like a banana" adds something new to the description.

2. Write the clichés on page 255 on the board. Ask the students to change them into more original similes by changing the object of comparison. For example, instead of "slow as molasses," one might say "slow as sap in early spring."

3. Review the Guides for Writing Similes on page 255.

4. Do Exercise A on page 256 in class.

5. Assign Exercise B. Discuss the example. Point out that for each item one must add a verb, the word *like, as,* or *than,* and the object of comparison. Ask students to read their favorite similes in class.

Part 2 Writing Similes

In the sentences below, the writers compare one thing to another.

1. The grass feels like a soggy sponge.
2. The room grew as quiet as a pine forest.
3. The steam shovel snorted and puffed like a dinosaur.

Each sentence contains a simile. A **simile** is a comparison between two unlike things that have something in common. The writer joins the two parts of the comparison with *like, as,* or *than.*

In the first sentence the writer compares the grass to a soggy sponge. A "soggy sponge" is full of water. It also springs back when you squeeze it. The comparison helps you feel what the grass is like.

Now look at sentences 2 and 3. How is the room like a pine forest? What do the steam shovel and a dinosaur have in common?

Here is a famous simile. It describes Santa Claus.

> He had a broad face
> And a little round belly
> That shook when he laughed
> Like a bowl full of jelly.

Now let's try to describe Santa without the simile.

> He had a broad face
> And a little round belly
> That shook when he laughed.

Without the simile, the lines have lost their magic. They are flat and dull.

Many children have chanted this jump-rope rhyme.

> Down in the valley
> Where the green grass grows
> There sat Mary
> As sweet as a rose.

Can you find the simile?

Sometimes we use one simile too often. It loses its freshness. An overworked simile is called a **cliché.**

Here are some clichés you hear often.

warm as toast	silly as a goose
sick as a dog	slow as molasses

Avoid clichés when you can. Try to make your similes fresh and interesting.

The guides below will help you write lively similes.

Guides for Writing Similes

1. Compare two unlike things that have something in common.

2. Use *like, as,* or *than* to join the two parts of the comparison.

3. Be sure your simile makes sense.

4. Avoid using clichés.

---

6. Before students write the paragraph for Exercise C on page 256, it would be helpful to get their imaginations working by talking about some possibilities for each topic. Assign Exercise C, and ask students to read their paragraphs out loud.

Extending the Lesson

Plan a display of similes for the bulletin board. Have students look for similes in their readers and in library books, especially books of poems. Ask them to record each simile they find on a separate sheet of paper. Depending on the ability of the class, you might also ask for the name of the selection in which the simile was found, and the name of the author. Encourage students to illustrate their similes. Use the illustration on page 255 as an example. How does it show that Mary and the rose have something in common?

Exercises   Writing Similes

A. Complete the similes below. Try to make your comparisons fresh and interesting. *These are possible answers.*

1. The machine sputtered like ___a Chinese firecracker___.
2. Her hair streamed behind her like ___a flag in the wind___.
3. The skin on his hand was as wrinkled as ___a turtle's neck___.
4. The thorns pricked my fingers like ___needles___.
5. The clouds raced across the sky like ___wild horses___.
6. My horse gallops faster than ___summer vacation___.
7. Her voice pierced the silence like ___a sharp knife___.
8. The workmen swarmed over the building like ___bees___.

B. Make up a simile to describe each item below. Use complete sentences.

Example: Your legs

Possible Answer: My legs are like toothpicks.

Now write similes for the following. Use complete sentences.

1. A balloon
2. Your teeth
3. A baby's cry
4. A spider's web
5. A sudden leap through the air
6. A skyscraper
7. Your pencil
8. The roar of a jet

C. Write a paragraph on one of the topics below, or choose one of your own. Include two similes in your paragraph. Underline the similes.

my favorite relative	stroking a cat	the storm
building a snowman	running	my room
roasting marshmallows	chicken soup	raking leaves

Part 3 Writing Metaphors

A poet wrote the lines below.

> I stood in the shelter of a great tree,
> Hiding from the wind that galloped over the land.
>
> —RAMONA GARDEN, from "Tumbleweed."

In the poem the writer compares the wind to a galloping horse. However, she does not say the wind is *like* a horse. She tells us only that the wind gallops. The rest is left to our imagination.

The poet's comparison is a **metaphor.** A metaphor resembles a simile. It also is a comparison between two things that are different but have something in common.

A metaphor, however, does not contain the words *as, like,* or *than.* In this way it is different from a simile.

Part 3

Objectives

1. To recognize and compose metaphors
2. To distinguish between similes and metaphors

Presenting the Lesson

1. Read page 257. Discuss the comparison between the wind and a horse. Point out that the speaker "hides." Is she afraid of the wind? Would she be afraid of a horse that "galloped over the land"? The wind and a horse are alike in two ways: (a) they both move fast; (b) they can both cause fear. Are there any other in which the wind and a horse are similar?

2. Read and discuss the examples and Guides for Writing Metaphors on page 258. Make sure the students recognize the differences in form between the similes and metaphors listed on the page. Ask them to identify the simile and the

metaphor in the following comparisons:

a. The moon was lighted and hung in the sky.
b. The moon was shining like a lantern.

3. Do Exercise A on page 259. For this exercise, it may be helpful to work in small groups or together as a class. The activity will prepare students for Exercises B and C.

4. Exercise B is important for increasing reading comprehension skills. Insist that students be precise in defining the literal meaning expressed by each metaphor. It is recommended that several sentences be worked out together in class. Students should then work independently on the sentences that remain.

5. Assign Exercise C. The concept of metaphor will be difficult for some students. You may wish to work in a small group with those who have trouble. When students have finished the assignment, ask each student to read one or two original metaphors to the class.

Let's look at some examples of similes and metaphors.

1. Simile: The rope looked like a snake.
   Metaphor: The rope snaked along the ground.

2. Simile: The clouds looked like huge white balloons.
   Metaphor: The clouds were huge white balloons.

3. Simile: The waves rose like wild horses in the storm.
   Metaphor: The waves reared and plunged in the storm.

To write good metaphors, follow the guides below.

Guides for Writing Metaphors

1. Compare two things that are different but have something in common.

2. Do not use *like, as,* or *than.*

3. Be sure your comparison makes sense.

Exercises Writing Metaphors

A. The sentences below all contain comparisons. Some are similes. Others are metaphors. Number your paper from 1 to 10. After the number for each sentence, tell whether the sentence contains a *simile* or a *metaphor*.

1. My father's cheeks are as scratchy as sandpaper. simile
2. Jenny's eyes are black beads. metaphor
3. The peacock was a living jewel. metaphor
4. Carla's words stung me. metaphor
5. Mike's skin is tougher than shoe leather. simile
6. The moon glowed like a jack-o'-lantern. simile
7. Marta dripped honey when she spoke. metaphor
8. Her feelings are more fragile than glass. simile
9. The stone looked like a piece of dough. simile
10. The hungry man wolfed his food. metaphor

B. The sentences below all contain metaphors. Write out, in your own words, what each metaphor means. The basic meanings of the metaphors are given below. Specific answers may vary.

Example: That character is made of ice.

Possible Answer: That character has no feelings.

1. My mind is a sieve. My mind can hold nothing.
2. Jack is turning into a bookworm. Jack does nothing but read.
3. John is a bear when he gets angry. John is fierce when he gets angry.
4. His voice purred in the next room. His voice sounded quietly happy in the next room.
5. The basement was a swamp. The basement was full of water.
6. The snow feathered in the sky. The snow filled the sky.
7. The officer barked a warning. The officer spoke a loud, curt order.
8. The basketball soared into the net. The basketball moved gracefully upward into the net.

C. Write five metaphors of your own. Try to make them as fresh and interesting as possible. Be sure that they make sense. Take turns reading your metaphors aloud in class. Add the ones you like best to your own list.

Extending the Lesson

Ask the students to illustrate the metaphors in Exercise B on page 259, or their own metaphors for Exercise C. They will find this a challenging and entertaining activity, and should become more aware of the need for vivid, concrete language.

Optional Practice

After students complete Exercise C, have them change their metaphors to similes. Check to be sure they can distinguish between similes and metaphors.

Chapter 19

Writing a Composition

Chapter Objectives

1. To understand the function and organization of a five-paragraph composition
2. To develop a method for finding a subject for a composition
3. To develop a method for gathering and organizing ideas for a composition
4. To write a good introductory paragraph
5. To write the body of a composition
6. To write a good ending paragraph
7. To apply a method for revising and correcting a composition

Preparing the Students

On the chalkboard write these pairs of subjects:

a sandwich/Thanksgiving dinner
a tree/a forest
a baseball/how to play baseball

Point out that the first subject in each pair could easily be covered in one paragraph, while the second subject would require several paragraphs to be covered adequately. Explain that in this chapter the students will learn how to write a five-paragraph composition about one subject.

Read the introduction to the chapter on page 261.

Additional Resources

Mastery Test—pages 478 and 479 in this T.E. Recommended for use after teaching the chapter.

Additional Mastery Test—Recommended for use after any necessary reteaching. (In separate booklet, *Mastery Tests, Silver Level,* pages 41 and 42.)

Skills Practice Book—pages 99–106
Duplicating Masters—pages 99–106

You now know what goes into writing a good paragraph. You also know how to write three kinds of paragraphs. Sometimes, though, a paragraph is just not long enough to cover a topic. You need to write several paragraphs. For example, you might want to write about the summer that everyone worked together to improve the looks of the camp.

A longer piece of writing on one topic is called a **composition**. In this chapter you will learn how to write a composition.

Part 1

Objective

To understand the function and organization of a five-paragraph composition

Presenting the Lesson

1. Read the first two paragraphs in Part 1, on page 262. Recall for the class the definition of *paragraph* (a group of sentences that explain a main idea). Review the function and position of a topic sentence. Emphasize that paragraphs are the building blocks of a composition.

2. Direct students' attention to the sample composition on page 262. (If you anticipate that some or all, of your class may have difficulty relating the explanation to the sample composition, duplicate the composition and direct the students to underline the topic sentences and to mark the three parts as they are discussed.)

Point out the indented lines that signal the beginning of each paragraph. Ask volunteers to read the composition.

3. Read The Introductory Paragraph on page 263. Note that the introductory paragraph is comparable to the topic sentence of a paragraph in that it presents the main idea.

Part 1   What Is a Composition?

A composition is like a paragraph, only longer. While a paragraph is made up of sentences, a composition is made up of paragraphs. The paragraphs work together to explain an idea.

Following is a composition. It is made up of five paragraphs. The main idea of the composition is getting rid of warts. Each paragraph tells something about this idea.

CURES FOR WARTS

Cures for warts have been around as long as warts themselves. Some cures have used unusual things like caterpillars and eel skins. Others have used everyday things in unusual ways. What is important about all the cures is that people believed in them. They were sure that the cures would work.

Long ago the Romans used peas to get rid of warts. They touched each wart with a pea. They wrapped the peas in a package and put the package where someone would find it. When someone found it, the warts went away. However, the unlucky person who found the package got warts.

Many people believed in touching warts with something that would rot. Most of the time they used a piece of fruit, vegetable, or meat. Sometimes they used string. They tied a knot in the string for each wart. As the food or string began to rot, the warts began to disappear.

People have made special wart ointments, too. They have used things like mashed caterpillars and eel skins. One well-known ointment was made from spunk water. This is rain water taken from a tree stump on the night of a full moon.

What is surprising to us is that these cures sometimes worked. It's almost as if people believed so strongly that the cures would work that they did. You might say they "thought" their warts away.

The Introductory Paragraph

A composition is divided into three parts. The first part tells what the composition is about. It is called the **introductory paragraph.** It "introduces" the main idea.

The introductory paragraph of the sample composition lets you know that the composition is about cures for warts. The introductory paragraph is like most good paragraphs. It opens with a topic sentence: "Cures for warts have been around as long as warts themselves." The other sentences explain this idea:

> Some of the cures have used unusual things.
>
> Other cures have used everyday things in unusual ways.
>
> What is important about the cures is that people believed in them.

The Body Paragraphs

Three paragraphs follow the introductory paragraph. They make up the second part of a five-paragraph composition. They form the **body** of the composition. They explain the idea presented in the introductory paragraph.

In the sample composition, the introductory paragraph lets you know that the composition is about cures for warts. The body paragraphs describe three types of cures. They tell about the Roman cure, the rot cure, and special ointments. The three cures are described in separate paragraphs. If you look at the paragraphs, you will see that each begins with a topic sentence. The sentence tells what the paragraph is about. The rest of the sentences in the paragraph explain that idea.

---

4. Read The Body Paragraphs on page 263. Ask volunteers to read the three body paragraphs of the sample composition. Then ask students to explain the main idea of each body paragraph, and to identify the topic sentence that presents that main idea.

5. Read The Ending Paragraph on page 264. Explain that this final paragraph signals the reader that the writer has said everything that he or she intends to say.

6. Assign and discuss the Exercise on page 264.

The Ending Paragraph

The third part of a composition is the **ending.** It is the last paragraph in the composition. In the sample composition, the ending ties everything together. It explains that sometimes the cures worked. It also tells why this might be so. The ending paragraph, like the others in the composition, begins with a topic sentence: "What is surprising to us is that these cures sometimes worked." The rest of the sentences explain this idea. They give a possible reason why the cures sometimes worked.

Exercises   Studying the Composition

On a sheet of paper complete this sentence:

A composition is _several paragraphs_ on one topic.

Then, below your sentence, answer the following four questions in complete sentences.

1. A composition is made up of how many parts? _three_
2. The first part of a composition is called _the introductory paragraph_. It tells _the main idea_.
3. The next part of a composition is called _the body_. It explains _the main idea_.
4. The last part of a composition is called _the ending_. It _ties everything together_.

Part 2 Finding a Subject

Now that you have learned about compositions, you are ready to work on one of your own. Where do you begin? First decide what to write about. This is called **finding a subject.**

For your first compositions, it's a good idea to write about things you know well. These are usually things that have happened to you. You might say, "Nothing exciting ever happens to *me!*" Well, maybe you haven't stowed away on a ship or captured a jewel thief single-handed. Even so, you probably have done many things that would be interesting to write and read about. This lesson will help you to remember them.

Thinking About a Subject

Sit down with a pencil and paper and answer the following questions. As you do this, write down any other ideas that come to you.

Think about the past week. Did anything funny happen? Did you do anything special with your family? Did you do anything with your friends? Did you build or make anything?

Think about the school year so far. Has anything surprising happened? What holidays have you had? Have you gone on a field trip? Have you done any special projects?

Think about your life. What is the nicest thing you've ever done for someone? When did you feel most like a winner? What relative do you admire most? Did you ever take a trip with your family? Have you gone to a carnival?

Now ask yourself these questions:

1. Have you ever earned money? How? What happened?
2. Did you ever climb or ride to a high place? What did you see? How did you feel?
3. What is your favorite outfit? What does it look like?

Part 2

Objective

To develop a method for finding a subject for a composition

Presenting the Lesson

1. Read and discuss the introduction to Part 2 and Thinking About a Subject on pages 265 and 266. Give the class time to begin listing possible subjects for compositions. Most of the suggestions and questions lead to topics for narrative compositions. However, the students should not necessarily be limited to this type of composition.

2. Read Making a Final List on page 266. Caution the students to be alert for subjects that are too broad or too narrow for five-paragraph compositions.

3. Assign the Exercise on page 266. Most students will need some help in finalizing their subject choices. It is suggested that you divide the class into groups of four or five students. Spend time with each group discussing the feasibility of various subjects until each student in the class has made a choice that lends itself to development into a five-paragraph composition.

4. Have you ever gone to a birthday party? What games did you play?
5. Were you ever in a place where you didn't know anyone? What did you do?
6. Were you ever accused of doing something you didn't do?
7. What is your favorite sport? What one game do you remember best?
8. Did you ever try to grow anything? What happened?

Making a Final List

You now have many things to write about. It's time to get rid of some of them. Look over your list. Cross out any things that you really don't want to write about. Cross out subjects that need more than five paragraphs. You will then have a list of possible subjects for compositions.

One writer answered the questions in this lesson. He then crossed out those things he didn't want to write about. His final list of possible subjects looked like this:

My dad took my brother and me to the stock car races.

I made "The Droids." It's the best basketball team in school.

I made a "balloon from outer space" as an art project.

Aunt Kit served a real Pilgrim dinner for Thanksgiving.

The class visited the mayor's office.

I took care of Harvey's pet snake for a weekend.

I sold apples before a football game.

When I was in second grade, I got lost in a shopping center.

Exercise   Choosing a Subject

Study your list of possible subjects. Think what you might write about each one. Choose one for your composition.

Part 3 Planning the Composition

Most things you do will turn out better if you follow some kind of plan. This is true of having a party, growing vegetables, or making cookies. It's also true of writing compositions. The next step in writing your composition, then, is to make a plan.

Listing the Main Ideas

To begin your plan, list the points you want to cover in your composition. Your list should include only the main ideas. You will have a chance to add more ideas later.

Part 2 gave eight subjects listed by one writer. He chose one subject from that list. He decided to write about the time he sold apples. Next he began his plan. He listed six things he wanted to talk about in his composition:

1. How I prepared the apples
2. Where I got the apples
3. How I set up a stand
4. Why I decided to sell apples
5. Figuring out what I had earned
6. Selling the apples

Exercise Listing the Main Ideas

Think about the subject you have chosen for your composition. List the main points you want to write about. Don't worry about listing them in any special order.

Arranging the Main Ideas

Think back to the lesson on narrative paragraphs. You learned that they tell what happened. You also learned that the ideas are arranged in a time sequence. They tell what happened first, what happened next, and so on.

You are now getting ready to write a composition about something that happened. You will, therefore, need to arrange your ideas in a time sequence.

The writer of the composition about selling apples arranged his ideas in the following way.

1. Why I decided to sell apples
2. Where I got the apples
3. How I prepared the apples
4. How I set up a stand
5. Selling the apples
6. Figuring out what I had earned

His list begins with deciding to sell apples. This is what happened first. It ends with figuring his earnings. This is what happened last. In between are the other things that happened. They are in the order that they happened.

Exercise   Arranging the Main Ideas

Study your list of main points. Arrange them in the order that they happened.

Adding Details

To finish the plan you must add details. Details are important. They help to let your readers know exactly what happened. They also make your composition more interesting.

The writer of the "selling apples" composition added the following details to his list.

1. Why I decided to sell apples

    Live close to a stadium
    Needed money
    Mother suggested I sell something

2. Where I got the apples

    Rode my bike to a farm stand
    Bought a bushel of apples
    Loaded apples into my bike baskets

3. How I prepared the apples

    Got my sister and her friends to wash and shine them
    Sorted them by size

4. How I set up the stand

    Used a card table
    Made a sign saying "Apples   Large 10¢   Small 5¢"

5. Selling the apples

    Sold to people walking by the stand
    Sold all the apples before the game

6. Figuring out what I had earned

    Totaled $5.20
    Subtracted $2.50 for expenses
    Made $2.70

Exercise **Adding Details**

Add details to your list of ideas. You now have a plan for your composition. Keep this plan. You will use it when doing Parts 4, 5, and 6.

Part 4

Objective

To write a good introductory paragraph

Presenting the Lesson

1. Read and discuss pages 270 and 271. Emphasize the twofold function of an introductory paragraph: to present the main idea of the composition and to catch the reader's attention. Note that in the introductory paragraph for the "selling apples" composition the topic sentence is not in its usual opening position, but rather concludes the paragraph.

2. Assign the Exercise on page 271. Suggest that the students consider the first parts of their plans when deciding what to include in their introductory paragraph.

Optional Practice

Select several examples—both good and bad—of introductory paragraphs written by the students. Type them on a sheet of paper or duplicating master, then make a copy for each person in the class. Direct the students to do the following with each paragraph:

1. Explain in one sentence what the composition will be about.
2. Underline the topic sentence.

Part 4 Writing the Introductory Paragraph

The first paragraph in a composition is called the introductory paragraph. It lets you know what the composition is about because it presents the main idea. Here is an example of an introductory paragraph.

> On the first day of our village school in Japan, there was a boy missing. None of us really knew him. He was nicknamed Chibi because he was very small. Chibi means "tiny boy." —TARO YASHIMA

The paragraph tells you that the composition is about a boy called Chibi. It begins with the topic sentence, "On the first day of our village school in Japan, there was a boy missing." This sentence lets you know that the introductory paragraph is about a missing boy.

Catching the Reader's Interest

An introductory paragraph does a second important thing. It makes you want to read the composition. Let's look at another example.

> Going into the last game of our season, we were tied with the Elks. By a miracle they had lost their last game. It wasn't exactly a miracle; it was the virus. Two of their three great left-handers had gotten it. Our last game would determine the league championship. I know that games that break a tie for the championship happen so often in stories. Maybe that is because that happens so often in real life.
> —E. L. KONIGSBURG

This introductory paragraph leaves you wanting to find out more. After reading the paragraph, you want to find out who won the championship.

The writer who planned a composition about selling apples wrote the following introductory paragraph. It explains why he decided to sell apples in the first place. Look at his plan in Part 3. You can see that this is the first main idea in the plan.

> I live one block from a high school football stadium. I never thought much about it. One day, though, I decided I needed money. My mother suggested that, with all the people walking past our house almost every Saturday, I might try to sell something. That's when I came up with my great idea—selling apples.

The paragraph does two things:

1. It lets you know that the composition is about selling apples.
2. It makes you want to find out what happened.

Exercise **Writing an Introductory Paragraph**

You are now ready to write the introductory paragraph to your composition. When you finish, ask yourself these questions:

1. Does the paragraph tell what the composition is about?
2. Does it have a topic sentence?
3. Will it make the readers want to read the rest of the composition?

Part 5

Objective

To write the body of a composition

Presenting the Lesson

1. Read and discuss page 272. Guide the students in understanding how each idea in the plan on page 269 was incorporated into the body of the composition. Note that a title has been added to the composition.

2. Read Explaining the Main Idea on page 273. Examine closely the time sequence of the body paragraphs in the sample composition.

3. Assign the Exercise on page 273. It may be helpful to hold a "writing workshop" for those students who need help in using the ideas in their plans as the basis for paragraph development. Help each student to write one paragraph, based on a main idea and its related details. Then have the students work independently on the other two paragraphs.

Part 5 Writing the Body

The middle of a composition is called the **body.** It is made up of several paragraphs. Each paragraph adds something to the main idea given in the introductory paragraph. All the paragraphs work together to explain the main idea.

In writing the body of your composition, it is important to follow your plan. The writer of the composition on selling apples did so. He had covered the first idea in his plan in the introductory paragraph. He now covered the next four ideas in the body paragraphs. Here is the introductory paragraph and the body of his composition.

SELLING APPLES

I live one block from a high school football stadium. I never thought much about it. One day, though, I decided I needed money. My mother suggested that, with all the people walking past our house almost every Saturday, I might try to sell something. That's when I came up with my great idea—selling apples.

The next Thursday afternoon I rode my bike to a farm stand. The farmer was selling bushels of just-picked apples. I chose the best bushel I could find. I then loaded the apples into the rear and front baskets of my bike and headed for home.

On Friday I made my little sister and her friends "partners for a day." I put them in charge of washing and shining the apples. I was in charge of sorting them. I put the big ones into one pile and the smaller ones into another.

Saturday was the day of a big game. That morning I set up my apple stand on a card table. I hung a sign on it saying, "Apples. Large 10¢. Small 5¢." Around noon people started walking past the stand. I started selling apples. Long before the game began, I had sold every single apple.

Explaining the Main Idea

The writer first explains why he decided to sell apples. He does this in the introductory paragraph. He then explains the following:

    Where he got the apples
    How he prepared the apples
    How he set up the stand
    How he sold the apples

He covers these four ideas in three paragraphs. The first body paragraph tells what he did on Thursday. The second paragraph tells what he did on Friday. The third tells what he did on Saturday. All three paragraphs work together. They explain what happened when the writer decided to sell apples.

Exercise   **Writing the Body of Your Composition**

Write the three body paragraphs of your composition. Be sure to include all the ideas you listed for the body of your composition. Be sure also to describe what happened in the same order as in your plan.

Part 6

Objectives

1. To write a good ending paragraph
2. To apply a method for revising and correcting a composition

Presenting the Lesson

1. Read the examples and explanatory material on page 274. Mention that the ending paragraph of a composition may include ideas from the plan, brought together in a satisfying way. The ending should not introduce new ideas not already discussed in the composition.
2. Assign the Exercise at the top of page 275. Remind students to refer to their plans when writing their final paragraph.
3. Read and discuss Checking the Composition on page 275. Emphasize specific points that regularly cause problems for many or most of the students in the class.
   You should also mention at this time any specific requirements that you wish to add to those in the text: for example, you may prefer the student's final copy to be in ink, or written on only one side of the paper.
4. Assign the Exercise on page 275.

Extending the Lesson

Assemble the completed compositions into several "books" (of five to eight compositions each) that can be kept in the classroom for student reading. You might choose a committee to create colorful covers for the books.

Part 6 Completing the Composition

Writing the Ending

The final paragraph in a composition is the ending. There are many different kinds of endings. Some are very short:

> I had now found my first friend. My life had truly begun.

Others are longer:

> After that I rode my bike around every day. I explored every street in Rosemont. I knew all the stores downtown. I found my junior high. I found the football field. I found the park. I wished it were September. —JUDY BLUME

> After that incident, the whole crew grew very fond of my mongooses. They brought the animals whatever food they had to spare. In the evening I often had a hard time finding Ruchnaia. The friendly mongoose was always visiting with someone. Eventually Dikaia also became quite tame. When the journey ended, I brought both mongooses home with me.
> —BORIS ZHITOV

A good ending paragraph lets your readers know that you have finished the composition. It leaves them feeling satisfied. They know that you have said everything you wanted to say.

The writer of the composition on selling apples wrote this ending. It describes what happened after he had sold the apples.

> I then sat down to figure what I had earned. I counted five dollars and twenty cents. I subtracted the dollar and a half I had paid for the apples. I subtracted another dollar that I had paid my partners. I was two dollars and seventy cents richer. I began thinking of expanding my business.

The ending tells how much money the writer had earned. This is the last main idea in his plan. The paragraph also tells how the writer felt. He wanted to sell apples again.

Exercise **Writing the Last Paragraph**

Write the ending to your composition. Make sure that it will leave your readers feeling satisfied.

Checking the Composition

Writing the last paragraph does not mean that you are finished with your composition. You still must do one more thing—check your composition. It's a good thing to do this in two steps.

First, read the composition to make sure of the following:

1. Each paragraph begins with a topic sentence.
2. All the sentences in the paragraph are complete.
3. All the sentences stick to the main idea of the paragraph.
4. All the paragraphs explain the main idea of the composition.

You may find things that do not sound quite right. If you do, revise them. Make a new copy of your composition.

Second, check the whole composition to make sure of the following:

1. The beginnings of sentences and proper names are capitalized.
2. Periods, commas, and other punctuation marks are in the correct places.
3. All words are spelled correctly. If you have a question about a word, look it up in the dictionary.
4. Each paragraph is indented.

Exercise **Making a Final Copy**

Check your composition in the two steps. Then make a final copy. Be sure that your final copy includes your revisions and corrections.

Chapter 20

Writing a Story

You have studied groups of paragraphs called compositions. Some compositions tell about things that happened to the writers. Others paint pictures with words. In this chapter you will study another kind of composition. You will learn how to write a story.

The girl and boy in the photograph on the opposite page wrote a story about their model airplane. In the story, the airplane acted on its own, like a person. One day the model airplane decided that it wanted to be a real airplane. One night when everyone was asleep, it rose from the table, flew out the window, and climbed into the night sky. It had an exciting adventure when it helped to rescue a man drifting alone on the ocean. It was honored for its good deed.

Chapter Objectives

1. To recognize the basic elements of a story, and to understand the use of time sequence in organizing the ideas in a story

2. To apply a method for planning a story

3. To write a five-paragraph story, organized into introductory paragraph, body, and ending

Preparing the Students

Read several opening paragraphs of stories familiar to the students. Ask them to identify the characters (without using that term) and to describe briefly what happens in each story. Explain that in this chapter they will learn to write their own stories.

Read the introduction to the chapter on page 277. Emphasize that the story written by the children is about what happens to the model airplane.

Additional Resources

Mastery Test—pages 480 and 481 in this T.E. Recommended for use after teaching the chapter.

Additional Mastery Test—Recommended for use after any necessary reteaching. (In separate booklet, *Mastery Tests, Silver Level*, pages 43 and 44.)

Skills Practice Book—pages 107–111

Duplicating Masters—pages 107–111

Part 1

Objective

To recognize the basic elements of a story, and to understand the use of time sequence in organizing the ideas in a story

Presenting the Lesson

1. Read pages 278 and 279. Guide the class in defining a story as a group of paragraphs that tell about something that happened to someone. Clarify the terms *characters* and *time sequence*. Recall that narrative paragraphs and explanatory paragraphs that tell "how" are also organized into time sequence.

2. Read Using Details on page 280. Help the students to identify details in the story "Ghosts!" You might want to concentrate on one type of detail or on one type at a time: strong verbs (*flashed, crawl, crept, quaking*), adjectives (*rustling, wet, cold, scared, dry*), or specific nouns (*hedge, branches, Leadback Road*).

3. Read Another Kind of Story on page 280. Ask the class for examples of imaginary characters, and of stories that are completely or partially fanciful. Suggest superheroes such as Superman and Wonder Woman and several fairy tales to stimulate thinking.

4. Assign and discuss the Exercise on page 280.

Optional Practice

Reassign the Exercise on page 280 with one variation: Tell the students to find an example of a story that could *not* have happened in real life.

Part 1 What Is a Story?

Stories can be about migrant workers or pirates or ghosts. They can be about Native American chiefs or space explorers or divers. They can be about very different things. Yet all stories are alike in some important ways.

For one thing, stories tell what happened. They tell what happened to the **characters** in them. The characters are invented, or made up, by the writer.

The writer of a story creates a special world. It comes from the imagination. When you read a story, you share another person's special world. When you write a story, you create a special world of your own.

Stories That Seem Real

Some stories are about things that could have happened in real life. The characters in them act like real people. They may remind you of people you know. The stories take place in ordinary houses on ordinary streets in ordinary towns.

The following story was made up by the writer. It is about a person who thinks she sees a ghost. It could have happened in real life. People often imagine things, especially late at night.

GHOSTS!

Geeder awoke with a start. The grass beyond the tip of her toes was wet with dew. She pulled the blankets more tightly around her, tucking her feet safely inside. She had closed her eyes again when she heard a rustling sound on Leadback Road.

Some old animal, she thought. The sound grew louder, and she could not think what it was. Suddenly the thought flashed through her mind, "Ghosts!"

It took all her courage to crawl out of the covers. She crept the few feet over the wet grass up to the hedge. She shook with fear but peeked through the hedge anyway. What she saw made her bend low, hugging the ground for protection. Truthfully, she wasn't sure what she saw. The branches of the hedge didn't allow much of a view.

Something tall and white was moving down the road. It didn't quite touch the ground. Geeder could hear no sound of footsteps. She couldn't see its head or arms. Beside it and moving with it was something that squeaked. The white, very long figure made a rustling sound. It passed by toward town.

Geeder watched, moving her head slowly until she could no longer see it. After waiting for what seemed hours, quaking at each sound of the night, she crept back to bed. She pulled the covers over her eyes. She lay, cold and scared, unable to think and afraid even to clear her dry throat. This way, she fell asleep. —VIRGINIA HAMILTON

The story is about Geeder. She is the main character. Things happen to Geeder while she is sleeping outside one night.

She wakes up.

She hears a sound on the road.

She peeks through the hedge.

She thinks she sees something tall and white moving down the road.

She goes back to bed.

She falls asleep.

The writer tells what happened first, what happened next, and so on. This is called a **time sequence.** It is the way most stories are told.

Using Details

The writer includes many details. She describes the grass as "wet with dew." She describes the "white, very long figure." These details help you to see the scene in your mind.

The writer also describes Geeder's thoughts and feelings. You know when Geeder begins to be afraid. You share her feelings as she "lay, cold and scared," under the covers. The writer makes Geeder's experience real for you.

Another Kind of Story

You have probably read stories about animals that can talk or about heroes like Paul Bunyan. These stories tell about things that couldn't happen in real life. They could happen only in a writer's imagination. In Parts 2 and 3 of this chapter you will learn more about this kind of story.

Exercise   Studying a Story

Find an example of a story that could have happened in real life. Name the characters. If you can, tell where the story takes place. Finally, list the things that happen in the story. Are they arranged in a time sequence?

Part 2 Planning a Story

A story is a kind of composition. When writing a story, you follow the steps for writing a composition. Here they are:

1. Find a subject.
2. Develop a plan.
3. Write the introductory paragraph.
4. Write the body paragraphs.
5. Write the ending.
6. Check the composition.
7. Make a final copy.

In this lesson you will find a subject and plan a story. It will be a special kind of story. It will tell about something that couldn't possibly happen in real life.

Finding a Subject

The first thing to decide is *who* you want to write about. This will be your **main character.** You might choose to write about a girl or boy like yourself. You might choose an animal or plant. You might make up an imaginary creature.

One writer thought about some possible kinds of main characters. She made this list.

1. A giant, fast-growing plant
2. A girl who is bored
3. A boy who loves to sleep
4. The fastest turtle in the world
5. A super-smart turkey
6. An ant who likes to travel
7. A girl who wants to play on a basketball team
8. A gentle dragon
9. A citizen of the planet Thor
10. A cat with magical powers

Part 2

Objective

To apply a method for planning a story

Presenting the Lesson

1. Read and discuss the steps for writing a composition summarized at the top of page 281. Be sure that the students understand the meanings of the terms *subject, plan, introductory paragraph,* and *body paragraphs.*

2. Read Finding a Subject on pages 281 and 282. Ask the students for additional ideas for main characters. List them on the chalkboard. Ask for suggestions about things that might happen to each character, and add these ideas to the chalkboard list.

3. Assign and discuss the Exercise on page 282. Suggest that some students might choose one of the subjects listed in the text or on the chalkboard.

4. Read Beginning a Plan on page 283. Emphasize the concept of time sequence.

5. Read Adding Details on pages 283 and 284. Explain that developing a complete plan is the most difficult and probably the most important step in writing a story.

6. Assign and discuss the Exercise on page 284.

Optional Practice

Conduct a timed brainstorming session for those students who have difficulty inventing characters or situations. Accept all ideas, even the most wildly improbable. After the timed period, work with the group in identifying the most workable ideas for stories.

She then thought of things that might happen to each character. She added these ideas to her list:

1. A giant, fast-growing plant takes over a town.
2. A girl who is bored drinks a potion and becomes invisible.
3. A boy who loves to sleep sleeps for twenty years.
4. The fastest turtle in the world loses the big race.
5. A super-smart turkey learns to play chess and becomes the world champion.
6. An ant who likes to travel leaves a colony in the country and goes to a big city.
7. A girl who wants to play on a basketball team suddenly grows two feet taller.
8. A gentle dragon is driven from his home and finds a new one.
9. A citizen from the planet Thor lands on earth in the middle of a school playground.
10. A cat with magical powers decides that all dogs should be the size of a peanut.

The writer ended up with ten subjects for stories. Each was about something that couldn't happen in real life. For her story she chose this one: A girl who is bored drinks a potion and becomes invisible.

Exercise   Choosing a Subject

Now it's your turn to do what the writer did. Begin by making a list of five characters. Add ideas to your list. Then choose one of the subjects for your story.

Beginning a Plan

Your next step is to decide what will happen in your story.

As you know, one writer chose this subject: A girl who is bored drinks a potion and becomes invisible. She then listed things that happen to her main character. Here is her list:

1. Blanca is bored and wishes that something would happen.
2. A little orange man appears.
3. The man gives Blanca a tiny bottle of orange liquid.
4. She drinks it.
5. She becomes invisible.
6. She thinks of good and bad things about being invisible.
7. She decides she doesn't want to be invisible.
8. The orange man appears again.
9. He gives her another bottle of orange liquid.
10. Blanca drinks the liquid and becomes visible again.

These are the important things that happen to the main character. They are listed in **time sequence.** What happens first is listed first. What happens second is listed second, and so on.

Adding Details

The writer next added details to her plan.

1. Blanca is bored and wishes that something would happen.
   It's raining.
   Her best friend has moved to a suburb.
   She has a cold.

2. A little orange man appears.
   He is about six inches tall.
   He is dressed in orange.
   He is wearing a pointed hat.
   He has a long cape.

3. The man gives Blanca a tiny bottle of orange liquid.
   He takes the bottle from a pouch on his belt.
   The potion smells like roses, freshly baked bread, and rain-soaked earth.

4. She drinks it.
   It tastes delicious.

5. She becomes invisible.
   She feels light.
   She gets up and goes into the hall.
   She looks in the mirror and doesn't see herself.

6. She thinks of good and bad things about being invisible.
   The good things are these: could come and go without house keys; could get into movies free; would not have to help with the dishes.
   The bad things are these: couldn't eat pizza; couldn't play in Little League; couldn't talk on the phone; couldn't hug her little sister or anyone else. She remembers her birthday.

7. She decides she doesn't want to be invisible.
   She decides she would rather be her regular visible self.

8. The orange man appears again.

9. He gives her another bottle of orange liquid.
   It smells like bus fumes, rotten potatoes, and dirty socks.

10. Blanca drinks the liquid and becomes visible again.
    The orange man disappears.
    Blanca is her regular self, only not bored.

Now the writer knew exactly what her story would be about.

Exercise Making a Plan

It is time for you to decide what will happen in your story. First do some thinking. Then list the important things that will happen. Add details. Finally, check to see that your plan is arranged in a time sequence. Save your finished plan. You will need it for Part 3 of this lesson.

Part 3 Writing a Story

A story has three parts. The first part is the introductory paragraph.

The Introductory Paragraph

An introductory paragraph usually tells *who* a story is about. It introduces the main characters. It tells *where* the story takes place. It also gives some idea of *what* the story is about. Here is an introductory paragraph. It begins a story.

> Once upon a time, in a little French town, lived an old lady whose name was Madame Louise Bodot. She had one son who was in Africa studying reptiles. One morning the mailman brought her a peculiar O-shaped box. Madam Bodot screamed when she opened it. It was a snake her son had sent her for her birthday. —TOMI UNGERER

This paragraph begins a story about Madame Louise Bodot. She lives in a little French town. The story is about what happens when she gets a snake from her son.

The paragraph tells you what the story is about. It does something else, too. It makes you want to read more.

The writer who made the sample plan in Part 2 wrote the following introductory paragraph.

> Blanca was bored. She was home alone, and it was raining. Her best friend had just moved to a far-away suburb. She had a cold. She wished that something, anything, would happen. Something did.

From this paragraph you learn that the story is about a girl named Blanca. Blanca is at home. Blanca is bored. You learn that something ends Blanca's boredom. After reading the paragraph, you probably want to find out what happened.

Part 3

Objective

To write a five-paragraph story, organized into introductory paragraph, body, and ending

Presenting the Lesson

1. Read and discuss page 285. Emphasize the three elements introduced in the opening paragraph of a story: who, where, and what.
2. Assign and discuss the Exercise on page 286.
3. Read The Body on pages 286 and 287. Ask volunteers to read sections of the plan and the corresponding paragraphs, to demonstrate how the writer incorporated the main ideas and details of her plan into the body of the story.
4. Assign and discuss the Exercise on page 287.
5. Read The Ending on page 287. Ask a student to read the final three points of the plan to show how these ideas were incorporated into the ending of the story. Ask another student to read the entire story, from beginning to end.
6. Assign and discuss the Exercise on page 287. The steps for checking a composition are on page 275.

Extending the Lesson

Explain that there are many mediums for story telling, such as plays, television programs, radio shows, comic strips, pantomime, dance, songs, movies, story boards, and puppet shows. Direct each student to choose one of these alternate methods of story telling and to translate his or her written story into this new format. Provide time for the students to share their stories.

Exercise Writing the Introductory Paragraph

Write the introductory paragraph to your story. The paragraph should introduce your main character. It should also catch your reader's interest.

The Body

The middle paragraphs in a story form the body. They tell what happens to the characters. The writer of the story about Blanca wrote three body paragraphs.

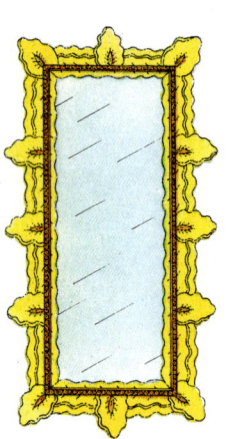

    On the arm of her chair appeared a tiny person. He was about six inches tall. He was dressed in orange, from the top of his high pointed hat to the hem of his long cape. He took a tiny bottle from a pouch on his belt. It was filled with orange liquid. He handed the bottle to Blanca without a word. She pulled out the cork and sniffed. It smelled like roses and freshly baked bread and rain-soaked earth all mixed together. She sipped it. It was delicious. She drank the rest, wishing he had given her more.

    Suddenly Blanca felt strangely light. She got up from her chair and half-floated, half-walked into the hall. As she passed the hall mirror, she turned to see if she looked any different. She wasn't even there!

    Blanca tried to decide what to do. She thought of good things about being invisible. She could come and go without using house keys. She could get into movies free. She could watch her brothers do the dishes without having to help. She felt happy. Then she began to think of bad things. She couldn't eat pizza or chocolate ice cream. She couldn't play on her Little League team. She couldn't talk on the phone with her friends. She couldn't hug her little sister, or anyone else. Suddenly she remembered that tomorrow was her birthday. That did it! Blanca decided she would much rather be her regular visible self.

The writer covers points 2, 3, and 4 of her plan in the first body paragraph. She covers point 5 in the second body paragraph. She covers points 6 and 7 in the third paragraph.

The plan lists events in a time sequence. So do the body paragraphs. That's because the writer followed her plan closely.

Exercise   Writing the Body.

Write the body of your story. Be sure to follow your plan.

The Ending

The last paragraph in a story ties up the loose ends. It lets the readers know that the story has ended. Here is the last paragraph in the story about Blanca.

> Blanca covered her eyes and wished as hard as she could. The little orange man appeared again. He handed Blanca another tiny bottle. It, too, was filled with something orange. This orange stuff, though, smelled terrible—like bus fumes and rotten potatoes and dirty socks. Blanca held her nose and drank. The little man disappeared. Little by little Blanca returned to her regular self. It was still raining. Her best friend was still gone. She still had a cold. She ran to the mirror, and there she was! She wasn't bored anymore.

This paragraph covers points 8, 9, and 10 of the writer's plan. After reading it, you know that the story about Blanca is finished.

Exercise   Finishing Your Story

Write the last paragraph of your story. After you finish, check your story. Follow the steps for checking a composition. They are given in Chapter 19, Part 6. Then make a final copy of your story.

Chapter 21

Group Discussion

Sometimes you need to talk with others about a single idea or problem. You want to keep the conversation moving in a certain direction. This kind of talk is called **discussion.**

Part 1 Taking Part in a Discussion

When you are having a discussion with others, follow these guides.

1. Be ready to make things clear when people get confused.
2. Ask questions that will help the discussion move forward.
3. Add any information you have that others don't know.
4. When you disagree, say so.
5. Always remember to speak courteously.

Chapter Objectives

1. To discover the nature of effective discussion
2. To learn how to lead a discussion
3. To become a helpful participant in discussion

Preparing the Students

Read the first paragraph on page 289. Ask students to examine the picture on page 280 and tell you what they think the boys are talking about.

Explain the difference between conversation and discussion. Conversation means "talking together." Discussion is a conversation with a particular purpose. In discussion, the people who are talking try to explore one subject. Everyone who takes part in a discussion should help keep it moving in a certain direction.

Point out examples of discussions you have held in class. This might be a good opportunity to explain that in a good discussion, everyone works. No one should remain silent, but neither should a single person dominate.

Part 1

Objective

To discover the nature of effective discussion

Presenting the Lesson

1. Read page 289 and discuss the guides.
2. Read the introductory paragraphs on page 290. Assign roles and ask students to read Part 1 of

the sample discussion. Then have them answer the questions.

Here are possible answers to questions, page 290:

1. Nan states the topic for discussion clearly and asks for suggestions from members of the group.
2. Jason's first comment is negative. Perhaps he could have said, "We need more equipment for older students."
3. Carmen's idea is that safety considerations are important, especially since the merry-go-round is dangerous.
4. Carlos is asking Carmen to clarify her statement. He wants to know exactly what is dangerous about the merry-go-round. Carlos also points out that the children enjoy it.
5. Jason is attacking Carmen instead of contributing ideas. The others should probably ignore his remark and get on with the subject of discussion. It is better not to further interrupt the discussion by criticizing Jason, unless he insists on being disruptive.

3. Assign roles and ask students to read Part 2 of the sample discussion on page 291. Then answer the questions on pages 291 and the top of 292.

Here are possible answers to the questions on pages 291 and 292.

1. Carmen states firmly that she knows what she is talking about. She further explains that she thinks older children should help take care of first-graders.
2. Susan tries to calm Jason down. Then she asks Carmen to explain her statement.

A Sample Discussion

The class has been invited by the P.T.A. to help with the school's project to improve the playground. Carlos, Susan, Carmen, Jason, and Nan will serve as a committee to figure out what to suggest to the P.T.A. Nan will be the chairperson.

Let's look at their discussion. You will see that it has been divided into three sections. After you read each part, try to answer the questions that follow it.

Part 1

NAN: We have to decide how we want the playground area used. We must also decide what equipment should be added or removed. Any ideas?

JASON: I don't like that playground. There's too much stuff for the little kids.

CARMEN: I think we should talk about safety. The merry-go-round is dangerous.

CARLOS: What's dangerous about it? The kids love it.

JASON: C'mon, Carmen. What are you, a traffic cop? You don't know anything about safety.

Questions   Part 1

1. How does Nan get the discussion off to a good start?
2. What was Jason's first point? How could he have stated it in a more positive way?
3. Carmen contributes the first good idea. What is it?
4. Why is Carlos' question a good one?
5. Jason interrupts with a rude remark. What do you think the other students should do to help the discussion move forward? How can they help Jason think more clearly about the issue?

Part 2

CARMEN: I *do* know about safety. I believe we should think about the first-graders. We're older and ought to feel responsible for them.

JASON: What a bunch of junk!

SUSAN: Wait a minute, Jason. Maybe Carmen should tell us why she thinks the merry-go-round is dangerous.

CARMEN: First of all, the big kids push it too fast and scare the little ones. The other problem is that the little kids can be pulled under it.

CARLOS: Maybe Carmen is right. Let's ask Ms. Jansen about it later. She's the real expert on first-graders. I have another idea. Do you think the playing field should be made any larger?

JASON: Super! Maybe the sliding board and swings could be moved closer together to give the older kids more room. We need some climbing bars, too.

SUSAN: Right, Jason. That would help with safety, too. There could be a special place for the little kids to play. Their equipment should be close together. Then the teachers could watch them more easily.

3. Carmen says that the merry-go-round is dangerous for two reasons:
   a. Little children are frightened when older ones push the merry-go-round too fast.
   b. Little children can be pulled underneath the merry-go-round.
4. Carlos introduces a new part of the problem, the idea of space on the playground.
5. Jason is thinking now. He contributes positive, concrete ideas.
6. Susan connects the problem of safety to the idea of expanding the space for older children.

Questions   Part 2

1. How does Carmen react to Jason's insult? What special responsibility does she think older students should have?
2. Susan speaks for the first time. How does she help the discussion move along?
3. Carmen states her reasons clearly. What are they?
4. Once again, Carlos asks a question. How does it open up the discussion?

4. Assign roles and ask students to read Part 3 of the sample discussion, on page 292. Then answer the questions at the bottom of the page.

Here are possible answers to the questions on page 292.

1. By asking a question, Nan returns the group to the subject of the merry-go-round. Carlos and Susan make suggestions for gathering more information.
2. Carmen summarizes the conclusion of the group: to suggest a playground near the building for young children and a larger playing field and climbing bars for older students, to be located farther from the building
3. Nan's question suggests a new angle for the discussion, one that will stimulate more thinking. It lets the group members know they have not finished discussing the topic. Questions of this kind keep a discussion moving toward its goal.
4. The group ignored Jason's rudeness and continued the discussion. (See Sample Discussion, Part 1, Question 5 and Part 2, Questions 1 and 2.)

5. How can you tell that Jason's attitude has changed?
6. How does Susan's point begin to pull the discussion together?

Part 3

NAN: What about the merry-go-round?

CARLOS: Maybe we should talk to someone who knows more about the equipment.

SUSAN: Let's ask Ms. Jansen if she can suggest a safety expert.

CARMEN: Good thinking. Now let's see. So far we think we should have two areas, right? We want a playground for the little kids near the building. We'd like a larger playing field and climbing bars for the older ones farther away.

NAN: I think we've reached a good stopping point for now. We can talk some more tomorrow. By the way, do you think that we ought to ask for a garden plot? It could be for a special class project. There might be room over by the bike racks.

JASON: Terrific! I think we're getting somewhere.

Questions   Part 3

1. Nan doesn't want to see the merry-go-round problem left hanging. How does she steer the group at this point? How do Carlos and Susan respond?
2. How does Carmen summarize the discussion?
3. Nan concludes the discussion. She then asks a question. How does her question create interest in tomorrow's meeting? Discuss how questions can be helpful in discussion.
4. Think about Jason. Earlier he made a rude remark. How did the group keep it from destroying the discussion?

Part 2   Roles in a Group Discussion

Leading a Discussion

It is usually helpful for someone involved in a discussion to serve as its leader or chairperson. Below are some suggestions that will help you lead a discussion in an organized way.

Guides for Leading a Discussion

1. When you begin the discussion, state the problem or ask someone else to do so.
2. Ask questions when a point is not clear.
3. Keep order. Make sure everyone takes turns talking.

The person who leads the group should be a helper and a guide. In the best discussions, the leader is well-informed and organized. He or she keeps the discussion moving forward.

Participating in a Discussion

When a group of people tries to solve a problem, everyone should work together. If you do not speak up, no one will know what you think or how you feel about the problem. As a responsible member of a group, always try to add something new or to ask a question.

You are always free to say what you think. However, you must also listen to others and respond to what they say. Group discussion helps you learn to think in an orderly way. It also teaches you to talk reasonably with other people in order to solve a common problem.

Part 2

Objectives

1. To learn how to lead a discussion
2. To become a helpful participant in discussion

Presenting the Lesson

1. Read Leading a Discussion on page 293. Discuss Nan's performance as leader in A Sample Discussion (pages 290–292). How did she follow the Guides for Leading a Discussion?
2. Read Participating in a Discussion on pages 293 and 294. Give special emphasis to the Guides for Participating in a Discussion. It is recommended that you spend some extra time on the importance of asking questions. Make sure that students understand the three reasons for asking questions in a discussion (Guide 3).
3. Assign Exercise A. Students should answer the questions independently and then discuss their answers in class.
4. Assign Exercise B. For reticent students, the topic for the sample discussion may be the one on paper and glass collection suggested in Exercise A. However, if some students want to launch a new topic, you may wish to encourage their initiative.

Extending the Lesson

Apply the principles of group discussion to a social studies lesson. Divide the class into small groups and assign topics for discussion. Ask students to follow the Guides for Participating in a Discussion on page 294. Monitor the groups.

Guides for Participating in a Discussion

1. Be informed. Be sure you have done any necessary reading and research.

2. Stay on the subject.

3. Ask questions:
    a. To clarify a point
    b. To get information
    c. To help the discussion move forward

4. Listen to others.

5. Always be polite, especially when you disagree.

Exercises Group Discussion

A. Pretend your class wants to help people recycle glass and paper to save energy. You have decided to collect old newspapers and glass from the people who live near your school. Here is your problem for discussion: How should the class be organized for picking up the newspapers and glass from your neighbors?

1. What questions can you ask to help the group explore the problem? Write two of these questions on your paper.

2. Read through the comments below. Then be ready to discuss them in class.

    a. I think we should collect the papers and glass on Saturday morning.

    b. What are we going to do with the money we get at the recycling center?

c. I read that colored glass should be separated from clear glass.

   d. Old newspapers are a fire hazard.

   e. My sister cut her hand on broken glass and had five stitches.

Discuss these questions in class.

   a. Which comments might help move the discussion forward?

   b. Which comments seem out of place?

Explain your answers.

B. For these exercises, divide into groups of four or five.

1. Let each group write a sample discussion. First, choose a leader. Then state the problem clearly. Write the discussion following the style in the sample discussion. Follow the Guides for Participating in a Discussion.

2. Exchange discussions. Read aloud the discussion that another group wrote. Check it for the following points:

   a. Is the problem stated clearly?

   b. Did the group explore all aspects of the problem?

   c. Did the members of the group stay on the subject?

   Write out two suggestions for improving the discussion your group read.

Chapter 22

Telling Stories

A really good storyteller knows how to bring a story to life. The listeners feel the excitement. The suspense grips them. A good storyteller helps the listeners follow the action. They listen to every word, eager to find out what happens next.

You will probably enjoy telling stories. Just be sure to learn your story well. People want their storyteller to be prepared.

This chapter is divided into three parts. Each part will help you learn one aspect of storytelling. Let's first discuss how to choose a good story.

Chapter Objectives

1. To choose a story that will interest listeners
2. To discover how a particular story is put together, and to learn how to study it for effective retelling
3. To tell a story in a lively way

Preparing the Students

Before beginning this chapter, let students hear a good story. Either tell one yourself—perhaps "The Snakebit Hoe Handle" on pages 300 and 301—or find some other competent storyteller who would be willing to share a favorite tale with the class. For purposes of this chapter, the story should be told, not read. Although there are some excellent recordings of stories, the live experience is preferable. Students will learn a great deal by interacting with a storyteller who talks with them in person.

After students listen to the story, discuss the experience. These questions will help get the discussion started: (a) What was the most exciting moment in the story? (b) How did the story make you feel?

When you are ready for students to learn to tell their own stories, read page 297. Discuss the responsibilities of the storyteller. What responsibilities does the listener have?

It would also be helpful, before discussing Part 1, to begin to assemble books containing stories that students might like.

Part 1

Objective

To choose a story that will interest listeners

Presenting the Lesson

1. Read the introduction to Part 1 and Where to Find the Story on page 298. Talk about stories that students know and like. Are there any favorites that they can remember from early childhood?

2. Read How You Should Feel About Your Story on page 298. Discuss how students can practice telling stories. Each telling of the story should improve it.

3. Read What to Look For in a Story on pages 298 and 299. Emphasize the importance of choosing a short tale. The story students choose should be about the same length as "The Snakebit Hoe Handle" (pages 300–301).

4. Write *plot* and its definition on the chalkboard. Ask students to summarize the plot of a story you have read or heard recently in class.

5. Discuss the Guides for Choosing a Story on page 299.

6. Assign Exercise A. Let students work independently but help them find stories to tell. Remind them that some of the best stories may come from their families or from their memories. More advanced students may be encouraged to write down a family or personal story at this time. They may then use these stories for later assignments in this chapter. Average students will probably feel more comfortable using a story

Part 1 Choosing a Story

It is important to choose a story that will capture the interest of your listeners. You may need to read several tales before you find one that is just right for you.

Where To Find a Story

Take plenty of time when you look for a story to tell. Ask your teacher or librarian to suggest tales that you might like. Read through them carefully. Look for stories among your books at home, too.

You might like to tell a story about yourself or someone close to you. Ask your parents and relatives if they remember any good family tales. Sometimes they have been handed down for generations.

How You Should Feel About Your Story

Your feelings about your story should be very strong. You should be eager to share it with others. If a story does not hold your interest, you should not tell it.

The more you practice telling your story, the closer you will feel to it. Try to make it part of you. It should feel as comfortable as an old shoe.

What To Look For in a Story

The story you choose should have important features:

1. **It should be short and simple.** Find a story that comes to the point quickly. A short tale is easy to remember. You can spend your time learning to tell it well. It's best to make your listeners wish you would tell more.

2. **It should have a lot of action.** An action story grips you. It makes you feel its excitement. A good action story will have a strong plot. The **plot** is the series of events that the author weaves together. A strong plot makes you follow the events eagerly. You want to know what happens next. Your listeners will share your feeling of suspense.

Guides for Choosing a Story

1. Ask your teacher, librarian, and parents to help you find stories to tell.

2. Read or listen to several of those stories.

3. Choose two stories that you especially like.

4. Check your stories. Are they short, simple, and strong in action? If not, look for others.

Exercise Choosing a Story

The exercise below will give you practice in choosing a story to tell. Be sure to follow the guides. When your teacher returns your paper, save it. You will use it in Parts 2 and 3.

A. Find five stories you might wish to tell. Read them or listen to them carefully. Write their titles and authors on your paper.

B. From the stories you have found, choose two that would be good stories to tell. On your paper, answer the following questions about each one of them:

1. What is the most exciting event in the story?
2. Why do you think this story would be a good one to tell?

published in an anthology or a magazine.

Another excellent resource is the nursery tale, such as "Goldilocks and the Three Bears." Stories for younger children are easy to tell because they contain repetition, suspense, and uncomplicated action. Stories that are more sophisticated may be too difficult for the beginning storyteller to handle. Caution students to find stories with simple plots.

7. Assign Exercise B. Help students cast aside stories that will not work. At this point the students will need much encouragement. They can easily become frustrated by the process of choosing a story.

Part 2

Objective

To discover how a particular story is put together, and to learn how to study it for effective retelling

Presenting the Lesson

1. Read the introduction on page 300. Ask students to tell why they like the stories they have chosen.

2. Read "The Snakebit Hoe Handle" on pages 300 and 301 in class. Have students tell what they like about the story.

3. Read The Introduction on pages 301 to 303. Examine the three steps for preparing the introduction of a story. In storytelling, the character of the narrator becomes very important since he or she controls the listener's point of view. *Narrator* may be a new term to students. Explore it carefully. It may be helpful to talk about narrators in other stories students know. Make sure students can identify the narrators. If they are not familiar with any other stories told by narrators, do the exercise suggested in Extending the Lesson. In "The Snakebit Hoe Handle," the narrator is the main character in the story. He is a farmer who lives in the Southern mountains. He has a vivid imagination and speaks in colorful language. His last question shows that he has a sense of humor.

Part 2 Studying the Story

Now that you have chosen a story, do you know why you like it so well? Do you like it because it is exciting? Does it remind you of something you yourself have done? Once you know why you enjoy your story, you are ready to study its parts.

First let's look at a tale told by a farmer who lives in the Southern mountains.

THE SNAKEBIT HOE HANDLE

One day, like any other day, I was out hoeing my corn. From the corner of my eye, I saw something moving across the ground. It was a huge copperhead snake. He was heading straight towards me.

I began hitting him with the hoe. He thrashed around. He bit the hoehandle a couple of times. Finally, I killed him. I hung him on the fence.

Then I went back to hoeing my corn. Before long my handle felt thicker. I looked it over. Sure enough, it was swelling. The poison from the snakebite was working through it.

I tried hoeing with it a little longer. The handle was growing fatter and fatter. Suddenly, the head of the hoe popped right off!

I didn't think too much about it at the time. I just wanted to get my work done. I threw that handle over by the fence and got another hoe from the shed. I finished hoeing my corn about dark.

Two weeks passed. One day I took a walk through my cornfield. A huge new log lay at the end of my fence. I looked closer. It was that hoe handle! The poison had made it as big as a tree trunk.

I took the log to the sawmill. It made twenty or thirty boards. There was just enough lumber to build a new chicken house.

First I nailed the boards together. Then I mixed my paint with some turpentine. I painted the chicken house a beautiful red, from top to bottom.

Early the next morning, I walked over to admire my new chicken house. All I could see was an empty field. I ran down the corn rows toward the fence. There was my chicken house, snug against a fencepost. It was no bigger than a shoe box!

I finally figured out what happened. During the night my chicken house had shrunk. The turpentine in the paint must have cured the snake bite. It had taken out all the swelling.

I guess I was pretty lucky. What if I had already put my chickens in that new house?

Now let's see how a writer puts the parts of a story together.

The Introduction

Study the introduction of your story. Knowing it well will help you feel relaxed. You will win the trust of your listeners. They will be eager to hear the rest of your story.

The introduction is the first part of a story. It lets you meet the characters. It also gives you the background of the story. The introduction stops when the main action starts. The main action is the body of the story.

The introduction of "The Snakebit Hoe Handle" is short. It is contained in the first paragraph. Let's read that paragraph again.

> One day, like any other day, I was out hoeing my corn. From the corner of my eye, I saw something moving across the ground. It was a huge copperhead snake. He was heading straight towards me.

The introduction stops here. The body of the story begins when the farmer kills the snake.

4. Assign Exercise A on page 303. Those students who have chosen a family story or other story that is not in print should write an original introduction that includes all the information requested.

After the students have prepared by completing Exercise A, assign Exercise B on page 304. It may be helpful to have the students form the same groups for each group exercise in this chapter. By having them meet together several times before they actually tell stories to one another, you will help them feel at ease.

5. Read The Body on pages 304 and 305. Point out that the list of events does not include every sentence or minor happening in the story. Only the events having a direct effect on the plot are listed. Write *climax* on the chalkboard. Check to be sure students can find the climax of the story.

6. Before assigning Exercise A, remind students to list only those events which affect the plot, not every detail mentioned. Assign Exercises A and B on page 305.

7. Read The Conclusion on pages 305 and 306. Discuss the farmer's question at the end of the story.

8. Assign Exercises A and B on page 306.

9. Use the Guides for Studying a Story on page 307 as a basis for review.

Extending the Lesson

This exercise may help students become aware of the importance of the point of view presented by a narrator. Ask students to imagine how a familiar story would be told by different characters in the story. For example, in "The Three Little Pigs," how would the serious pig tell what happened? How would one of the careless pigs tell the story? How would the wolf?

A storyteller prepares the introduction of a story by following three steps.

1. Learn the facts.
2. Picture the setting.
3. Feel the mood.

Each step helps you learn the story well enough to share it with others.

Let's look at these steps one at a time.

Step 1. Learn the Facts. You must first find out as much as you can about the narrator. The narrator is the person who tells the tale. In "The Snakebit Hoe Handle," the narrator is the farmer. We see everything through his eyes.

When you tell a story out loud, you will play the part of the narrator. Your listeners will see everything through your eyes. Try to be as much like the narrator in the story as you can.

The introduction will also give you the background of the story. It will answer some or all of these questions:

1. *Who* is the story about?
2. *What* is happening?
3. *Where* does the story take place?
4. *When* do the events occur?

The introduction to "The Snakebit Hoe Handle" answers all four questions:

1. *Who?* The story is about a farmer and a copperhead snake.
2. *What?* The farmer is hoeing his corn. The snake is heading toward him.
3. *Where?* The story takes place in a cornfield.
4. *When?* The events happen on an ordinary day.

Step 2. Picture the Setting. Your next step is to picture the setting. The setting is the objects and places named in the story. In our story, the cornfield, hoe, and snake are all part of the setting.

Memory can help you picture these things. Have you ever seen a cornfield? Perhaps you can remember the straight rows of tall green plants.

Step 3. Feel the Mood. The introduction also creates a mood. The **mood** is the feelings that surround the events of the story.

Think again about "The Snakebit Hoe Handle." How do you feel when the snake appears? Are you afraid? Are you curious? Are you tense?

A storyteller must help the listeners sense the mood. Let your voice and your face show the narrator's feelings. In your story, the snake comes closer and closer. How can you make the listeners feel the growing suspense?

Exercises   The Introduction

A. Read again one of the stories that you chose in Part 1 of this chapter. Copy the introduction on your paper. Be sure that you copy the whole introduction. It may include more than one paragraph.

Answer these questions on your paper. Write your answers in complete sentences.

1. *Who* is the story about?
2. *What* is happening?
3. *Where* does the story take place?
4. *When* do the events occur?
5. Does the introduction tell you anything about the *narrator* of the tale?

B. Divide into groups of four or five. Take turns telling the introduction to "The Snakebit Hoe Handle" to the other people in your group. Try to picture the setting. Help your listeners feel the mood. After you have taken your turn, ask the others to tell you how you did.

The Body

The body of a story begins when one of the characters performs an important action. In "The Snakebit Hoe Handle," the body begins when the farmer kills the snake.

This first action sets the plot in motion. Each time a character does something, the plot grows. The body of the story contains all the events that make up the plot. The storyteller must know these events in their proper order.

Learning the Events. When you prepare to tell a story, it is helpful to list the events on paper. Then go over them until you are sure you know them in order.

Here are the events that make up the plot of "The Snakebit Hoe Handle."

1. The farmer kills the snake with the hoe.
2. The hoe handle swells.
3. The head of the hoe pops off.
4. The farmer throws the handle on the ground.
5. The hoe handle grows as big as a tree trunk.
6. The farmer has it sawed into boards.
7. He uses the boards to build a chicken house.
8. The farmer paints the chicken house.
9. The chicken house shrinks.

The body ends with the last event. After that comes the conclusion of the story.

Preparing for the Climax. The climax is the most surprising or exciting moment in the story. It is always the last event in the body of the tale. In "The Snakebit Hoe Handle," the climax comes when the farmer finds that the chicken house has shrunk.

A storyteller must prepare the listeners for the climax. You should make them feel the suspense growing. For example, you might want to speak slowly when you come close to the climax. When you reach the climax, show your excitement in your voice and body. Don't hold back. The climax is the most important moment in your story.

Exercises The Body

A. Read again the story you chose in Part 1. List the events in the body of the story. Be sure to write them in order. Underline the event that is the climax.

B. Divide into groups of four or five. Take turns reading aloud the following paragraph:

> Early the next morning, I walked over to admire my new chicken house. All I could see was an empty field. I ran down the corn rows toward the fence. There was my chicken house, snug against a fencepost. It was no bigger than a shoe box!

Try to picture each thing that happens. Let your voice and body show your feelings.

The Conclusion

The conclusion of a story tells how everything ends. It ties up the details of the plot. It also shows what happens after the climax.

In "The Snakebit Hoe Handle," the conclusion comes in the last two paragraphs. Let's look at them again:

> I finally figured it out. During the night my chicken house had shrunk. The turpentine in the paint must have cured the snake bite. It had taken out all the swelling.
>
> I guess I was pretty lucky. What if I had already put my chickens in that new house?

Earlier, the farmer had seen that his chicken house was now the size of a shoe box. That was the climax. What happened next?

The farmer figured everything out. He thought about his experience. His thinking is the conclusion of the story.

Now look at the last line of the story. It is a question. How does the question tie together the details of the plot?

A good question makes you think. The farmer's question takes you back through the story. It allows you to use your imagination.

Be sure you know the conclusion of your story. After you have told the climax, come to the end quickly. If you ramble, the listeners won't pay attention to you. It is very important to learn the last line of your story.

Exercises The Conclusion

A. Find the conclusion of the story that you chose for yourself in the last two exercises. Write it out on paper. Answer these questions in complete sentences:

1. What happens after the climax?
2. How does the last line tie the parts of the story together?

B. Divide into small groups. Take turns telling each other the conclusion of "The Snakebit Hoe Handle." Pretend that you are the farmer. Let your listeners see you thinking. Afterwards, ask the others how you did.

Putting the Story Together

You are ready to study your whole story. The guides below will help you remember the parts of a story.

Guides for Studying a Story

The Introduction

1. Decide what questions are answered. Learn the answers.
2. Picture the setting.
3. Feel the mood.

The Body

1. List the events in order.
2. Underline the climax.

The Conclusion

1. Think about what happens after the climax.
2. Learn the last line of the story.

Part 3

Objective

To tell a story in a lively way

Presenting the Lesson

1. Read page 308. Step by step, discuss the Guides for Telling a Story.

2. If students are timid about speaking before a group, you may wish to assign a preliminary exercise at this point. See Optional Practice at the end of this lesson for suggestions.

3. Assign Exercise A on page 309.

4. Assign Exercise B. Remind students that their stories should be short. For students at this level, two or three minutes is long enough. "The Snakebit Hoe Handle" can be told in that period of time.

Optional Practice

These icebreaker exercises will help students feel at ease when they talk before a group.

1. Divide into small groups. Ask each student to prepare to describe someone he or she knows well. The description should be very short, about thirty seconds. Urge students to include very specific details. Give the groups a minute or two of silence so that students can think about what they want to say. Before anyone speaks, review numbers 3, 4, and 5 in the Guides for Telling a Story on page 308. Insist that when one student talks, the others look at the speaker and listen attentively.

Part 3   Telling the Story

In the first part of this chapter, you learned to choose a good story. Then you learned how to prepare to tell it. Now you are ready to share your story with your friends.

When you tell your story, you should know it backwards and forwards. Show your listeners your eagerness. They will share your excitement and listen closely.

Practice is very important. To learn your story, tell it out loud, over and over again. Practice in front of your family or friends. When you practice, try to keep your voice and expressions lively.

The best advice is to *be natural*. Don't worry about special skills. Your purpose is to bring your story to life. To do that, relax and have fun telling it.

Here are some guides to help you tell your story.

Guides for Telling a Story

1. Learn your story so well that you can tell it without stumbling. Be sure to tell the events in the proper order.

2. Try to build suspense. Make your listeners eager to find out what happens next.

3. Speak loudly enough so that everyone can hear you.

4. Look into the eyes of the people listening to you.

5. Watch your listeners for reactions. Try to draw them into your story. Make them feel a part of it.

Exercises Telling a Story

A. Go back to one of the stories you chose in the exercise on page 299. Read it again and review your answers to the exercise questions.

Your goal now will be to tell your story to a small group of people. Follow these directions carefully:

1. Study the introduction, the body, and the conclusion of your story. Follow the guides for preparing to tell a story.

2. Practice telling your story out loud. Go over it at least four times.

3. Form several small groups. Tell your story to the other people in your group.

When you are the storyteller, remember to share your enthusiasm with the others. When you are listening to someone else's story, pay attention and show your interest.

B. Prepare to tell a story about yourself. In choosing what to tell, think about something exciting, frightening, or surprising that has happened to you. Talk over your ideas with your family, your teacher, and your friends. They may be able to help you remember an experience that would make a good story. Be sure to follow the Guides for Choosing a Story.

Once you have decided what story to tell, look again at the Guides for Studying a Story. Figure out how to put your story together. Even though it is about you, you must have an introduction, a body that builds to a climax, and a conclusion.

After you have put your story together, you are ready to practice telling it out loud. At this point you should review the Guides for Telling a Story. Be sure to follow them when you share your story with others.

2. At first, students may think this exercise is silly, but it will help to relieve them of self-consciousness. Encourage students to have fun with the exercise.

First gather together several different hats. Then have everyone in the class memorize this line: "Yesterday it snowed, but today I'm going to see the tigers in the zoo."

Ask students, one by one, to do the following exercise:

1. Choose a hat.
2. Make up a character to go with the hat.
3. Moving and speaking in character, walk across the front of the room, wearing your hat and saying the line you have learned.

Chapter 23
Oral and Written Reports

You learn how to prepare reports in language arts class. However, you will use this skill in many different classes. You will use it in social studies and music. You will use it in art and science. You may even use it in math.

As you know, a composition can be about anything. It can be about something that happened to you or to someone you know. A report, however, is a little different. It is usually about a subject you must study and learn about. In other words, a report is based on learned information.

In this chapter you will learn how to prepare both oral and written reports. You will learn how to do the following:

1. How to find a subject
2. How to find and record information
3. How to make a plan
4. How to write a report
5. How to give an oral report

Chapter Objectives

1. To develop a method for finding a subject for a report
2. To gather and record information for a report
3. To develop a method for organizing information, and to master the skill of outlining
4. To write a report, organized into introductory paragraph, body, and ending
5. To learn techniques for presenting an effective oral report

Preparing the Students

Discuss briefly some of the reports that students have given in subjects such as science and social studies. Point out that reports can be either oral or written. Explain that in this chapter the students are going to learn a method for doing reports that will help them in all their classes.

Read and discuss page 311.

Additional Resources

Mastery Test—pages 482 and 483 in this T.E. Recommended for use after teaching the chapter.

Additional Mastery Test—Recommended for use after any necessary reteaching. (In separate booklet, *Mastery Tests, Silver Level*, pages 45 and 46.)

Skills Practice Book—pages 112–118

Duplicating Masters—pages 112–118

Part 1

Objective

To develop a method for finding a subject for a report

Presenting the Lesson

1. Read page 312 and the first paragraph of page 313. As you read, write on the chalkboard these steps for finding a subject.

1. Choose a general subject.
2. Look for books on that subject.
3. List possible subjects for reports.
4. Check reference books.
5. Add to your list of possible subjects.
6. Check magazines.
7. Add more ideas to your list of subjects.

Pause to review library skills, if necessary.

2. Read Deciding on a Subject on page 313. Emphasize that a subject must be narrow enough to be covered in a short report. Give these examples of subjects that are too broad and subjects that are appropriate for short reports:

1. insects that live underground
   how ants build their nests
2. cooking
   how to decorate a birthday cake
3. Native Americans
   Geronimo

3. Assign and discuss the Exercise on page 313. Guide students in choosing a subject that is narrow enough for a short (five or six paragraph) report.

Part 1 Finding a Subject

Many times you will be assigned a subject for a report. Other times you may be asked to choose from a list of subjects. Sometimes, however, you will need to find a subject on your own.

Using the Library

The best place to look for a subject is in a library. You learned in Chapter 14 that every nonfiction book has a number. You learned also that books on the same general topic have similar numbers. For example, books on astronomy are numbered between 500 and 599. When you need ideas for a subject, go to the part of the library that has books on the general topic you are studying. It might be astronomy or mammals or American artists. Look through several books. Begin a list of possible subjects.

Next check the reference books. Encyclopedias, almanacs, and dictionaries on special topics are some of the reference books that may help you. If you find a book or an article, look through it for ideas. Add the ideas to your list.

A third place to check is the magazine shelf. You might also ask a librarian for the back issues of magazines. Magazines can be especially helpful if you are going to prepare a report on plants or animals. *National Geographic World* and *Ranger Rick* are full of ideas for subjects.

Remember, at this point you are only getting ideas. You are not gathering information.

Deciding on a Subject

You will probably end up with many possible subjects. Your next job is to decide on one. Go over your list. Circle the subjects that seem most interesting. Make sure that each of them could be covered in a short report. Then make your final choice.

Optional Practice

Arrange for a class visit to the school or local library during which students can begin their lists of subjects.

Exercise Choosing a Subject

Choose a general subject from the list below. Go to the library and look through books and magazines. The general subjects below are too large for a report. You must look for a small part of any of them. This will be the **topic** for your report. For example, under "flying insects" you may find an insect that is unusual. You may want to write a report on that one insect.

Make a list of possible short topics for a report. Then choose one of them.

musical instruments
stars
flying insects
unusual plants
animal homes
masks

party ideas
women athletes
endangered species
crafts
television
legends

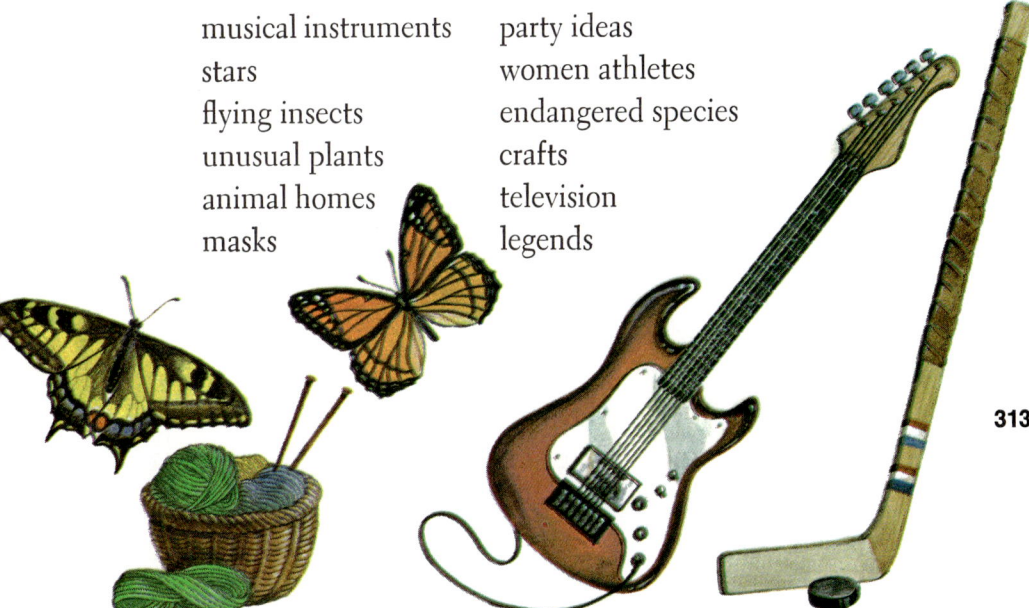

Part 2

Objective

To gather and record information for a report

Presenting the Lesson

1. Read and discuss page 314. Point out that three sources of information are mentioned: books, reference books, and magazines. Ask the class for examples of each and for their locations in the library. If necessary, review Chapter 14, Using the Library.

2. Read the explanations and study the note cards on pages 315 and 316. Ask questions that direct the students to each specific item of information, for example: What is the name of the encyclopedia on Note Card 1? Point out that each note card contains one fact and that the facts are recorded in complete sentences. Emphasize that students should paraphrase the information, writing it in their own words. If sentences are copied directly from the source, they must be set off by quotation marks.

3. Assign and discuss the Exercise on page 316.

Optional Practice

Provide each student with three 3 x 5 cards. Direct the students to find the following information and to record the facts on the cards in the format presented in the lesson.

1. One fact about sports, taken from a magazine
2. One fact about holidays, taken from a reference book
3. One fact about ocean creatures, taken from a book

Part 2 Gathering Information

You have decided on a topic. Now you must go back to the library again. This time you will look for specific information.

First, check the card catalog. Make a list of books that might have information about your topic. Next check the indexes of the general encyclopedias. Write down the name of the encyclopedia and the volume and page numbers where you might find information. You will also want to record the names of other reference books related to your topic.

You may need to review how to use the card catalog and indexes of books for information. If so, turn to pages 193 to 203 of this book.

Reading About Your Subject

Your next step is to learn more about your topic. On the library shelves, find each book that you listed. Then read the part of the book that deals with your topic.

In your search for possible topics, you may have come across magazine articles on the topic you chose. If so, read those articles now.

Taking Notes

As you read, you will need to take notes. Notes will help you remember facts or ideas to put into your report.

Many writers take notes on 3 x 5 cards. They write each fact or idea on a separate card.

One writer chose the topic "spider webs" for a report. She got her information from an encyclopedia, a book, and a magazine article. Here are three of her note cards.

Note Card 1

This note card shows information from an encyclopedia. The note card gives the name and date of the encyclopedia and the volume and page number of the article.

Name / **Date**
World Book Encyclopedia, 1978,
Volume 18, page 615
Volume / **Page**

Some webs are as small as a postage stamp. Others are two feet across.
Information

Note Card 2

This note card shows information from a book. It gives the title and author of the book.

Title
Animals and Plants That Trap
by Philip Goldstein
Author

Spiders produce several kinds of silk. Some silk forms sticky threads or droplets. Other silk forms dry threads.
Information

Note Card 3

This note card shows information from a magazine. It gives the name and date of the magazine. It also gives the title and page numbers of the article. Some magazine articles give authors' names. These, too, can be written on this type of note card.

Magazine: National Geographic World, November 1975
Title: "Spiders: Nature's Master Builders," *Pages:* pages 5-6
Information: Each species of spiders spins its own type of web.

Exercise Gathering Information

Return to the library. This time, make a list of books and encyclopedias that might have information about your topic. Read about your topic in these books. Also, read any magazine articles that have to do with your topic. As you read, take notes on 3 x 5 cards. Save your note cards. You will need them to plan your report.

Part 3 Making a Plan

The next step in doing a report is to make a plan. A plan involves the following:

1. Organizing your notes
2. Listing four or five main ideas
3. Making an outline

Organizing Your Notes

Organizing your notes is important. While doing this, you are doing something even more valuable. You are organizing your thoughts. You are deciding exactly what you want to say in your report.

To begin, read each 3 x 5 card. Put the cards that deal with the same idea together. You may want to put them in separate piles. You can also join them together with paper clips.

The writer who chose spider webs as a topic sorted her cards into five groups. These were the groups:

1. Cards with facts about where spiders build webs
2. Cards about different types of webs
3. Cards about how spiders build webs
4. Cards about spiders' silk
5. Cards about how spiders use webs

When you sort your cards, you should end up with four or five groups. You will probably have some cards that don't seem to fit with any others. Set these aside. You may not be able to use them for your report.

Exercise Organizing Your Notes

Sort your 3 x 5 cards into four or five groups. Each group should have facts related to the same idea.

Presenting the Lesson

1. Although the process of planning a report is presented step by step, it might be confusing to students who are encountering the tasks of organizing information, formulating main ideas, and outlining for the first time. Try to identify these students before introducing Part 3. Then work with these students in a group to complete each Exercise.

2. Read page 317. Emphasize that organizing notes is the first step in making a plan. Point out that having only one fact or idea on each card allows for flexibility when the time comes to group the cards.

3. Assign the Exercise on page 317.

4. Read and discuss Listing Main Ideas on page 318. The thought process required of the students for this step is similar to that required for writing a topic sentence. They must formulate a general idea from a group of specific ideas.

Listing Main Ideas

Next you will want to read each group of cards. Think about the one main idea that pulls all the facts together.

The writer of the spider web report read these facts:

1. Spider webs are found on mountains.
2. Spider webs are found in tropical forests.
3. Spiders build webs inside folded leaves.
4. Some spiders build webs under ground.
5. One type of spider builds webs under water.
6. Spider webs are found inside houses.

The facts showed that spiders build webs just about everywhere. The writer wrote the following main idea for this group of cards:

Spider webs are found everywhere, inside and out.

The writer did this for each group of cards. Her final list of main ideas was this:

1. Spider webs are found everywhere, indoors and out.
2. Each kind of spider builds its own type of web.
3. A spider builds a web thread by thread.
4. Spiders use their webs in many ways.
5. All spider webs are made from silk.

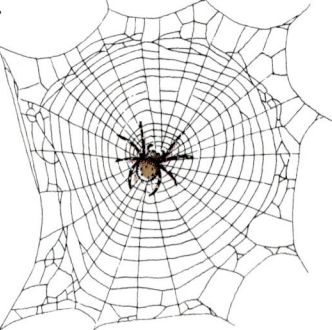

Exercise Making a List of Main Ideas

Read each group of cards. For each group, decide on one main idea. It should pull the facts together. Make a list of the four or five main ideas covered by your cards.

Making an Outline

An outline is a way of arranging ideas. It shows how ideas fit together. Let's look at a short sample outline. It was made to plan a shopping trip.

SHOPPING **Title**

I. Hardware store **Main Topic**
   A. Nails ⎤
   B. Hammer ⎦ **Subtopics**

II. Grocery Store **Main Topic**
   A. Milk ⎤
   B. Eggs ⎥
   C. Bread ⎥ **Subtopics**
   D. Jelly ⎦

The hardware store and the grocery store are the two main stops on the shopping trip. They are the two main ideas on the outline. They are called **main topics.**

Look at the outline again. Notice the following:

> 1. Each topic is numbered with a Roman numeral followed by a period.
>
> 2. The first letter of each main topic is capitalized.
>
> 3. The main topics are lined up under each other.

Several items are listed under each main topic. "Nails" and "Hammer" are under "Hardware store." "Milk," "Eggs," "Bread," and "Jelly" are under "Grocery store." These are called **subtopics.** There must always be at least two subtopics.

Notice the following:

> 1. Subtopics are labeled with capital letters followed by periods.
>
> 2. The first letter in each subtopic is capitalized. The subtopics are not complete sentences.
>
> 3. Subtopics are indented. They begin under the first letter of the main topic.
>
> 4. Subtopics are lined up under each other.

Topics and subtopics can be words, phrases, or sentences. The outline "shopping" uses phrases for the main topics. It uses words for the subtopics. Here is the important thing to remember:

> 1. All the main topics should be in the same form.
>
> 2. All the subtopics should be in the same form.

Besides topics and subtopics, an outline has a **title.** It tells what the outline is about. Sometimes you will use an outline to plan a composition. You will use the title of the composition as the title of the outline. Remember this:

> All the important words in a title are capitalized.

Outlining can help you when you need to organize your thoughts. It can help you plan a report. It can help you plan a composition. It can help you plan a book report or a speech.

Outlining Your Report

You have a list of main ideas. You are now ready to make an outline for your report.

First arrange your main ideas in some logical order. This will be the order you will follow in your outline. This will also be the order you will follow in writing your report. The main ideas on your list will become the main topics of your outline. The facts from your 3 x 5 cards will become the subtopics.

The writer of the spider web report arranged her main ideas in the following order:

1. Spider webs are found everywhere, indoors and out.
2. All spider webs are made from silk.
3. A spider builds a web thread by thread.
4. Each kind of spider builds its own type of web.
5. Spiders use their webs in many ways.

She decided that her general idea uniting all five ideas was that spider webs are wonders of nature.

Each of the five ideas became a main topic in her outline. The related facts were listed as subtopics. Here is her finished outline:

SPIDER WEBS

I. Introduction: Spider webs are wonders of nature found everywhere, indoors and out.
  A. On mountains
  B. In tropical forests
  C. Underground
  D. Underwater
  E. Inside folded leaves
  F. Inside houses

II. All spider webs are made from silk.
  A. Made in special glands
  B. Carried by tubes to spinnerets
  C. Comes sticky and dry

III. A spider builds a web thread by thread.
   A. Begins with dry thread
   B. Anchors thread to starting point
   C. Bites off extra threads
   D. Joins certain threads
   E. Weaves threads in and out
   F. Creates pattern

IV. Each kind of spider builds its own type of web.
   A. Spiders born knowing how
   B. Some webs small as postage stamps
   C. Some webs two feet across
   D. Some jumbles of tangled threads
   E. Some perfect circles and triangles
   F. Some bowl-shaped, dome-shaped, or tent-shaped
   G. Some platforms, funnels, and mazes

V. Spiders use their webs in many ways.
   A. As homes
   B. As places to lay eggs
   C. As food catchers: Insects fly or walk into a web and are caught by sticky threads. The spider bites the captive to paralyze it. It wraps the captive in silk and saves it.

VI. Ending

As an introduction, the writer decided to write about where spider webs are found. She added an ending as a sixth main topic. When she finished her outline, she had a detailed plan for her report.

Exercise   Planning Your Report

List your main ideas in logical order. Then make an outline. Use the main ideas as the main topics of your outline Use the facts from your 3 x 5 cards as the subtopics.

Part 4 Writing Your Report

Like a composition, a written report has three parts.

1. It has an introductory paragraph. This paragraph gives the main idea of the report.
2. It has body paragraphs. These explain the main idea.
3. It has an ending. It pulls all the ideas together.

When you are writing the three parts of a report, be sure to follow your outline. The outline includes all the ideas you want to cover. The ideas are arranged in logical order.

It is also important to refer to your note cards once in a while. In that way, you won't forget details not on the outline.

The Introductory Paragraph

The introductory paragraph presents the topic of the report. It may also include facts about the topic.

Here is the introductory paragraph of the report on spider webs.

> Spider webs are wonders of nature. They are found everywhere, indoors and out. They can be high on a mountain slope or deep in a tropical forest. They can be underground or underwater. They can be inside a folded leaf or in a corner of your living room.

The paragraph lets you know that the report is about spider webs. It also gives you some information about spider webs. The paragraph makes you want to learn more.

Exercise Writing the Introductory Paragraph

Write the introductory paragraph of your report.

Part 4

Objective

To write a report, organized into introductory paragraph, body, and ending

Presenting the Lesson

1. Read the introduction to Part 4 on page 323. Remind the students to keep their outlines and their notes cards in front of them as they write their reports.
2. Select several examples of catchy opening paragraphs from magazines such as *Cricket* and *National Geographic World*. Read each to the class, then follow with these two questions:
    1. What is the report going to be about?
    2. Do you want to find out more about the topic?
3. Read The Introductory Paragraph on page 323. Note that the paragraph incorporates the main topic under Roman numeral I and its related subtopics from the outline on page 321.
4. Assign the Exercise on page 323. Remind the students that they are writing rough drafts, which they will revise and recopy at the end of Part 4.
5. Read The Body on pages 324 and 325. Refer to the outline on pages 321 and 322 to show how the main topics of the outline became the topic sentences of the body and how the subtopics were incorporated into the supporting sentences in each paragraph.

6. Assign the Exercise on page 325. Remind the students again that they are writing rough drafts.

7. Read The Ending on page 325. Explain that the final paragraph of a report does not have to include facts from note cards. However, its message must relate directly to what has been said in the body. It may not introduce a totally new idea. Mention that many ending paragraphs pull together the main topics in a brief summary.

8. Read Giving Credit on pages 325 and 326. Have the students turn back to the sample note cards on pages 315 and 316. Point out that the information for the list of sources at the end of the report was taken directly from the note cards. Explain that page numbers are not included for the book, and that the page numbers for the magazine and reference sources are those for the entire article. It may also be helpful to discuss the use of capitalization and punctuation in the references.

9. Assign the Exercise on page 326.

Optional Practice

Give the students the following list of sources. Ask them to identify the item or items of information that are missing from each.

    a. *Compton's Encyclopedia,* 1979, pages 314–316
    b. *Ranger Rick,* December, pages 10–13
    c. *Wildlife in Danger*
    d. *World Book Encyclopedia,* Volume 4

The Body

The middle paragraphs are called the body of the report. These paragraphs give many facts about the topic. Each paragraph begins with a topic sentence. This sentence is usually a main topic from the outline. The rest of the sentences explain the idea in the topic sentence. They cover the subtopics on the outline. In other words, each paragraph in a report covers a main topic and its subtopics.

Here are the four body paragraphs of the report on spider webs. Notice how closely the writer has followed her outline.

    All spider webs are made from silk. Silk comes from special glands. They are inside a spider's body. Tubes connect the glands to openings on a spider's underside. The openings are called spinnerets. Some spinnerets have silk that stays sticky. Others have silk that hardens into dry threads.

    A spider builds a web thread by thread. It first draws a thread of dry silk out of a spinneret. It attaches the thread to a starting point with a drop of sticky silk. As it builds its web, the spider bites off extra threads. It discards them. It joins certain threads and weaves others in and out. Little by little the spider forms an intricate pattern.

    Each kind of spider builds its own type of web. A spider is born knowing how to build its special web. Some webs are as small as a postage stamp. Others measure two feet across. Some webs look like jumbles of tangled threads. Others form perfect circles or triangles. Webs can be shaped like bowls, domes, tents, platforms, or funnels. Some webs are complicated mazes.

    Spiders use their webs in many ways. They use them as homes and as places to lay their eggs. They don't have to worry about getting caught in their own sticky threads. Their bodies are coated with an oil that prevents sticking. Other creatures aren't as lucky. When they walk or fly into a spider web, they are caught by the sticky threads. The spider bites each captive and paralyzes it. The spider then wraps its victim in silk and saves it.

Each paragraph begins with a topic sentence. It is taken from the outline. The rest of the paragraph gives many facts about spider webs. The paragraphs work together to explain the subject of the report.

Exercise Writing the Body Paragraphs

Write the body paragraphs of your report. Make sure that you follow your outline. Check your note cards to make sure you don't leave out any details.

The Ending

The last paragraph in a report is the ending. It lets your readers know that you are finished. It tells them that you have said everything you are going to say about the subject.

An ending does not have to be long. For example, the ending of the report on spider webs is only three sentences long.

> Web-building spiders cannot live without their webs. Think about that the next time you are tempted to brush away a web. You may decide not to destroy it after all.

A report is made up of facts. However, a writer may want to include a personal opinion. The ending is a good place for it. The writer of the spider web report cautioned her readers to think before destroying a web.

Giving Credit

You write a report in your own words. However, you get the information you use from outside sources. It is important to give credit to these sources. You do this at the end of your report. There, you list the books and magazines from which you got information.

The writer of the report on spider webs used three sources. She listed them at the end of her report.

I got my information from the following sources:

1. *Animals and Plants That Trap* by Philip Goldstein
2. *National Geographic World,* November 1975, "Spiders: Nature's Master Builders," pages 5–6
3. *World Book Encyclopedia,* 1978, Volume 18, page 615

Exercise   Finishing Your Report

Write the final paragraph for your report. Give credit to your sources. Then check the entire report. First, reread the report to make sure that the paragraphs stick to the main idea. Check to see that each paragraph is written correctly. Then correct the capitalization, punctuation, and spelling. If you need to review the steps for checking a composition, turn back to page 275, Checking the Composition. The last thing to do is to make a final copy of your report.

Part 5   Giving an Oral Report

Not all reports are written. Some are oral. Oral reports are like written reports in many ways. They, too, are based on learned information. They are developed by following many of the same steps.

Using Notes

Most people use notes when they give an oral report. Notes keep them on the right track. They also help them to remember main ideas.

Part 5

Objective

To learn techniques for presenting an effective oral report

Presenting the Lesson

1. Read pages 326 and 327. Explain that the steps in preparing an oral report are the same as those for a written report up through making an outline. Recall the steps:
   1. Choose a subject.
   2. Make a list of sources.
   3. Read and take notes.
   4. Organize the notes.
   5. List main ideas.
   6. Make an outline.

Notes can be written in several ways. One way is in outline form. A speaker would record each main topic of the outline and its subtopics on a separate 3 x 5 card. Cards are easy to hold. Also, a card can be set aside after that part of the report has been given.

The person doing the spider web report recorded her outline on note cards. Her card for her second topic looked like this.

> II. All spider webs are made from silk.
>   A. Made in special glands
>   B. Carried by tubes to spinnerets
>   C. Comes sticky and dry

Exercise Preparing Notes

Prepare the notes you will use for your report. Write each main topic and its subtopics on separate 3 x 5 cards.

2. Assign the Exercise on page 327.

3. Read Using Pictures on page 328.

4. Assign the Exercise on page 328. Give individual students suggestions of sources for pictures. Encourage them to ask a librarian for additional suggestions.

5. Read and discuss Practicing Your Report on page 329. Suggest that students might practice with partners, checking each other on the points listed.

Extending the Lesson

When the students are preparing to give their reports, suggest several alternatives to the "stand-in-front-of-the-class" style of reporting. These might include:

  a. reporting to a small group that is sitting on chairs in a circle; speaker is also sitting
  b. reporting to a small group that is sitting around a table; speaker is sitting at the same table
  c. reporting to a small group that is sitting on the floor; speaker is in the same position
  d. reporting to the entire class; speaker is standing behind or next to a desk in front of the group
  e. reporting to the entire class and alternating between two or three positions in front of the group

After several students have presented their reports, discuss the advantages and disadvantages of each style.

Using Pictures

Pictures can make an oral report more interesting. The kind of pictures you use depends upon your subject. You can show pictures during a report. You can pass pictures around after a report. You may also be able to display pictures in the classroom.

The person who gave the spider web report could have used several pictures. She could have shown different kinds of webs. She could have shown a spider building a web or catching food.

Exercise **Looking for Pictures**

Think about your report. Would pictures help to make it more interesting? If so, look for some pictures to use. Decide how and when you will show them to your listeners.

Practicing Your Report

You have prepared your report. Your notes are ready. You know what you are going to say. You have decided on the pictures you are going to use. Now it's time to practice.

A good way to practice is in front of a mirror. Present the report to yourself just as you will present it to the class. Make sure of the following:

1. Try to stand still.
2. Keep your eyes on your listeners most of the time.
3. Try not to distract your listeners from what you are saying.

Another good way to practice is with a tape recorder. Record your report. Then play it back. As you're listening, ask yourself the following:

1. Am I speaking slowly enough?
2. Am I stressing the main points?
3. Am I using correct English?
4. Do I sound natural?
5. Does my report seem interesting?

Practice until you feel relaxed about giving your report.

Exercise Getting Ready To Give Your Report

Practice your report. When you are ready, arrange with your teacher to give the report. You can give it to a small group or to the entire class.

Chapter 24

Writing Letters

Chapter Objectives

1. To become familiar with the organization and correct form of a friendly letter
2. To differentiate between friendly letters and social notes in purpose and form, and to use each form where it is appropriate
3. To differentiate between the form of the friendly letter and the form of the business letter, and to use each form where appropriate
4. To understand the purpose of the letter of request and the order letter
5. To use the correct form for addressing envelopes

Preparing the Students

Read the chapter introduction on page 331. Ask the students if any of them have written letters recently, and what the purpose of the letter was. Let them know that they will be writing letters while studying this chapter, and ask for suggestions for topics of letters. Use the picture on page 330 to help stimulate discussion. Ask the class to imagine that the boy is visiting a farm. What should he write about to a friend in the city?

Read the chapter introduction on page 331.

Additional Resources

Mastery Test—pages 484 and 485 in this T.E. Recommended for use after teaching the chapter.

Additional Mastery Test—Recommended for use after any necessary reteaching. (In separate booklet, *Mastery Tests, Silver Level,* pages 47 and 48.)

Skills Practice Book—pages 119–127

Duplicating Masters—pages 119–127

Letters are written for many different purposes. We write letters to keep in touch with friends and relatives. We use them to share news, to invite guests, and to thank people. In letters, we can order materials or get needed information.

Each type of letter has its own special form. This chapter will help you to learn and practice the forms of letters.

Part 1 Writing a Friendly Letter

Writing a letter to a friend is like a conversation on paper. You want your letter to sound natural and friendly. Here are some guides that will help you.

Part 1

Objective

To become familiar with the organization and correct form of a friendly letter

Presenting the Lesson

1. Read and discuss pages 331 and 332. Point out the conversational tone used in the sample letter. Emphasize that the letter should sound natural, almost as if the writer were speaking to the friend.

A Friendly Letter

Point out, also, the arrangement of ideas into separate paragraphs. Have students identify the specific parts of the letter that follow the guidelines listed above the letter.

2. Read pages 333 and 334, stopping after each subtopic to refer to the sample letter on page 332. Discuss the purpose of each part in the letter.

3. Assign and discuss Exercise A on page 334.

4. Before students write the letter for Exercise B on page 334, it would be helpful to spend some class time discussing possible topics. Make it clear that students are not limited to the suggestions in the text. Assign and discuss Exercise B.

Optional Practice

1. Students may enjoy making a collection of the letters written for Exercise B on page 334. Several collections could be made and put on display in the room.

Guides for Writing a Friendly Letter

1. Write about people and events that your friend will be interested in.
2. Express interest in what your friend is doing.
3. Arrange your information in paragraphs. Start a new paragraph each time you change your subject.

Read the following sample letter. Look carefully at each part.

Heading
7500 South State Street
Midvale, Utah 84047
May 12, 1980

Greeting
Dear Michelle,

Body
I just got your letter. When are you moving back to Midvale? Do you know your new address yet? I hope it's near me!

My brother and I are learning kite-making at the Y. When you come, I can teach you, too.

Write back soon. Tell me all about your move.

Closing Your friend,
Signature Danielle

The Parts of a Friendly Letter

Each part of a friendly letter has a specific purpose and should be written in a certain way. Follow these rules for writing each part correctly:

1. Heading. The heading tells where you are and when you are writing. It is written in the upper right-hand corner. The heading has three lines in the following order.

> house address and name of street
>
> city, state, and ZIP code
>
> month, day, and year

Follow these punctuation and capitalization rules for writing the heading:

1. Capitalize all proper names.
2. Place a comma between the city and the state.
3. Put the ZIP code after the state. No comma is needed to separate the state and the ZIP code.
4. Place a comma between the day and the year.
5. Avoid abbreviations.

2. Greeting. The greeting is the way you say "hello" to your friend. Here are examples of some common greetings:

Dear Ted,

    Hi Friend,

        Greetings, Kathryn,

Write the greeting on the line below the heading and begin at the left margin. Do not indent the greeting. Capitalize the first word and all proper nouns. Place a comma after the greeting.

2. Have students write a letter to a real or imaginary friend describing a circus, carnival, or state fair they have attended. Stress that the description should use vivid details that will give the friend the feeling of being there. Suggest, also, that the students illustrate the letter.

3. Body. The body of the letter is where you talk to your friend. Begin the body on the line below the greeting. Indent the first line. Always arrange your information in paragraphs. Use your best handwriting.

4. Closing. The closing is where you say "goodbye" to your friend. Capitalize only the first word. Place a comma at the end. Here are some suggestions for closings:

Love,   Your friend,   Sincerely,
Always,   Missing you,   Yours truly,

The closing lines up with the heading.

5. Signature. Your signature should be written clearly. If you don't know the person very well, include your first and last name. Write your signature below the closing.

Exercises   Writing Friendly Letters

A. Copy the following words and phrases. Capitalize and punctuate them as if they were in a letter.

1. 4802 page street
2. yankton, south dakota 57078
3. january 18, 1980
4. dear uncle dave,
5. your nephew,
6. mike larsen

B. Write a complete letter to a real or imaginary friend. If you wish, you may use some of the following situations:

1. A class field trip
2. What your pet has been up to
3. A sports event you attended
4. A new hobby you started
5. A movie you saw
6. A church picnic

Part 2 Writing Social Notes

Writing a social note is a polite way to thank someone for a gift, to invite someone to an event, or to accept an invitation.

Writing a Thank-You Note

Write a thank-you note as soon as possible. This is important. Your promptness will show your appreciation. There are three occasions on which you should write thank-you notes:

1. When you have received a gift
2. When someone has done you a special favor
3. When you have stayed overnight at someone's house

Here is an example of a thank-you note. Notice that only the date is needed in the heading.

February 24, 1980

Dear Mr. Owen,
 Thank you for letting me have that old tricycle. I plan to fix it up and paint it for my younger brother. He will really be surprised.
 You certainly are a good neighbor. I hope I can do a favor for you sometime.

Sincerely,
Doug Martin

Part 2

Objective

To differentiate between friendly letters and social notes in purpose and form, and to use each form where it is appropriate

Presenting the Lesson

1. Read the introductory sentence about social notes on page 335. This sentence should point out to students that each type of social note has a very specific purpose. Courtesy should be emphasized as the general purpose of all social notes.

A Thank-You Note

2. Read Writing a Thank-You Note and the sample on page 335. Point out that the heading is simpler than the heading in a friendly letter. Stress the need to use specific details in referring to a favor. On the board list the other two purposes for writing thank-you notes (gifts and visits), and make a list of the details that could be included. Here are some suggestions: type of gift; size and color of the gift; how the gift will be enjoyed or used; date of visit; events or activities enjoyed during visit.

3. Read and discuss Writing an Invitation on page 336. Students will probably be familiar with the commercial invitations sold in stores. Ask students to bring in examples of packaged invitations, and compare their contents with details listed on page 336. The packaged invitations may include *RSVP*. You may wish to write the actual French translation on the board: *Répondez, s'il vous plaît.* (Respond, if you please.) Explain that an RSVP is needed when the host or hostess needs to know exactly how many will attend.

4. Read the sample invitation on page 336. Point out that the heading includes a return address, and ask students why this information is needed. Have students locate in the sample the information that must be included in an invitation. Stress that a handwritten invitation is more personal and friendly than a packaged invitation.

5. Read and discuss Answering an Invitation and the samples on page 337. Emphasize the need for punctuality in responding. Students may prefer the simpler approach of telling the writer whether they are coming to the event. Help them to see that with a note, the person planning the event will have a record of who is coming, in order to make plans. In discussing the note of regret, point out that it is polite to give a reason for not attending.

6. Assign and discuss Exercises A and B on page 338. The situations for Exercise A may be real or imaginary. Both exercises should emphasize the details that should be included in each type of social note.

Optional Practice

Have the students write a class letter inviting a famous person to speak to the class.

Writing an Invitation

When you are inviting someone to a party or an event, include the following details:

1. What the activity is
2. Why the activity is being held
3. Where the activity will take place
4. When the activity will be held: day, date, and time
5. Any special instructions

The following example will help you. Notice that your address should be included in the heading so that the person can respond to your invitation.

An Invitation

108 Clayton Street
Denver, Colorado 80206
April 7, 1980

Dear Aunt Alice and Uncle Frank,

I would like to invite you both to our school play, "The Case for Two Detectives." I play the part of a rich old lady. The play will be performed on Friday, April 18, at 7 P.M. The address is Roosevelt School, 1864 Cherry Hill Road. I hope you can come.

Love,
Sandy

Answering an Invitation

When you receive an invitation, you should reply as soon as possible. You reply with either a note of acceptance or a note of regret.

A Note of Acceptance

> April 10, 1980
>
> Dear Sandy,
>   Your Uncle Frank and I would love to attend your play. We will be there early so we can get a good seat.
>   Good luck in your part!
>
>   Love,
>   Aunt Alice

A Note of Regret

> April 10, 1980
>
> Dear Sandy,
>   I wish your Uncle Frank and I could come to your play, but I have to take him to the airport that evening. When he gets back you can tell us all about the play.
>   I'm very sorry we can't attend.
>
>   Love,
>   Aunt Alice

Exercises   Writing Social Notes

A. Write a thank-you note for one of the following situations. Check your punctuation and use your best handwriting.

1. Thank a friend for a birthday gift.
2. Thank a friend of your parents for the information he or she gave you for a report.
3. Thank a relative for a Christmas gift.
4. Thank your neighbor for letting you spend the weekend.
5. Thank your uncle for the tickets to the baseball game (or for some other event).

B. Write an invitation for a party you would like to have. Exchange invitations with a classmate and reply to your classmate's invitation.

Part 3   Writing Business Letters

A business letter is very useful. You may use it to request information for a report. This kind of business letter is called a **letter of request.** Also, you may use a business letter to order materials from a magazine or coupon. This kind of business letter is called an **order letter.** The writing in a business letter should be clear and to the point. Use only the necessary details for your request or order.

The Parts of a Business Letter

A business letter has one part that a friendly letter doesn't have. This new part is called the **inside address.** Read the following information about each part of a business letter. Pay close attention to the details included in each part.

1. Heading. The heading of a business letter is the same as the heading for a friendly letter. Write your street address on the first line in the upper right-hand corner. Write your city, state, and ZIP code on the second line. Write the date on the third line. Remember to follow capitalization and punctuation rules.

2. Inside Address. The inside address tells the name and address of the person or company you are writing to. This is the same address you will use on the envelope. This address follows the same capitalization and punctuation rules as the heading. Write the inside address below the heading but at the left margin. See the sample letters on pages 341 and 342.

3. Greeting. The greeting of a business letter is more formal than in a friendly letter. If you are writing to a specific person, use *Dear* and then the person's name.

Dear Ms. Courtney:

Dear Mr. Dylan:

Many times you will be writing directly to a company. In this case you use a general greeting such as *Dear Sir or Madam*, or *Ladies and Gentlemen*. The greeting begins two lines below the inside address and ends with a colon (:).

4. Body. The body of a business letter is usually short. It should be polite and state very clearly the subject you are writing about. Follow these suggestions for writing a letter of request or an order letter:

Letter of Request

1. Tell *what* specific information you need.

2. Tell *why* you need that information.

3. Tell *when* you need the information.

attention to punctuation (especially the use of the colon), the inside address, and the formal greeting and closing.

Point out the difference in tone between the formal business letter and the conversational friendly letter. The business letter uses precise information whereas the friendly letter uses colorful details.

3. Have students read and compare the letter of request on page 341 and the order letter on page 342. Ask them to locate the information that should be included in each.

4. Emphasize that neatness and organization are necessary in a business letter if the writer expects to receive a response.

5. Assign and discuss Exercises A and B on page 343. After the letters are corrected, you may wish to have the students make a good copy in ink, not pencil, as if they were actually going to send the letters.

Extending the Lesson

Have students write to businesses in the community to request information on careers or a topic being studied in social studies, science, or other subject. Students should be given class time to share their replies.

Order Letter

1. Tell the name of the product and how many you want.
2. Tell where you saw the product advertised.
3. Tell the catalog number, size, and color.
4. Tell the price of the item, and list the fee for postage and handling separately.
5. Tell the total price of the order.
6. Tell what you are enclosing with the letter, such as a check or a coupon.

5. Closing. Write the closing on the first line below the body. Line it up with the heading. The most common closings for a business letter are these:

Sincerely,

Yours truly,

Very truly yours,

Respectfully yours,

Notice that you capitalize only the first word of the closing, and put a comma after the closing.

6. Signature. Print your name four spaces below the closing. Then write your signature in the space between. In this way the reader will have no trouble reading your name so that he or she can reply to you.

Louise Chin

Louise Chin

A Letter of Request

9204 Palm Drive
Tampa, Florida 33603
October 4, 1980

Science and Health Reports
Division of Research Resources
National Institutes of Health
Bethesda, Maryland 20014

Dear Sir or Madam:

    In our fifth-grade science class we have four white mice and two guinea pigs. I am writing a report about how these animals are used in research. Do you have any brochures or information on this topic? I would appreciate any information you have available.

    I need this information by November 1 for my report. Thank you for your help.

Respectfully,
Jacob Corley

An Order Letter

32 Caroline Avenue
Toledo, Ohio 43612
June 15, 1980

All-Breed, Dept. BH-8
400 1st Avenue
Minneapolis, Minnesota 55403

Dear Sir or Madam:

    I would like to order one of your T-shirts as seen in <u>Better Homes and Gardens</u>. Please send me the following order:

1 light blue T-shirt with a picture of a German shepherd	$6.95
postage and handling	.75
total	$7.70

I am enclosing a money order for $7.70 for my order.

Sincerely,
Janice Hess

Exercises Writing Business Letters

A. Write a letter of request for one of the following items. Use the proper business letter form and your best handwriting.

1. Request a free catalog of the many different telephones you can buy from The Telephone Booth, One Tandy Center, Dept. AP, Fort Worth, Texas 76102.

2. Request information about the George Rogers Clark Memorial for your family's summer vacation. Write to the following: George Rogers Clark National Historical Park, Vincennes, Indiana 47591.

3. Request a free subscription to *Boom in Bikeways* newsletter because you want to start a bike club. Write to Bicycle Manufacturers Association of America, 1101 15th Street N.W., Washington, D.C. 20005.

4. Request the brochure "Our Nation's Flags" for your report for social studies on the history of flags. Write to Dept. PR-B, State Mutual of America, 440 Lincoln Street, Worcester, Massachusetts 01605.

B. Write an order letter for one of the following products. Use the correct form and your best handwriting.

1. Order one copy of *Stained Glass Windows Coloring Book* for $1.50 plus 35 cents handling from Dover Publications, 180 Varick Street, New York, New York 10014.

2. Order *The Kid's Garden Book* at $3.95 from Nitty Gritty Productions, P.O. Box 457, Concord, California 94522.

3. Order two copies of the book *Further Adventures in Cardboard Carpentry* for $3.50 each from Workshop for Learning Things, 5 Bridge Street, Watertown, Massachusetts 02172.

4. Order one set of 500 self-stick address labels for $2.50 plus 24 cents postage from W. Yarborough, Dept. BH-558, 5768 Venice Blvd., Los Angeles, California 90019.

Part 4

Objective

To use the correct form for addressing envelopes

Presenting the Lesson

1. Read and discuss pages 344 and 345. Emphasize accuracy and neatness. Ask students for reasons for providing a return address.

2. Assign and discuss Exercises A and B on page 345. Again, stress accuracy and neatness.

Extending the Lesson

Obtain from the school secretary, or from your own mail, a variety of envelopes or mailing labels from sales brochures, catalogs, and other commercial mail. Have the students find on a map all the locations printed in the return addresses.

Part 4 Addressing Envelopes

Once you have written a friendly letter or a business letter, you want to make sure that it gets where it's supposed to go. This is why addressing envelopes correctly is so important. Use the following guides for preparing the envelope for mailing:

Guides for Addressing Envelopes

1. Make sure the envelope is the right size for the paper. You should not fold the paper more than three times.

2. Make sure the envelope is right-side up.

3. Write the address almost half-way down the envelope, and indented about one-fourth to one-third of the way from the left edge.

4. Put your own address, called the return address, in the upper left-hand corner.

5. Check the accuracy of street numbers and ZIP codes.

6. Write as neatly as possible.

Study the following example of an envelope.

```
Miss Nancy Shafer
92 Laurel Trail
Wheeling, Illinois 60090


                        Ms. Naomi Martinez
                        423 St. Catherine Avenue
                        Phoenix, Arizona 85040
```

Envelopes for social notes are often smaller in size. In this case, the return address may be put on the back of the envelope, as in the following example:

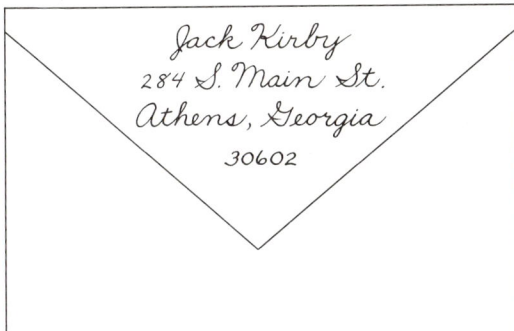

Exercises   Addressing Envelopes

A. Choose three companies or offices listed in Exercises A and B on page 343. Then draw three envelopes on your paper and address them correctly. Use your own home or school address as the return address.

B. Using your local telephone directory, look up the names and addresses of three of the following businesses. As in Exercise A, draw three envelopes on your paper and address them correctly. Use your own home or school address as the return address.

1. a sporting goods store
2. an arts and craft store
3. a bicycle repair shop
4. a record store
5. a pharmacy
6. a pet store
7. a music store
8. a dentist

Chapter 25

Capitalization

Part 1 Capitalizing Proper Nouns, Proper Adjectives, and *I*

A **common noun** is the name of a whole group of persons, places, and things.

    hero   country   planet

A **proper noun** is the name of one particular person, place, or thing.

    Hercules   Switzerland   Mars

> Begin every proper noun with a capital letter.

Chapter Objectives

1. To understand and apply the general rules for capitalizing proper nouns and adjectives, and the pronoun *I*

2. To understand and apply the specific rules for capitalizing names, initials, titles, and abbreviations

3. To understand and apply specific rules for capitalizing other proper nouns

4. To understand and apply the rules for capitalizing first words in sentences, direct quotations, poetry, outlines, and letters

5. To understand and apply the rules for capitalization in titles

Preparing the Students

Chapters 25, 26, and 27 constitute the *Silver Level* Handbook: The Mechanics of Writing. The material is arranged in an easy-to-consult form so that students can make frequent use of the chapters for reference. It is recommended that you introduce the three chapters in a brief overview at the beginning of the year. It is also suggested that you present and assign the material in these chapters periodically.

Additional Resources

Diagnostic Test—page 435 in this T.E. Recommended for use before teaching the chapter.

Mastery Test—pages 486–487 in this T.E. Recommended for use after teaching the chapter.

Additional Mastery Test—Recommended for use after any necessary reteaching. (In separate booklet, *Mastery Tests, Silver Level,* pages 49–60.)

Skills Practice Book—pages 128–133

Duplicating Masters—pages 128–133

Part 1

Objective

To understand and apply the general rules for capitalizing proper nouns and adjectives, and the pronoun *I*

Presenting the Lesson

1. Read and discuss pages 347 and 348. Point out how the sample common nouns are made more specific by the sample proper nouns (*planet, Mars*) and how those proper nouns are changed to proper adjectives (*Martian*). Ask students to give other examples of proper nouns and adjectives.

2. Assign and discuss Exercises A and B on pages 348 and 349.

3. Use Exercise A on page 359 as additional practice or review.

Optional Practice

Distribute copies of the list below or put the list on the board. Have students number their papers from one to twelve. Explain that they are to find on the list a common noun and a proper noun that match. They are to write the two nouns together on the same line (common noun first), and capitalize where needed.

Example: month—December

snickers, dog, city, kennedy, buick, asia, superdog, comic book character, holiday, philadelphia, president, car, continent, tuesday, road runner, explorer, balboa, state, spiderman, bird, candy, day, south dakota, thanksgiving

---

The words below are proper nouns. They are made up of two words. Both words are part of the name. Both begin with capital letters.

Independence Day	South America	February
Exton Mall	Lake Erie	Mary Shelley

A **proper adjective** is an adjective made from a proper noun.

Herculean strength (made from *Hercules*)   *Swiss* cheese (made from *Switzerland*)   *Martian* atmosphere (made from *Mars*)

> Begin every proper adjective with a capital letter.

Proper adjectives are usually used with common nouns. Do not capitalize the common noun.

Proper Adjective	**Common Noun**	**Adjective and Noun**
English	language	English language
Roman	numerals	Roman numerals
Canadian	mountains	Canadian mountains
Indian	corn	Indian corn

Most pronouns are treated like common nouns, and are not capitalized. The pronoun *I*, however, is capitalized.

> Always capitalize the word *I*.

Exercises   Using Capital Letters

A. Number your paper from 1 to 12. Copy each word in this list, changing small letters to capitals where necessary. After each word, write the group that the word belongs to: *common noun, proper noun,* or *proper adjective*.

1. boston **PN**   5. easter **PN**   9. coca-cola **PN**
2. city **CN**   6. woman **CN**   10. food **CN**
3. thursday **PN**   7. german **PA**   11. union school **PN**
4. pocahontas **PN**   8. doctor **CN**   12. louis pasteur **PN**

CN = Common Noun
PN = Proper Noun
PA = Proper Adjective

B. Number your paper from 1 to 10. Copy the sentences below, using capital letters where they are needed.

1. I live on forest hills road.
2. I have lived there since last december.
3. We moved in on the wednesday before christmas.
4. We used to live on a road near lake erie.
5. Before that, i lived in chicago.
6. Some of my new friends are margie, bobby, and bobby's sister, judy.
7. The school i go to is noble road elementary school.
8. My teacher is miss conlin.
9. In august i will be twelve years old.
10. On my birthday i am going to see the white house.

Part 2 Some Kinds of Proper Nouns

There are many kinds of proper nouns. The rules in this part, and Part 3, will help you recognize proper nouns so that you can capitalize them correctly.

Names and Initials

Capitalize the names of people and pets.

Carla   Michael   Snoopy

Begin every word in a person's name with a capital letter.

Maria Tallchief   James Earl Jones

Optional Practice

Have students copy the following list, changing small letters to capital letters where necessary.

1. all my aunts, including aunt georgina
2. queen elizabeth, the queen of england
3. the doctor at the clinic, dr t. j. calloway
4. franklin d. roosevelt, elected president four times
5. the superintendent of schools, ms bessie clark
6. smokey the bear, the forest rangers' friend
7. the speaker, professor paul jablonski
8. the head nurse, mrs. arlene grover

An **initial** stands for a name.

Capitalize an initial and follow it with a period.

C. G. Rossetti   O. J. Simpson
Mary B. Martin   Elwood P. Dowd

Capitalize words for family relations when they are used as names of specific people.

Father	Mother	Aunt Em
Dad	Mom	Uncle Henry
Pa	Ma	Grandma Smith

Titles and Their Abbreviations

You may have noticed that many people have special words before their names. Your dentist has the word *Doctor* before his name. So has your doctor. These special words are **titles**. Titles in names are capitalized.

Doctor Brown	Superintendent Ames	Judge Clark
Governor Smith	Reverend A. B. Hill	Senator Louis
Professor Jones	President Collins	Secretary Allen

There are also short forms for many titles. A shortened form of a word is an **abbreviation**. Abbreviations for titles are capitalized and followed by a period.

Doctor = Dr.   Mister = Mr.   Mistress = Mrs.

The title *Ms.* has no long form. It is always capitalized and marked with a period. The title *Miss* has no short form. Do not place a period after the word *Miss* in a title.

Capitalize titles and their abbreviations when you use them with names. Follow an abbreviation with a period.

Exercises   Using Capital Letters Correctly

A. Number your paper from 1 to 10. Copy the following sentences. Change small letters to capital letters wherever necessary.

1. We live next door to dr. l. e. brown.
2. My brother luis met superintendent julia f. jones.
3. My father knows judge mercedes blake and senator steven thomas.
4. The mayor presented an award to miss allen.
5. Last thursday senator phyllis r. grimes and professor a. e. ames visited our school.
6. The writer charles lutwidge dodgson used the pen name lewis carroll.
7. Perhaps i'll name my new puppies pepper and salt.
8. The best players on rhonda's team are rhonda and i.
9. Some famous indian leaders are chief joseph, sitting bull, and cochise.
10. At the state capitol, clara and her cousin b. j. met governor ridge.

B. Follow the directions for Exercise A.

1. A dog named benji adopted us.
2. Yes, aunt aretha and i met doctor cooley.
3. My neighbor, mrs. avellini, repairs cars.
4. Kathy moran's cousin produces a television show.
5. My favorites are princess leia and luke skywalker.
6. One champion golfer is judy rankin.
7. The bill was introduced by senator s. i. hayakawa.
8. "Stamp out forest fires," smokey tells us.
9. Yesterday, grandma and jeremy made fudge.
10. Timothy bottoms and joseph bottoms are brothers.

Part 3

Objective

To understand and apply specific rules for capitalizing other proper nouns

Presenting the Lesson

1. Read and discuss pages 352 and 353. Ask students for further examples. Point out that the two-letter state abbreviations are written without periods

2. Assign and discuss the Exercise on page 353.

3. Read and discuss page 353. Ask students for further examples.

4. It is suggested that you do Exercise A on page 354 with the class. Assign and discuss Exercises B and C.

5. Use Exercise C on page 360 as additional practice or review.

Optional Practice

Distribute copies of the paragraph below. Have students find the errors in capitalization, and write the words correctly.

Our Vacation

My family lives in missouri. Every summer we spend a week with my cousins in sioux falls, south dakota. We usually arrive on july 3, the day before independence day. Last year we visited mount rushmore, where the heads of four famous men have been carved out of the side of the mountain. The men are presidents george washington, thomas jefferson, abraham lincoln, and theodore roosevelt. I like the head of president lincoln the best. The carvings are so immense that they make me feel very small.

Part 3 More About Proper Nouns

Proper nouns are not limited to specific people. Here are some other types of proper nouns to watch for.

Months, Days and Holidays

Capitalize the names of months, days, and holidays.
Do not capitalize names of seasons, such as spring and summer.

> We observe Lincoln's Birthday on February 12.
> Next Friday is the first day of summer.

Particular Places and Things

Capitalize the names of particular places and things.
Capitalize cities, states, and countries.

> Did you live in Kansas City, Kansas, or Kansas City, Missouri?
> The United States shares borders with Mexico and Canada.

Capitalize both letters of the two-letter abbreviations for states, used especially in addresses.

> California = CA   Maine = ME   Wisconsin = WI

Capitalize streets, bridges, and buildings, such as schools.

> Chambers Elementary School is on Shaw Avenue.
> The Oakland Bay Bridge was being repainted.

Capitalize all geographic names. Also capitalize such words as *north, south, east,* and *west* when they refer to a section of the country. Do not capitalize them when they are used as directions.

Father Jacques Marquette began his explorations at Lake Michigan. His party traveled south along the Mississippi River toward the Gulf of Mexico.

Exercise   Using Capital Letters Correctly

Number your paper from 1 to 10. Copy these sentences. Change small letters to capital letters wherever necessary.

1. Cactus grows in the Southwest.
2. Vacation begins on Tuesday.
3. The Danube River flows into the Black Sea.
4. My friend Miya Osaka has relatives in Japan.
5. On May 5 Harper School will hold a carnival.
6. A time for picnics is Independence Day, July 4.
7. The Swedish ship passed through the Panama Canal.
8. The first Monday in September is Labor Day.
9. Last summer Dad and I crossed the Golden Gate Bridge.
10. The Aleutian Islands are southwest of Alaska.

Religions, Nationalities, and Languages

Capitalize the names of religions, nationalities, and languages.

Three of the major faiths are Christianity, Judaism, and the Muslim religion.

Many Mexicans speak both Spanish and English.

Clubs, Organizations, Businesses

Capitalize the names of clubs, organization, and business firms.

Mary Ann belongs to the Junior Photographers' Club.
The Campfire Girls took a tour of the Bell Telephone Company office.

Extending the Lesson

You may want to divide the students into small groups for this exercise. Distribute copies of the following lists of states and two-letter mailing abbreviations. Direct students to match each state with its abbreviation, and write the abbreviation next to the state, using proper capitalization. Then have the students look up the capital city of each state and write it after the state abbreviation.

States	Abbreviations
1. kentucky	a. ia
2. missouri	b. co
3. colorado	c. or
4. idaho	d. ky
5. delaware	e. mi
6. maine	f. mo
7. georgia	g. in
8. minnesota	h. ga
9. oregon	i. mn
10. arizona	j. vt
11. arkansas	k. tx
12. michigan	l. ar
13. indiana	m. id
14. iowa	n. wy
15. wyoming	o. de
16. utah	p. ut
17. florida	q. ri
18. vermont	r. az
19. rhode island	s. fl
20. texas	t. me

Exercises Using Capital Letters Correctly

A. Number your paper from 1 to 8. Copy the following sentences. Change small letters to capital letters wherever necessary.

1. The sierra club holds nature outings each summer.
2. Last december russian dancers performed here.
3. Jeb and i admired the israeli leader golda meir.
4. The national geographic society has a good magazine.
5. Yes, aunt nancy, schwinn makes racers.
6. One indian craft is bead design.
7. There is a ponderosa steakhouse on south grand avenue.
8. Many chinese people practice buddhism.

B. Follow the directions for Exercise A.

1. My sister jeannine has posters of african kings.
2. The polish scientist madame curie discovered radium.
3. In october, logan school started the snowflake club.
4. Candy stover has folk dolls from portugal and brazil.
5. The amateur bicycle league holds races on august 5.
6. The boston children's museum is open from october to june.
7. The white house is at 1600 pennsylvania avenue.
8. Last spring mom and i flew a delta jet to miami.

C. Copy the paragraph below, using capital letters where they are needed.

Our teacher, miss abbott, told us about woodrow wilson the other day. At princeton university, professor wilson taught politics. He later became president of princeton university. Then he was known as doctor wilson. In 1912 the people elected him to the presidency of the united states. After that he was called president wilson.

Part 4 First Words

Any word is capitalized if it appears in certain places in written work.

Sentences

Capital letters are important sentence signals. They tell when a new sentence begins.

Begin every sentence with a capital letter.

> My brother likes mushrooms on his pizza.
> Does February have twenty-nine days this year?
> Duck!

Direct Quotations

When you write the exact words somebody else said, you are **quoting** that person. The words are a **direct quotation.**

Capitalize the beginning of every direct quotation.

> "Today we can expect two inches of snow," said the forecaster.

Usually, when you are writing what a person said, you add some words before or after the direct quotation to tell who said it. If these explaining words come at the beginning of your sentence, use a capital letter there. Use another capital letter at the beginning of the direct quotation.

> "It's raining," my brother said.
>   (Direct quotation at beginning of sentence)
> My mother asked, "Is your cake still in the oven?"
>   (Direct quotation after explaining words)

Part 4

Objective

To understand and apply the rules for capitalizing first words in sentences, direct quotations, poetry, outlines, and letters

Presenting the Lesson

1. Read and discuss page 355. Give particular attention to the use of two capital letters in a sentence ending with a direct quotation.
2. Assign and discuss the Exercise on page 356. Stress the importance of copying the punctuation (commas, end marks, and quotation marks) exactly as shown in the text.
3. Read and discuss pages 356 and 357. Point out that most poems that rhyme also use capital letters to begin each line; poems that do not rhyme often do not use capital letters in this way. Make sure that students notice the last example under Letters. Stress that they capitalize only the first word in the closing of a letter.
4. Assign and discuss the Exercise on page 357.
5. Use Exercise D on pages 360 and 361 as additional practice or review.

Extending the Lesson

Have each student write a four- or six-line poem about a favorite cartoon or comic book character. Then the student should write a brief letter that could be sent with the poem to a friend. If you wish, have the students illustrate their letters and poems.

Optional Practice

Make copies of the dialogue below for the students. Have them rewrite it, changing small letters to capital letters where needed.

Telephone Conversation

joshua called his friend and said, "hi, daniel. this is josh. would you like to go to the museum tomorrow?"

daniel replied, "that sounds like fun. i'd really like to go. i've never been there before."

"good! i'll tell my mother. she said she'd take us. we'll come for you at nine o'clock," joshua said.

"that's great! i'll be waiting," said daniel.

Exercise   Using Capital Letters Correctly

Number your paper from 1 to 10. Copy the sentences below. Change small letters to capital letters where needed.

1. giant reptiles lived long ago. [G]
2. "a robot has no brain," mr. rodriquez said. [A, M, R]
3. maria asked, "may i use the microscope?" [M, M, I]
4. "would you like to take a bike trip?" roosevelt asked. [W, R]
5. wildflowers grow in the forest. [W]
6. i explained, "a spaceship has gone to mars." [I, A, M]
7. a kayak is similar to a canoe. [A]
8. mother reminded me, "your fish must be fed." [M, Y]
9. mona asked, "did you find any animal tracks?" [M, D]
10. the teacher said, "admiral byrd was the first to fly over the south pole." [T, A, B, S, P]

Poetry

Capitalize the first word in most lines of poetry.

> An emerald is as green as grass;
>   A ruby red as blood;
> A sapphire shines as blue as heaven;
>   A flint lies in the mud.
> A diamond is a brilliant stone,
>   To catch the world's desires;
> An opal holds a fiery spark;
>   But a flint holds fire.
>
> —CHRISTINA GEORGINA ROSSETTI, "Precious Stones"

Outlines

Capitalize the first word of each line of an outline.

The major ideas of an outline are marked with Roman numerals. Roman numerals are followed by capital letters.

Systems of Measurement
  I. The British system
     A. Inch, foot, yard, mile
     B. Ounce, pound, ton
     C. Cup, pint, quart, gallon
  II. The metric system
     A. Meter
     B. Gram
     C. Liter

Letters

Capitalize the greeting and the closing of a letter.

Dear Sir: Dear Lucy,
   Sincerely,   Your friend,

Exercise   Using Capital Letters Correctly

Copy the following poem and outline. Capitalize them correctly.

1. the steam digger
   is much bigger
   than the biggest beast i know.
   he snorts and roars
   like the dinosaurs
   that lived long years ago.
                —ROWENA BENNETT, "The Steam Shovel"

2. The Lewis and Clark Expedition
      I. why it was needed
         a. the Louisiana Purchase of 1803
         b. lack of good maps
      II. why Lewis and Clark were chosen
         a. achievements of Meriwether Lewis
         b. achievements of William Clark

Part 5

Objective

To understand and apply the rules for capitalization in titles

Presenting the Lesson

1. Read and discuss page 358. Explain that in printed material, such as the textbook, titles of books are usually set in italics rather than underlined. Have the students copy the three example titles, underlining the first one and using quotation marks around the second and third.

2. Assign and discuss the Exercise on page 358.

3. Use Exercise E on page 361 as additional practice or review.

Optional Exercise

Have students imagine that they are editors for a publishing company. Their job is to capitalize these titles as necessary.

101 dalmatians (movie)
wind in the willows (book)
superman (movie)
where the wild things are (book)
"rudolph is tired of the city" (poem)
"the plaint of the camel" (poem)
i sailed on the mayflower (book)
the ugly duckling (movie)
what dinosaur is it? (book)
the red balloon (movie)

Extending the Lesson

Have each student make up a title to an imaginary book he or she would like to write. Then the student is to write a short book review telling what the story is about and listing a few good things about the book that would encourage others to read it. You may want to have students make illustrated book jackets (with their reviews inside) for display.

Part 5 Capitalizing Titles

Capitalize the first word, the last word, and any other important words in a title.

Do not capitalize a little word such as *the, in, for, from, by, a,* or *an,* unless it comes first or last.

From the Mixed-Up Files of Mrs. Basil E. Frankweiler (book)

"The Legend of Sleepy Hollow" (story)

"Casey at the Bat" (poem)

Titles are also enclosed in quotation marks or underlined. Rules for using these marks are given on page 379. In general, use quotation marks around the titles of short works, such as stories, poems, television programs, newspaper articles, and reports. Underline the titles of longer works, such as books, movies, and magazines. In printed books, these titles are in italics instead of being underlined.

Exercise   Using Capital Letters Correctly

Copy the following titles. Capitalize them correctly.

1. *little house in the big woods* (book)
2. "east of the sun and west of the moon" (story)
3. *alice's adventures in wonderland* (book)
4. *and now miguel* (book)
5. "the pied piper of hamelin" (poem)
6. *a christmas carol* (book and movie)
7. "the top ten on television" (newspaper article)
8. *newsweek* (magazine)
9. "the horses of the sea" (poem)
10. *fantasia* (movie)

Additional Exercises

Capitalization

A. Capitalizing Proper Nouns, Proper Adjectives, and *I*
(Use after page 348.)

Number your paper from 1 to 12. Copy each word below, changing small letters to capitals where necessary. After each word, write the group that the word belongs to: *common noun, proper noun,* or *proper adjective.*

CN = Common Noun
PN = Proper Noun
PA = Proper Adjective

1. flower — CN
2. british (B) — PA
3. actress — CN
4. cicely tyson (C, T) — PN
5. mark twain (M, T) — PN
6. july (J) — PN
7. whale — CN
8. wrestler — CN
9. georgia (G) — PN
10. balloon — CN
11. disneyland (D) — PN
12. park — CN

B. Capitalizing Names, Initials, and Titles
(Use after page 350.)

Number your paper from 1 to 10. Copy the following sentences. Change small letters to capital letters wherever necessary.

1. My sister toni (T) rode a horse named diamond (D).
2. For breakfast i (I) ordered french (F) toast.
3. Will mom (M) or dad (D) take us to the movie?
4. My teacher, ms. (M) burnett (B), knows magic tricks.
5. Did aunt (A) marianne (M) give you a donny (D) osmond (O) album?
6. From 1837 to 1901, queen (Q) victoria (V) ruled.
7. Janie tyler (T) joined the track team.
8. The first american (A) poet was ann (A) bradstreet (B).
9. One expert on flying saucers is professor (P) j. (J) hynek (H).
10. Amelia earhart (E) was a well known american (A) flyer.

C. Capitalizing Other Proper Nouns (Use after page 353.)

Number your paper from 1 to 10. Copy the following sentences. Change small letters to capital letters wherever necessary.

1. Celebrate arbor day in april by planting a tree.
2. Ms. amy conti teaches ballet on wednesdays.
3. We will stay at the palace hotel on may 9.
4. Many TV shows are made in los angeles, california.
5. The george washington bridge spans the hudson river.
6. Yes, i have pen pals in germany and austria.
7. Snow fell west of the rocky mountains.
8. The first basketball game was played at springfield college.
9. On april 6, 1909, admiral r. e. peary reached the north pole.
10. The oldest city in the south is st. augustine, florida.

D. Capitalizing First Words (Use after page 357.)

Copy the following poem, outline, and letter. Capitalize them correctly.

1. it's such a shock, i almost screech,
   when i find a worm inside my peach!
   but then, what really makes me blue,
   is to find a worm who's bit in two!

   —WILLIAM COLE

2. The Lion
   I. location
      a. africa
      b. southwest asia
      c. western india

II. appearance
   a. short yellow or brown hair
   b. up to ten feet long
   c. weighs up to 500 pounds

III. eating habits
   a. hunts large and small animals
   b. eats dead animals

3.   april 19, 1980

dear officer bolden,

   thank you for talking to the children in room 148 about careers in police work. everything you said was interesting. the best part was when you answered my question. i asked, "what was the most exciting thing that ever happened to you?"
   i think i'd like to be a police officer someday, too.

                                             your friend,
                                             lillian mays

E. Capitalizing Titles (Use after page 358.)

Copy the following titles. Capitalize them correctly.

1. *escape from witch mountain* (movie)
2. *abe lincoln grows up* (book)
3. *roll of thunder, hear my cry* (book)
4. "the steadfast tin soldier" (story)
5. "bank robbery suspect held" (newspaper article)
6. *island of the blue dolphins* (book)
7. "i saw a man down in the well" (poem)
8. "the singing bone" (story)
9. *encyclopedia brown takes the case* (book)
10. *the adventures of robin hood* (book and movie)

Chapter 26

Punctuation

Chapter Objectives

1. To use the period correctly after sentences, initials, and abbreviations, and in outlines
2. To use the question mark correctly after sentences
3. To use the exclamation mark correctly after sentences
4. To use the comma correctly in dates, addresses, sentences, and letters
5. To use the apostrophe correctly to form possessives and contractions
6. To use the hyphen correctly to divide words at the end of a line
7. To use quotations marks correctly in direct quotations and titles
8. To use underlining correctly in titles

Preparing the Students

It is suggested that you present the material in this chapter periodically rather than as a single unit. If you overview the chapter at the beginning of the year, you can have students use this chapter as a reference independently.

Additional Resources

Diagnostic Test—page 436 in this T.E. Recommended for use before teaching the chapter.

Mastery Test—pages 488–490 in this T.E. Recommended for use after teaching the chapter.

Additional Mastery Test—Recommended for use after any necessary reteaching. (In separate booklet, *Mastery Tests, Silver Level*, pages 51–53.)

Skills Practice Book—pages 134–143

Duplicating Masters—pages 134–143

Part 1 Using the Period

The period (.) is used in several different positions for different purposes. Part 1 discusses four of those positions.

The Period at the End of Sentences

A period is used at the end of a declarative sentence and at the end of an imperative sentence. The period is a signal that the sentence has ended. When you are reading aloud, the period tells you to drop your voice.

(Declarative)   Navaho Indians built homes called hogans.

(Imperative)   Describe a tepee.

Use a period at the end of a declarative sentence and after most imperative sentences.

Part 1

Objective

To use the period correctly after sentences, initials, and abbreviations, and in outlines

Presenting the Lesson

1. Read and discuss pages 363 to 366. Review the definition and use of the declarative sentence and the imperative sentence. Explain that the period is used at the end of any imperative sentence that does not show strong emotion. Ask students to give examples for each rule concerning use of the period.

2. On page 365, point out the list of metric abbreviations that do not use periods. Mention that other frequently-used abbreviations that do not use periods are the two-letter abbreviations for states used in addresses, such as *ME*.

3. Assign and discuss the Exercise on page 366.

4. Use Exercise A on page 381 for additional practice or review.

Optional Practice

1. Have students copy the names and addresses of the people listed below inserting periods where needed.

  Example: Supt. M. R. Richardson
  10 Apple Tree Ln.
  Chattanooga, Tenn.

1. Rev Caleb R Zimmerman
   129 Cottonwood Rd
   Los Angeles, Calif
2. Mr John H Kingston
   209 E 9th St
   New York, N Y
3. Mrs. H L Crawford
   2312 S E Washington Blvd
   Louisville, Ken

The Period After an Initial

An **initial** is the first letter of a name, followed by a period. It is used to stand for that name. The letter is always capitalized.

  Nancy L. Kassebaum   John F. Kennedy

Use a period after an initial in a name.

The Period After an Abbreviation

A short form for a word is an **abbreviation.**
An abbreviation is usually followed by a period.
Here are abbreviations of the days of the week. Can you tell the word that each abbreviation stands for?

  Sun. Mon. Tues. Wed. Thurs. Fri. Sat.

Some abbreviations stand for more than one word and have more than one period.

  District of Columbia   D.C.
  New York   N.Y.
  before noon (ante meridiem)   A.M.
  after noon (post meridiem)   P.M.

Below is a list of common abbreviations with the words that they stand for.

Titles		**Geographic Terms**	
Reverend	Rev.	Road	Rd.
Mister	Mr.	Avenue	Ave.
Mistress	Mrs.	Street	St.
(no long form)	Ms.	Boulevard	Blvd.
Doctor	Dr.	Florida	Fla.

English Measure

ounce(s)	oz.	inch(es)	in.
pound(s)	lb.	foot (or feet)	ft.
minute(s)	min.	yard(s)	yd.
dozen	doz.	mile(s)	mi.

Other Terms

Company	Co.	continued	cont.
Post Office	P. O.	anonymous	anon.
Junior	Jr.	noun	n.
Senior	Sr.	pronoun	pron.
Before Christ	B. C.	verb	v.
Anno Domini	A. D.	adjective	adj.
(Year of Our Lord)		adverb	adv.

Not all abbreviations use periods. Here are some examples of this second type:

Metric Measure

meter	m	gram	g
centimeter	cm	milligram	mg
decimeter	dm	liter	l
kilometer	km	milliliter	ml

Most abbreviations are used only in lists, addresses, arithmetic problems, or other special forms of writing. They would not be used in regular sentences. For example, on an application for a library card, or on an envelope, you may write your address in this way:

2176 So. Taylor Rd.

In a sentence, you should write this:

I live at 2176 South Taylor Road.

As a rule, the only abbreviations you should use in sentences are titles with names, *A.M.* and *P.M.*, and *B.C.* and *A.D.*

4. Ms Janet S Reed
   1633 N Ashland Ave
   Chicago, Ill
5. Prof Irma G Hanson
   63 Circle Dr
   Kalamazoo, Mich
6. Dr Joseph E Scanlon
   14320 S Dixie Hwy
   Miami, Fla

2. Have students abbreviate the days and months in the following phrases. Remind them to check the dictionary if they are unsure of the abbreviations.

1. Tuesday, February 10
2. Wednesday, July 29
3. Monday, January 2
4. Saturday, August 17
5. Thursday, September 8
6. Friday, April 30
7. Sunday, October 12
8. Tuesday, March 8
9. Friday, November 5
10. Wednesday, December 28

The Period After Each Number or Letter in an Outline

Use a period after each number or letter that shows a division of an outline.

How the Months Got Their Names

I. Months named for real people
   A. July
   B. August
II. Months named for gods
   A. January
   B. March
   C. May
   D. June
III. Other months

Exercise Using Periods Correctly

Copy these sentences. Use periods correctly.

1. The Rev. Jesse Jackson spoke at our school.
2. Make yourself comfortable.
3. Ms. Sue Schneider refereed the game.
4. J. Fred Muggs is a chimpanzee.
5. Ask Dr. Dale Casey for an appointment.
6. Be sure to bring warm mittens.
7. Capt. Pierce talked to Col. Sherman Potter.
8. Capt. James Cook sailed across the ocean.
9. Send your questions to Mr. Thomas N. Sane.
10. Author P. L. Travers wrote about Mary Poppins.
11. The Capitol is in Washington, DC.
12. Our troop leader is Mrs. Jean Carmody.
13. Sammy Davis, Jr., recorded that song.
14. Please call back tomorrow.

Part 2 Using the Question Mark

A **question mark** (?) is used at the end of every interrogative sentence. It is a signal that a question has been asked. When you are reading aloud, the question mark tells you to raise the pitch of your voice.

Are you ready to go?   What did you say?

Use a question mark at the end of every interrogative sentence.

Exercises   Using Question Marks Correctly

A. Copy these sentences. Use either a period or a question mark at the end of each sentence.

1. I built a sandcastle.
2. Does Jason collect stamps?
3. Fill out this application form.
4. What is batik?
5. Can you grow a plant from orange seeds?
6. How does this camera work?
7. Mom made the costumes.
8. Tell me a riddle.
9. Have you made granola?
10. Recycle glass bottles.

B. Follow the directions for Exercise A.

1. Shari Lewis is a puppeteer.
2. Are you babysitting?
3. Measure in metrics.
4. I make paper airplanes.
5. Can you tie a half-hitch?
6. Come and join our game.

Part 2

Objective

To use the question mark correctly after sentences

Presenting the Lesson

1. Read and discuss page 367. Review the definition and use of the interrogative sentence.
2. Assign and discuss Exercises A and B on page 367.
3. Use Exercise B on page 381 for additional practice or review.

Optional Practice

Have students write two questions beginning with each of the following interrogative words: *who, what, where, when, why,* and *how.*

Extending the Lesson

Give students a short list of people, places, events, and things from their other studies (science, social studies), or have them make their own list from what they are studying. Ask them to write a question beginning with *who, what, where,* or *when* for each item on the list, and to write an answer for the question. You might want to use the questions for a review in that subject, or for a contest.

Examples: a. larynx
  What is your larynx?
  The larynx is your voice box.
  b. July 4, 1776
  When was the Declaration of Independence adopted?
  The Declaration of Independence was adopted on July 4, 1776.

Part 3

Objective

To use the exclamation point correctly after sentences

Presenting the Lesson

1. Read and discuss page 368. Review the definition and use of the exclamatory sentence. Point out that an imperative sentence or a declarative sentence showing strong emotion is punctuated like an exclamatory sentence.

Exclamatory: How hot it is today!
Declarative: This is great ice cream!
Imperative: Stop that dog!

2. Assign and discuss the Exercise on page 368.

3. Use Exercise C on pages 381 and 382 for additional practice or review.

Optional Practice

Have students find in other books five examples of sentences ending in an exclamation point. Have them copy the sentences and briefly explain why the exclamation point was used for each one.

Extending the Lesson

Have students read the sentences in the Exercises on pages 367 and 368 with proper intonation. Direct them to be conscious of the way their voices rise and/or drop depending on the type of sentence.

Part 3 Using the Exclamation Point

An **exclamation point** (!) is used at the end of every exclamatory sentence and after words or phrases that show strong feeling.

It tells the reader that the sentence or words should be read with strong feeling. The exclamation point signals surprise, joy, fear, excitement, or shock.

Don't open that door!   Help!   Fire!
That's exactly the bicycle I wanted!   Good grief!

Use an exclamation point at the end of an exclamatory sentence or word.

Exercise Using Exclamation Points Correctly

Copy these sentences. Use either a period, question mark, or exclamation point at the end of each sentence.

1. Do you have a sweet tooth?
2. Hooray! We won!
3. Oh, no! The bus has gone!
4. Get help fast!
5. Where is your prize?
6. We went to the spook house.
7. Let's sing some songs.
8. May I use the shovel?
9. Start with a simple project.
10. Halt!
11. Kurt opened an account at the bank.
12. How is a butterfly different from a moth?
13. Run for cover!
14. What is a spelunker?
15. What a strong current this river has!

Part 4 Using the Comma

The **comma** (,) generally signals a pause in a sentence, or a separation between related ideas. When you are reading aloud, the comma tells you to pause briefly.

There are eight uses of the comma that you should know.

Use a comma to separate the day of the month from the year.

Thomas Jefferson died on July 4, 1826.

If the date appears in the middle of the sentence, place a comma after the year, also.

Peace came on November 11, 1918, to the nations of Europe.

Use a comma to separate the name of a city from the state or country in which it is located.

Toronto, Canada   Detroit, Michigan

If the name appears in the middle of a sentence, place a comma after the state or country.

We lived in Cherry Valley, Ohio, for several years.

Use a comma to set off the name of a person spoken to.

Will you close the door, Juan?
Miss Bristol, may I leave early today?
I think, Nancy, that I'll be late today.

Use a comma after words such as *yes, no,* and *well.*

No, planets are not stars.
Yes, an accident might happen.
Well, everyone else is going.

2. Have students copy the following phrases from the board or a worksheet, inserting commas when necessary.

Dates:
January 1 1979
October 25 1792
June 3 1903
April 10 1686
February 29 1970

Cities and Countries:
Acapulco Mexico
Buenos Aires Argentina
Geneva Switzerland
Dublin Ireland
Tokyo Japan

Series:
planets stars and moons
eye ear nose and throat
movies books television programs and articles
sugar honey jam and jelly
soccer football baseball and hockey

Use a comma to set apart words or names in a series.

Two words or names are not a series. There are always three or more in a series.

We had watermelon and cake for dessert. (No series)
We had cake, ice cream, and melon for dessert. (Series)

Use a comma before or after a direct quotation.

The crowd shouted, "Run to third base!"
"I like swimming best," Ted replied.

Use a comma after the greeting of a friendly letter and the closing of any letter.

Dear Joseph,   Yours truly,

Use a comma at the end of the first complete thought in a sentence with two thoughts.

Casey struck out, and the game was over.
The cookies burned, but we ate them anyway.

Exercises Using Commas Correctly

A. Copy the following sentences. Put in commas where they are needed.

1. Dad, where did you find my gloves?
2. Julie, answer this riddle.
3. The Declaration of Independence was signed July 4, 1776.
4. Amelia Earhart was born in Atchison, Kansas.
5. Yes, you may have another piece of cake.
6. A Kentucky Derby winner must be stouthearted, fast, and strong.
7. Do you always stop, look, and listen at crossings?
8. "You'll feel better after a rest," the nurse said.
9. The birdcage fell, and my parakeet screeched.
10. Courtney said, "Pick a card."

B. Follow the directions for Exercise A.

1. Well, I'd rather have soup.
2. Stacey said, "Try this trick."
3. The Astrodome is in Houston, Texas.
4. This lake is cool, deep, and clear.
5. The guide arrived, and the tour began.
6. Debbie, did you see the seahorse?
7. "I'll be outside," Larry said.
8. The baby cried, and Mom picked her up.
9. The fielder caught, dropped, and recovered the ball.
10. Sputnik was launched on October 4, 1957.

Part 5 Using the Apostrophe

The **apostrophe** (') is used for two different purposes. When you are reading aloud, it has no effect on how you say the word in which it appears.

The Apostrophe To Show Possession

A **possessive** is a word that shows that someone or something possesses something else.

To form the possessive of a singular noun, add an apostrophe and an s.

The tent that belongs to James is James's tent.

To form the possessive of a plural noun that does not end in s, add an apostrophe and an s.

The hats that belong to men are men's hats.

To form the possessive of a plural noun that ends in s, add only an apostrophe.

The costumes of actresses are the actresses' costumes.

apostrophes where necessary. In a second column they are to list all the words or phrases that contain contractions, adding the necessary apostrophes.

1. havent gone
2. gardeners hoe
3. my brothers car
4. shed probably go
5. wouldnt budge
6. after youve eaten
7. the babys formula
8. the race drivers helmets
9. since were students
10. the tennis players tournament

2. Put the sentences below on a worksheet, with a short blank before each sentence and a longer blank after it. If the apostrophe is used in a contraction, the student should write **C** in the first blank, and the two words that the contraction stands for in the second blank. If the apostrophe is used for possession, students should write **P** in the first blank, and the noun modified by the possessive word in the second blank.

Examples:
C a. We haven't tried skiing yet. have not
P b. The singer's voice was off key. voice

1. I'd like to fly a biplane.
2. I think we'll be late.
3. The jockey's horse was nervous.
4. It's not easy to water ski.
5. My friend's new roller skates were expensive.
6. My neighbors said they're going to the pool.
7. The team's victory put them in first place.
8. There were no eggs in the eagle's nest.

Exercises Using Apostrophes To Show Possession

A. Make these words show possession. Write the possessive form.

1. Sarah's
2. skaters'
3. people's
4. riders'
5. boss's
6. lady's
7. workers'
8. builders'
9. gardener's
10. chief's
11. ranchers'
12. hostess's

B. Copy the groups of words below. Make the underlined word in each group show possession.

1. the kittens' mother
2. the catcher's mitt
3. bus drivers' uniforms
4. Ann's cousin
5. the children's library
6. your grandparents' house
7. the captain's orders
8. the woman's office
9. Geraldo's uncle
10. the canary's cage

The Apostrophe in Contractions

Do you often use the word *don't*? You use it as a short way of saying *do not*. The apostrophe shows that a letter has been left out.

A word made up of two words combined into one by leaving out a letter or letters is called a **contraction**. Here are some contractions used frequently:

isn't	is not	it's	it is
doesn't	does not	I'll	I will
don't	do not	I'm	I am
can't	cannot	they're	they are
won't	will not	we're	we are
haven't	have not	you've	you have
wouldn't	would not	she'd	she would

Use an apostrophe in a contraction to show where a letter or letters have been omitted.

Wherever you use an apostrophe in cursive writing, in possessives or in contractions, do not connect the letters before and after the apostrophe. The apostrophe should separate the two letters.

I'm   it's   student's

Exercises Using Apostrophes To Show Contractions

A. Below is a list of words we often say as contractions. Write each pair of words, and opposite it write the contraction. Use the apostrophe where the letters have been left out.

1. have not haven't
2. does not doesn't
3. it is it's
4. was not wasn't
5. would not wouldn't
6. were not weren't
7. I am I'm
8. did not didn't
9. are not aren't
10. had not hadn't
11. you are you're
12. she would she'd

B. Copy the sentences below. Put in apostrophes where they are needed to show possession or to identify contractions.

1. Isn't that racket yours?
2. Who's building the fire?
3. I can't play backgammon.
4. Doesn't your town have a children's museum?
5. You'll enjoy Barry's records.
6. Vic's room is full of pets.
7. It's a picture of a lion's den.
8. The kittens are Mandy's and hers.
9. They're in Mr. Baxter's guitar class.
10. The box won't stand on its end.

C. Write sentences using each of the contractions you made for Exercise A. Answers will vary.

Part 6

Objective

To use the hyphen correctly to divide words at the end of a line

Presenting the Lesson

1. Read and discuss page 374. Stress the importance of referring to the dictionary for help in deciding where to divide a word.

2. It is suggested that Exercise A on page 374 be done as a class activity. Assign and discuss Exercise B on page 375.

Optional Practice

1. Using a spelling or vocabulary list, ask students to identify the words that can be divided. Then have them copy those words, dividing them according to the rules given in Part 6. Remind students to use the dictionary for any difficult word.

2. Follow the directions above, using the following list.

1. calendar
2. hyphen
3. punctuation
4. secret
5. manufacture
6. apartment
7. lottery
8. television
9. write
10. restaurant
11. ninth
12. equal
13. today
14. smile
15. divide
16. tacos

Part 6 Using the Hyphen

Often when you are writing you run out of space at the end of a line and cannot fit in all of the next word. When this happens, you write part of the word, followed by a **hyphen** (-), on that line. You write the rest of the word at the beginning of the next line.

Use a hyphen after the first part of a word divided into two parts at the end of a line.

Only words of two or more syllables can be divided at the end of a line. Never divide words of one syllable, such as *pound* or *might*. If you are in doubt about dividing a word, look it up in a dictionary.

A single letter must not be left at the end of a line. For example, this division would be wrong: *a-part*. A single letter must not appear at the beginning of a line either. It would be wrong to divide *dictionary* like this: *dictionar-y*.

Exercises Using the Hyphen

A. Decide whether you can divide each of these words into two parts, each part having more than one letter. Check the word in a dictionary to be sure. If you can, divide the word as you would at the end of a line. Add the necessary hyphen. If the word cannot be divided, just copy it.

Example: arithmetic

    arith- or arithme-
    metic   tic

1. bury
2. adventure
3. sail
4. music
5. owl
6. copy
7. groceries
8. marbles
9. live
10. honest
11. together
12. hungry

B. Follow the directions for Exercise A.

1. banner
2. collection
3. strange
4. pony
5. equal
6. history
7. sketch
8. amazing
9. body
10. measure
11. neighborhood
12. crafts

Part 7 Using Quotation Marks

When you write exactly what someone says, you are **quoting** that person. If you write the person's exact words, you write a **direct quotation. Quotation marks** (" ") are the sign that someone is being quoted exactly.

Use quotation marks before and after the words of every direct quotation.

Read this sentence carefully:

Molly called, "The game starts in ten minutes."

Notice these things about the sentence above:

1. There is a comma (,) before the quotation.
2. Only the speaker's exact words are placed inside the quotation marks.
3. The quotation begins with a capital letter.
4. The punctuation at the end of the sentence is placed *inside* the quotation marks.

Study each of these sentences. See how each one follows the four rules.

Kenneth yelled, "There is a fire in the kitchen!"
Della asked, "Did anybody find a red glove?"
The director insisted, "Speak slowly and clearly."

Part 7

Objective

To use quotation marks correctly in direct quotations and titles

Presenting the Lesson

1. Read and discuss pages 375 and 376.

2. It is suggested that you do Exercise A on page 376 with the class. Assign and discuss Exercises B and C on pages 376 and 377. Please note that, as in Part 4 Exercises, there is not always adequate space in the Teacher's Answer Key to show the correct order of punctuation marks. If a comma or end mark should be placed after a word and before quotation marks, but there is no room for it, that comma or end mark has been placed *under* the word.

3. Read and discuss pages 377 and 378. Stress that quotation marks enclose only what is actually spoken. Make it clear that if the actual quotation is one sentence, it should be treated as one sentence even if it is interrupted by phrases such as *he answers, she said,* or *he replied.* It is not correct to capitalize the word after the interrupting phrase. If there are two sentences, they should be treated as two standard sentences, both beginning with capital letters and ending with proper punctuation.

4. It is suggested that Exercise A on page 378 be done as a class activity. Assign and discuss Exercise B.

5. Read and discuss page 379. Remind students of the need for capitalization in titles, also.

6. Assign and discuss the Exercise on page 379. Stress that students are to copy the capital letters exactly as given.

7. Use Exercise F on page 383 for additional practice or review.

Optional Practice

You may want to put this exercise on a worksheet. Leave enough space between each set of sentences so that students have room to rewrite one of the sentences. Explain that one of the two sentences in each pair is correct, but the other needs quotation marks and may also need capitalization. Students should write **C** after the correct sentence in each pair. In the space beneath each pair, students should rewrite correctly the sentence containing errors.

Example: a. Roger wanted to know where Eric was.   **C**
b. Where is Eric? Roger asked.
"Where is Eric?" Roger asked.

1. a. He asked me if I wanted to go.
   b. He asked, do you want to go?
2. a. The baby cried, Waaa! Waaa!
   b. The baby cried when he was hungry.
3. a. I can fix the computer, the robot said.
   b. It was the robot that fixed the computer.
4. a. The librarian asked if I liked to read biographies.
   b. The librarian asked, do you like to read biographies?
5. a. One of the questions on the test was about the planet Saturn.
   b. Do you know which planet has rings around it? the teacher asked.

A Quotation at the Beginning of a Sentence

Sometimes the quotation is placed at the beginning of a sentence.

"This plant needs water," Mr. Crockett said.

Notice that the comma ending the quotation is placed inside the quotation marks. Notice that the punctuation ending each of the following quotations is also placed inside the quotation marks. Notice, too, that there is punctuation at the end of the sentence, as well.

"There is a fire in the kitchen!" yelled Kenneth.
"Did anybody find a red glove?" Della asked.
"Speak slowly and clearly," the director insisted.

Exercises   Punctuating Quotations Correctly

A. Copy these sentences. Add all the punctuation marks that are needed.

1. "Make up your mind," Dennis urged.
2. "I finished the puzzle," he announced.
3. JoAnn asked, "Is that a robin?"
4. The zookeeper warned, "Don't disturb the panda."
5. "Where is the North Star?" she asked.
6. "What causes a storm?" Lauren asked.
7. "Mom raises bees," said Jeff.
8. "A chameleon changes color," Terri noted.
9. Dad asked, "Where are your gloves?"
10. Mr. Owens said, "Sing that verse again."

B. Follow the directions for Exercise A.

1. "What happened to my room?" Caroline asked.
2. The doctor called, "I need a bandage!"
3. "Put your feet in the stirrups," she said.
4. "Here's the entrance!" Kyle yelled.

5. Charlene asked, "What's your favorite color?"
6. "The monarch is a butterfly," Alonzo explained.
7. Steve shouted, "My kite string broke!"
8. Emily said, "I have a Venus flytrap."
9. I asked, "Have you read the comic strips?"
10. "Where is the Snoopy book?" Alison asked.

C. Each of these five sentences has one mistake in it. Write the sentences correctly.

1. "Mary said, "I will be home soon."
2. "Do you deliver the newspaper?" Ms. Conklin asked?
3. Jeff yelled, "look out for the car!"
4. Lawuana said, "You may use my skateboard".
5. "My watch broke," Spencer" complained.

Divided Quotations

Sometimes a quotation is divided. Words that tell who is talking, like *she said* or *she asked*, sometimes come in the middle of the sentence.

"After three hamburgers," Vic admitted, "dessert will be too much."

Divided quotations follow the capitalization and punctuation guidelines presented already. In addition, these rules apply:

1. Two sets of quotation marks are used.
2. The words that tell who is talking are followed by a comma or a period. Use a comma if the second part of the quotation does not begin a new sentence. Use a period if the second part of the quotation is a new sentence.

"Did you know," Katherine asked, "that mammoths once lived here?"

---

6. a. My mother yelled to my little sister, stay out of the street!
   b. My mother yelled at my little sister to stay out of the street.
7. a. The conductor on the train said, tickets, please.
   b. The conductor on the train asked us for our tickets.
8. a. The announcer said that the center fielder fumbled the ball.
   b. The announcer said, the center fielder fumbled the ball.
9. a. The imaginary lion won't scare us.
   b. I'll try not to scare you, roared the imaginary lion.
10. a. The ski instructor told us to bend our knees.
    b. Bend your knees, directed the ski instructor.

Extending the Lesson

Your more advanced students may enjoy this activity.

Have students write an imaginary interview with one of the characters listed below (or another favorite character). They should write six questions and answers using phrases such as *I said, I asked*, or *he replied*, each time someone talks. Ask students to write each question and answer in a separate paragraph.

Snoopy   Lois Lane
Lucy   Kermit the Frog
Spiderman   Miss Piggy

"Turn off the TV," Larry suggested. "Nothing good comes on now."

3. The second part of the quotation begins with a capital if it is the start of a new sentence, as in the second example above. Otherwise, the second part begins with a small letter.

Exercises **Punctuating Divided Quotations Correctly**

A. Copy these sentences. Add punctuation and capital letters where they are needed.

1. "Some people," Josh noted, "don't laugh much."
2. "I'm tired," Suzanne said. "Let's rest."
3. "Will you write to me," Jeff asked, "after you move?"
4. "During the summer," Amy said, "we make ice cream."
5. "What's cooking?" I asked. "It smells good."
6. "We're late," Mom said. "The show has started."
7. "When does camp start?" Sonia asked. "I'm ready."
8. "I have a layout," Bill said, "for a model railroad."
9. "I made sculptures," Tom said, "out of soap."
10. "We've looked at stars," Linn said. "We used a telescope."

B. Follow the directions for Exercise A.

1. "My favorite ballplayer," Kelly said, "is Pete Rose."
2. "Drop the anchor," Tandra called. "We'll fish here."
3. "The space shuttle *Enterprise*," Marilyn reported, "can be used many times."
4. "Chants and drumbeats," the teacher noted, "were early music."
5. "Thread the needle," Dad said. "Then make a knot."
6. "Eric made a film," I explained, "with clay figures."
7. "Try this sauce," my sister said. "It's very good."
8. "Throw the boomerang," Judith said. "It will return."
9. "What's a tangram?" Jorge asked. "Is it a puzzle?"
10. "What do fossils tell us," Elena asked, "about history?"

Titles

Quotation marks are used to mark titles as well as direct quotations.

Put quotation marks around the titles of stories, poems, television programs, reports, articles, and chapters of a book.

"Windwagon Smith" (story)
"Sea Fever" (poem)
"Zoom" (television program)
"The Koala Bear" (student report)
"Fog Causes Traffic Jam" (newspaper article)

Exercise Using Quotation Marks with Titles

Copy the following titles, using quotation marks correctly.

1. "To a Nightingale" (poem)
2. "Star Trek" (TV show)
3. "How the Camel Got His Hump" (story)
4. "Swift Things Are Beautiful" (poem)
5. "Eskimo Life" (student report)
6. "Hurricane" (poem)
7. "To Build a Fire" (story)
8. "The First Women in America" (chapter)
9. "Owens Runs for Office" (newspaper article)
10. "Nonsense Verses" (chapter)

Part 8 Underlining

Underlining is used in written work to set off certain titles.

Underline the title of a book, magazine, or motion picture.

When these titles are set in print, they are in *italics*.

<u>Charlotte's Web</u> by E. B. White   (book title in writing)
Charlotte's Web by E. B. White   (book title in print)

magazines. Both are underlined. Make sure students understand what italic print looks like.

2. Assign and discuss Exercises A and B on page 380.

3. Use Exercise G on page 383 for additional practice or review.

Optional Practice

1. Have students write sentences using each of the titles in Exercise B on page 380 or Exercise G on page 383.

2. Have students choose three chapters from their textbooks, three articles from a newspaper, and three articles from a magazine, and write a sentence for each according to the pattern of the example below. They must use capital letters, quotation marks, and underlining correctly.

> Example: "Yankee Doodle" is the title of a chapter from the book, <u>American History</u>.

Ebony Junior (magazine)
Peter Pan (motion picture)

Exercises   Using Underlining Correctly

A. Copy the following titles, underlining them.

1. <u>Frankenstein</u> (movie)
2. <u>Cheaper by the Dozen</u> (book)
3. <u>Time</u> (magazine)
4. <u>Homer Price</u> (book)
5. <u>Miracle on 34th Street</u> (movie)
6. <u>Follow My Leader</u> (book)
7. <u>Misty of Chincoteague</u> (book)
8. <u>Sports Illustrated</u> (magazine)
9. <u>The Red Balloon</u> (movie)
10. <u>A Dipperful of Stars</u> (book)

B. Copy the following titles. Use quotation marks or underlining as needed.

1. "Two Escape from Jail" (newspaper article)
2. <u>Cricket</u> (magazine)
3. <u>Sounder</u> (movie)
4. "The Emperor's New Clothes" (story)
5. "The Ice Ages" (chapter)
6. <u>The Reason for Seasons</u> (book)
7. "The Legend of Bigfoot" (student report)
8. <u>Caddie Woodlawn</u> (book)
9. "Foul Shot" (poem)
10. <u>Ranger Rick's Nature Magazine</u> (magazine)

Additional Exercises

Punctuation

A. Using Periods Correctly (Use after page 366.)

Copy these phrases, using periods where necessary.

1. J.P. Duffy, Jr.
2. Morton Salt Co.
3. 111 N. Canal St.
4. 12 oz.
5. Ms. M.K. Evans
6. 200 B.C.
7. Dec. 7, 1941
8. U.S.A.
9. 6 min.
10. P.O. Box 29, New York, N.Y.

B. Using Question Marks Correctly (Use after page 367.)

Copy these sentences. Use either a period or a question mark at the end of each sentence.

1. What should I feed my hamster?
2. I've made many new friends.
3. Help me with this tent.
4. Will you teach me to knit?
5. Arnette baked six dozen cookies.
6. Jamie fixed her bike chain.
7. How is film developed?
8. What did Ben Franklin invent?
9. Hang the mobile here.
10. Have you read about deep-sea divers?

C. Using Exclamation Points Correctly (Use after page 368.)

Copy these sentences. Use either a period, question mark, or exclamation point at the end of each sentence.

1. Look out

Additional Exercises

If these Exercises were not used with each lesson, they may now be used for chapter review.

2. Would you like to be on TV?
3. Ector explored the mountains.
4. Have you been to the pet store?
5. Help! I can't swim!
6. Turn in your math papers.
7. The Model T was an early car.
8. Come and visit us next summer.
9. Wow! What luck you have!
10. The Vikings came from Norway.

D. Using Commas Correctly (Use after page 370.)

Copy the following sentences. Put in commas where they are needed.

1. Todd makes candles, jewelry, and pottery.
2. The ship set sail on September 16, 1620.
3. No, I've never seen a wombat.
4. Katy, are you playing in Little League?
5. The tournament is in Shaker Heights, Ohio.
6. Sean asked, "Where is my backpack?"
7. Michael rowed, and Bonnie bailed water.
8. On January 24, 1848, gold was discovered.
9. "I know that song," Juanita said.
10. Lightning, winds, and waves battered the ship.

E. Using Apostrophes Correctly (Use after page 373.)

Copy the sentences below. Put in apostrophes where they are needed to show possession or to identify contractions.

1. I'll tell some riddles.
2. Your tulips haven't bloomed.
3. The tree fort is Curtis's and ours.
4. The monkey's tail was wrapped around the limb.
5. Wouldn't you like a ride?

6. It's a ghost town now.
7. The dog couldn't catch its tail.
8. We're going to Marguerite's house.
9. You'll like Ogden Nash's poems.
10. Who's been to the children's zoo?

F. Using Quotation Marks Correctly (Use after page 379.)

Copy these sentences. Add all the punctuation marks that are needed.

1. "Be careful!" Dad yelled. "It's broken glass!"
2. Lucinda called, "Come home for dinner!"
3. Cary asked, "Where is Zaire?"
4. The poem "Jabberwocky" uses nonsense words.
5. "Do you want a hamburger," Mom asked, "or a hot dog?"
6. "Where do pineapples grow?" Chuck asked.
7. Noah announced, "It's halftime now."
8. "This book," Rafael said, "is the story of whales."
9. "The Raiders scored again," Angela said.
10. "Christine Loock," I explained, "is a champion diver."

G. Underlining Titles (Use after page 380.)

Copy these titles. Use quotation marks or underlining.

1. <u>A Month of Sundays</u> (book)
2. <u>Child Life</u> (magazine)
3. "The Life of Eleanor Roosevelt" (student report)
4. <u>A Thousand Clowns</u> (movie)
5. "Sitting Bull" (chapter)
6. <u>Star Trek</u> (movie)
7. <u>The Wizard of Oz</u> (movie)
8. "Hurricane Hits Florida" (newspaper article)
9. <u>Are You There, God? It's Me, Margaret</u> (book)
10. "Happy Days" (TV show)

Chapter 27

Improving Your Spelling

When you speak, you never have to think about how a word is spelled. But when you write, correct spelling is absolutely necessary. Sometimes a misspelled word looks like a different word that makes no sense in the sentence.

    Marisma *moped* the floor with a sponge.

More often the misspelled word simply makes no sense at all.

    She was wearing her new blue *shurt*.

Because you want your writing to make sense, you will want to be a good speller.

You can become a good speller by developing a few good habits and understanding a few basic rules. These habits and rules will help you to write clearly almost as easily as you speak.

Chapter Objectives

1. To develop habits for good spelling
2. To understand and apply common spelling rules

Preparing the Students

It is suggested that it might be more helpful to do parts of this chapter periodically so that students will not have too many spelling rules to learn all at once; instead, they can concentrate on a few at a time. Perhaps you can coordinate learning some of the rules with other spelling lessons or vocabulary work.

Read and discuss the introduction to the chapter on page 385. Bring up the fact that the rules to be discussed in this chapter will not tell how to spell every word, but will make most words easier to figure out. The rules will also give clues to help students find the more difficult words in the dictionary.

Additional Resources

Diagnostic Test—page 437 in this T.E. Recommended for use before teaching the chapter.

Mastery Test—pages 491–492 in this T.E. Recommended for use after teaching the chapter.

Additional Mastery Test—Recommended for use after any necessary reteaching. (In separate booklet, *Mastery Tests, Silver Level,* pages 54–55.)

Skills Practice Book—pages 144–150

Duplicating Masters—pages 144–150

End-of-year Test—pages 493–496 in this T.E. Recommended for use

after teaching this chapter, to review Chapters 14 through 27.
Additional End-of-year Test—Recommended for use after any necessary reteaching. (In separate booklet, *Mastery Tests, Silver Level*, pages 56–59.)

Part 1

Objective

To develop habits for good spelling

Presenting the Lesson

1. Read and discuss pages 386 to 388. Ask students for examples of words they find difficult to spell correctly. Write the words on the board and ask other students if they can think of any memory devices that would help someone remember the correct spelling. Using a few of the most difficult words on the board, have the class go through the Steps for Mastering Specific Words. Erase the words and test the class on them. Let students check their own papers to help each one discover personal strengths or weaknesses.
2. You may find it helpful to do Exercise A on page 388 with the class. Assign and discuss Exercises B and C.
3. Use Exercise A on page 395 as additional practice or review.

Part 1 Plan Your Study of Spelling

There may always be a few words that will give you trouble. But you will be able to master most words quickly if you work at developing the following habits.

Habits for Improving Your Spelling

1. Make a habit of looking at words carefully.

When you come to a new word, be sure you know its meaning. If you are not certain, look up the word in a dictionary.

Practice seeing every letter. Many people see a word again and again but don't really look at it. When you see a new word, or a tricky word, like *government*, look at all the letters. To help yourself remember them, write the word several times. Use pencil and paper if they're handy. Otherwise, draw the word with your finger.

2. When you speak, pronounce words carefully.

Some words are spelled wrong just because they are not pronounced right. If you leave out the sound of certain letters, you will have a hard time spelling words right.

Here is a list of words that cause trouble because they are often pronounced wrong. The letters in dark print are the letters that are often left out in spelling because they are left out in pronouncing the words.

1. Feb**r**uary
2. lib**r**ary
3. hund**r**ed
4. stren**g**th
5. **re**member
6. regular
7. hist**o**ry
8. pro**b**ably
9. interesting
10. Saturday
11. poem
12. violet

3. Find out your own spelling enemies and attack them.

Look over your past papers and make a list of the misspelled words. Also keep a list of new words that are difficult for you. Study these words until you can spell them correctly and easily.

4. Find memory devices to help with problem spellings.

Some words do not follow regular spelling patterns or rules. It may be that there is no rule applying to a certain word.

In these cases, a **memory device** may help you. A memory device is a trick, or a catchy sentence about the word, that you can remember easily. The device tells you how to spell the word. Here are some examples:

friend—She is a fri**end** to the end.

know—If you thin**k,** you will **k**now the answer.

hear—You h**ear** with your ear.

believe—Never be**lie**ve a lie.

piece—Take a **pie**ce of pie.

separate—Only a rat makes us sep**arat**e.

principal—The princi**pal** is my pal.

When you find a word that is a particular problem for you, think of a memory device for that word.

5. Proofread what you write.

To make sure that you have spelled all words correctly, re-read your work. Examine it carefully, word for word. Don't let your eyes race over the page and miss misspellings.

Steps for Mastering Specific Words

When you notice that you are having trouble with a certain word, take a few minutes to study it carefully. Give it all your attention. If you spend the time and energy to learn it correctly once, you will save yourself all the trouble of correcting it many times.

Optional Practice

1. Divide the class into small groups. Have each student list five words he or she finds difficult to spell, circling each trouble spot. The groups should discuss ways that might be helpful for students to remember the correct spellings. They should compile a group list, making a copy for each group member. Any suggestions that were made to help remember the spellings should be noted next to the word on the list. Before the students study the entire list, check the words to see that they are practical. The students should then take their lists home and study the words according to the directions in the text. Have the groups form again later for post-tests.

2. Combine all the lists from each group from the optional exercise above and use them for a spelling bee. Distribute copies to students for study beforehand.

Follow these steps to master a specific word.

1. Look at the word and say it to yourself. Pronounce it carefully. If it has two or more syllables, say it again, one syllable at a time. Look at each syllable as you say it.

2. Look at the letters and say each one. If the word has two or more syllables, pause between syllables as you say the letters.

3. Without looking at the word, write it.

4. Now look at your book or list to see if you have spelled the word correctly. If you have, write it once more. Compare it with the correct spelling again. For best results, repeat the process once more.

5. If you have misspelled the word, notice where the error was. Then repeat steps 3 and 4 until you have spelled the word correctly three times in a row.

Exercises   Developing Good Habits

A. Here are some words that are often pronounced carelessly and then misspelled. Look at each letter of every word. Pronounce the words correctly to yourself. Write the words in alphabetical order.

7 regular	2 general	11 strength
10 Saturday	9 ruin	4 poem
6 probably	5 police	12 violet
3 geography	8 remember	1 finally

B. Write each word listed in Exercise A in a good sentence. Check your spelling each time you write the word.

C. Read through some of your recent papers to find words you have misspelled. Make a list of five to ten of your personal spelling enemies. Study them, following the steps given in Part 1. Then write each word in a good sentence.

Part 2 Rules for Spelling

Many words in our language follow certain patterns. Studying the following rules should help you with these words.

Spelling Words with *ie* and *ei*

Many boys and girls, and adults too, find it hard to tell whether *i* comes before or after *e* in spelling certain words. Your mother and father probably learned this old rhyme about the problem.

> *I* before *e*
> Except after *c*,
> Or when sounded as *a*
> As in n*ei*ghbor or w*ei*gh.

This rhyme does help. Look at the words below. Decide which lines of the rhyme work for each of these words.

1. believe
2. niece
3. relief
4. receive
5. conceit
6. ceiling
7. weigh
8. weight
9. eight

The rule will help you with most words. But you will have to study and remember these four words. They do not follow the rule.

either   neither   seize   weird

Exercise Writing Words with *ie* and *ei*

Write sentences using all of the words listed above. Try to use more than one *ie* or *ei* word in each sentence. Be sure to use at least ten different *ie* or *ei* words. Underline the *ie* and *ei* words. You may use each word more than once.

Example: My n*ie*ce r*ec*eived *ei*ght presents.

Part 2

Objective

To understand and apply common spelling rules

Presenting the Lesson

1. Read and discuss page 389. Ask students for other examples of *ie* and *ei* words.
2. Assign and discuss the Exercise on page 389.
3. Read and discuss page 390. Ask students for examples of other prefixes, and other words that follow the two suffix rules.
4. Assign and discuss the Exercise on page 391.
5. Read and discuss page 391 and the first paragraph of page 392. Make sure students recognize and can use the words listed as examples and exceptions.
6. Assign and discuss the Exercise on page 392.
7. Read and discuss page 392 and the first three lines of page 393. Ask students for examples of other words ending in *y* to which suffixes may be added. Have the students tell whether the *y* in each of those words will be changed to *i*.
8. Assign and discuss the Exercise on page 393.
9. Read and discuss page 393. Ask students for examples of other words that need the final consonant doubled.
10. Assign and discuss the Exercise at the top of page 394.
11. Use Exercise B on page 395 as additional practice or review.

Optional Practice

1. Have students copy these words, filling in the blanks with *ie* or *ei*.

1. br___f
2. rec___ve
3. f___ld
4. ___ther
5. n___ce
6. ch___f
7. w___gh
8. ___ght
9. th___r
10. n___ther
11. gr___f
12. bel___ve
13. w___ght
14. misch___f
15. sl___gh
16. th___f
17. rel___f
18. v___n
19. w___rd
20. c___ling

2. Have students write the base word and a brief definition for each word in the list below.

1. staring
   starring
2. hoping
   hopping
3. planed
   planned
4. riding
   ridding
5. robing
   robbing

Extending the Lesson

Discuss how the various suffixes change words from one group of words to another. For example, the *ly* ending changes an adjective to an adverb. The *er* ending changes an adjective that simply tells *what kind* to an adjective that compares two things. Ask the students to find other ways suffixes affect the base words.

Adding Prefixes

A **prefix** is a syllable or group of syllables that is added to the beginning of a word to change its meaning. Here are some common prefixes and examples of their use:

Prefix	Basic Word	New Word
re- (again)	write	rewrite (write again)
un- (not)	able	unable (not able)
in- (not)	formal	informal (not formal)
im- (not)	possible	impossible (not possible)
pre- (before)	view	preview (see before)

When a prefix is added to a word, the spelling of the word stays the same.

Adding the Suffixes *-ly* and *-ness*

A **suffix** is a letter or syllable added to the ending of a word to change its meaning. For example, the suffix *-s* is added to a singular noun to make it plural. The suffix *-ed* is added to a verb to change the action to the past. Adding a suffix sometimes adds a spelling problem to a word.

The suffix *-ly* added to an adjective changes it to an adverb.

Adjective

My mother is a *careful* driver.

Adverb

My mother drives *carefully*.

When the suffix -ly is added to a word ending with *l*, both *l*'s are kept.

The suffix *-ness* added to an adjective changes it to a noun.

Adjective

Kirk is *open* and honest.

Noun

I admire Kirk's *openness*.

When the suffix -ness is added to a word ending with *n*, both *n*'s are kept.

Exercise   Adding Prefixes and Suffixes

Find the misspelled words in these sentences and spell them correctly.

1. I liked the eveness of Tammy's haircut. evenness
2. Spencer thoughtfuly brought a gift. thoughtfully
3. A dog is unnable to climb a tree. unable
4. Winding this watch is unecessary. unnecessary
5. The thiness of this pencil makes it hard to hold. thinness
6. Some people misstrust cats. mistrust
7. We admired the salesperson's openess. openness
8. Those hints were awfuly misleading. awfully
9. Holmes uncovered a totaly new clue. totally
10. We usualy see movie preeviews. usually, previews

Adding Suffixes to Words Ending in Silent e

Notice what happens when you add suffixes beginning with vowels to words that end in silent *e*.

hope + ing = hoping   fame + ous = famous
refuse + al = refusal   pale + er = paler
expense + ive = expensive   like + able = likable

When a suffix beginning with a vowel is added to a word ending in silent e, the e is usually dropped.

Now see what happens when you add suffixes beginning with consonants to words that end in silent *e*.

care + ful = careful   move + ment = movement
lone + ly = lonely   nine + ty = ninety
score + less = scoreless   bore + dom = boredom

When a suffix beginning with a consonant is added to a word ending in silent e, the e is usually kept.

The following words are exceptions to these two rules:

truly   argument   ninth   judgment   wholly

Exercise   Adding Suffixes Correctly

Add the suffix given for each word. Write each new word in a sentence.

1. place + ing *placing*
2. use + able *usable*
3. sure + ly *surely*
4. confuse + ion *confusion*
5. hope + ful *hopeful*
6. come + ing *coming*
7. make + er *maker*
8. safe + ty *safety*
9. like + ly *likely*
10. save + ing *saving*
11. desire + able *desirable*
12. remove + al *removal*

Adding Suffixes to Words Ending in y

See what happens when you add suffixes to words that end in *y* following a consonant.

1. baby + es = babies
2. empty + er = emptier
3. happy + ly = happily
4. lazy + ness = laziness
5. carry + ed = carried
6. story + es = stories

When a suffix is added to a word that ends with y following a consonant, the y is usually changed to i.

However, the *y* is not changed when the suffix *-ing* is added.

empty + ing = emptying   carry + ing = carrying
fly + ing = flying   apply + ing = applying

Notice, too, what happens when you add suffixes to words that end in *y* following a vowel.

boy + s = boys   play + ed = played
buy + er = buyer   stay + ing = staying

When a suffix is added to a word that ends with *y* following a vowel, the *y* usually is not changed.

The following words are exceptions: *paid, said.*

Exercise Adding Suffixes Correctly

Add the suffix given for each word. Write each new word correctly.

1. hurry + ing — hurrying
2. story + es — stories
3. heavy + est — heaviest
4. fly + er — flyer
5. enjoy + ed — enjoyed
6. play + er — player
7. fly + ing — flying
8. sky + es — skies
9. ready + ness — readiness
10. easy + ly — easily
11. carry + ed — carried
12. happy + ness — happiness
13. early + est — earliest
14. toy + s — toys
15. cry + ing — crying

Doubling the Final Consonant

What happens to these words when you add suffixes?

spin + ing = spinning   fat + er = fatter
hot + est = hottest   scrub + ed = scrubbed

You can see that the last letter is doubled when suffixes beginning with a vowel are added to these words. Look at the vowels and final letters of the base words. How are these parts alike?

Words of one syllable, ending with a consonant following one vowel, double the final consonant before adding -ing, -ed, -en, -er, or -est.

The final consonant is not doubled when it follows *two* vowels.

trail + er = trailer   shout + ed = shouted
steam + ing = steaming   float + er = floater
peel + ed = peeled   shoot + ing = shooting

Exercise   **Doubling the Final Consonant**

Add the suffix given for each word. Write each new word correctly.

1. fat + est   *fattest*
2. stop + ed   *stopped*
3. sad + er   *sadder*
4. hear + ing   *hearing*
5. pat + ed   *patted*
6. bit + en   *bitten*
7. soon + est   *soonest*
8. get + ing   *getting*
9. plan + ed   *planned*
10. big + est   *biggest*
11. put + ing   *putting*
12. hot + er   *hotter*
13. leak + ed   *leaked*
14. rot + en   *rotten*
15. hop + ed   *hopped*

Review Exercises   **Using the Spelling Rules**

A. Find the misspelled words in these sentences and spell them correctly.

1. The surface of this desk is very iregular.   *irregular*
2. The wagons moved into the openess of the plains.   *openness*
3. Beth recieved a carefuly wrapped gift.   *received, carefully*
4. Mom ordered a Spiderman cake specialy made.   *specially*
5. I reecopied on a clean peice of paper.   *recopied, piece*
6. I beleive I hear a mysteryous sound.   *believe, mysterious*
7. The theif easly opened the safe.   *thief, easily*
8. Shopers spoted the bargains.   *shoppers, spotted*
9. We're geting excited about the upcomeing play.   *getting, upcoming*
10. Hikeing and bikeing are two camp activitys.   *hiking, biking, activities*

B. Add the suffix given for each word below and write the new word.

1. bite + ing   *biting*
2. stay + ed   *stayed*
3. play + ing   *playing*
4. try + ed   *tried*
5. heat + er   *heater*
6. shop + ed   *shopped*
7. hike + ing   *hiking*
8. enjoy + s   *enjoys*
9. waste + ing   *wasting*
10. fry + ed   *fried*
11. hope + ing   *hoping*
12. tiny + est   *tiniest*
13. pet + ing   *petting*
14. big + er   *bigger*
15. hope + ful   *hopeful*

Review Exercises

Assign and discuss Review Exercises A and B on page 394.

Additional Exercises

Improving Your Spelling

A. Developing Good Habits (Use after page 388.)

Here are some words that are often pronounced carelessly and then misspelled. Look at each letter of every word. Pronounce each word correctly to yourself. Write the words in alphabetical order.

- 9 memory
- 1 asked
- 11 twelfth
- 12 violent
- 4 history
- 10 surprise
- 6 interesting
- 2 athlete
- 8 library
- 3 February
- 5 hundred
- 7 introduce

B. Using the Spelling Rules (Use after page 393.)

Find the misspelled words in these sentences and spell them correctly.

1. Leona faithfuly attended Cycle Club meetings. *faithfully*
2. The banner flaped in the brisk wind. *flapped*
3. Renee sayed she would be makeing popcorn tonight. *said, making*
4. Niether dog retreived the stick. *neither, retrieved*
5. What are the cheif animals of the polear region? *chief, polar*
6. Finaly, Barry applyed another coat of glaze. *finally, applied*
7. Children were skiping, runing, and leaping to the song. *skipping, running*
8. King Solomon imediately settled the arguement. *immediately, argument*
9. We noticed the uneveness of the coastline. *unevenness*
10. One dinosaur had extremly sharp spikes. *extremely*

Additional Exercises

If these Exercises were not used with each lesson, they may be assigned for chapter review.

395

Index

a, an, the (articles), 192, 226—227, 236—237, 358
  in book titles, 192, 358
  before nouns, 226—227
Abbreviations
  capitalization of, 350—351
  defined, 350, 364
  in dictionary entries, 216
  lists of, 364—365
  periods with, 350, 364—365, 366, 381
  of titles, 350—351
Accent mark, 213—214
Action verbs, 54—55, 127—130, 152
Addresses
  business letters, 338—339
  envelopes, 344—345
  social letters, heading of, 333
Adjectives, 219—237
  adverbs or, distinguishing, 244—247, 249
  articles, 192, 226—227, 236—237, 358
  comparisons with, 230—233, 237
  defined, 219—221
  proper, 348—349, 354, 359
  in sentence patterns, 234
  telling how many, 223—225, 236
  telling what kind, 222—223, 225, 235—236
  telling which ones, 224—225, 228—229, 236—237
Adverbs, 239—249
  adjectives or, distinguishing, 244—247, 249
  comparisons with, 242—243, 248—249
  defined, 239—242
Alphabetical order
  dictionary words, 206
  fiction books, 192—193
  in index of book, 202
  titles in card catalog, 196—199, 201

Apostrophe
  in contractions, 147—149, 155, 169—170, 372—373, 382—383
  in possessives, 120—122, 125, 168, 371—373, 382—383
Articles, 192, 226—227, 236—237, 358
  See also a, an, the.
Author card in card catalog, 197—198, 201
Auxiliary verbs. *See* Helping verbs.

Base word, 1—3, 10—11
be, forms of, 131, 138—142, 153—154
  See also is, was, are, were.
Biography, 194
Body of business letter, 339—340
Body of composition, 272—273
  See also Compositions.
Body of friendly letter, 334
Body of story, 301, 304—305, 307
Body paragraphs
  in compositions, 263—264, 272—273
  in written reports, 323—325
  in stories, 281, 286—287
Books, finding and using in library. *See* Library, using the.
Business letters. *See* Letters.

Call numbers of library books, 196
Capitalization, 347—361
  first words, 355—357, 360—361
    of outlines, 356—357, 360—361
    of poetry lines, 356—357, 360—361
    of quotations, 355—356, 375, 378
  I, 348—349, 351, 353—354, 359
  proper adjectives, 347—349, 359
  proper nouns, 347—354, 356, 359—361
  rules for, 347—358
  titles
    of persons, 350—351, 359

of written works, 358, 361
Card catalog, 196—201
   author cards, 197—198, 201
   cross reference cards, 200
   guide cards, 196—197, 201
   subject cards, 199, 201
   title cards, 198, 201
Characters in story, 278—282, 285—286
Cliché, 255
Climax in story, 305
Closing in letters, 334, 340
Colon, 339
Comma
   with adjectives, 220
   with city and state or country, 369—371, 382
   after complete thought in sentences, 370—371, 382
   as context key to restatement, 16—17
   in dates, 369—371, 382
   in letters, 370
   with name of person spoken to, 369—371, 382
   in quotations, 370—371, 375—378, 382—383
   in series, 370—371, 382
   rules for use, 369—370
   after *yes, no, well,* 369—371, 382
Common nouns, 115—116, 124—125, 347—349
Comparisons
   with adjectives, 230—233, 237
   with adverbs, 242—243, 248—249
Compositions, 261—275
   body paragraphs in, 263—264, 272—273
   checking, 275
   defined, 261—262
   details in, 268—269
   ending paragraph in, 264, 274—275
      introductory paragraph in, 263—264, 270—271
   main ideas in, 267—268, 270—275
   parts of (paragraphs), 263—264, 270—275

   planning, 267—269
   subjects for, 265—266
   time sequence in, 268
   topic sentences in, 263—264, 270—271, 275
Conclusion of story, 305—307
Context, 13—21
   learning word meanings from
      by definition, 14—15, 19—21
      by example, 18—21
      by restatement, 16—17, 19—21
Contractions, 147—151, 155, 372—373, 382—383
   apostrophe in, 147—149, 155, 372—373, 382—383
   it's and *its,* 169—170
   lists of, 147, 372
   negatives, 148—149, 155
   n't not included in verb, 134—135
Cross reference cards in card catalog, 200
Cursive handwriting, 186—189

Dashes, as key to restatement in context, 16—17
Declarative sentences
   defined, 45—46
   period with, 45, 47—49, 64—65, 363, 366
   subject in, 50—53, 56—60, 65—67
Definitions in dictionary, 215—217
Descriptive paragraphs, 99, 104—107, 111
Details
   in compositions, 268—269
   in paragraphs, 91—95, 97, 104—107
   in stories, 280, 283—284
Dewey Decimal System, 193—196
Dictionary, 205—217
   alphabetical order in, 206
   definitions, 215—217
   entries, information in, 211—217
      definitions, 215—217
      part of speech, 216—217
      respellings, decoded by pronunciation key, 213—214, 217

syllables, 211—212, 217
entry words, 206—211
guide words, 208—210
Directions, writing, 108—111
Direct object of the verb, 136—137, 153
Discussion, group, 289—295
example of, 290—292
guides for, 289, 294
practicing, 294—295
roles in, 293
Double negatives, 148—149, 155

Encyclopedia, 312, 314—316
Ending paragraph
in compositions, 264, 274—275
in reports, 323, 325
in stories, 287
Envelopes, addressing, 344—345
Example(s), used to develop paragraph, 95—97
Exclamation point
with exclamatory sentences, 46—49, 64—65, 368, 381—382
with imperative sentences, 48—49, 64—65
Exclamatory sentences
defined, 46
exclamation point with, 46—49, 64—65, 368, 381—382
Explanatory (how-to) paragraphs, 99, 108—111

Fiction books, 192—193
Fragments, sentence, 40—43, 64
Friendly letters. *See* Letters, friendly.

good, bad, forms of, 232—233
good, bad, well, badly, use of, 246—247
Greeting (salutation) in letters, 333, 339
Guide cards in card catalog, 196—197, 201
Guide words in dictionary, 208—210

Handwriting, 183—189
cursive, 186—189
guides for, 184
manuscript, 185—186, 189
Heading in letters, 333, 339
Helping verbs, 131—135, 152—153, 177—180
"How-to" paragraphs, 108—111
Hyphen, 374—375

I
capitalization of, 348—349, 359
after state-of-being verbs, 164, 172
as subject of sentence, 161—163, 171
verb forms with, 138—139, 153, 175—176
ie, ei, 389
Imperative sentences
defined, 46
exclamation point with, 48—49, 65
period with, 46—49, 64—65, 363, 366
subject in, 61—62, 67
Indenting first line of paragraph, 78
Index, 202—203, 314
Information
finding in a book, 202—203
gathering for reports, 312—316
giving credit to sources of, 325—326
Initials
in abbreviations, 364—365
defined, 350, 364
from first letters of names, 364
Inside address of business letters, 338—339
Interrogative sentences (questions)
defined, 45—46
question mark with, 45, 47—49, 64—65, 367, 381
Introduction of story, 301—304, 307
Introductory paragraph
in compositions, 263—264, 270—271
in reports, 323
in stories, 285—286
Invitations. *See* Letters, social notes.
Irregular verbs
defined, 180

principal parts, list of, 181
rules for past form, 180
is, was, are, were
   agreement with subject, 138—139, 153—154
   after *here, there, where*, 140—142, 154
Italics
   defined, 216
   in dictionary entries, 216
   underlining for, 379—380
it's and *its*, 169—170

Language, lively
   metaphors, 257—259
   similes, 254—256, 259
   strong verbs, 252—253
let, leave, 143—144, 154
Letters, 331—345
   business, 338—343
      capitalization in, 339—340
      order letter, 338, 340, 342—343
      parts of, 338—341
      punctuation in, 339—340
      request letter, 338, 339, 341, 343
   envelopes, addressing, 344—345
   friendly, 331—334
      capitalization in, 333—334
      example of, 332
      parts of, 332—334
      punctuation in, 333—334
   social notes, 335—338
      of acceptance, 337—338
      of invitation, 336, 338
      of regret, 337—338
      thank you, 335, 338
Library, using the, 191—203, 312—316
   call numbers, 193—196
   card catalog, 196—201, 314
   classification and arrangement of
      fiction and nonfiction books, 192—195
   Dewey Decimal System, 193—195
      finding a particular book, 196—201
      finding information in nonfiction books, 202—203
   reference books, 312—314
Linking verbs. *See* State-of-being verbs.
Lively language. *See* Language, lively.
Logical order
   in paragraphs, 105—106
   in reports, 321—323

Magazines, using for reports, 312—316
Main character in story, 281, 285—286
Main idea
   in compositions, 262—264, 267—268, 270—275
   in paragraphs, 78—89
   See also Topic sentence.
Main verbs, 131—135, 152—153
Manuscript handwriting, 185—186, 189
may, can, 145—146, 154
Memory devices for spelling, 387
Metaphor, 257—259
Modifiers, 220. *See also* Adjectives, Adverbs.
Mood in story, 303—304
more, most
   with adjectives, 231—233, 237
   with adverbs, 242—243, 248—249

Narrator in story, 302
Negatives
   defined, 148
   double, 148—149, 155
   not part of verb, 134
no-words, *not*-words. *See* Negatives.
Nonfiction books, 193—196, 202—203, 312—314
Note cards
   for oral reports, 326—328
   for written reports, 314—317
Notes, social. *See* Letters, social notes.
Nouns, 113—125
   common, 115—116, 124—125, 347—349
   defined, 113—114
   as objects of verbs, 150
   plural forms of, 117—119, 125

possessive forms of, 120—122, 125,
  371—372, 382—383
proper, 115—116, 124—125
  capitalization of, 347—354, 356,
    359—361
  in sentence patterns, 123, 150—151,
    234
  singular forms of, 117
    changing to plural, 117—119, 125

Object of the verb, 136—137, 150, 153,
  165—166, 172
Object pronouns, 165—166, 172
or, as key to restatement in context,
  16—17
Oral reports, 326—329. See also Reports.
Outlines, 319—322
  capitalization in, 356—357, 360—361
  punctuation in, 366

Paragraphs, 77—89, 91—97, 99—111
  body, 263—264, 272—273, 281, 286—
    287, 323—325
  in compositions, 261—275
  descriptive, 99, 104—107, 111
    details in, 104—107
    natural order in, 106
  details in, 91—95, 97, 104—107
  developing, 91—97
    using details, 92—95, 97
    using example(s), 95—97
  ending, 264, 274—275, 287, 323, 325
  explanatory, 99, 108—111
    giving directions in, 108—111
    time sequence in, 108
  indenting first line in, 78
  introductory, 263—264, 270—271,
    285—286, 323
  kinds of, 99—111
  main idea in, 78—89
  narrative, 99—103, 111
    order in, 101
    natural order in, 106

in reports, 323—326
in stories, 281, 285—287
time sequence in, 101, 108
topic sentence in, 82—89
Parentheses, as key to restatement
  in context, 16—17
Parts of speech, 216
  See also Adjectives, Adverbs, Nouns,
    Pronouns, Verbs.
Past forms of verbs, 176—181
Period
  in abbreviations, 350, 364—365, 366,
    381
  in initials, 350, 364, 366, 381
  in outlines, 366
  with quotation marks, 375—378, 383
  in sentences, 45—49, 363, 366
Plot in story, 299, 304
Plural forms. See Nouns, Pronouns,
  Verbs.
Possessive nouns, 120—122, 125, 371—
  372, 382—383
  apostrophe in, 121—122, 125, 168,
    371—373, 382—383
Possessive pronouns, 168—170, 173
Predicate of the sentence
  complete, 50—53, 65—66
  defined, 50
  simple (the verb), 53—55, 58, 66
Prefixes, 4—6, 10—11
Present forms of verbs, 175—181
Principal parts of common irregular
  verbs, 181
Pronouns, 157—173
  defined, 158
  as objects, 165—166, 172
  plural forms of, 159
  possessive forms of, 168—170, 173
  singular forms of, 159
  after state-of-being verbs, 164, 172
  as subjects, 161—163, 171
  used for nouns, 158—160, 171
  we, us, 167—168, 173
Pronunciation, in dictionary entry,
  213—214

Pronunciation key in dictionary, 213—214
Proofreading for spelling, 387
Proper adjectives, 348—349, 354, 359
Proper nouns, 115—116, 124—125, 347—354, 356, 359—361
Punctuation, 363—383
   apostrophe, 120—122, 125, 147—149, 155, 168—170, 371—373, 382—383
   colon, 339
   comma, 16—17, 220, 369—371, 375—378, 382
   dashes, 16—17
   end marks. *See* Exclamation point, Period, Question mark.
   exclamation point, 46—49, 64—65, 368, 381—382
   hyphen, 374—375
   in letters, 333—334, 339—340
   parentheses, 16—17
   period, 45—49, 350, 364—366, 375—378, 381, 383
   question mark, 45, 47—49, 64—65, 367, 381
   quotation marks, 375—380, 383

Question mark
   after interrogative sentences, 45, 47—49, 64—65, 367, 381
   with quotation marks, 375—378, 383
Questions. *See* Interrogative sentences.
Quotation marks, 375—378, 383
Quotations
   direct, 375—378, 383
   divided, 377—378, 383

Reading and study skills, 23—37
   getting ready to study, 24—26, 36
   ways of reading (reading rate), 27—35, 37
      for enjoyment, 33—35
      scanning, 27—28
      skimming, 28—29
      study-type, 30—32, 37
   timing reading rate, 33—35

Reading rate, 27—35
Reference books, 312—314
Regular verbs, 175—179
   past forms of, 176—179
Reports, 311—329
   oral, 326—329
      notes for, 326—327
      opening and closing statements in, 327—328
   written, 311—326
      body paragraphs in, 324—325
      checking, 326
      ending paragraph in, 325
      gathering information for, 314—316
      introductory paragraph in, 323
      logical order in, 321—323
      main ideas in, 318
      note cards for, 314—316
      outlines for, 319—322
      parts of (paragraphs), 323—325
      planning, 317—322
      sources of information, giving credit to, 325—326
      subjects for, 312—313
      topic sentences in, 324—325
Return address, 344—345
Run-on sentences, 69—71, 74

s', 's. *See* Apostrophe, in possessives.
Salutation. *See* Greeting in letters.
Scanning, 27—28
Sentence patterns, 63, 123, 150, 151, 234
Sentences, 39—67, 69—75
   complete, 40—43, 64
   complete predicate in, 50—53, 65—66
   complete subject in, 50—53, 65—66
   declarative, 45—49, 64—65, 363, 366
   end punctuation in, 48—49, 65. *See also* Exclamation point, Period, Question mark.
   exclamatory, 46—49, 64—65, 368, 381—382
   fragments of, 40—43, 64
   imperative, 46—49, 61—62, 64—65, 67, 363, 366

 interrogative, 45—49, 64—65, 367, 381
 kinds of, 44—49
 parts of, 50—53
 run-on, 69—71, 74
 simple predicate (the verb) in, 53—55, 58, 66
 simple subject (subject of the verb) in, 56—62, 66—67
 stringy, 72—75
 topic, 82—89, 263—264, 270—271, 275
set, *sit*, 143—144, 154
Setting of story, 303
Signature in letters, 332, 334, 340, 341
Simile, 254—256, 259
Simple predicate (the verb), 53—55, 58, 66. *See also* Verbs.
Simple subject (subject of the verb), 56—62, 66—67, 161—163, 171
Singular forms. *See* Nouns, Pronouns, Verbs.
Skimming, 28—29
Social notes. *See* Letters, social notes.
Sources of information, 202—203, 312—316
 giving credit to, 325—326
Speaking. *See* Discussion, Reports, Stories.
Spelling, 385—395
 habits for improving, 386—387
  memory device, 387
 proofreading, 387
 rules for, 389—395
  adding prefixes, 390—391
  adding suffixes, 390—394
  words with *ie* or *ei*, 389
 ways to master, 387—388
State-of-being verbs, 54—55, 129—130, 152, 164, 172
 list of, 129
Stories, telling, 297—309
 choosing a story, 298—299
 studying the story, 300—307
  guides for, 307

story elements
 climax, 305
 mood, 303—304
 narrator, 302
 plot, 299, 304
 setting, 303
story parts
 body, 301, 304—305
 conclusion, 305—306
 introduction, 301—304
telling the story, 308—309
 guides for, 308
Stories, writing, 277—287
 learning about stories, 278—280
  characters in, 278—280
  details in, 280
  time sequence in, 279
  kinds of
   could happen in real life, 278
   couldn't happen in real life, 280
 planning a story, 281—284
  choosing subject for, 281—282
   main character, 281
  steps for, 281
  time sequence, 283—284
 writing a story, 285—287
  body, 286—287
  ending, 287
  introductory paragraph, 285—286
Stringy sentences, 72—75
Study skills. *See* Reading and study skills.
Study-type reading, 30—32, 37
Subject cards in card catalog, 199, 201
Subject of the sentence
 complete, 50—53, 65—66
 defined, 50
 in imperative sentences, 61—62, 67
 nouns as, 123, 150, 151, 234
 pronouns as, 161—163, 171
 simple (subject of the verb), 56—62, 66—67
Subject of the verb, 56—62, 66—67
 finding, 56—62, 66—67, 140—142, 154
 in imperative sentences, 61—62, 67

in unusual positions, 59—60, 67
Subjects
  for compositions, 265—266
  for reports, 312—313
  for stories, 281—282
Subtopics in outlines, 320—322
Suffixes, 7—11, 390—394
Syllables
  as shown in dictionary entries, 211—212
  dividing words into, 374—375

Table of contents, 202—203
Talking. *See* Discussion, Reports, Stories.
teach, taught, learn, 145—146, 154
Tenses of verbs. *See* Present forms of verbs, Past forms of verbs.
Thank you notes. *See* Letters, social notes.
them, those, 228—229, 237
there, here, where, introducing sentences, 140—142, 154
this kind, that kind, 228—229, 237
Time sequence
  in compositions, 268
  in explanatory paragraphs, 108
  in narrative paragraphs, 101
  in written stories, 279, 283—284
Titles
  capitalization of, 350—351, 358—359, 361
  of persons, 350—351, 359
    abbreviations, 350—351
  of written works, 358, 361, 379—380, 383
    alphabetizing, 192—193
    quotation marks with, 358, 379—380, 383
    underlining for italics, 358, 379—380, 383
Topic sentences
  in compositions, 263—264, 270—271, 275
  defined, 82—83
  in paragraphs, 82—89
Topics in outline, 319—322

Underlining certain titles for italics, 358, 379—380, 383
Understood subject (*you*), 61—62, 67

Verb, the (simple predicate), 53—55, 58, 66. *See also* Verbs.
Verbs, 53—58, 127—155, 175—181
  action, 54—55, 127—130, 152
  defined, 53
  forms of, 175—181
  helping, 131—135, 152—153, 177—180
  irregular, 180—181
    principal parts of, 181
  main, 131—135, 152—153
  object of, 136—137, 153, 165—166, 172
  past forms of, 176—181
  present forms of, 175—181
  regular, 175—179
  in sentence patterns, 123, 150, 151, 234
  subjects of, 56—62, 66—67
  with *there, here, where,* 140—142, 154
Vocabulary, developing, 1—11

we, us, 167—168, 173
well, badly, 246—247
Word, base, 1—3
Word beginnings, 1—6, 10—11
Word endings, 1—3, 7—11
Word parts, 1—11
Writing. *See* Compositions, Paragraphs, Reports, Sentences, Stories.

you
  as understood subject, 61—62, 67
  and verb forms, 138—139, 153, 175—176

ZIP code, 333, 339

Acknowledgments

Atheneum Publishers: For a selection from *Rosie and Michael* by Judith Viorst. Copyright © 1974 by Judith Viorst.

William Collins Publishers, Inc.: For a selection from *Rhyme Giggles*, edited by William Cole and illustrated by Tomi Ungerer. Copyright © 1967 and 1970 by William Cole and Tomi Ungerer.

William Collins Publishers, Inc.: For the dictionary excerpt reproduced on page 209, from *Webster's New World Dictionary for Young Readers*, copyright © 1976 by William Collins + World Publishing Company, Inc.

Thomas Y. Crowell, Publishers: For an adapted excerpt from *Chains, Webs, and Pyramids: The Flow of Energy in Nature* by Laurence Pringle. Copyright © 1975 by Laurence Pringle.

Macmillan Publishing Company, Inc.: For a selection from *Zeely* by Virginia Hamilton. Copyright © 1967 by Virginia Hamilton.

New Dimensions Publishing Company: For a selection from *Puerto Rico* by Natalie Nelson. Copyright © 1970 by New Dimensions Publishing Company, Inc.

World Book—Childcraft International: For an excerpt from *The World Book Encyclopedia*. Copyright © 1979 by World Book-Childcraft International, Inc.

Zaner-Bloser, Inc.: For the alphabets (pages 185 and 186) from *Creative Growth in Handwriting*. Copyright © 1975, 1979 by Zaner-Bloser, Inc., Columbus, Ohio.

Photographs

Cover: Dennis Brokaw

Woodfin Camp: Dan Budnik, 126, 174; Timothy Eagan, 310; John Wehrheim, 330.
Magnum: Burk Uzzle, 12; Paul Fusco, 22, 218, 260, 362; Dennis Stock, 112; Rene Burri, 204, 250.
James L. Ballard: ii, xii, 38, 68, 76, 90, 98, 156, 182, 190, 238, 276, 288, 296, 346, 384.

Illustrations

SUPERMAN (page 7) is a registered trademark of DC Comics, Inc. and is used with their permission.

THE INCREDIBLE HULK (page 7) is copyright © 1980 by Marvel Comics Group, a division of Cadence Industries Corporation. All rights reserved.

Karen Ackoff: 2, 6, 16, 17, 18, 34, 35, 48, 50, 120, 128, 136, 162, 163, 166, 192, 207, 220; Len Ebert: 3, 4, 42, 44, 54, 57, 58, 101, 144, 145, 179, 184, 212, 230; Michael Deas: 7, 24; Kip Lott: 14, 70, 79, 82, 83; Steve Sullivan: 25, 26, 31, 32, 84, 170, 203, 267, 269, 295; Philip Smith: 28; Linda Gist: 33, 95, 96, 160, 224, 225, 253, 262, 263, 279, 280, 282; Robert Barner: 81; Rodica Prato: 85, 255, 257, 258, 264, 283, 286, 287, 316, 317, 318, 324; Lyle Miller: 105; Wayne Bonnett: 106, 116, 119, 271, 273, 312, 313; Gregory Hergert: 133, 161, 167, 200, 208, 244, 245, 252, 327, 328; Carolyn Croll: 140; Lane Yerkes: 142; Lyn Lazarus: 188, 189; Gary Cooley: 215, 227; Bill Schmidt: 300, 301, 303, 307, 345. Ken Izzi: 197, and mechanical artwork; Jeanne Seabright: handwritten letters.

Copy Masters

Practice Pages on Usage of Irregular Verbs

The next nineteen pages are an extension of Chapter 12, **Using Irregular Verbs Correctly,** and are recommended for use after class discussion of that chapter. The pages have been designed for the teacher's convenience in reproducing them. The publisher grants permission to the classroom teacher to reproduce any of the practice pages as needed.

A brief pretest on the usage of irregular verbs is provided on page 406. It is recommended that the teacher use the results of this pretest to group students and assign practice pages as needed. Not more than three pages should be assigned at one session.

NAME _____

Practice Pages on Irregular Verbs

There are a few irregular verbs that are especially troublesome. Many people get confused about which form is used alone to mean the past, and which form is used with helping verbs.

To find the verbs that are difficult for you, do the exercise below. Then study the practice page for each verb that you used incorrectly or were unsure of.

Exercise Using Irregular Verbs

Underline the correct word from the two given in the parentheses.

1. A relief pitcher has (began, begun) to warm up.
2. That driver has (broke, broken) the law.
3. Joan has (chosen, chose) to stay with us.
4. My dog had always (came, come) when I called.
5. Has Bert (done, did) what he promised?
6. The robin (drank, drunk) from the birdbath.
7. Christopher has (ate, eaten) a whole box of candy.
8. Alicia had (fallen, fell) from the balance beam before.
9. Dolores has (gave, given) an excellent report.
10. The Johnsons have (gone, went) on vacation.
11. The sunflower has (grew, grown, growed) five feet high.
12. Barry (knew, known, knowed) the rules of the game.
13. Your teammates have (ran, run) as fast as you.
14. I (seen, saw) you at the mall.
15. The choir has (sang, sung) that song every year.
16. The students have (taken, took) four tests this week.
17. Who (threw, throwed, thrown) that ball?
18. Jennifer has (wrote, written) some funny jokes.

1. begun
2. broken
3. chosen
4. come
5. done
6. drank
7. eaten
8. fallen
9. given
10. gone
11. grown
12. knew
13. run
14. saw
15. sung
16. taken
17. threw
18. written

NAME _____

Hear It Right   Say It Right

Began and *begun* are used correctly in these sentences. *Began* is used alone, without a helping verb. *Begun* is used with a helping verb. Say each sentence to yourself.

Begin
Began
Begun

1. The little boy *began* to cry.
2. Suddenly the airplane *began* flying in a circle.
3. My mother *has begun* her spring housecleaning.
4. She *began* by washing the kitchen windows.
5. I *had* just *begun* packing for the trip.
6. *Have* you *begun* your social studies report?
7. Many forest fires *are begun* by careless campers.
8. I *have* finally *begun* to get along with my sister.

> Use *began* alone, without a helping verb.
> Use *begun* with the helping verbs *is*, *are*, *was*, *were*, *has*, *have*, and *had*.

Write It Right

Underline the correct verb in the parentheses. Then say the sentence to yourself, using the correct verb.

1. We have (began, begun) a new unit in science class.
2. My father (began, begun) cooking lessons last month.
3. By evening the hurricane had (began, begun) to lose force.
4. The next day people (began, begun) to return home.
5. I have (began, begun) to think of careers.
6. Mr. Jansen, have you (began, begun) to correct our tests yet?
7. Eight people (began, begun) the race, but only three finished.
8. The mayor (began, begun) her speech with a joke.
9. While we were setting up the tent, it (began, begun) to rain.
10. The hamburgers were ready, so we (began, begun) eating.

1. begun
2. began
3. begun
4. began
5. begun
6. begun
7. began
8. began
9. began
10. began

Building English Skills, Silver Level, Teacher's Edition.
Copyright © 1981 by McDougal, Littell & Company, Evanston, Illinois

NAME _____

Break
Broke
Broken

Hear It Right   Say It Right

Broke and *broken* are used correctly in these sentences. *Broke* is used alone, without a helping verb. *Broken* is used with a helping verb. Say each sentence to yourself.

1. What *broke* in the kitchen?
2. Paula *has broken* a plate.
3. My bike *broke* down on the way home.
4. Have you ever *broken* a bone?
5. I once *broke* a finger.
6. The clock radio *is broken*.
7. Ms. Berger *broke* up the argument in the hall.
8. Lorne *had broken* his promise.

> Use *broke* alone, without a helping verb.
> Use *broken* with the helping verbs *is, are, was, were, has, have,* and *had*.

Write It Right

Underline the correct verb in the parentheses. Then say the sentence to yourself, using the correct verb.

1. The chick has (broke, broken) out of the shell.
2. My pencil (broke, broken) again.
3. The sand dollars on the beach are all (broke, broken).
4. The lamp was (broke, broken) into a hundred pieces.
5. I shouldn't have (broke, broken) my glasses.
6. Mitch has finally (broke, broken) in his new shoes.
7. The bus (broke, broken) down on the way.
8. Has Babe Ruth's home run record ever been (broke, broken)?
9. Roger Maris (broke, broken) it in 1961.
10. The child has (broke, broken) the toy.

1. broken
2. broke
3. broken
4. broken
5. broken
6. broken
7. broke
8. broken
9. broke
10. broken

NAME _____

Hear It Right   Say It Right

Chose and *chosen* are used correctly in these sentences. *Chose* is used alone, without a helping verb. *Chosen* is used with a helping verb. Say each sentence to yourself.

Choose
Chose
Chosen

1. Who *chose* chocolate ice cream for dessert?
2. Vicky *has chosen* a name for her puppy.
3. I *chose* to sit alone at lunch.
4. Eddie *was chosen* to speak at the assembly.
5. *Have* you *chosen* a good topic for your report?
6. Sue's brother *chose* to go to college.
7. We *chose* Sam to be captain of our team.
8. Maria *had* never *been chosen* to sing a solo before.

> Use *chose* alone, without a helping verb.
> Use *chosen* with the helping verbs *is, are, was, were, has, have,* and *had.*

Write It Right

Underline the correct verb in the parentheses. Then say the sentence to yourself, using the correct verb.

1. chosen
2. chose
3. chosen
4. chose
5. chosen
6. chosen
7. chosen
8. chosen
9. chosen
10. chose

1. Adele was (chose, chosen) to lead the volleyball team.
2. Mom (chose, chosen) to walk to work today.
3. Which dress has Karen (chose, chosen)?
4. She (chose, chosen) the red one instead of the blue one.
5. Do the shoes she has (chose, chosen) go with it?
6. An Irish setter was (chose, chosen) as the best dog.
7. Todd could have (chose, chosen) to go to a movie instead.
8. I still haven't (chose, chosen) a gift for Dad's birthday.
9. Mary would have (chose, chosen) to buy a new record album.
10. Mr. Hernandez (chose, chosen) the five best spellers.

Building English Skills, Silver Level, Teacher's Edition.
Copyright © 1981 by McDougal, Littell & Company, Evanston, Illinois

NAME _____

Come
Came
Come

Hear It Right   Say It Right

Came and *come* are used correctly in these sentences. *Came* is used by itself, without a helping verb. *Come* is used with a helping verb. Say each sentence to yourself.

1. Mark *came* late to football practice.
2. You should *have come* to the party.
3. What *came* in the mail?
4. The ambassador *had come* for the peace talks.
5. Roberto's father *came* from South America.
6. *Has* your dog *come* home yet?
7. My mom *came* to pick me up.
8. The patrol *came* to a sudden halt.

> Use *came* alone, without a helping verb.
> Use *come* with the helping verbs, *has, have,* and *had.*

Write It Right

Underline the correct verb in the parentheses. Then say the sentence to yourself, using the correct verb.

1. We just (came, come) home from our vacation.
2. Have you (came, come) to this restaurant before?
3. The repairman has (came, come) to fix the TV.
4. Hilary (came, come) with refreshments.
5. My dress hasn't (came, come) back from the cleaners.
6. We (came, come) from behind to win the game.
7. My cousin Vicky has (came, come) to visit.
8. See if the delivery truck has (came, come).
9. Why haven't you (came, come) for extra help?
10. Cathy (came, come) home early from the fair.

1. came
2. come
3. come
4. came
5. come
6. came
7. come
8. come
9. come
10. came

NAME _____

Hear It Right   Say It Right

Did and *done* are used correctly in these sentences. *Did* is used alone, without a helping verb. *Done* is used with a helping verb. Say each sentence to yourself.

Do
Did
Done

1. I *did* my homework before dinner.
2. Gerry *had* never *done* woodworking before.
3. Denise *did* everything she could to help.
4. Who *hasn't done* the assignment?
5. The cast *did* an extra show.
6. *Have* you ever *done* needlepoint?
7. The cleanup crew *did* a great job.
8. What *was done* about the leaky faucet?

Use *did* alone, without a helping verb.
Use *done* with the helping verbs *is, are, was, were, has, have,* and *had.*

Write It Right

Underline the correct verb in the parentheses. Then say the sentence to yourself, using the correct verb.

1. did
2. done
3. done
4. did
5. done
6. did
7. done
8. done
9. did
10. did

1. I (did, done) all I could to pass my test.
2. What have you (did, done) with your report card?
3. Those pictures were (did, done) by Carlos.
4. Mary (did, done) the fifty-yard dash in 6.7 seconds.
5. I haven't (did, done) a thing about the broken window.
6. The racing car (did, done) 120 miles an hour.
7. Has Mike (did, done) his homework?
8. I should have (did, done) better on my painting.
9. Jack (did, done) more push-ups than anyone else.
10. Faith (did, done) an excellent science project.

Building English Skills, Silver Level, Teacher's Edition.
Copyright © 1981 by McDougal, Littell & Company, Evanston, Illinois

Hear It Right   Say It Right

Drink
Drank
Drunk

Drank and *drunk* are used correctly in these sentences. *Drank* is used by itself, without a helping verb. *Drunk* is used with a helping verb. Say each sentence to yourself.

1. No one *drank* the warm pop.
2. *Have* you *drunk* your milk?
3. I *drank* two glasses.
4. My cat *has* always *drunk* apple juice.
5. The knights *drank* a toast to their king.
6. Dad left before he *had drunk* his coffee.
7. Who *drank* my milkshake?
8. The dog *has drunk* all of its water.

> Use *drank* alone, without a helping verb.
> Use *drunk* with the helping verbs *is, are, was, were, has, have,* and *had.*

Write It Right

Underline the correct verb in the parentheses. Then say the sentence to yourself, using the correct verb.

1. The cocoa we had (drank, drunk) helped us to warm up.
2. The sparrows (drank, drunk) from the bird bath.
3. Tea is (drank, drunk) more than coffee in England.
4. Why haven't you (drank, drunk) your orange juice?
5. My dog Peppy (drank, drunk) from the garden hose.
6. The parched land (drank, drunk) up the rain.
7. Matt couldn't have (drank, drunk) all of the punch.
8. Pam has never (drank, drunk) buttermilk.
9. I could have (drank, drunk) a gallon of water.
10. After exercising, Antoinette (drank, drunk) a cup of water.

1. drunk
2. drank
3. drunk
4. drunk
5. drank
6. drank
7. drunk
8. drunk
9. drunk
10. drank

NAME _____

Hear It Right   Say It Right

Ate and *eaten* are used correctly in these sentences. *Ate* is used alone, without a helping verb. *Eaten* is used with a helping verb. Say each sentence to yourself.

Eat
Ate
Eaten

1. What *have* you *eaten* for breakfast?
2. I *ate* eggs and toast this morning.
3. Skip *has eaten* the kitten's food.
4. Paula *ate* a delicious ice cream sundae.
5. Johnny *had* never *eaten* oysters before.
6. Hot peppers *are eaten* in Mexico.
7. We *ate* a small lunch before the race.
8. *Have* you *eaten* yet?

> Use *ate* alone, without a helping verb.
> Use *eaten* with the helping verbs *is, are, was, were, has, have,* and *had.*

Write It Right

Underline the correct verb in the parentheses. Then say the sentence to yourself, using the correct verb.

1. eaten
2. eaten
3. ate
4. eaten
5. eaten
6. eaten
7. eaten
8. ate
9. eaten
10. eaten

1. The sparrows have (ate, eaten) all the crumbs.
2. Teddy has (ate, eaten) the last piece of pie.
3. Shelly (ate, eaten) dinner with us last night.
4. Al had just (ate, eaten) breakfast when the phone rang.
5. We should have (ate, eaten) our lunch in a shady spot.
6. I dreamed that my sister was (ate, eaten) by a dragon.
7. By morning, the raccoons had (ate, eaten) all of our food.
8. Kevin (ate, eaten) his lunch in a hurry.
9. Why haven't you (ate, eaten) your broccoli?
10. Ruth must have (ate, eaten) one of my cookies.

Building English Skills, Silver Level, Teacher's Edition.
Copyright © 1981 by McDougal, Littell & Company, Evanston, Illinois

Fall
Fell
Fallen

Hear It Right   Say It Right

Fell and *fallen* are used correctly in these sentences. *Fell* is used by itself, without a helping verb. *Fallen* is used with a helping verb. Say each sentence to yourself.

1. The vase *fell* from the shelf.
2. I *have fallen* over your shoes three times now.
3. Sherry tripped and *fell* on the stairs.
4. Rain *had* not *fallen* for several weeks.
5. *Has* that picture *fallen* off the wall again?
6. My grades *fell* when I stopped doing my homework.
7. The children *fell* in love with the kitten.
8. The leaves *had* all *fallen* by late September.

> Use *fell* alone, without a helping verb.
> Use *fallen* with the helping verbs *has, have,* and *had*.

Write It Right

Underline the correct verb in the parentheses. Then say the sentence to yourself, using the correct verb.

1. The satellite must have (fell, fallen) to the earth.
2. The pants have (fell, fallen) from the hanger.
3. Some ashes (fell, fallen) from the grill.
4. Amy has (fell, fallen) in love again.
5. Chuck (fell, fallen) into the pool by accident.
6. Six inches of snow have (fell, fallen) overnight.
7. The dictionary has (fell, fallen) to the floor.
8. The horse slipped on a rock and (fell, fallen) .
9. Stock market prices have (fell, fallen) again today.
10. Those keys must have (fell, fallen) out of his pocket.

1. fallen
2. fallen
3. fell
4. fallen
5. fell
6. fallen
7. fallen
8. fell
9. fallen
10. fallen

Hear It Right   Say It Right

Gave and *given* are used correctly in these sentences. *Gave* is used alone, without a helping verb. *Given* is used with a helping verb. Say each sentence to yourself.

Give
Gave
Given

1. Who *gave* you that ice cream?
2. The rollercoaster *has given* me a stomach ache.
3. Ting *gave* John some tips on ice skating.
4. The ticket taker *had given* me the wrong change.
5. Tom *gave* me a ride home yesterday.
6. *Have* you *given* your report yet?
7. Our team *gave* a cheer for Coach Long.
8. Ellen *has given* me her new address.

> Use *gave* alone, without a helping verb.
> Use *given* with the helping verbs *is, are, was, were, has, have,* and *had.*

Write It Right

Underline the correct verb in the parentheses. Then say the sentence to yourself, using the correct verb.

1. given
2. gave
3. given
4. given
5. gave
6. given
7. given
8. gave
9. given
10. given

1. My mom has (gave, given) me fifty cents for lunch.
2. The visitor (gave, given) a talk on traffic safety.
3. Calculators were (gave, given) as door prizes.
4. The manager had (gave, given) my sister a raise.
5. Linda (gave, given) me a piece of chocolate cake.
6. I was (gave, given) a bike for my birthday.
7. Eric may have (gave, given) the book to Ms. Coleman.
8. The class (gave, given) Sandi a going-away party.
9. I had (gave, given) Bobby my best matchbox car.
10. Has Lois (gave, given) you a copy of the contest rules?

Building English Skills, Silver Level, Teacher's Edition.
Copyright © 1981 by McDougal, Littell & Company, Evanston, Illinois

NAME _____

Go
Went
Gone

Hear It Right   Say It Right

Went and *gone* are used correctly in these sentences. *Went* is used alone, without a helping verb. *Gone* is used with a helping verb. Say each sentence to yourself.

1. Why *has* Laurie *gone* home early?
2. She *went* home sick.
3. My notebook *is gone* again.
4. Jill *went* to the band concert with her cousin.
5. I *had gone* sailing before.
6. Everyone but Peter *went* to the picnic.
7. *Have* you ever *gone* to California?
8. Nina *went* on an errand.

> Use *went* alone, without a helping verb.
> Use *gone* with the helping verbs *is, are, was, were, has, have,* and *had*.

Write It Right

Underline the correct verb in the parentheses. Then say the sentence to yourself, using the correct verb.

1. Do you know where Ken's family (went, gone)?
2. They have (went, gone) camping again.
3. Fortunately, the hurricane had (went, gone) out to sea.
4. It seems that vacation is (went, gone) in no time.
5. We haven't (went, gone) to a baseball game lately.
6. Miss Jamison (went, gone) to Hawaii last year.
7. My family has always (went, gone) south for Christmas.
8. Last year, we (went, gone) to Florida.
9. The entire sixth grade has (went, gone) on a field trip.
10. When we looked, the deer was (went, gone).

1. went
2. gone
3. gone
4. gone
5. gone
6. went
7. gone
8. went
9. gone
10. gone

Building English Skills, Silver Level, Teacher's Edition.
Copyright © 1981 by McDougal, Littell & Company, Evanston, Illinois

Hear It Right   Say It Right

Grew and *grown* are used correctly in these sentences. *Grew* is used alone, without a helping verb. *Grown* is used with a helping verb. Say each sentence to yourself.

Grow
Grew
Grown

1. Hank's puppy *has* really *grown*.
2. The injured starfish *grew* a new leg.
3. *Have* you ever *grown* a cactus?
4. The farmer *grew* all sorts of vegetables.
5. The lioness *had grown* too old to hunt.
6. Delicious strawberries *are grown* in Michigan.
7. The noisy crowd *grew* larger and larger.
8. The tomatoes *have grown* rapidly.

Use *grew* alone, without a helping verb.
Use *grown* with the helping verbs *is, are, was, were, has, have,* and *had*.

Write It Right

Underline the correct verb in the parentheses. Then say the sentence to yourself, using the correct verb.

1. The horses had (grew, grown) tired.
2. The class (grew, grown) tired of Larry's jokes.
3. The flood (grew, grown) deeper as the rain continued.
4. I have (grew, grown) much closer to my dad.
5. Thick, green ivy has (grew, grown) all over the house.
6. Rita finally (grew, grown) tall enough to play basketball.
7. The pollution problem has (grew, grown) even larger.
8. I (grew, grown) weary of reading, and fell asleep.
9. Some pineapples are (grew, grown) in Puerto Rico.
10. Palm trees have (grew, grown) all over the island.

1. grown
2. grew
3. grew
4. grown
5. grown
6. grew
7. grown
8. grew
9. grown
10. grown

NAME _____

Know
Knew
Known

Hear It Right   Say It Right

Knew and *known* are used correctly in these sentences. *Knew* is used alone, without a helping verb. *Known* is used with a helping verb. Say each sentence to yourself.

1. Judy *knew* that she had passed the test.
2. Our family *has known* the O'Neills for years.
3. *Had* you *known* that Mother was worried?
4. North Carolina *is known* for furniture making.
5. We *knew* that the snow would melt by morning.
6. I always *knew* that Frank was forgetful.
7. How long *have* you *known* Susan?
8. Dogs *are known* for their loyalty.

> Use *knew* alone, without a helping verb.
> Use *known* with the helping verbs *is, are, was, were, has, have,* and *had.*

Write It Right

Underline the correct verb in the parentheses. Then say the sentence to yourself, using the correct verb.

1. Only Gail (knew, known) how to repair the bicycle.
2. John Galvani is (knew, known) as Jackie to his friends.
3. I have never (knew, known) anyone as stubborn as Debra.
4. No one could have (knew, known) that answer.
5. Steve has (knew, known) Carlos since first grade.
6. Our cat Eleanor (knew, known) how to protect herself.
7. Dad never (knew, known) his cousin Rosemary very well.
8. If only I had (knew, known) you were home!
9. Everyone (knew, known) that Mary Ellen was creative.
10. Teachers always (knew, known) when I could do better.

1. knew
2. known
3. known
4. known
5. known
6. knew
7. knew
8. known
9. knew
10. knew

Building English Skills, Silver Level, Teacher's Edition.
Copyright © 1981 by McDougal, Littell & Company, Evanston, Illinois

Hear It Right   Say It Right

Ran and *run* are used correctly in these sentences. *Ran* is used alone, without a helping verb. *Run* is used with a helping verb. Say each sentence to yourself.

Run
Ran
Run

1. The meeting *ran* late.
2. The grocery store *has run* out of milk.
3. Michelle *ran* for class president.
4. *Have* you ever *run* a mile?
5. Our dog never *ran* away.
6. The old car *had* not *run* for years.
7. Who *ran* the record player last?
8. Marathon races *are run* in many cities.

> Use *ran* alone, without a helping verb.
> Use *run* with the helping verbs *is, are, was, were, has, have,* and *had.*

Write It Right

Underline the correct verb in the parentheses. Then say the sentence to yourself, using the correct verb.

1. run
2. ran
3. run
4. run
5. ran
6. run
7. ran
8. run
9. ran
10. run

1. I have never (ran, run) a lawnmower before.
2. Mom stopped writing because she (ran, run) out of ink.
3. Our gym class hasn't (ran, run) the fifty-yard dash yet.
4. Bicycle races are (ran, run) on a bowl-shaped track.
5. Paul (ran, run) the popcorn machine at the circus.
6. The team had (ran, run) out of energy.
7. Cara (ran, run) every morning last summer.
8. The stalled truck must have (ran, run) out of gas.
9. Franklin D. Roosevelt (ran, run) for President four times.
10. Many foreign airlines are (ran, run) by the state.

Building English Skills, Silver Level, Teacher's Edition.
Copyright © 1981 by McDougal, Littell & Company, Evanston, Illinois

NAME _____

Hear It Right Say It Right

See
Saw
Seen

Saw and *seen* are used correctly in these sentences. *Saw* is used alone, without a helping verb. *Seen* is used with a helping verb. Say each sentence to yourself.

1. *Have* you *seen* Billy?
2. I *saw* him in gym.
3. Angeline *has seen* three plays.
4. We *saw* a mysterious looking man.
5. I thought I *had seen* him somewhere before.
6. Darrin *saw* him, too.
7. The cat *was* last *seen* this morning.
8. Who *has seen* Cindy's pocketbook?

> Use *saw* alone, without a helping verb.
> Use *seen* with the helping verbs *is, are, was, were, has, have,* and *had*.

Write It Right

Underline the correct verb in the parentheses. Then say the sentence to yourself, using the correct verb.

1. Joey says he once (saw, seen) a U.F.O.
2. Lorna says she has (saw, seen) a Great White Shark.
3. I think they both have (saw, seen) too many movies.
4. We had (saw, seen) that card trick before.
5. Patty (saw, seen) deer and wild turkey on the island.
6. The game wasn't (saw, seen) on local TV.
7. Have you ever (saw, seen) Johnny Bench in person?
8. Terry (saw, seen) her guests to the door.
9. Has anyone (saw, seen) my pencil?
10. No one (saw, seen) Mark run out the back door.

1. saw
2. seen
3. seen
4. seen
5. saw
6. seen
7. seen
8. saw
9. seen
10. saw

Hear It Right   Say It Right

Sang and *sung* are used correctly in these sentences. *Sang* is used alone, without a helping verb. *Sung* is used with a helping verb. Say each sentence to yourself.

Sing
Sang
Sung

1. Mrs. Hansen usually *sang* while she ironed.
2. Luther *sang* only when there was no one around.
3. "Yankee Doodle" *is* often *sung* on the Fourth of July.
4. After she *had sung* the song twice, Bonita knew it by heart.
5. Mr. Levee *has sung* at all my cousins' weddings.
6. The first graders all *sang* in the Christmas play.
7. *Has* the group *sung* at many concerts?
8. Everyone *sang* the last chorus of the school song.

> Use *sang* alone, without a helping verb.
> Use *sung* with the helping verbs *is, are, was, were, has, have,* and *had.*

Write It Right

Underline the correct verb in the parentheses. Then say the sentence to yourself, using the correct verb.

1. Sam (sang, sung) louder than anyone else in the church.
2. You must have (sang, sung) that song ten times today.
3. During the show, Val (sang, sung) several songs.
4. The bus driver usually (sang, sung) for his passengers.
5. The nightingale (sang, sung) near my window.
6. The opera singer had (sang, sung) several times for royalty.
7. How many movies has Barbra Streisand (sang, sung) in?
8. My family loved the songs my grandfather (sang, sung).
9. Has Fred ever (sang, sung) in the chorus?
10. The fans have (sang, sung) the national anthem.

1. sang
2. sung
3. sang
4. sang
5. sang
6. sung
7. sung
8. sang
9. sung
10. sung

Hear It Right Say It Right

Take
Took
Taken

Took and *taken* are used correctly in these sentences. *Took* is used alone, without a helping verb. *Taken* is used with a helping verb. Say each sentence to yourself.

1. Mom *took* the twins to the movies.
2. *Have* you *taken* your vitamins?
3. Tim *took* his sled to Squirrel Hill.
4. This seat *is taken*.
5. What *took* you so long?
6. Ginger *has taken* her sister to school.
7. I *took* first prize in the art fair.
8. Betty *had* often *taken* a bus before.

> Use *took* alone, without a helping verb.
> Use *taken* with the helping verbs *is, are, was were, has, have,* and *had*.

Write It Right

Underline the correct verb in the parentheses. Then say the sentence to yourself, using the correct verb.

1. Shouldn't we have (took, taken) the Taylor Road bus?
2. Keith (took, taken) out a book about tennis.
3. It has (took, taken) me an hour to get home.
4. Good friends are sometimes (took, taken) for granted.
5. Aunt Charlene might have (took, taken) me to a play.
6. Who (took, taken) the clothes to the cleaners?
7. It has (took, taken) you long enough to get ready.
8. Lucia (took, taken) many pictures on her trip.
9. Peter (took, taken) the baby in the carriage.
10. The injured boy was (took, taken) to the nurse's office.

1. taken
2. took
3. taken
4. taken
5. taken
6. took
7. taken
8. took
9. took
10. taken

NAME _____

Hear It Right   Say It Right

Threw and *thrown* are used correctly in these sentences. *Threw* is used alone, without a helping verb. *Thrown* is used with a helping verb. Say each sentence to yourself.

Throw
Threw
Thrown

1. The baby *threw* all the toys on the floor.
2. Who *threw* my homework in the wastebasket?
3. *Have* you *thrown* out some bread for the birds?
4. Marcia's friends *threw* a surprise party for her.
5. I *have thrown* away those old sneakers of yours.
6. The pitcher *threw* out the runner at first base.
7. My father *had thrown* away all the rusty garden tools.
8. The rider *was thrown* from her horse.

> Use *threw* alone, without a helping verb.
> Use *thrown* with the helping verbs *is, are, was, were, has, have,* and *had.*

Write It Right

Underline the correct verb in the parentheses. Then say the sentence to yourself, using the correct verb.

1. threw
2. thrown
3. threw
4. thrown
5. thrown
6. thrown
7. thrown
8. thrown
9. threw
10. thrown

1. Who (threw, thrown) that rock into the water?
2. Jake had (threw, thrown) the football into the end zone.
3. I finally (threw, thrown) my scrapbook away.
4. Have you (threw, thrown) your dirty clothes into the washer?
5. Kirk had never (threw, thrown) a Frisbee before.
6. Margie had (threw, thrown) water on our old campfire.
7. Many glass bottles are (threw, thrown) away.
8. Who has (threw, thrown) those cards all over the table?
9. Ms. Joski (threw, thrown) the master switch.
10. Jed had (threw, thrown) snow all over the sidewalk.

Hear It Right   Say It Right

Write
Wrote
Written

Wrote and *written* are used correctly in these sentences. *Wrote* is used alone, without a helping verb. *Written* is used with a helping verb. Say each sentence to yourself.

1. Janie *wrote* the note in green ink.
2. *Has* anyone *written* to Uncle George?
3. I *wrote* to him the other day.
4. The report *was written* neatly.
5. *Have* you *written* your name on your paper?
6. Donna *wrote* another story about her brother.
7. Louis *had* never *written* a poem before.
8. Alexis *wrote* her name in Greek.

> Use *wrote* alone, without a helping verb.
> Use *written* with the helping verbs *is, are, was, were, has, have,* and *had.*

Write It Right

Underline the correct verb in the parentheses. Then say the sentence to yourself, using the correct verb.

1. I like the poems that you (wrote, written).
2. Sue has (wrote, written) her name on Richard's cast.
3. Lupé's letter was (wrote, written) in Spanish.
4. My neighbor has (wrote, written) a mystery.
5. Ms. Jacobson (wrote, written) the year in Roman numerals.
6. Have you (wrote, written) to your pen pal?
7. Geraldo should have (wrote, written) in ink.
8. I had (wrote, written) so much that my hand hurt.
9. Have you ever (wrote, written) to a newspaper?
10. I must have (wrote, written) five letters to Sally.

1. wrote
2. written
3. written
4. written
5. wrote
6. written
7. written
8. written
9. written
10. written

Building English Skills, Silver Level, Teacher's Edition.
Copyright © 1981 by McDougal, Littell & Company, Evanston, Illinois

Copy Masters

Diagnostic and Mastery Tests

The Diagnostic Tests. These tests should be given to students before their study of this text. The purpose of the tests is to diagnose which skills the students have mastered from their study of the preceding level of *Building English Skills*.

The tests diagnose the students' skills in the following areas: sentence structure and grammar, usage, capitalization, punctuation, and spelling.

For each test, the maximum score is 100 points.

The Mastery Tests. Each test is designed to be administered immediately after the students have studied the corresponding chapter in *Building English Skills, Silver Level*. The tests measure students' mastery of vocabulary, writing skills, grammar and usage, capitalization, punctuation, and spelling.

Midyear and end-of-year tests are also provided for the purpose of measuring achievement. The midyear test reviews skills included in the mastery tests through Chapter 12; the end-of-year test reviews skills included in the remaining mastery tests.

For each test, the maximum score is 100 points.

McDougal, Littell & Company grants permission to the classroom teacher to reproduce these tests as needed.

Class Record Sheet

May be duplicated for teacher's use

Names

Diagnostic Tests

1.	Learning About Sentences	p. 428
2.	Writing Good Sentences	429
3.	Using Nouns	430
4.	Using Verbs	431
5.	Using Pronouns	432
6.	Using Adjectives	433
7.	Using Adverbs	434
8.	Capitalization	435
9.	Punctuation	436
10.	Spelling	437

Mastery Tests

Chapter	1	Learning New Words	pp. 438–439
Chapter	2	Learning Word Meaning from Context	440–441
Chapter	4	Learning About Sentences	442–445
Chapter	5	Writing Good Sentences	446–447
Chapter	6	Writing Good Paragraphs	448–449
Chapter	7	Ways of Developing Paragraphs	450–451
Chapter	8	Kinds of Paragraphs	452–453
Chapter	9	Using Nouns	454–455
Chapter	10	Using Verbs	456–459
Chapter	11	Using Pronouns	460–461
Chapter	12	Using Irregular Verbs Correctly	462–463

Building English Skills, Silver Level, Teacher's Edition.
Copyright © 1981 by McDougal, Littell & Company, Evanston, Illinois

Names

Mastery Tests continued

Midyear Test	pp. 464–467
Chapter 14 Using the Library	468–469
Chapter 15 Using a Dictionary	470–471
Chapter 16 Using Adjectives	472–473
Chapter 17 Using Adverbs	474–475
Chapter 18 Making Language Lively	476–477
Chapter 19 Writing a Composition	478–479
Chapter 20 Writing a Story	480–481
Chapter 23 Oral and Written Reports	482–483
Chapter 24 Writing Letters	484–485
Chapter 25 Capitalization	486–487
Chapter 26 Punctuation	488–490
Chapter 27 Improving Your Spelling	491–492
End-of-Year Test	493–496

Building English Skills, Silver Level, Teacher's Edition.
Copyright © 1981 by McDougal, Littell & Company, Evanston, Illinois

NAME _____ SCORE _____

Diagnostic Test 1 **Learning About Sentences**

Part 1 Sentences Write **S** on the line before each complete sentence. Write **NS** before each word group that is not a complete sentence. (6 points each)

1. _____ Entered three races.   1. NS
2. _____ French fries and a chocolate shake.   2. NS
3. _____ Laura and Lisa are twins.   3. S
4. _____ Skated all afternoon.   4. NS
5. _____ The bus stops here.   5. S
6. _____ Carol's blue eyes.   6. NS
7. _____ Mr. Guerrero collects music boxes.   7. S
8. _____ Invited Frank and Robin to the party.   8. NS
9. _____ On top of the building.   9. NS
10. _____ The sky is gray.   10. S

Part 2 Kinds of Sentences After each sentence, place the end mark needed. On the line, name the kind of sentence. Write **S** for Statement, **C** for Command, **Q** for Question, or **E** for Exclamation. (8 points each answer)

1. _____ How silly the clown was   1. ! E
2. _____ The elevator stopped at the main floor   2. . S
3. _____ What is your teacher's name   3. ? Q
4. _____ Please pass the salt   4. . C
5. _____ What a great singer she is   5. ! E

NAME _____   SCORE _____

Diagnostic Test 2 **Writing Good Sentences**

Part 1 Recognizing Run-on Sentences Some of these sentences are good sentences and some are run-on sentences. If it is a good sentence, write **S** on the line. If it is a run-on sentence, write **RO** on the line. Also, draw a line between the two ideas in the sentence. (10 points each)

1. RO
     shining | the

2. S

3. RO
     gumball | what

4. RO
     march | there

5. S

6. S

7. RO
     hole | my

1. The sun is shining the sky is blue. _____

2. We visited Mammoth Cave National Park in Kentucky. _____

3. I got a gumball what did you get? _____

4. The band played a march there was a trumpet solo. _____

5. New York City has a very busy harbor. _____

6. On clear nights, you can see many stars. _____

7. My boots have a hole my shoes are wet. _____

Part 2 Improving Stringy Sentences Each of these sentences has 3 thoughts. Take these stringy sentences and separate them into 2 or 3 sentences. Write the new sentences on the line. (10 points each)

1. late. I missed the
     bus. I
     or
     bus. I came
     or
     late. I missed

2. picnic. We played
     baseball. We
     or
     picnic. We played
     or
     baseball. We all

3. pencil. Neil

1. I woke up late and I missed the bus and I came late to school.

_____

_____

2. We went on a picnic and we played baseball and we all took a hike.

_____

_____

3. Kim loaned Neil a pencil and Neil gave it back but it was broken.

_____

_____

Building English Skills, Silver Level, Teacher's Edition.
Copyright © 1981 by McDougal, Littell & Company, Evanston, Illinois

NAME _____ SCORE _____

Diagnostic Test 3 **Using Nouns**

Part 1 Finding Nouns Underline all of the nouns in the following sentences. (7 points each sentence)

1. Motorbikes are very popular in Europe.
2. Rayna found a cat at her back door.
3. The soldiers at Valley Forge showed great courage.
4. The first subway in the United States was built in Boston.
5. My uncle writes for a newspaper.
6. Janice is saving money for a radio.
7. February has an extra day every fourth year.
8. The storm brought strong winds and hail.

1. Motorbikes, Europe
2. Rayna, cat, door
3. soldiers, Valley Forge, courage
4. subway, United States, Boston
5. uncle, newspaper
6. Janice, money, radio
7. February, day, year
8. storm, winds, hail

Part 2 Plurals Write the plural form of each noun. (2 points each)

1. pin _____
2. party _____
3. half _____
4. foot _____
5. lunch _____
6. deer _____
7. woman _____
8. table _____
9. penny _____
10. wish _____

1. pins
2. parties
3. halves
4. feet
5. lunches
6. deer
7. women
8. tables
9. pennies
10. wishes

Part 3 Nouns Showing Ownership Write the underlined word to show possession. (6 points each)

1. the <u>children</u> game _____
2. <u>Pat</u> new radio _____
3. the <u>students</u> test papers _____
4. <u>Jess</u> boots _____

1. children's
2. Pat's
3. students'
4. Jess's

NAME _____   SCORE _____

Diagnostic Test 4 Using Verbs

Part 1 Finding Verbs   Underline the complete verb in each sentence. On the line, tell whether it is an **action** verb or a **state-of-being** verb. (8 points each sentence)

1. gathered   action

2. will finish   action

3. eats   action

4. packed   action

5. has been
    state-of-being

6. grow   action

7. are
    state-of-being

8. found   action

9. can live   action

10. will ride   action

1. _____ The beekeeper gathered honey.

2. _____ Carmine will finish his homework after dinner.

3. _____ Tommy's pet crab eats lettuce.

4. _____ Janet and Marie packed the crates.

5. _____ The sky has been cloudy for days.

6. _____ Roses grow in my garden.

7. _____ My shoes are blue with white stripes.

8. _____ Alicia found a rare nickel.

9. _____ These trees can live for a century.

10. _____ David will not ride his bike tomorrow.

Part 2 Choosing the Correct Verb   Underline the correct verb for each sentence. (4 points each)

1. were

2. itch

3. am

4. gone

5. wins

1. You (was, were) working on that model for weeks.

2. These insect bites (itch, itches).

3. I (be, am) late for school.

4. Emily has (gone, went) home already.

5. Our team (wins, win) the game!

Building English Skills, Silver Level, Teacher's Edition.
Copyright © 1981 by McDougal, Littell & Company, Evanston, Illinois

NAME _____   SCORE _____

Diagnostic Test 5 Using Pronouns

Part 1 Finding Pronouns Underline the pronouns in the following sentences. (6 points each sentence)

1. I saw Ms. Graham in her new car.
2. His raincoat looks just like mine.
3. He and I will paint the signs.
4. The puppy pulled at its leash.
5. My rollerskates cost less than yours.
6. They sent us a postcard from Ontario.
7. She grabbed the ball and passed it to me.
8. Their track team outran ours.
9. You should send your drawings to them.
10. Our apartment is in the same building as theirs.

1. I, her
2. His, mine
3. He, I
4. its
5. My, yours
6. They, us
7. She, it, me
8. Their, ours
9. You, your, them
10. Our, theirs

Part 2 Choosing the Correct Pronoun Underline the correct pronoun in each sentence. (4 points each)

1. Greg and (he, him) are cousins.
2. Sherri coached Chris and (I, me).
3. (Us, We) dancers worked hard.
4. Our dog has lost some of (its, it's) energy.
5. Phillip phoned (we, us) from Chicago.
6. After school (we, us) band members practice.
7. (She, Her) was the host of the show.
8. Bess bought tickets for Pete and (I, me).
9. That mural was painted by (we, us) girls.
10. Raul took a picture of (she, her).

1. he
2. me
3. We
4. its
5. us
6. we
7. She
8. me
9. us
10. her

Building English Skills, Silver Level, Teacher's Edition.
Copyright © 1981 by McDougal, Littell & Company, Evanston, Illinois

NAME _____ SCORE _____

Diagnostic Test 6 Using Adjectives

Part 1 Finding Adjectives On the first line, write the adjective in each sentence. Write the word modified by the adjective on the second line. Ignore *a, an,* and *the.* (3 points each answer)

	Adjective	Word Modified
1.	two	runs
2.	youngest	brother
3.	several	deer
4.	good	food
5.	those	apples
6.	forty	thieves
7.	popular	music
8.	muddy	boots
9.	magic	trick
10.	steep	hill

1. _____ _____ Carlos batted in two runs.
2. _____ _____ The youngest brother is an artist.
3. _____ _____ Several deer slept under the trees.
4. _____ _____ The restaurant serves good food.
5. _____ _____ Put those apples in a basket.
6. _____ _____ Forty thieves hid inside the cave.
7. _____ _____ I listen to popular music.
8. _____ _____ Mike wore muddy boots.
9. _____ _____ Lucia tried a magic trick on me.
10. _____ _____ Carrie climbed the steep hill.

Part 2 Choosing the Correct Adjective Underline the correct adjective for each sentence. (5 points each)

1. Those
2. that
3. better
4. shortest
5. smallest
6. most
7. an
8. hardest

1. (Them, Those) skate blades are too dull.
2. Have you tried (that, those) new kind of paint?
3. Of the two sweaters, the first looks (better, best) on you.
4. Which day is the (shorter, shortest) day of the year?
5. Let's buy the (smaller, smallest) of the three radios.
6. The rose is the (more, most) beautiful flower I know.
7. The plane is over (a, an) hour late.
8. A triple flip is the (most hard, hardest) move to learn.

Building English Skills, Silver Level, Teacher's Edition.
Copyright © 1981 by McDougal, Littell & Company, Evanston, Illinois

NAME _____   SCORE _____

Diagnostic Test 7 Using Adverbs

Part 1 Finding Adverbs Find the adverbs in these sentences. Write them on the lines. (6 points each)

1. _____ We quickly raised the flag.   1. quickly
2. _____ That team always wins the basketball games.   2. always
3. _____ Tom, sit here.   3. here
4. _____ The dog growled angrily.   4. angrily
5. _____ Molly saw that movie yesterday.   5. yesterday
6. _____ The paperboy sometimes forgets our house.   6. sometimes
7. _____ Our class played kickball outside.   7. outside
8. _____ Cats can walk silently.   8. silently
9. _____ Nervously, Josh began his speech.   9. Nervously
10. _____ Tina carefully lifted the butterfly.   10. carefully

Part 2 Using Adverbs Underline the correct word for each sentence below. (5 points each)

1. Of all the motors, this one starts (easiest, most easily).   1. most easily
2. Leon writes (more carefully, carefullier) than Joan.   2. more carefully
3. The team played (bad, badly) in today's game.   3. badly
4. The cat moved (more fast, faster) than the bird.   4. faster
5. This song can be played (more quietly, most quietly) than you play it.   5. more quietly
6. Of the three authors, he writes (more, most) clearly.   6. most
7. Cary handled that problem (good, well).   7. well
8. Snow fell (heavy, heavily) all day long.   8. heavily

NAME _____ SCORE _____

Diagnostic Test 8 **Capitalization**

Part 1 Use Capitals Correctly In these sentences, find the words that should be capitalized. Write them on the line and capitalize correctly. (10 points each sentence)

1. We traveled in south dakota last july.
_____

2. Our neighbor, mr. phil jordan, has a dog named skipper.
_____

3. Many chinese americans live in california.
_____

4. My cousin, dr. jane m. stephens, has her office in this building.
_____

Part 2 First Words and Titles Circle each letter that should be capitalized. (10 points each number)

1. lisa enjoyed reading *little house in the big woods.*

2. "can you do a handstand?" asked wilma.

3. martin said, "all my dreams are in color."

4. paper is two kinds, to write on, to wrap with.

   if you like to write, you write.

   if you like to wrap, you wrap.

   some papers like writers, some like wrappers.

   are you a writer or a wrapper?
   —CARL SANDBURG

5. hans christian andersen wrote "the emperor's new clothes".

6. dear aunt ruth,

Margin answers:

1. South Dakota, July

2. Mr. Phil Jordan, Skippper

3. Chinese, Americans, California

4. Dr. Jane M. Stephens

1. Lisa, Little, House, Big, Woods
2. Can, Wilma
3. Martin, All
4. Paper
   If
   If
   Some
   Are
5. Hans, Christian, Andersen, The, Emperor's, New, Clothes
6. Dear, Aunt, Ruth

Building English Skills, Silver Level, Teacher's Edition.
Copyright © 1981 by McDougal, Littell & Company, Evanston, Illinois

NAME _____ SCORE _____

Diagnostic Test 9 **Punctuation**

Part 1 End Marks Put periods, question marks, and exclamation points where they are needed. (5 points each sentence)

1. P T Barnum was a famous showman
2. This vase was made around 1000 B C
3. What a catch that was
4. Did you see Dr Burnett this morning
5. Robert E Lee was a Civil War general
6. My dancing class begins at 4:00 P M

Part 2 Commas and Apostrophes Put in commas and apostrophes where they are needed in each sentence. (5 points each sentence)

1. Yes Bill Ill call you tonight.
2. The potter molded fired and glazed the bowl.
3. Ms. Marshall was born on May 25 1934 in Ontario Canada.
4. Isnt that Hectors bicycle?
5. Its your turn at bat Andy.
6. "The baby is taking a nap" said Dad.

Part 3 Quotation Marks Punctuate the following sentences correctly. (8 points each sentence)

1. The poem There Will Come Soft Rains is in this book
2. Danny asked Have you done your homework
3. Lets walk to the mailbox said Ronald
4. Where is the bike rack asked Mary Kay
5. Time for lunch yelled the camp cook

---

1. P. T.
   showman.
2. B. C.
3. was!
4. Dr.
   morning?
5. E.
   general.
6. P. M.

1. Yes, Bill,
   I'll
2. molded,
   fired,
3. 25, 1934,
   Ontario,
4. Isn't
   Hector's
5. It's
   bat,
6. nap,"

1. "There . . .
   Rains"
   book.
2. asked, "Have . . .
   homework?"
3. "Let's . . .
   mailbox,"
   Ronald.
4. "Where . . .
   rack?"
   Kay.
5. "Time . . .
   lunch!"
   cook.

Building English Skills, Silver Level, Teacher's Edition.
Copyright © 1981 by McDougal, Littell & Company, Evanston, Illinois

NAME _____   SCORE _____

Diagnostic Test 10 **Spelling**

Part 1 Prefixes and Suffixes Combine the following root words with the suffixes or prefixes given. Drop, change, or add the necessary letters. (5 points each)

1. fattest   6. carefully

2. dislike   7. happier

3. player   8. stopped

4. unlucky   9. thinness

5. famous   10. saving

1. fat + est _____   6. careful + ly _____

2. dis + like _____   7. happy + er _____

3. play + er _____   8. stop + ed _____

4. un + lucky _____   9. thin + ness _____

5. fame + ous _____   10. save + ing _____

Part 2 Finding Spelling Errors Find the misspelled words in the following sentences. Write them correctly on the line. (10 points each sentence)

1. prettiest

1. I think May is the prettyest month of the year.

2. Neither, received

2. Niether runner recieved a prize.

3. busily, pieces

3. Working busyly, Luis sawed the log into peices.

4. their

4. The umpires took thier places.

5. friends, coming

5. Liz's freinds will be comeing to see her.

Building English Skills, Silver Level, Teacher's Edition.
Copyright © 1981 by McDougal, Littell & Company, Evanston, Illinois

NAME _____ SCORE _____

Mastery Test Chapter 1 **Learning New Words**

Part 1 Base Words Underline the base word in each word. (2 points each)

1. misprint
2. trainer
3. relight
4. unafraid
5. marvelous
6. rewrite
7. thankful
8. prewar
9. enjoyable
10. unbutton
11. spoonful
12. shameless
13. quicker
14. nonmember
15. courageous

1. print   9. enjoy
2. train   10. button
3. light   11. spoon
4. afraid   12. shame
5. marvel   13. quick
6. write   14. member
7. thank   15. courage
8. war

Part 2 Prefixes Find the base word and the prefix in each word. Write the word parts on the two lines. (3 points each word)

1. reorder _____ + _____
2. mismanage _____ + _____
3. unpack _____ + _____
4. nonsense _____ + _____
5. rehire _____ + _____
6. prearrange _____ + _____
7. reheat _____ + _____
8. unplug _____ + _____
9. mispronounce _____ + _____
10. misunderstand _____ + _____

1. re + order
2. mis + manage
3. un + pack
4. non + sense
5. re + hire
6. pre + arrange
7. re + heat
8. un + plug
9. mis + pronounce
10. mis + understand

Building English Skills, Silver Level, Teacher's Edition.
Copyright © 1981 by McDougal, Littell & Company, Evanston, Illinois

**Mastery Test
Chapter 1**

NAME _____

Part 3 Suffixes Combine the base word and the suffix. Write the new word. Then, on the line below, write the meaning of the new word. (2 points for the new word, and 2 points for the meaning)

Word   Meaning

1. cheerful—having cheer

1. cheer + ful = _____
_____

2. humorless— without humor

2. humor + less = _____
_____

3. mountainous— full of mountains

3. mountain + ous = _____
_____

4. preacher— a person who preaches

4. preach + er = _____
_____

5. affordable—can be afforded

5. afford + able = _____
_____

6. friendless— without a friend

6. friend + less = _____
_____

7. washable—can be washed

7. wash + able = _____
_____

8. governor— a person who governs

8. govern + or = _____
_____

9. odorous—having an odor

9. odor + ous = _____
_____

10. pocketful—means a pocket that is full

10. pocket + ful = _____
_____

NAME _____ SCORE _____

Mastery Test Chapter 2 **Learning Word Meanings from Context**

Part 1 A Definition in Context   Write the meaning of the underlined word in each sentence. (5 points each)

1. The ship sailed into the fiord. A fiord is a narrow inlet of the sea with steep cliffs.

2. Mark excels in swimming. That is, he is better than the rest.

3. The museum guide showed us a lute, which is an old stringed instrument.

4. Becky and Tom entered a cavern, which is a large cave.

5. You could become an architect, who is a person who designs buildings.

6. The pale yellow rose is exquisite. In other words, it is especially beautiful.

7. The tired hikers discovered a glen. A glen is a mountain valley.

8. Mother took Brad to a pediatrician, who is a doctor who treats children.

1. a narrow inlet of the sea with steep cliffs

2. is best

3. an old stringed instrument

4. a large cave

5. a person who designs buildings

6. especially beautiful

7. a mountain valley

8. a doctor who treats children

Mastery Test
Chapter 2

NAME _____

Part 2 A Restatement in Context Underline the word being defined. Write which kind of key helps you find its meaning. Write one of these: **or**; **D** (for dash); **C** (for command), or **P** (for parentheses). (5 points each line)

1. axis, D

1. The earth rotates on its axis—an imaginary line through its center. _____

2. flint, P

2. He started the fire with flint (a hard stone that makes sparks when struck against steel). _____

3. phantoms, **or**

3. In Dickens's *A Christmas Carol,* three phantoms, or ghosts, appear. _____

4. transformation, **or**

4. The caterpillar underwent a transformation, or change. _____

5. optimist, D

5. Jane is an optimist—one who is always hopeful. _____

6. arsenal, C

6. The troops attacked an arsenal, a place for making or storing weapons. _____

Part 3 An Example in Context Underline the words that tell the definition of the word in italics. (5 points)

1. childhood diseases

1. This shot protects against *diphtheria* and other serious childhood diseases.

2. German cakes

2. I love Grandma's German cakes, especially apple *kuchen*.

3. foreign dishes

3. The restaurant serves foreign dishes, such as *beef stroganoff.*

4. shade-loving plants

4. The gardener chose many shade-loving plants, for instance, *impatiens.*

5. sit-ups and push-up

5. *Calisthenics* like sit-ups and push-ups develop body strength.

6. members of the cat family

6. The zoo has some members of the cat family, for example, *cougars.*

NAME _____ SCORE _____

Mastery Test Chapter 4 **Learning About Sentences**

Part 1 What Is a Sentence?   Write **S** before each group of words that is a complete sentence. Write **F** before each group of words that is only a fragment. (1 point each)

1. _____ On the side of the road.   1. F
2. _____ After the tennis match.   2. F
3. _____ Stirred the fire with a poker.   3. F
4. _____ Timmy jumped.   4. S
5. _____ We forgot.   5. S
6. _____ Janet helps at the newsstand.   6. S
7. _____ Since the last blizzard.   7. F
8. _____ Slowly she opened the door.   8. S
9. _____ The team and its coach.   9. F
10. _____ Voted for class president.   10. F

Part 2 Kinds of Sentences   Add the correct end punctuation mark to each sentence. On the line, write **D** if the sentence is Declarative, **INT** if it is Interrogative, **IMP** if it is Imperative, and **E** if it is Exclamatory. (2 points each)

1. _____ Hundreds of people came to the festival   1. D   .
2. _____ What a fantastic drive that was   2. E   !
3. _____ Sharpen your pencil   3. IMP .
4. _____ What tricks can your dog do   4. INT ?
5. _____ Turn the key the other way   5. IMP .
6. _____ Carolyn likes ice cream sodas   6. D   .

Building English Skills, Silver Level, Teacher's Edition.
Copyright © 1981 by McDougal, Littell & Company, Evanston, Illinois

Mastery Test Chapter 4 NAME _____

Part 3 Complete Subjects and Complete Predicates Draw a line between the complete subject and the complete predicate. (1 point each sentence)

1. Betsy reads fast.
2. Scott O'Dell is a relative of Sir Walter Scott.
3. The trumpeter played a solo.
4. Streaks of lightning flashed through the clouds.
5. Superman came from a faraway planet.
6. That skater practices three hours each day.
7. Ken has a painting in the art show.
8. The farmer's fields were flat and dusty.
9. My grandmother carved that wooden figure.
10. The football player's helmet protects his head.

Part 4 The Simple Predicate, or Verb Draw a line under the simple predicate, or verb, of each sentence. (2 points each sentence)

1. Orville's aunt drives a van.
2. Icy winds blew south from Canada.
3. Roy worked long and hard on his speech.
4. Molly carefully sanded the edge of the pencil holder.
5. The whole family has chicken pox.
6. Ms. Fandell is a birdwatcher.
7. Beverly swam in the Great Salt Lake in Utah.
8. We went to my cousin's wedding last Saturday.
9. That drawing of a chipmunk won first prize.
10. Jim Bridger told tall tales about his adventures.

Side answer key:

Part 3:
1. Betsy | reads
2. Scott O'Dell | is
3. ... trumpeter | played
4. ... lightning | flashed
5. Superman | came
6. ... skater | practices
7. Ken | has
8. ... fields | were
9. ... grandmother | carved
10. ... helmet | protects

Part 4:
1. drives
2. blew
3. worked
4. sanded
5. has
6. is
7. swam
8. went
9. won
10. told

Building English Skills, Silver Level, Teacher's Edition.
Copyright © 1981 by McDougal, Littell & Company, Evanston, Illinois

Mastery Test Chapter 4   NAME _____

Part 5 The Simple Subject, or Subject of the Verb Draw one line under the simple subject in these sentences. (1 point each sentence)

1. This table is made of oak wood.
2. Steven will hang up his jacket.
3. The old lawnmower still does a good job.
4. Dana rides a 10-speed bicycle.
5. The restaurant on the corner makes good ham sandwiches.
6. The smell of lilacs is in the air.
7. The boys in my Scout troop went on a campout.
8. The sailboat on the lake belongs to my aunt.

1. table
2. Steven
3. lawnmower
4. Dana
5. restaurant
6. smell
7. boys
8. sailboat

Part 6 The Subject in Unusual Positions Draw one line under the simple subject and two lines under the verb in each sentence. (1 point each answer)

1. All through the night, the snow fell.
2. After the ghost story nobody slept.
3. Upstream swam the salmon.
4. Last Wednesday our class went on a field trip.
5. On the ceiling a spider crawled.
6. Up the tree scampered the squirrel.
7. Above the clouds the fireworks exploded.
8. Down the street marched the band.
9. In the back yard Sam planted tomatoes.
10. Into the woods ran the fox.

	subjects	verbs
1.	snow	fell
2.	nobody	slept
3.	salmon	swam
4.	class	went
5.	spider	crawled
6.	squirrel	scampered
7.	fireworks	exploded
8.	band	marched
9.	Sam	planted
10.	fox	ran

Mastery Test Chapter 4 NAME _____

Part 7 Tricky Subjects Write the simple subject (s.s.) and the verb (v.) on the lines below each sentence. If the subject is understood to be *you*, write (You). (1 point each line)

1. Buy the funniest mask in the store!

   S.S. _____ V. _____

2. The spaceship landed on a barren planet.

   S.S. _____ V. _____

3. Behind the bookcase was a secret staircase.

   S.S. _____ V. _____

4. Play "The Logical Song" for me.

   S.S. _____ V. _____

5. On a desert island Robinson Crusoe lived for years.

   S.S. _____ V. _____

6. During tryouts, Greg sounded nervous.

   S.S. _____ V. _____

7. At the back of the room was a huge statue.

   S.S. _____ V. _____

8. Let the parakeet out of its cage.

   S.S. _____ V. _____

9. Please follow the guide.

   S.S. _____ V. _____

10. After the game we went for a snack.

    S.S. _____ V. _____

	subject	verb
1.	(You)	buy
2.	spaceship	landed
3.	staircase	was
4.	(You)	play
5.	Robinson Crusoe	lived
6.	Greg	sounded
7.	statue	was
8.	(You)	let
9.	(You)	follow
10.	we	went

Building English Skills, Silver Level, Teacher's Edition.
Copyright © 1981 by McDougal, Littell & Company, Evanston, Illinois

NAME _____   SCORE _____

Mastery Test Chapter 5 **Writing Good Sentences**

Part 1 Run-On Sentences   Write **Correct** by each sentence that is one complete thought. Write **RO** by each run-on sentence. (4 points each)

#	Answer	Sentence	Key
1.	_____	Lynn entered the contest the first prize was a bike.	1. RO
2.	_____	Don't worry about the chair it was old anyway.	2. RO
3.	_____	Mary and Liz switched seats.	3. Correct
4.	_____	Michael knocked all the pins down it was his first bowling game.	4. RO
5.	_____	Billy rode his bike 25 miles in one day.	5. Correct
6.	_____	The apples are ripe now let's make applesauce.	6. RO
7.	_____	I like this book it is a mystery.	7. RO
8.	_____	His stories are always about the future.	8. Correct
9.	_____	Across the lake skimmed the sailboat.	9. Correct
10.	_____	Carlos is a born comedian he really makes me laugh.	10. RO
11.	_____	Chris is sick she has the flu.	11. RO
12.	_____	We made a huge pile of leaves in our back yard.	12. Correct
13.	_____	I rollerskate on the sidewalk sometimes the cracks trip me.	13. RO
14.	_____	The monster rose from the sea it ate the town.	14. RO
15.	_____	Tulips and daffodils bloom early in the year.	15. Correct

Building English Skills, Silver Level, Teacher's Edition.
Copyright © 1981 by McDougal, Littell & Company, Evanston, Illinois

MASTERY TEST   NAME
Chapter 5

Part 2 Avoiding Stringy Sentences Rewrite these stringy sentences as 2 or 3 sentences with correct capitalization and punctuation. (8 points each)

1. Kathy jumped into the pool and the water was cold and she got out again quickly.

   1. Kathy jumped into the pool. The water was cold. She got out again quickly.
      or
      Kathy jumped into the pool. The water was cold and she got out again quickly.

2. The repairman brought in his tools and he took apart the washer and he put in some new parts.

   2. The repairman brought in his tools. He took apart the washer. He put in some new parts.
      or
      . . . tools and he took apart the washer. He put. . . .
      or
      . . . tools. He took apart the washer and he put. . . .

3. Jon took his dog to the vet and the vet gave Jon's dog a shot.

   3. Jon took his dog to the vet. The vet gave Jon's dog a shot.

4. There was a great explosion and the planet blew up and only one spaceship escaped.

   4. There was a great explosion. The planet blew up. Only one spaceship escaped.
      or
      . . . explosion and the planet blew up. Only one. . . .

5. Our family rented a cabin last summer and we canoed on a nearby river and we hiked in the woods.

   5. Our family rented a cabin last summer. We canoed on a nearby river. We hiked in the woods.
      or
      . . . summer. We canoed on a nearby river and we hiked in the woods.

Building English Skills, Silver Level, Teacher's Edition.
Copyright © 1981 by McDougal, Littell & Company, Evanston, Illinois

NAME _____ SCORE _____

Mastery Test Chapter 6 **Writing Good Paragraphs**

Part 1 Sticking to the Main Idea Find the sentence that does **not** tell more about the main idea. Circle the letter of that sentence. (8 points each)

1. a. Many of the foods we eat today are native Indian foods.
   b. The early settlers learned about the foods from the Indians.
   c. Indians in North and South America learned to grow potatoes, corn, and tomatoes long before the white men came.
   d. When Columbus came to America, there were about 10 million people in the Inca tribes.

2. a. The snowshoe hare has a smart way of adapting to winter.
   b. In the winter, its hind feet grow long hairs and its toes spread wide to help it travel in the snow.
   c. Also, it turns from brown to white in the winter to match the snow.
   d. There are many kinds of rabbits.

3. a. On a spring walk you can find many colorful wildflowers.
   b. Wildflower seeds can be bought at garden stores.
   c. The yellow adder's tongue may be seen in the woods.
   d. Lovely bluebells grow in damp, rich soil.

4. a. Birds' nests can be very different.
   b. Some birds dig their nests in the ground.
   c. Many birds fly south in the winter.
   d. Robins build nests of twigs and weeds in tree branches.

5. a. Know your rules for bicycling safety.
   b. Bicycling is fun.
   c. Stop at all stop signs.
   d. Ride on the right side of the road.

1. d.

2. d.

3. b.

4. c.

5. b.

Building English Skills, Silver Level, Teacher's Edition.
Copyright © 1981 by McDougal, Littell & Company, Evanston, Illinois

Mastery Test Chapter 6

NAME _____

Part 2 The Topic Sentence Read these paragraphs. Then write the topic sentence on the line. (10 points each)

 Breakfast is the most important meal of the day. When you eat a good breakfast, you can do better work all morning. You won't get tired so soon. You will be able to think more clearly.

The topic sentence is:

Breakfast is the most important meal of the day.

_____

_____

 People have made up stories about the stars for thousands of years. The ancient Greeks saw hunters, gods, and animals in the star groups. The American Indians saw other people and creatures in the stars. These people and animals were part of fantastic tales and legends.

The topic sentence is:

People have made up stories about the stars for thousands of years.

_____

_____

Part 3 Writing Good Topic Sentences Decide which of these sentences catch your attention. Circle the numbers of the good topic sentences. (8 points each)

Numbers to be circled: 1, 3, 4

1. Yellowstone National Park has some unbelievable sights.

2. Caterpillars change into butterflies.

3. I learned the hard way not to believe everything I read.

4. Not everyone can love a rat, but I love my pet rat Freddie.

5. Earth is the third planet from the sun.

Building English Skills, Silver Level, Teacher's Edition.
Copyright © 1981 by McDougal, Littell & Company, Evanston, Illinois

| NAME _____ | SCORE _____ |

**Mastery Test
Chapter 7** **Ways of Developing Paragraphs**

Part 1 Using Details Here is a list of phrases without details. Add details to each phrase. You may want to change words to make it more specific. (6 points each)

1. a tree _____

2. the sky _____

3. a nose _____

4. the beach _____

5. a garage _____

6. a parade _____

Answers will vary.

Part 2 Developing a Paragraph Using Details Read this paragraph. Make a list of four details the author uses to develop the paragraph. (10 points each)

> I can hardly describe the clothes. The figures were all robed and had crowns on their heads. Their robes were of crimson and silvery grey and deep purple and vivid green: and there were patterns, and pictures of flowers and strange beasts, in needlework all over them. Precious stones of astonishing size and brightness stared from their crowns and hung in chains round their necks.
> —C. S. LEWIS, *The Magician's Nephew*

1. _____

2. _____

3. _____

4. _____

Answers may vary. These are some possible answers:

Figures had robes and crowns.

Robes were of crimson, grey, purple, and green.

Robes had needlework patterns and pictures of flowers and beasts.

There were precious stones on their crowns.

The figures wore chains of precious stones round their necks.

Building English Skills, Silver Level, Teacher's Edition.
Copyright © 1981 by McDougal, Littell & Company, Evanston, Illinois

Mastery Test Chapter 7   NAME _____

Part 3 Developing a Paragraph Using an Example   Tell whether these paragraphs are developed by using details or an example. Write *Details* or *Example* on the line. (8 points each)

　　When water evaporates all by itself, it makes things feel cool. Before you get into your bath, you feel comfortable in the warm room. The warm water feels comfortable, too. But you may begin to shiver as soon as you step out of the tub. The water evaporating from your skin makes you feel cold.

—MAE AND IRA FREEMAN

1. Example   1. _____

　　The forest after a snowfall was unforgettable. The snow glistened like diamonds in the morning sunlight. Each branch of the pine trees looked soft and fluffy. There was not a single sound to disturb the peacefulness of the scene.

2. Details   2. _____

　　Water becomes bigger when it turns into ice. It spreads out and takes up more room. If you put a bottle full of water outdoors on a very cold day, the water will freeze. You will see the ice sticking up out of the bottle. You may cover the bottle as tightly as you can, but you will not stop the push of the ice. It will crack the glass.

—IRA AND MAE FREEMAN

3. Example   3. _____

Building English Skills, Silver Level, Teacher's Edition.
Copyright © 1981 by McDougal, Littell & Company, Evanston, Illinois

NAME _____   SCORE _____

Mastery Test Chapter 8 **Kinds of Paragraphs**

Part 1 The Narrative Paragraph and Time Sequence   Below is a list of events for a narrative paragraph. Number the events in the order they would happen. (4 points each)

1. _____   Ellen broke the window pane with her lamp and shouted, "Fire!"   1. 5

2. _____   Quickly, Ellen crawled on the floor over to the window.   2. 3

3. _____   The smoke alarm buzzed and woke Ellen up.   3. 1

4. _____   She saw smoke oozing under the door to her bedroom.   4. 2

5. _____   She tried to open the window, but it was stuck.   5. 4

Part 2 The Descriptive Paragraph   In this paragraph, the author uses natural order to describe the animal. Number these body parts in the order that he describes them. (4 points each)

    The beast had four big, flat feet about the size of a deflated volley ball. Four long legs with knobby knees came next. On top of the legs was a huge body covered with wooly hair. In the middle of the back were two great humps. Up front a long curved neck led up to an ugly, bony head with stiff hairy ears, big rubbery lips, long yellow front teeth, and beautiful warm brown eyes. It was a camel.

—FRED JOHNSON

1. _____   legs   1. 2

2. _____   neck   2. 4

3. _____   body and humps   3. 3

4. _____   feet   4. 1

5. _____   head and face   5. 5

Building English Skills, Silver Level, Teacher's Edition.
Copyright © 1981 by McDougal, Littell & Company, Evanston, Illinois

Mastery Test NAME _____
Chapter 8

Part 3 The Explanatory Paragraph Number the sentences of this explanatory paragraph in the correct time sequence. The first sentence would be number 1, and so on. (4 points each)

1. 4   1. _____ Tape the matched edges together with splicing tape.

2. 5   2. _____ Finally, run the tape through the projector and check your work.

3. 2   3. _____ First cut each of the broken ends of the film on an angle.

4. 1   4. _____ You can mend your family's broken movie film yourself.

5. 3   5. _____ Next, place the cut ends together so that the angles match up.

Part 4 Kinds of Paragraphs Tell whether each of the following topics would most likely be discussed in a *Narrative, Descriptive,* or *Explanatory* paragraph. (10 points each)

1. Explanatory   1. _____ You can make your own tapshoes using thumbtacks and metal washers.

2. Descriptive   2. _____ The view from the Sears Tower was impressive.

3. Narrative   3. _____ I was fourteen years old when I first met Grandpa.

4. Narrative   4. _____ One night, when I was alone in the house, I heard a strange noise in the basement.

Building English Skills, Silver Level, Teacher's Edition.
Copyright © 1981 by McDougal, Littell & Company, Evanston, Illinois

NAME	SCORE

Mastery Test Chapter 9 **Using Nouns**

Part 1 Finding Nouns Underline all of the nouns in each sentence. (4 points each sentence)

1. Karleen can play the banjo and the guitar.
2. Pepper was the first dog our family had.
3. Bill ate lunch on a hill by the Mississippi River.
4. Does Sharon want cocoa, milk, or lemonade?
5. Mr. Morales has an office in the Sears Tower.
6. The company moved to Houston.
7. Get a glass of cold water, please.
8. Dad lost a suitcase at the airport.
9. My brother saw the Cowboys play in Dallas.
10. Terry draws dragons and unicorns.

Part 2 Proper Nouns Write the proper nouns from each sentence on the blank lines. Capitalize them correctly. (4 points each)

1. Off the coast of california lies catalina island.

_____

2. marcus read books by armstrong sperry and marguerite henry.

_____

3. uncle abe's favorite reporter on "sixty minutes" is dan rather.

_____

4. The poet emily dickinson lived in amherst, massachusetts.

_____

5. kathy visited starved rock state park in illinois.

_____

1. Karleen, banjo, guitar
2. Pepper, dog, family
3. Bill, lunch, hill, Mississippi River
4. Sharon, cocoa, milk, lemonade
5. Mr. Morales, office, Sears Tower
6. company, Houston
7. glass, water
8. Dad, suitcase, airport
9. brother, Cowboys, Dallas
10. Terry, dragons, unicorns

1. California, Catalina Island
2. Marcus, Armstrong Perry, Marguerite Henry
3. Uncle Abe, "Sixty Minutes," Dan Rather
4. Emily Dickinson, Amherst, Massachusetts
5. Kathy, Starved Rock State Park, Illinois

Mastery Test Chapter 9   NAME _____

Part 3 Plural Nouns Write the plural form of the following words.
(2 points each)

1. thief _____   6. wife _____

2. stereo _____   7. tax _____

4. desk _____   8. pony _____

4. sheep _____   9. woman _____

5. tooth _____   10. bunch _____

Answers (left margin):
1. thieves   6. wives
2. stereos   7. taxes
3. desks   8. ponies
4. sheep   9. women
5. teeth   10. bunches

Part 4 Possessive Nouns Make each underlined noun show possession. Write the possessive form of the noun in the blank. (2 points each)

1. _____ My <u>father</u> key chain broke.

2. _____ The <u>girl</u> jacket caught in the door.

3. _____ Where is the <u>children</u> jungle gym?

4. _____ The <u>women</u> group meets on Mondays.

5. _____ Is that <u>Ms. Jones</u> briefcase?

6. _____ The <u>doctor</u> office is on Hay Street.

7. _____ Everyone can fit into <u>Mother</u> car.

8. _____ The <u>boys</u> team lost at volleyball.

9. _____ These <u>animals</u> cages are too small.

10. _____ The <u>dancer</u> costume glittered.

Answers (left margin):
1. father's
2. girl's
3. children's
4. women's
5. Ms. Jones's
6. doctor's
7. Mother's
8. boys'
9. animals'
10. dancer's

Building English Skills, Silver Level, Teacher's Edition.
Copyright © 1981 by McDougal, Littell & Company, Evanston, Illinois

NAME _____   SCORE _____

Mastery Test Chapter 10   **Using Verbs**

Part 1 Action Verbs and State-of-Being Verbs   Underline the verb in each sentence. On the blank, write **A** for Action and **S** for State-of-being. (2 points each sentence)

		Verb
1. _____	Danielle mowed the lawn on Saturday.	1. A mowed
2. _____	I used my allowance on this magazine.	2. A used
3. _____	Leanne's father is from Holland.	3. S is
4. _____	Albert has a good sense of humor.	4. A has
5. _____	That homemade fudge tastes delicious.	5. S tastes
6. _____	Paula juggled three oranges and an apple.	6. A juggled
7. _____	The fire truck raced to the fire.	7. A raced
8. _____	Cary seems tired today.	8. S seems

Part 2 Main Verbs and Helping Verbs   Write the helping verb or verbs on the first blank (**HV**). Write the main verb on the second blank (**MV**). (1 point each answer)

1. Tyrone has written a book of poems.

   HV _____   MV _____

2. The newspapers should have printed the story.

   HV _____   MV _____

3. Mozart could compose whole symphonies in his head.

   HV _____   MV _____

4. Dale probably should have sung the solo part.

   HV _____   MV _____

5. Phoebe's mother has never missed a day of work.

   HV _____   MV _____

HV	MV
1. has	written
2. should have	printed
3. could	compose
4. should have	sung
5. has	missed

Mastery Test Chapter 10 NAME _____

Part 3 Direct Objects Underline the verb in each sentence. Circle the direct object of the verb. (2 points each sentence)

	V.	D. O.
1.	made	planter
2.	checked	wires
3.	wrote	play
4.	hit	Kansas
5.	sang	song
6.	practiced	tricks
7.	may have	pancakes
8.	builds	models

1. Geraldine made this planter.

2. The repairman checked the wires.

3. Alan Alda wrote that play.

4. Last week tornadoes hit Kansas.

5. Cathy and Ilsa sang a song together.

6. Merlin practiced his old tricks.

7. May we have pancakes for breakfast?

8. Mr. Alveraz builds models of famous ships.

Part 4 Using the Right Form of *Be* Underline the correct form of *Be* in each sentence. (2 points each)

1. are
2. am
3. am
4. were
5. were
6. have been
7. was
8. has been

1. Darla and Jean (is, are) co-captains of the team.

2. Tomorrow I (is, am) going to the soccer game.

3. I (be, am) late for baseball practice.

4. I didn't know you (was, were) from Maine.

5. (Was, Were) Brad and Dave still working when you left?

6. I (been, have been) in this theater before.

7. The concert (was, were) well done.

8. Ms. Thomas (been, has been) looking for you.

Mastery Test Chapter 10   NAME _____

Part 5 Using the Right Verb After *There*, *Here*, and *Where* Underline the correct verb in these sentences. (1 point each)

1. Where (is, are) my boots? 1. are
2. Here (is, are) the Van Gogh painting. 2. is
3. There (is, are) two points between the teams. 3. are
4. Where (is, are) the North Star? 4. is
5. There (is, are) twenty-five children in the class. 5. are
6. There (is, are) a fly in my soup. 6. is
7. Here (is, are) your slippers. 7. are
8. Where (is, are) my garden tools? 8. are
9. Here (is, are) Nancy's favorite puzzle. 9. is
10. There (is, are) thirty shopping days until Christmas. 10. are

Part 6 Some Confusing Verbs Underline the correct verb for each sentence. (2 points each)

1. Will those players (set, sit) on the bench for the whole game? 1. sit
2. (Can, May) I invite a friend to dinner? 2. May
3. Carla wouldn't (leave, let) me help her. 3. let
4. Dawn's uncle (taught, learned) her how to play the banjo. 4. taught
5. Mike (can, may) play chess very well. 5. can
6. Be sure to (set, sit) the picnic basket in the shade. 6. set

**Mastery Test
Chapter 10**

NAME _____

Part 7 Contractions Make contractions from the words in parentheses. Write them in the blanks. (1 point each blank)

1. Can't, what's

1. (Can not) you tell me (what is) going on here?

_____   _____

2. We'll, I'm

2. (We will) win the game, (I am) sure.

_____   _____

3. She's, doesn't

3. (She is) a player who just (does not) get tired.

_____   _____

4. He's, isn't

4. (He is) sure that the suspect (is not) the robber.

_____   _____

5. She'd, weren't

5. (She would) help us with the wiring if she (were not) so busy.

_____   _____

Part 8 Using Negatives Correctly Choose the right word from the parentheses. Underline it. (2 points each sentence)

1. any

1. Can't we have (no, any) free time today?

2. anything

2. There wasn't (anything, nothing) left in the refrigerator.

3. any

3. I didn't make (no, any) mistakes on my test.

4. anywhere

4. We didn't go (nowhere, anywhere) on our vacation.

5. none

5. Bill has seen (any, none) of the snapshots yet.

NAME _____ SCORE _____

Mastery Test Chapter 11 **Using Pronouns**

Part 1 Finding Pronouns   Underline all the pronouns in the following sentences. (2 points each sentence)

1. We fanned the fire to keep it going.
2. Laura wrote to him and me from England.
3. Is the mistake yours or mine?
4. They found an old lantern in their cabin.
5. She is my second cousin.

1. We, it
2. him, me
3. yours, mine
4. They, their
5. She, my

Part 2 Using Pronouns   Underline the correct pronoun in each sentence. (2 points each sentence)

1. Francisco and (me, I) are tied for first place.
2. The checkers champs are June and (me, I).
3. The Perlmans gave (us, we) their new address.
4. Mr. Ebsen and (he, him) run a grocery store.
5. The dogs' trainers watched (they, them) carefully.
6. The club's members are Elena and (her, she).
7. (They, Them) and we shared the cost of renting bicycles.
8. The surprise witness was (him, he)!
9. Their neighbors helped (they, them) after the fire.
10. Show (they, them) the poncho you made.
11. (I and Tracey, Tracey and I) both live on Erie Street.
12. Mom gave Kim and (I, me) apples in our lunches.
13. Lia and (him, he) will take swimming lessons.
14. Dad and (we, us) built a picnic table.
15. The tree fell near Brian and (I, me).

1. I
2. I
3. us
4. he
5. them
6. she
7. They
8. he
9. them
10. them
11. Tracey and I
12. me
13. he
14. we
15. me

Building English Skills, Silver Level, Teacher's Edition.
Copyright © 1981 by McDougal, Littell & Company, Evanston, Illinois

Mastery Test Chapter 11   NAME _____

Part 3 Using *We* and *Us*   Decide whether *we* or *us* should be used in each of the sentences below. Write your choice in the blank. (4 points each)

1. _____ dog lovers believe that dogs have feelings.

2. Mr. Krenz sent _____ members an invitation.

3. _____ tourists listened to the museum guide.

4. Those extra pieces of cake are for _____ three.

5. _____ students can make this food drive a success.

Part 4 Possessive Pronouns   On the blank in each sentence, write a possessive pronoun using the information given in parentheses. (4 points each)

1. Did you see _____ new skates? (The skates belong to him.)

2. The trophy is _____. (The trophy belongs to us.)

3. The records and tapes are _____. (The records and tapes belong to them.)

4. The groundhog saw _____ shadow. (The shadow belongs to it.)

5. May we use _____ sewing machine? (The sewing machine belongs to you.)

Part 5 Using *Its* and *It's*   Insert apostrophes where they are needed. (4 points)

1. Its my first day of vacation.

2. My kitten chases its toy mouse.

3. The oak tree has lost all its leaves.

4. Its going to be a hot day.

5. The battleship fired its cannon.

Answers (left margin):

Part 3:
1. We
2. us
3. We
4. us
5. We

Part 4:
1. his
2. ours
3. theirs
4. its
5. your

Part 5:
1. It's
2. (none needed)
3. (none needed)
4. It's
5. (none needed)

NAME _____   SCORE _____

Mastery Test Chapter 12 **Using Irregular Verbs Correctly**

Part 1 Regular Verbs Write the indicated verb form on the line. Remember to use a helping verb when it is needed. (3 points each)

(Helping verbs may vary.)

1. _____ Carol (*love*, present) the book *The Hobbit*. — 1. loves
2. _____ Everyone (*squeeze*, past) into the car. — 2. squeezed
3. _____ Ben's sister (*work*, past) at a bakery last summer. — 3. worked
4. _____ Mr. Grant often (*walk*, past) to his office. — 4. walked
5. _____ I (*try*, past with helping verb) to remember the answer. — 5. have tried
6. _____ Hillary (*climb*, past) the highest mountain. — 6. climbed
7. _____ Lucia sometimes (*trade*, present) her lunch with Fran. — 7. trades
8. _____ A family (*move*, past with helping verb) into the house next door. — 8. has moved
9. _____ The pirates (*bury*, past) the treasure. — 9. buried
10. _____ It (*stop*, past with helping verb) raining. — 10. has stopped
11. _____ The cat (*lick*, past) her paws. — 11. licked
12. _____ Some wrens (*live*, present) in our birdhouse. — 12. live
13. _____ We (*plant*, present) marigolds every spring. — 13. plant
14. _____ Our team (*win*, past with helping verb) the game. — 14. has won
15. _____ We (*hike*, past) up the mountain trail. — 15. hiked
16. _____ Dan (*start*, past with helping verb) a new project. — 16. has started
17. _____ Kate (*paint*, past) a self portrait. — 17. painted
18. _____ Adam and I (*save*, present) string. — 18. save
19. _____ The race car (*crash*, past with helping verb) into the fence! — 19. has crashed
20. _____ The strong winds (*push*, past with helping verb) our boat off course. — 20. have pushed

Building English Skills, Silver Level, Teacher's Edition.
Copyright © 1981 by McDougal, Littell & Company, Evanston, Illinois

Mastery Test Chapter 12 NAME _____

Part 2 Verb Forms Fill in the verb forms for each of the following verbs. (1 point each answer)

	Present	**Past**	**Past with Helping Verb**
1. speak, spoke	1. _____	_____	spoken
2. run, run	2. _____	ran	_____
3. sang, sung	3. sing	_____	_____
4. threw, thrown	4. throw	_____	_____
5. fall, fallen	5. _____	fell	_____
6. taught, taught	6. teach	_____	_____
7. wrote, written	7. write	_____	_____
8. brought, brought	8. bring	_____	_____
9. grow, grown	9. _____	grew	_____
10. began, begun	10. begin	_____	_____
11. drank, drunk	11. drink	_____	_____
12. ride, ridden	12. _____	rode	_____
13. take, took	13. _____	_____	taken
14. knew, known	14. know	_____	_____
15. choose, chosen	15. _____	chose	_____
16. rose, risen	16. rise	_____	_____
17. swam, swum	17. swim	_____	_____
18. break, broke	18. _____	_____	broken
19. did, done	19. do	_____	_____
20. see, seen	20. _____	saw	_____

Building English Skills, Silver Level, Teacher's Edition.
Copyright © 1981 by McDougal, Littell & Company, Evanston, Illinois

NAME _____   SCORE _____

Midyear Test

Part 1 Prefixes and Suffixes Find the base word and the prefix or suffix for each word. Write them on the lines. (1 point each word)

1. shinier = _____ + _____   1. shiny + er

2. unafraid = _____ + _____   2. un + afraid

3. cheerful = _____ + _____   3. cheer + ful

4. likable = _____ + _____   4. like + able

5. reorder = _____ + _____   5. re + order

Part 2 Word Meanings from Context On the first line, write the word that is being defined. On the second line, write the key words or key punctuation that help you find its meaning. (2 points each answer)

1. Magma, that is, molten rock deep in the earth, is extremely hot.
_____ _____
    1. magma
       that is

2. He convinced his partners that his plan was feasible, or possible.
_____ _____
    2. feasible
       or

3. The movie showed many unusual sea creatures, such as a manta ray.
_____ _____
    3. manta ray
       such as

4. Dr. Warshaw is an archeologist—one who studies the life and culture of ancient peoples.
_____ _____
    4. archaeologist
       — (dash)

5. Corrine looked pensive. In other words, she looked thoughtful.
_____ _____
    5. pensive
       in other words

Building English Skills, Silver Level, Teacher's Edition.
Copyright © 1981 by McDougal, Littell & Company, Evanston, Illinois

Midyear Test NAME _____

Part 3 Sentences Write **S** before each group of words that is a complete sentence. Write **NS** before each group of words that is not a complete sentence. (2 points each)

1. _____ Kia chased Brett.

2. _____ Trained in judo and karate by a black belt instructor.

3. _____ On the beach with his brother and sister.

4. _____ The shop was full of toys.

5. _____ The princess danced until midnight.

1. **S**
2. **NS**
3. **NS**
4. **S**
5. **S**

Part 4 Complete Subject and Complete Predicate Draw a line between the complete subject and the complete predicate. (2 points each sentence)

1. The hot sand burned my feet.
2. Mom's wedding ring has three diamonds.
3. The baseball bounced off the fence in left field.
4. Encyclopedia Brown solves difficult cases.
5. The tire on Steve's bike was flat.

1. ... sand | burned
2. ... ring | has
3. ... baseball | bounced
4. ... Brown | solves
5. ... bike | was

Part 5 Run-On and Stringy Sentences Tell whether the sentence is **run-on, stringy,** or **correct.** (2 points each sentence)

1. _____ I went to a ball game and I ate a hot dog and I caught a foul ball.

2. _____ The rain has stopped the sun is shining.

3. _____ The movie was exciting and it was about a race horse and its owner was a little girl.

4. _____ Sharon moved to Florida last year.

5. _____ That singing group is very popular it has a hit record.

1. stringy
2. run-on
3. stringy
4. correct
5. run-on

Building English Skills, Silver Level, Teacher's Edition.
Copyright © 1981 by McDougal, Littell & Company, Evanston, Illinois

Midyear Test NAME _____

Part 6 Paragraphs Read this paragraph. Answer the questions that follow it. (3 points each)

    Linda's lucky tennis shoes were comfortable, but they were an eyesore. The right shoe had a ragged hole at the toe and the shoelace had been broken and retied in two places. The left shoe had lost the stitching around the heel and showed the beginnings of a hole in the toe identical to the right shoe's. Linda was ten years old. Their original white color was now a dirty, unattractive grey.

1. What is the main idea of this paragraph?
_____

2. Underline the topic sentence of this paragraph.
_____

3. Is this paragraph *narrative, descriptive,* or *explanatory?*
_____

4. Was this paragraph developed by *details* or *example?*
_____

5. Draw a line through the sentence that does *not* tell more about the main idea
_____

(Answers may vary.)
1. Linda's lucky tennis shoes were an eyesore.
2. The line should be under the first sentence.
3. descriptive
4. details
5. The line should be through the sentence: Linda was ten years old.

Part 7 Nouns Make the underlined nouns in each sentence show possession. Write it on the line. Also, circle all the other nouns in each sentence. (2 points each sentence)

1. _____ Mrs. Gonzales restaurant serves tacos and tortillas.

2. _____ The old horse leg is lame.

3. _____ Mr. Trent antique clock tells the time perfectly.

4. _____ The three dancers costumes are hanging on the rack.

5. _____ The nurse put bandages on the children cuts.

1. Mrs. Gonzales's
   Circle: restaurant, tacos, tortillas.
2. horse's
   Circle: leg.
3. Mr. Trent's
   Circle: clock, time.
4. dancers'
   Circle: costumes, rack.
5. children's
   Circle: nurse, bandages, cuts.

Building English Skills, Silver Level, Teacher's Edition.
Copyright © 1981 by McDougal, Littell & Company, Evanston, Illinois

Midyear Test NAME _____

Part 8 Verbs Underline the verb in each sentence. Remember that some verbs may need helping verbs. (2 points each sentence)

1. Janice threw another log on the fire.
2. I have found a four-leaf clover.
3. The local theater is showing a monster movie.
4. A porpoise is intelligent and friendly.
5. The hunter could not follow the trail past the creek.

1. threw
2. have found
3. is showing
4. is
5. could follow

Part 9 Choosing the Right Verb Underline the right verb from the verbs in parentheses. (2 points each)

1. Kip (was, were) interested in volcanoes.
2. The mother bird (brought, brang) worms to her babies.
3. Electric power (been, has been) cut by the storm.
4. Sue (chose, choosed) a royal blue bicycle.
5. The club president (call, called) the meeting to order an hour ago.

1. was
2. brought
3. has been
4. chose
5. called

Part 10 Pronouns Underline the right pronoun from the pronouns in parentheses to complete the sentence. (2 points each)

1. Colleen and (me, I) found a robin's egg.
2. Give (them, they) a taste of your tomato sauce.
3. (We, Us) players were really tired.
4. The guide showed the White House to (we, us) visitors.
5. The ocean liner *Titanic* sank on (it's, its) first voyage.

1. I
2. them
3. We
4. us
5. its

NAME _____   SCORE _____

Mastery Test Chapter 14 **Using the Library**

Part 1 Arranging Fiction Books Put the fiction books in this list in the order that you would find them on a library shelf. Number from 1 to 6, with 1 being the first book you would find on the shelf. (5 points each)

_____	Peyton, K. M. *Thunder in the Sky*	4
_____	Wier, Ester. *The Wind Chasers*	6
_____	Neufeld, John. *Edgar Allen*	2
_____	McCaffey, Anne. *Dragonsong*	1
_____	Wier, Ester. *The Loner*	5
_____	North, Sterling. *Rascal: A Memoir of a Better Era*	3

Part 2 Nonfiction Books Decide whether each book in the list is fiction or nonfiction. Write **F** for Fiction and **NF** for Nonfiction. (5 points each)

1. _____ *The Lion, the Witch, and the Wardrobe* — 1. **F**
2. _____ A book about Theodore Roosevelt — 2. **NF**
3. _____ *Betty Crocker's Cookbook for Boys and Girls* — 3. **NF**
4. _____ The adventures of a talking donkey — 4. **F**
5. _____ A mystery about a treasure in an old trunk — 5. **F**
6. _____ A book on how to play better tennis — 6. **NF**

Building English Skills, Silver Level, Teacher's Edition.
Copyright © 1981 by McDougal, Littell & Company, Evanston, Illinois

Mastery Test NAME _____
Chapter 14

Part 3 Using the Card Catalog If you were using a card catalog to find these items, would you be looking for an **author** card, a **title** card, or a **subject** card? (4 points each)

1. title

2. author

3. subject

4. title

5. subject

6. title

7. author

1. _____ *Song of the Shaggy Canary*

2. _____ books by Joan Aiken

3. _____ a book about sharks

4. _____ *Watching the Wild Apes*

5. _____ a book about Clara Barton

6. _____ *Chocolate War*

7. _____ books by Edward Eager

Part 4 Finding Information in a Book Complete these sentences. (4 points each)

1. table of contents

2. index

3. index

1. At the front of every nonfiction book is a _____ _____. It lists the title of every chapter and the page on which it begins.

2. At the end of most nonfiction books is an _____. It is an alphabetical list of topics discussed in the book.

3. If you are looking for specific information such as definitions, lists, or dates, look in the _____.

Building English Skills, Silver Level, Teacher's Edition.
Copyright © 1981 by McDougal, Littell & Company, Evanston, Illinois

Mastery Test Chapter 15 **Using a Dictionary**

Part 1 Using Alphabetical Order Rewrite these three sets of words in alphabetical order. (2 points each word)

1. _____ stall
2. _____ fright
3. _____ mirror
4. _____ bundle
5. _____ movable

1. _____ alley
2. _____ ability
3. _____ amber
4. _____ allure
5. _____ address

1. bundle   1. ability
2. fright   2. address
3. mirror   3. alley
4. movable 4. allure
5. stall   5. amber

1. _____ mound
2. _____ middle
3. _____ muddy
4. _____ munch
5. _____ mold

1. middle
2. mold
3. mound
4. muddy
5. munch

Part 2 Using Guide Words By using the sample guide words, write the page on which each of the given words would be found. (5 points each)

304	305	306
dare-demand	**deputy-diction**	**diet-disturb**

1. _____ dialect
2. _____ decoy
3. _____ dilute

4. _____ daughter
5. _____ direct
6. _____ describe

1. 305   4. 304
2. 304   5. 306
3. 306   6. 305

470

Building English Skills, Silver Level, Teacher's Edition.
Copyright © 1981 by McDougal, Littell & Company, Evanston, Illinois

470

Mastery Test Chapter 15 NAME _____

Part 3 Using a Dictionary Entry Answer the questions about the following dictionary entry from *Websters New World Dictionary for Young Readers*. (5 points each)

> **hall** (hôl), *n.* **1.** a passageway from which doors open into various rooms. **2.** a room or passageway at the entrance of a building. **3.** a large room used for meetings, shows, dances, etc. **4.** a building containing public offices or a headquarters of some sort [the city *hall*]. **5.** any of the buildings of a college, especially a dormitory. **6.** the large country house of a baron, squire, etc.

1. Copy the pronunciation of *hall*. _____

2. How many syllables are there in *hall*? _____

3. Are there any accent marks in the respelling of *hall*? _____

4. What part of speech is *hall*? _____

How is *hall* used in the following sentences? Write the number of the correct definition next to the sentence.

5. _____ The company rented a hall for the convention.

6. _____ His office is down at the end of the hall.

7. _____ There will be a rally at the town hall next Thursday.

8. _____ At college, my brother lives in Murphy Hall.

---

1. hôl
2. one
3. No
4. noun
5. 3
6. 1
7. 4
8. 5

NAME _____   SCORE _____

Mastery Test Chapter 16 **Using Adjectives**

Part 1 Finding Adjectives Draw a line under the adjectives in each sentence. Ignore *a, an,* and *the.* (3 points each sentence)

1. I took the biggest cookie on the plate.
2. The hopeful runner trained for the big race.
3. Some people skated on the icy pond.
4. The fastest swimmer won the race.
5. A bright light flashed a warning.
6. The happy guests brought colorful presents.
7. A poisonous spider crawled under the leaves.
8. Three girls are working the difficult puzzle.
9. These flowers bloom in the shade.
10. The beach is busy on hot days.

1. biggest
2. hopeful, big
3. some, icy
4. fastest
5. bright
6. happy, colorful
7. poisonous
8. Three, difficult
9. These
10. busy, hot

Part 2 Adjectives Tell *What Kind, How Many,* or *Which Ones* Decide whether the underlined adjective tells *what kind, how many,* or *which ones.* Write the answer on the line. (4 points each)

1. _____ The restless lion paced around his cage.
2. _____ A baseball team needs nine players.
3. _____ Is Kurt hiding among those trees?
4. _____ A sudden wind sprang up.
5. _____ Ms. Baker chose a few children for the project.

1. what kind
2. how many
3. which ones
4. what kind
5. how many

Mastery Test Chapter 16   NAME _____

Part 3 Using Adjectives Correctly Underline the correct word from the two or three in parentheses. (3 points each)

1. an
2. those
3. an
4. these
5. this
6. a
7. those
8. Those
9. those
10. that

1. Would you like (a, an) egg for breakfast?
2. Eddie picked some of (those, them) flowers for a bouquet.
3. The show begins in (a, an) hour.
4. The farm has (this, these, them) kinds of vegetables.
5. I forgot to study (these, this) kind of problem.
6. The mailman delivered (a, an) package.
7. Karen rollerskates with (them, those) girls every day.
8. (Them, Those) kinds of snakes are dangerous.
9. Where did you buy (them, those) jeans?
10. I always choose (those, that) kind of ice cream.

Part 4 Making Comparisons with Adjectives Draw a line under the correct word in parentheses. (4 points each)

1. best
2. more
3. most beautiful
4. worst
5. sharper

1. This was the team's (better, best) year yet.
2. The second problem was the (more, most) difficult of the two.
3. The Badlands is one of the (beautifulest, most beautiful) places in the West.
4. That's the (worst, worse) song I ever heard.
5. Of the two cameras, that one takes (sharper, sharpest) pictures.

Building English Skills, Silver Level, Teacher's Edition.
Copyright © 1981 by McDougal, Littell & Company, Evanston, Illinois

NAME _____ SCORE _____

Mastery Test Chapter 17 **Using Adverbs**

Part 1 Finding Adverbs   Find each adverb. Write it on the first line under each sentence. On the second line, write the word that the adverb modifies. (2 points each answer)

	Adverb	Word Modified
1. This brass bed is very old.	1. very	old
2. Turn the pages of that book carefully.	2. carefully	turn
3. Winter vacation starts tomorrow.	3. tomorrow	starts
4. We quickly climbed the rocky cliffs.	4. quickly	climbed
5. I saw an awfully funny movie.	5. awfully	funny
6. The lion stalked the zebra silently.	6. silently	stalked
7. One old house was completely empty.	7. completely	empty
8. The raindrops splashed everywhere.	8. everywhere	splashed
9. I often telephone my friend Marcy.	9. often	telephone
10. Your package arrived early.	10. early	arrived

Mastery Test   NAME
Chapter 17

Part 2 Making Comparisons with Adverbs   Underline the correct word in each sentence. (3 points each)

1. The American team swam (faster, fastest) than the Canadian team.
2. Of all these model trains, the Zephyr runs (more smoothly, most smoothly).
3. Ronald does a handstand (more well, better) than Alan.
4. The movie started (later, more late) than it was supposed to.
5. Between radishes and carrots, I like radishes (less, least).
6. The falcon flew (more high, higher) than the other birds.
7. Jenny worked (harder, more harder) than anyone else.
8. Which animal walks (more quietly, most quietly), a mouse or a cat?
9. Donna sang (more better, better) after she took voice lessons.
10. Which of the three kites flies (higher, highest)?

1. faster
2. most smoothly
3. better
4. later
5. less
6. higher
7. harder
8. more quietly
9. better
10. highest

Part 3 Adjective or Adverb   Underline the correct word in each sentence. (3 points each)

1. Please handle those glasses (careful, carefully).
2. Emil looked (closely, close) at the coin.
3. Maria has a (bad, badly) cut on her finger.
4. Mr. Goodman keeps his room (warm, warmly).
5. Charles answered the phone (sleepy, sleepily).
6. Did you study (good, well) for the quiz?
7. Ms. Chase spoke (clearly, clear) over the loudspeaker.
8. The cat's eyes looked (bright, brightly).
9. Press (strong, strongly) on your pen to make three copies.
10. Darrell was (happy, happily) when he got back to school.

1. carefully
2. closely
3. bad
4. warm
5. sleepily
6. well
7. clearly
8. bright
9. strongly
10. happy

Building English Skills, Silver Level, Teacher's Edition.
Copyright © 1981 by McDougal, Littell & Company, Evanston, Illinois

NAME _____ SCORE _____

Mastery Test Chapter 18 **Making Language Lively**

Part 1 Using Strong Verbs Change each sentence by writing in the blank a stronger verb from the list. (3 points each)

galloped	struggled	pedaled	bloomed
spied	zig-zagged	strummed	hurled
shouted	triumphed	snatched	gripped

1. The bee flew from flower to flower.

    The bee _____ from flower to flower.   1. zig-zagged

2. The sergeant told the orders to his men.

    The sergeant _____ the orders to his men.   2. shouted

3. The country music star played his guitar.

    The country music star _____ his guitar.   3. strummed

4. The pitcher threw the ball to the catcher.

    The pitcher _____ the ball to the catcher.   4. hurled

5. The horses went around the race track.

    The horses _____ around the race track.   5. galloped

6. Mike caught the ball just before it went over the fence.

    Mike _____ the ball just before it went over the fence.   6. snatched

7. Many flowers were in the meadow.

    Many flowers _____ in the meadow.   7. bloomed

8. Our team won at the track meet.

    Our team _____ at the track meet.   8. triumphed

9. I saw a bluejay and a cardinal.

    I _____ a bluejay and a cardinal.   9. spied

10. Jerry rode his bicycle up the hill.

    Jerry _____ his bicycle up the hill.   10. pedaled

Building English Skills, Silver Level, Teacher's Edition.
Copyright © 1981 by McDougal, Littell & Company, Evanston, Illinois

Mastery Test   NAME _____
Chapter 18

Answers will vary.

Part 2 Writing Similes Complete each sentence with a simile. (5 points each)

1. His beard was as tangled as _____.

2. Diane balanced on the fence like a _____.

3. The hot, dry beach was like a _____.

4. The woodpecker sounds like a _____.

5. The basement was colder than _____.

6. The frightened bird flew off like a _____.

Part 3 Writing Metaphors Decide whether each sentence contains a **simile** or a **metaphor**. Write the answer on the line. (4 points)

1. Metaphor	1. _____	The rain hammered on the roof.
2. Simile	2. _____	The raccoon's call sounded like a child's cry.
3. Metaphor	3. _____	The dandelions are a carpet of gold.
4. Metaphor	4. _____	The sound of the horn cut through the fog.
5. Simile	5. _____	The baby opened his mouth for the bottle like a hungry baby bird.
6. Metaphor	6. _____	The locked car was an oven.
7. Metaphor	7. _____	The audience buzzed with excitement.
8. Simile	8. _____	The biscuit tasted like old cardboard.
9. Metaphor	9. _____	The aspen leaves whispered in the wind.
10. Metaphor	10. _____	His mind is a storehouse of information.

Building English Skills, Silver Level, Teacher's Edition.
Copyright © 1981 by McDougal, Littell & Company, Evanston, Illinois

NAME _____ SCORE _____

Mastery Test Chapter 19 — **Writing a Composition**

Part 1 What Is a Composition? Complete each sentence with the correct term. (8 points each)

composition   body paragraph
introductory paragraph   ending paragraph

1. A group of paragraphs that work together to explain an idea is a _____.   1. composition

2. A good _____ ties together the rest of the composition.   2. ending paragraph

3. The _____ tells what the composition is about.   3. introductory paragraph

4. A _____ explains the idea presented in the first paragraph.   4. body paragraph

Part 2 Finding a Subject The following list shows ideas for a composition about making a puppet. On the blank before each idea, write either **MI** for main idea or **D** for details. (8 points each answer)

1. _____ It was hard to find the right material for the hair.   1. **D**

2. _____ I drew the puppet outline on my material.   2. **MI**

3. _____ The puppet has a patch over its left eye.   3. **D**

4. _____ I found the materials I needed.   4. **MI**

5. _____ I decided to make a pirate puppet.   5. **MI**

Mastery Test Chapter 19 NAME _____

Part 4 The Introductory Paragraph This is **not** a good introductory paragraph. Tell two mistakes the author made in writing this paragraph. (10 points each)

> The usher showed us to our seats. My cousin was graduating from high school. She had extra tickets so mom and I went to the auditorium. I waved to my cousin as she marched into the room.

1. The order of sentences is mixed up.
2. The first sentence is dull and doesn't make you want to read the rest.
3. There is no indentation.
4. *Mom* should be capitalized.

1. _____

2. _____

Part 5 Writing the Body Paragraph and Completing the Composition One of these paragraphs is a body paragraph and one is an ending paragraph. Write **Body** next to the body paragraph and **Ending** next to the ending paragraph. (10 points each)

Ending _____ After all that work, I'm glad to say that the snow didn't melt soon. We were able to play in our forts every day for three weeks.

Body _____ Soon Joan and I decided that we both needed forts for protection from each other's snowballs. We rolled huge balls of snow and set them side by side. We packed snow between to hold them together. The completed snow forts faced each other across our back yards.

| NAME | SCORE |

Mastery Test Chapter 20 **Writing a Story**

Part 1 What Is a Story? Read this story. Then tell the main events of the story in the correct time sequence. (4 points each)

Roy loved his home near the ocean, but he was not perfectly happy. He liked walking down the beach and listening to the roar of the waves. But that was just not enough for him. He wished that he could be a fish himself and live in the sea.

One day, Roy was swimming in the ocean when a fish swam up to him and said, "Follow me." Roy looked down at himself and saw that he had turned into a fish. His wish had come true.

Roy followed the fish down to a beautiful cave. There he met other fish who were all friends because they were all in the same school.

Roy met a jellyfish and a seahorse. They were both very friendly too. "But be careful," said the fish. "Not everyone down here is your friend."

Suddenly, a shadow fell over the ocean floor. A huge shark glided by. He looked hungry. All the fish and other creatures swam away in fear. Roy decided it was time to go back home.

Soon the shark went on with his search. Roy thanked all his fish friends for their kindness and swam back to the surface. As soon as his head touched the air, he turned back into a boy. He was glad that he had had the chance to be a fish, but even more glad that he was again a boy who lived on dry land.

1. _____
2. _____
3. _____
4. _____
5. _____
6. _____

Answers may vary somewhat.
1. Roy wished to be a fish.
2. He turned into a fish.
3. He swam with a fish to a cave.
4. He met other fish and sea creatures.
5. A shark swam by.
6. Roy turned back into a boy.

Building English Skills, Silver Level, Teacher's Edition.
Copyright © 1981 by McDougal, Littell & Company, Evanston, Illinois

**Mastery Test
Chapter 20**   NAME _____

Answers will vary.

Part 2 Planning a Story   Here are some characters that could be used in a story. Tell, in a few words, something that could happen to them in a real or fantastic story. (10 points each)

1. A dog who can talk _____
_____

2. A Scout group on an overnight campout _____
_____

3. A family that buys a van that can fly _____
_____

4. A girl who invents a time machine _____
_____

5. A boy who moves to a new neighborhood _____
_____

Part 3 Writing a Story   Pick one of the story ideas you made up in Part 2. Write an introductory paragraph that will tell something about the story and characters, and will catch the reader's interest. (26 points)

Answers will vary.

_____
_____
_____
_____

Building English Skills, Silver Level, Teacher's Edition.
Copyright © 1981 by McDougal, Littell & Company, Evanston, Illinois

NAME _____ SCORE _____

**Mastery Test
Chapter 23** **Oral and Written Reports**

Part 1 Finding a Subject   Each of these subjects is too broad for a short report. Think of one small part of the subject that could be a topic for a short report. Write the topic on the line. (5 points each)

1. Birds _____

2. Energy sources _____

3. Holidays _____

4. Vegetables _____

5. Games children play _____

Answers will vary.

Part 2 Gathering Information and Making a Plan   This information could be found on note cards for a report. Read each group of ideas and decide what the main idea is. Write the main idea as a sentence. (10 points each)

   1. Wool is a cloth made from the hair of a sheep.
     Cotton cloth is made from the cotton plant.
     Some cloths are made from man-made fibers such as nylon and polyester.

_____

   2. Many people read books for pleasure.
     Some books are read for information.
     Small children sometimes use books just to look at the pictures.

_____

Answers will vary.
1. Different cloths are made in many different ways.

2. There are many reasons why people read books.

Building English Skills, Silver Level, Teacher's Edition.
Copyright © 1981 by McDougal, Littell & Company, Evanston, Illinois

Mastery Test Chapter 23   NAME _____

Part 3 Making an Outline   Organize these ideas into the outline below. (5 points each)

Planets far from the sun   Which planets have moons
How asteroids were formed   Where we find asteroids
How comets are formed   How moons were formed
Planets close to the sun   Where we find meteors

The Solar System

I. Introduction

II. Planets

   A. _____

   B. _____

III. Moons

   A. _____

   B. _____

IV. Asteroids

   A. _____

   B. _____

V. Meteors and Comets

   A. _____

   B. _____

VI. Ending

(Order of ideas may vary.)
- II. A. The planets close to the sun
  - B. The planets that are far from the sun
- III. A. How moons were found
  - B. Which planets have moons
- IV. A. How asteroids were found
  - B. Where we find asteroids
- V. A. Where we find meteors
  - B. How comets are formed

Part 4 Writing a Report   Here are some sentences that could be used in an ending paragraph for the report on the solar system. If the sentence is a **good** ending sentence, write **G.** If it is **not good**, write **NG.** (5 points each)

1. __**NG**__   So, the sun has many things going around it.

2. __**NG**__   That's all I know about the solar system.

3. __**G**__   Think of those wonderful neighbors of ours when you look up into the sky tonight.

Building English Skills, Silver Level, Teacher's Edition.
Copyright © 1981 by McDougal, Littell & Company, Evanston, Illinois

NAME _____ SCORE _____

Mastery Test Chapter 24 **Writing Letters**

Part 1 Writing a Friendly Letter Copy these words and phrases. Capitalize and punctuate them as if they were in a letter. (5 points each)

1. sincerely yours _____
2. 3865 bryden road _____
3. dear aunt sarah _____
4. lincoln nebraska _____
5. may 14 1981 _____

    1. Sincerely yours,

    2. 3865 Bryden Road

    3. Dear Aunt Sarah,

    4. Lincoln, Nebraska

    5. May 14, 1981

Part 2 Addressing Envelopes Address this envelope, using your own name and address in the return address. Address the envelope to Steven Parker, 1613 Third Street, Mentor, Ohio 44060.

10 points

10 points

Answers will vary for return address

Steven Parker

1613 Third Street

Mentor, Ohio 44060

Building English Skills, Silver Level, Teacher's Edition.
Copyright © 1981 by McDougal, Littell & Company, Evanston, Illinois

Mastery Test Chapter 24 NAME _____

Part 3 Writing Business Letters Write a letter of request asking for the following information. Use your own name and address, and today's date. Write to the State Department of Commerce of West Virginia to get information about campgrounds for a family vacation. The address is State Department of Commerce, Room 2022, Charleston, West Virginia 25305.

Answers will vary for all but Inside Address:

State Department of Commerce

Room 2022

Charleston, West Virginia 25305

Heading _____
_____
_____
(10 points)

Inside Address
_____
_____
_____ (15 points)

Greeting
_____ (5 points)

Body
_____
_____
_____
_____
(20 points)

Closing _____
(5 points)

Signature _____

NAME _____ SCORE _____

Mastery Test Chapter 25 **Capitalization**

Part 1 Proper Nouns and Adjectives Copy these words, changing small letters to capitals where it is needed. After each word, write the group it belongs to: **CN** for common noun; **PN** for proper noun, or **PA** for proper adjective. (2 points each answer)

1. alaska   _____ _____
2. christmas _____ _____
3. birthday _____ _____
4. irish   _____ _____
5. france   _____ _____
6. picnic   _____ _____
7. french   _____ _____

1. Alaska	PN	
2. Christmas	PN or PA	
3. birthday	CN	
4. Irish	PA or PN	
5. France	PN	
6. picnic	CN	
7. French	PA or PN	

Part 2 Some Kinds of Proper Nouns Circle the letters that should be capitalized in each sentence. (3 points each sentence)

1. One of hannah's favorite desserts is boston cream pie.
2. What do we call the mountains in chile?
3. The polio vaccine was first made by dr. jonas e. salk.
4. Many of the prayers in the jewish and christian religions are similar
5. My sister heard professor bernard speak at northwestern university.
6. In chicago, the swiss embassy is on michigan avenue.
7. On arbor day, oxford school has a tree planting ceremony.
8. The wright brothers made their first airplane flight on december 17, 1903.
9. president lincoln gave a memorable speech at gettysburg, pennsylvania.

1. Hannah's, Boston
2. Chile
3. Dr. Jonas E. Salk
4. Jewish, Christian
5. Professor Bernhard, Northwestern University
6. Chicago, Swiss, Michigan Avenue
7. Arbor Day, Oxford School
8. Wright, December
9. President Lincoln, Gettysburg, Pennsylvania

Mastery Test Chapter 25   NAME _____

Part 3 First Words and Titles Circle all letters that should be capitalized. (10 points each number)

1. **Poem**   twinkle, twinkle, little bat!

           twinkle, twinkle little bat

           how I wonder what you're at?

           up above the world you fly,

           like a tea-tray in the sky.

2. **Outline**   great buildings

          I. tallest

            A. sears tower

            B. world trade center

          II. largest ground area

            A. pentagon

            B. merchandise mart

3. **Letter**

dear kevin,

    thank you for the painting you sent me. i showed it to my art teacher. he said, "this is good work!"

                           sincerely,

                           peggy

Part 4 Capitalizing Titles Copy these titles. Capitalize them correctly. (3 points each)

1. "my favorite word" (poem) _____

2. "the red shoes" (story) _____

3. *a wrinkle in time* (book) _____

4. *breaking away* (movie) _____

5. *ben and me* (book) _____

Answers (left margin):

1. Twinkle, Twinkle Little Bat
   Twinkle
   How
   Up
   Like

2. Great Buildings
   Tallest
      Sears Tower
      World Trade Center
   Largest ground area
      Pentagon
      Merchandise Mart

3. Dear Kevin,
   Thank. . . . I. . . .
      He said, "This. . . .
         Sincerely,
      Peggy

1. "My Favorite Word"
2. "The Red Shoes"
3. *A Wrinkle in Time*
4. *Breaking Away*
5. *Ben and Me*

Building English Skills, Silver Level, Teacher's Edition.
Copyright © 1981 by McDougal, Littell & Company, Evanston, Illinois

Mastery Test Chapter 26 — **Punctuation**

Part 1 The Period Copy these phrases using the correct punctuation. Some phrases need no additional punctuation. (1 point each)

1. Dr Anita Perez _____ 1. Dr. Anita Perez
2. Dec 7, 1941 _____ 2. Dec. 7, 1941
3. 1 lb , 2 oz _____ 3. 1 lb., 2 oz.
4. 60 km _____ 4. 60 km
5. William C Kelly, Jr _____ 5. William C. Kelly, Jr.
6. 2:00 P M _____ 6. 2:00 P.M.
7. 79 A D _____ 7. 79 A.D.
8. 4 mm _____ 8. 4 mm
9. 10 min _____ 9. 10 min.
10. Euclid Ave _____ 10. Euclid Ave.

Part 2 The Period, Question Mark, and Exclamation Point Put the correct end punctuation on these sentences. (2 points each)

1. Is the forecaster predicting rain 1. ?
2. Hurry Follow that car 2. Hurry! Follow that car!
3. I found a sand dollar in a tidepool 3. .
4. How tall the grass has grown 4. !
5. Why is our galaxy called the Milky Way 5. ?

Mastery Test Chapter 26   NAME _____

Part 3 The Comma Insert commas in these sentences and phrases where they are needed. (2 points each)

1. The restaurant serves steaks chops and seafood.
2. Ryan you may give your report now.
3. On May 8 1945 World War II ended in Europe.
4. "Today is my birthday " said Maya.
5. Lightning flashed across the sky and thunder rumbled loudly.
6. My aunt lives in St. Paul Minnesota.
7. No that is not my jacket.
8. (letter) Dear Uncle Warren
9. Terry Kia and Darla went to the library.
10. Ms. Jackson visited Mexico City Mexico.
11. Is January 1 1990 the first day of the decade?
12. Dennis shouted "I'll race you home!"
13. (letter) Yours truly
14. I think Reggie that it is your turn.
15. The motor in the bus made strange noises but it finally started.

Part 4 Titles and Underlining Underline or put quotation marks around these titles. (2 points each)

1. The Wizard of Oz (book)
2. The Old Wife and the Ghost (poem)
3. Mount St. Helens Erupts (newspaper article)
4. Half Magic (book)
5. How the Leopard Got Its Spots (story)

Answers (margin):

1. steaks, chops,
2. Ryan,
3. 8, 1945,
4. birthday,
5. sky,
6. Paul,
7. No,
8. Warren,
9. Terry, Kia, and Darla
10. City,
11. 1, 1990,
12. shouted,
13. truly,
14. think, Reggie,
15. noises,

1. <u>The Wizard of Oz</u>
2. "The . . . Ghost"
3. "Mount . . . Erupts"
4. <u>Half Magic</u>
5. "How . . . Spots"

Building English Skills, Silver Level, Teacher's Edition.
Copyright © 1981 by McDougal, Littell & Company, Evanston, Illinois

Mastery Test NAME
Chapter 26

Part 5 The Apostrophe Write the underlined word with correct punctuation. (2 points each)

1. <u>shes</u> _____
2. the <u>dog</u> leash _____
3. <u>Nancy</u> cousin _____
4. <u>theyve</u> _____
5. <u>isnt</u> _____

6. the <u>snails</u> shells _____
7. <u>Im</u> _____
8. the <u>students</u> reports _____
9. <u>wont</u> _____
10. <u>James</u> sister _____

1. she's   6. snails'
2. dog's   7. I'm
3. Nancy's 8. students'
4. they've 9. won't
5. isn't   10. James's

Part 6 Quotation Marks Rewrite these sentences with the correct punctuation. (4 points each sentence)

1. Ms. Calabrese said We'll sing this song at the concert

2. This popcorn complained Josh has too much salt

3. Sally called Where did you put the door key

4. I'll go sledding with you said Matt

5. This rock is quartz Mr. Wright said.

1. Ms. Calabrese said, "We'll sing this song at the concert."

2. "This popcorn," complained Josh, "has too much salt."

3. Sally called, "Where did you put the door key?"

4. "I'll go sledding with you," said Matt.

5. "This rock is quartz," Mr. Wright said.

Building English Skills, Silver Level, Teacher's Edition.
Copyright © 1981 by McDougal, Littell & Company, Evanston, Illinois

NAME _____   SCORE _____

Mastery Test Chapter 27   **Improving Your Spelling**

Part 1 Recognizing Spelling Errors   There is one spelling error in each of the following sentences. Write the misspelled word correctly on the line. (4 points each sentence)

1. weird

1. We were glad when the wierd noises stopped.

2. misspelled

2. That sign has a mispelled word.

3. carried

3. The ski patrol carryed the injured skier down the slope.

4. stories

4. My favorite storys are about pioneers.

5. usually

5. Joanna usualy walks home from school with me.

6. hoping

6. I am hopeing you can come to my party.

7. said

7. Brad sayed that he would be late for dinner.

8. confusion

8. During all the confuseion, we were unable to find each other.

9. hiking

9. The earliest we ever went hikeing was 5 A. M.

10. biggest

10. The bigest package does not always have the best present.

Building English Skills, Silver Level, Teacher's Edition.
Copyright © 1981 by McDougal, Littell & Company, Evanston, Illinois

Mastery Test Chapter 27   NAME _____

Part 2 Prefixes and Suffixes Combine the root words with the prefixes and suffixes given. Drop, add, or change letters as needed. (3 points each)

1. im + mature _____
2. open + ness _____
3. spin + ing _____
4. same + ness _____
5. heavy + est _____

6. dis + appoint _____
7. carry + ing _____
8. pay + ment _____
9. use + able _____
10. lazy + ness _____

1. immature
6. disappoint
2. openness
7. carrying
3. spinning
8. payment
4. sameness
9. usable
5. heaviest
10. laziness

Part 3 Problem Spellings Underline the correct spelling of these problem words in each sentence. (3 points each)

1. I have made several new (freinds, friends) this year.
2. We can serve (either, iether) brownies or cookies.
3. Does anyone (believe, beleive) the legend of Paul Bunyan?
4. Begin the treasure hunt (hear, here).
5. Maybe the bunny would eat a (peice, piece) of lettuce.
6. Our (principal, principle) is Mr. Adams.
7. Julia (seperated, separated) the yolk from the white.
8. I (probly, probably) will want only one hot dog.
9. Carole (payed, paid) two dollars for a ticket.
10. The theater can seat three (hundred, hunderd) people.

1. friends
2. either
3. believe
4. here
5. piece
6. principal
7. separated
8. probably
9. paid
10. hundred

Building English Skills, Silver Level, Teacher's Edition.
Copyright © 1981 by McDougal, Littell & Company, Evanston, Illinois

End-of-year Test

Part 1 Using the Library If you were using the card catalog to find these items, would you look for an author card (**A**), a title card (**T**), or a subject card (**S**)? Write your answer on the line. (2 points each)

1. S   4. A

2. A   5. T

3. T

1. _____ a book about Hopi Indians
2. _____ books by E.B. White
3. _____ *Miracles on Maple Hill*
4. _____ a book by Elizabeth Coatsworth
5. _____ *The Kid Who Batted 1.000*

Part 2 Using the Dictionary Answer the questions about the following entry from *Webster's New World Dictionary for Young Readers*. Underline the right choice in the parentheses. (2 points each answer)

> **grat·er** (grāt′ər), *n*. **1.** a person or thing that grates. **2.** a kitchen tool with a rough surface for grating vegetables, cheese, etc.

1. entry word
2. respelling
3. *noun*
4. definitions
5. graphite—gravity

1. The (entry word, respelling) is grat·er.
2. The (entry word, respelling) is grāt′ ər.
3. The *n.* stands for (*north, noun*).
4. This entry gives two (pronunciations, definitions).
5. The guide words for this page are (graphite—gravity, grope—growth).

Part 3 Using Adjectives Choose the correct adjective from the parentheses. Underline it. (2 points each)

1. an
2. sweeter
3. better
4. those
5. highest

1. Have you ever seen (a, an) apple tree in bloom?
2. This frosting is (sweetest, sweeter) than candy.
3. I want a (better, more better) story than this one.
4. Don't scratch (them, those) records.
5. Jackie climbed to the (highest, higher) peak in the mountains.

End-of-year Test NAME _____

Part 4 Using Adverbs Choose the correct word from the parentheses. Underline it. (2 points each)

1. I am rowing as (even, <u>evenly</u>) as I can.
2. Of the two brothers, David eats (<u>slower</u>, slowest).
3. Now I understand (more well, <u>better</u>) than I did before.
4. The trees swayed (graceful, <u>gracefully</u>) in the wind.
5. Beth rides her bike (more carefully, <u>most carefully</u>) of all my friends.

1. evenly
2. slower
3. better
4. gracefully
5. most carefully

Part 5 Similes and Metaphors Decide whether the sentence contains a **simile** or a **metaphor**. (2 points each)

1. _____ The dew looked like diamonds scattered on the grass.
2. _____ The cold January wind howled around the cabin.
3. _____ The human eye is like a camera.
4. _____ The rain is hammering at my windows.
5. _____ The sand on the beach is as white as snow.

1. simile
2. metaphor
3. simile
4. metaphor
5. simile

Part 6 Compositions and Stories To write about these subjects, would you write a **composition** or a **story**? (1 point each)

1. _____ Magic glasses that made Jo see things before they happened
2. _____ A project you worked on one summer
3. _____ A night in a haunted house
4. _____ A character that you invent who joins the circus
5. _____ How people crossed the Atlantic in the 1800's

1. story
2. composition
3. story
4. story
5. composition

End-of-year Test   NAME _____

Part 7 Reports   Write a note card for this paragraph in your own words. Include all the information you would need to give credit to your source at the end of the report. (5 points for source, 5 points for note)

> There is enough salt in all the oceans to build a mountain higher than any now on earth. Some seas are saltier than others, and the Red Sea, which lies between the hot deserts of Arabia and Africa, is the saltiest of all.
> —BORIS ARNOV, JR. AND HELEN MATHER-SMITH MINDLIN, *Wonders of the Deep Sea*

Wonders of the Deep Sea
　by Boris Arnov, Jr., and Helen Mather-Smith Mindlin

(The rest of the note will vary.)

_____
_____
_____
_____
_____

Part 8 Letters   Copy the following phrases. Capitalize and punctuate them as if they were in a letter. (1 point each)

1. dear sir or madam   _____   1. Dear Sir or Madam:

2. february 17 1981   _____   2. February 17, 1981

3. sincerely yours   _____   3. Sincerely yours,

4. 1614 valley drive   _____   4. 1614 Valley Drive

5. cleveland ohio 44101   _____   5. Cleveland, Ohio 44101

End-of-year Test   NAME

Part 9 Capitalization   Copy the following words and phrases. Change small letters to capital letters where they are needed. (2 points each)

1. the state of vermont

2. "the highwayman"

3. harry truman

4. the swahili language

5. rainbow falls

1. the state of Vermont
2. "The Highwayman"
3. Harry Truman
4. the Swahili language
5. Rainbow Falls

Part 10 Punctuation   Punctuate the sentences correctly. (3 points each)

1. Ms. Ferguson said Youre doing a good job

2. Ill be in Paris France by 3:00 P M

3. Have you seen Glorias brother

4. Sean give your report now

5. Rob Gerry and Chris have visited Orlando Florida

1. Ms. Ferguson said, "You're doing a good job."
2. I'll be in Paris, France, by 3:00 P.M.
3. Have you seen Gloria's brother?
4. Sean, give your report now.
5. Rob, Gerry, and Chris have visited Orlando, Florida.

Part 11 Spelling   Choose the word that is spelled correctly from the two words in parentheses. Underline it. (1 point each)

1. Jeff wore his (heavyest, heaviest) coat today.

2. The (principle, principal) made an announcement.

3. My (friend, freind) always knocks at the back door.

4. The magician's rabbit (disappeared, dissappeared).

5. Do you mind (sharing, shareing) your candy bar?

1. heaviest
2. principal
3. friend
4. disappeared
5. sharing

Building English Skills, Silver Level, Teacher's Edition.
Copyright © 1981 by McDougal, Littell & Company, Evanston, Illinois

LETTER NUMBER 1

Date: _____

Dear Parent,

In this year's study of language arts, your child will be using *Building English Skills, Silver Level*. This text is designed to lead students toward mastery of essential writing, speaking and listening, vocabulary development, grammar, and other related language skills. It develops each topic fully, rather than fragmenting it throughout the text, and provides extensive exercises for development and drill.

Your assistance and reinforcement will add to the effectiveness of the text and your child's classroom experience. It would be helpful for you to become familiar with the subjects covered in the lessons and to encourage your child to share with you what he or she is studying.

No language arts program is complete if it is limited to study alone. Lessons in a text or classroom can develop the structure for a student's language experience, but cannot replace the language experience itself. Here are some ways you can contribute to your child's language development.

- Encourage your child in developing discussion skills by having relaxed family discussions.

- Guide your child's television viewing to include some of the better young people's specials and series. Talk about the programs with your child.

- Encourage your child to read by letting him or her see you read. Make sure that reading materials—books, newspapers, magazines—are present in your home.

- Provide a quiet place and time for reading, letter writing, or school assignments.

I am confident that, with your assistance, your child's understanding and effective use of language will increase throughout this year. If you have any questions or suggestions, please feel free to contact me.

Sincerely,

Date: _____

Dear Parent,

Throughout this past school year, your child has developed a variety of writing, speaking and listening, vocabulary development, grammar, and other related language skills through the classroom use of *Building English Skills, Silver Level.* It is important to maintain these skills at a high level throughout the coming vacation.

Here are some ways you can assist your child in maintaining these skills:

> Encourage reading for pleasure. Help your child to visit a library regularly. Accompany your child, if possible. It would also be helpful to have a dictionary for young people available at home, so that your child can continue to develop vocabulary and comprehension skills. Discuss with your child what she or he has learned or enjoyed in this independent reading.

> Encourage your child in writing letters, keeping a diary, or writing original stories or poems for fun. Offer to read your child's writing, not to criticize, but to provide an audience. This will give your child a stronger feeling for communication through writing, and will provide more incentive for clear and correct writing.

Encouraging your child to participate in more purposeful activities such as these will help to lessen an addiction to watching television throughout the summer.

I hope these suggestions will help to make the coming vacation stimulating as well as enjoyable for both you and your child.

Sincerely,